CHIEF WHIP

The author's grandfather, Aretas Akers-Douglas (1857-1926) was in his day called "The Prince of Whips". Starting in 1880 as a confederate of the brilliant but unorthodox Lord Randolph Churchill, he graduated in record time to the position of chief dispenser of the official Conservative party line and held it for ten exceptionally arduous years at the height of the Home Rule controversy with its complications, Liberal unionism, parliamentary sabotage and obstruction.

This position was rendered all the more responsible through the distaste felt by the two great leaders whom he served Lord Salisbury and A. J. Balfour—for the details of party management; and even after he had been moved to another office his advice continued to be sought on all questions relating to the party's domestic affairs.

Out of the intimate and informal correspondence received in these capacities Lord Chilston has made an entertaining political biography, unravelling a most complex period of parliamentary history and revealing much about Lord Salisbury, Lord Randolph Churchill, Joseph Chamberlain, A. J. Balfour and lesser figures, like the loyal and endearing W. H. Smith, Walter Long and Richard Middleton.

ERIC ALEXANDER AKERS-DOUGLAS was employed at the Royal Institute of International Affairs (Chatham House) during the period 1948-1952, where under the editorship of Professor Arnold Toynbee he wrote a much praised section of volume 3 of the survey for International Affairs for 1938. The past few years he has spent managing his Kentish estate and writing—mainly the present book and articles.

STUDIES IN POLITICAL HISTORY

Editor: Michael Hurst
Fellow of St. John's College, Oxford

'THE SPRIGHTLY WHIP'
(A. AKERS-DOUGLAS)

From the original drawing by Harry Furniss

CHIEF WHIP

The Political Life and Times of
ARETAS AKERS-DOUGLAS
1st Viscount Chilston

by
Eric Alexander
3rd VISCOUNT CHILSTON

UNIVERSITY OF TORONTO PRESS
TORONTO 1962

First published in Canada 1962
by University of Toronto Press

Reprinted in paperback 2015

ISBN 978-1-4426-3911-9 (*paper*)

London: Routledge & Kegan Paul Ltd.

EDITOR'S NOTE

UNLIKE so many history series this one will not attempt a complete coverage of a specific span of time, with a division of labour for the contributors based on a neat parcelling out of centuries. Nor will it, in the main, be a collection of political monographs. Rather, the aim is to bring out books based on new, or thoroughly reinterpreted material ranging over quite a wide field of chronology and geography. Some will be more general than others, as is to be expected when biography is included alongside of detailed treatment of some comparatively short period of crisis like the appeasement of the Axis Powers. Nevertheless, whatever mode of presentation may have been appropriate, each work should provide an exposition of its subject in context and thus enable the reader to acquire new knowledge amidst things he knows, or could have known.

MICHAEL HURST

St. John's College,
Oxford.

CONTENTS

PLATES

PREFACE

THE late Victorian and Edwardian periods are already profusely documented by scores of volumes of biographies and memoirs, but it is my hope that the present book may fill a gap among these works by presenting a side of politics with which they seldom concern themselves. It is that side which has to do with the functions of those who are responsible for managing a political party and who have to deal with all the day-to-day problems arising from the relationship between the individuals who compose the party and between them and their leaders. It is for this reason that a not inconsiderable part of the correspondence and other material presented here will be found to deal with minor, long-forgotten episodes and quarrels or to consist of informal and intimate exchanges of views on topics ranging from the bestowal of honours to the tactics in regard to an election or a debate. Yet, although such material may lack the portentous aura of the more formal 'historic document', it cannot but convey a greater sense of spontaneity and immediacy. It is also obviously more revealing of personal character and of the springs of action underlying the great events and movements of the time.

Apart from these considerations a Chief Whip's correspondence is apt to be, by the nature of his office, largely of this day-to-day kind: he is seldom concerned with what is known as 'high policy'—though Akers-Douglas was unique in being something of an exception in this respect. In any case, the more political affairs are analysed the more difficult it becomes to establish a point where party domestic affairs end and high policy begins. In fact, of course, the latter cannot become operative without the former being in good order. The party machine must be continually minded and oiled and kept at maximum efficiency for the leader to be able to impose his ideas upon it and, still more, to give them effect through it. Therefore, ideally, it is the function of the Chief Whip to keep his finger upon the pulse of the party so that he can give accurate forecasts of its reactions to any given line of policy and, ultimately, as to the likelihood of its compliance with such policy when a vote is to be taken. By ultra-conscientious, but extremely enlightened attention to these duties Akers-Douglas fulfilled this ideal to a truly unique extent and owing to this, and to the peculiar temperaments of his two great chiefs, Salisbury and Balfour, even extended the normal scope and influence of his office.

My grandfather left behind a wealth of letters from his political colleagues, including some of the greatest figures of the day—those most copiously represented being Lord Salisbury and W. H. Smith; though the batches from Lord Randolph Churchill, Joseph Chamberlain, Long, Labouchere and others are no less revealing and interesting for their comparative smallness. A letter-book of Richard Middleton, the Chief Party Agent, for the years 1885–92, which somehow found its way into his papers and today forms part of the collection, is a mine of interesting information. Of his own letters on party political matters he seldom kept copies, except for those rare ones which he deemed necessary to record for his own reference or for the benefit of posterity.

Most of his Whip's business was obviously transacted by word of mouth—partly because it was in keeping with his discreet and reticent nature to commit as little as possible to paper about the party's domestic affairs and partly because he simply had not the time to write. For much the same reasons, probably, he kept no journal beyond a purely factual diary of his appointments; nor did he leave any memoirs or jottings of impressions, as so many other politicians have done. This, it will be appreciated, has in many ways made my task a hard one, although I had the one inestimable advantage of having known him (though still in my teens when he died) and heard him speak—with occasional flashes of extreme candour, as well as humour—about his political life. At the same time, the dozen or so volumes of press-cuttings which he accumulated have been invaluable for their revelation of contemporary feeling and opinion.

The bulk of the correspondence which has survived is concentrated within the years of his Chief Whipship and after 1895 it declines sharply and becomes sporadic. This also made the writing of a balanced book difficult. But, though there are in the latter period a number of blank years in the matter of correspondence, the occurrence at intervals of several groups of extremely interesting and important letters (which incidentally reveal Akers-Douglas in his later role of *éminence grise* of the party) decided me to widen the scope of the book beyond the limits implied in its title.

Among the many acknowledgments which I have to make I would like first to place on record the deep debt of gratitude which I owe to Dr. Felix Hull, Kent County Archivist, with whom the whole collection of my grandfather's papers was deposited a few years ago and who enormously facilitated my task by the kindly promptness with which he and his staff compiled a catalogue, of which I was to be the first beneficiary. Secondly, my most grateful thanks must go to Dr. H. J. Hanham of Manchester University for considerable help and encouragement during the writing of the book, for reading my drafts and advising upon them, and for a number of valuable suggestions. For most generous assistance of a similar kind I am also indebted to Mr. Michael Hurst of St. John's College, Oxford, and to my old friend Mr. John Connell.

My sincere thanks go also to Dr. J. F. A. Mason of Christ Church, Oxford, custodian of the Salisbury Papers, for his courtesy and kindness in selecting the relevant papers for my inspection, and to Miss W. D. Coates of the National Register of Archives and her staff for similar kindness in regard to the Hambleden Papers. In particular, of course, I wish to thank the owners of these collections, the present Marquess of Salisbury and the Hon. David Smith, for their courtesy in allowing me access to them and for their kind permission to quote them.

By way of postscript I must add that neither the Chamberlain Papers nor the Balfour Papers were accessible before this book was put into the hands of the printers.

CHILSTON

Chilston Park,
near Maidstone,
Kent.

INTRODUCTION

I

ARETAS AKERS-DOUGLAS first entered Parliament in 1880, in his twenty-ninth year, as member for East Kent, and represented this constituency and subsequently the St. Augustine's Division (created by the Redistribution Act of 1885) uninterruptedly for thirty years—several times being returned without a contest. Within three years of his entry he had become one of the Conservative Whips, and within another two he had become Chief Whip. He was appointed First Commissioner of Works in 1895 in Salisbury's third and last ministry and then Home Secretary in 1902 under Balfour until the latter's resignation in 1905. He was made a peer at the Coronation in 1911. But, despite these later distinctions, it was the six years between 1886 and 1892, when he was Chief Government Whip, which was the supreme test of his exceptional abilities and which in some ways constituted his highest achievement. For, within the bounds of the same short period, there were concentrated an extraordinary sequence of portentous and intriguing events and a whole stage of party political evolution—all amid a fascinating interplay of great and celebrated personalities. It is at the same time the most fully documented portion of his career.

But, though he spent the best part of his life in politics—and much of this at the very heart of affairs—he remained throughout the country gentleman par excellence, and as such will always be remembered by those who knew him. Inheriting great estates at an early age, retaining always a profound interest in the land and a love of nature (and an equal prowess with gun, cricket-bat and butterfly-net), surrounding himself by preference with countrymen, horses, dogs and birds—he was the very antithesis of that distinctly urban conception—the 'professional politician'. For, though immensely vigorous, capable and shrewd—and often ruthless where his party's interests were at stake—he was singularly devoid of the self-seeking and hypocrisy so commonly found among politicians. His integrity, as well as his capacity for sound judgment of men and affairs, became increasingly respected as time went on and were seldom questioned by colleagues of either party. It was no doubt his possession of this fortunate blend of qualities and characteristics which was the clue to the unique charm which he held for his contemporaries and the source of his great influence in the councils of his party.

To say that he was born (in 1851) the son of a Kentish 'squarson', the Reverend Aretas Akers of Malling Abbey, might evoke little surprise in seeming to round off a thoroughly conventional picture. Yet in fact his origins were romantic—even exotic. The Akers family, far from having been rooted amongst the orchards of Kent since time immemorial—as no doubt many assumed both then and later—had been there for barely more than a generation. Before that there stretched a long history of sojourn in the West Indies—some six generations, in fact, of sugar-planters and slave-owners; though by a strange irony a celebrated pioneer of Slavery Abolition, the Reverend James Ramsay, married into the family in the middle of the eighteenth century and his daughter in turn married her cousin the Aretas Akers of the next generation. Yet it appears that it was not so much this potentially embarrassing connection that caused the Akerses to turn their backs upon St. Kitt's, as the hard fact that the French had stolen all their slaves in a raid on the island during the War of American Independence.

It was also in the mid-eighteenth century that the Akerses formed an alliance which was to have tremendous consequences for the subject of this book—well over a hundred years later—when an Aretas Akers married Jean Douglas, an heiress of the Douglases of Baads in Midlothian, who also owned plantations in the West Indies. It was in fact through this alliance and through the failure of heirs in the Douglas line that the large Douglas estates in Midlothian, Lanarkshire, Dumfriesshire and

Kent finally descended to the present subject, causing him to assume the additional surname of Douglas.[1]

This inheritance came to him in 1875, at the age of twenty-four, in which same year he married Adeline, daughter of Horatio Austen-Smith of Hayes Court, Kent. Here it may be said, once for all, that this union, though it brought him seven children to whom he was devoted, failed in later years to bring him the other benefits, in the way of support and sympathy, which a happy marriage can bring and which would have meant so much to him in the career which he had chosen. For, in his wife, a remarkable and gifted personality was marred by eccentricity to such an extent that a normal social life at home became increasingly difficult and, more serious still, he was handicapped in his career by feeling himself debarred from certain high offices where a gracious consort is almost indispensable. On the other hand, the Chief Whipship, with its total claims on his time and attention and by necessitating his almost continual presence in the House of Commons, provided the perfect 'escape' from this unhappy predicament. In this situation is largely to be found the key to his career.

Malling Abbey, the Akers home, having been left to his grandmother for life (both his father and grandfather had died and his mother had remarried) Akers-Douglas made his home and raised his family at that uniquely beautiful seat Chilston, near Lenham, which had come to him as part of the Douglas inheritance. After being educated at Eton and University College, Oxford, he had read for the Bar and had in fact been called by the Inner Temple in the very year of his inheritance and marriage. But, as a result of his new prospects and responsibilities, he proceeded no further with this career, devoting himself instead to the management of his far-flung estates, to the rebuilding of Chilston to accommodate the large family

[1] In *The Great Landowners of Great Britain and Ireland* by John Bateman (Harrison, 1883) the following details are given:

	Acres	*Gross annual value*
Kent	3,753	4,937
Dumfries	6,629	6,013
Midlothian	3,106	1,388
Lanark	2,190	752
	15,678	13,090

which quickly began to appear, to cricket and shooting, to the breeding of exotic waterfowl and the collection of butterflies, moths and birds' eggs.

As soon as he had settled down it was inevitable that, by virtue of the high position which automatically became his as one of the biggest landowners in Kent, he should be invited by his fellow magnates to shoulder some of the local responsibilities which then went—and to a lesser extent still go—with such status. He became a magistrate and was soon enveloped in all the multifarious duties which at that time—before the reform of local government—fell to the lot of these functionaries. He also made his first tentative acquaintance with national politics by interesting himself in his local Conservative Association, of which he soon became the chairman.

The energy, ability and tact which he showed in the latter role quickly drew upon him the interested gaze of that great territorial magnate and political potentate, William Nevill, 5th Earl and 1st Marquess of Abergavenny, who in the past had been Disraeli's principal party manager, was still his foremost unofficial adviser and who from his seat at Eridge, near Tunbridge Wells, still closely controlled the party's interests in Kent. Abergavenny's influence was potent but unseen: a more visible and official symbol of the party and agent of its Chief, who also took young Akers-Douglas under his wing, was another Kentish magnate, Sir William Hart Dyke, (7th Baronet) of Lullingstone Castle, M.P. for Mid Kent, Chief Whip and Patronage Secretary in the Government of the day (Disraeli's ministry of 1874–80).

It was thus that Kent had become not only a Conservative stronghold, but also a recruiting ground of the principal staff officers of the party—starting with Dyke and going on to such as Akers-Douglas and Middleton, the great Chief Party Agent, all of whom became known as the 'Kent Gang'. His own high place in the hierarchy of the county, added to his personal charm and distinction (and not least his growing reputation as one of the best game shots of his day), made Akers-Douglas a popular and regular member of the great house-parties held at Eridge and other county magnates' seats, where in an atmosphere of easy intimacy—outside the pheasant coverts or over the billiard table—the current problems of State and Party, from the appointment of Ministers to the selection of candidates, were discussed.

When, therefore, on the very eve of the General Election of 1880, the sudden retirement through illness of one of the two members for East Kent caused a vacancy, it was a matter of little surprise that Akers-Douglas was persuaded by his discerning and influential friends (I have heard it said at the suggestion of Disraeli himself) to offer himself as a candidate.

2

Akers-Douglas made his debut at a time when the whole character and climate of English politics was in course of changing. Despite the First Reform Act of 1832, in the main the old ways and conditions of the eighteenth century still persisted; though Disraeli's Second Reform Act of 1867, by nearly doubling the electorate, heralded the dawn of the age of Democracy. Even this for a time had little effect upon ingrained political and electoral habits; nevertheless the sudden expansion of the electorate automatically led to a more elaborate organization and a stricter marshalling of party forces. If this were not enough to sharpen the contest between the parties, their respective leaders, through their starkly opposite characters and mutual antipathy, provided all and more than was necessary by way of extra stimulus.

For seldom has the history and constitutional development of the country been so much influenced by the characters of its leading statesmen as it was in the days of Disraeli and Gladstone. The clash of their personalities coloured the whole of political life, intensifying the party spirit to a hitherto unknown degree and engendering a rancour and venom which startles us as much today as it would have startled the men of the first half of their own century. Akers-Douglas, in after years, would often dwell on this phenomenon, epitomizing it by quoting a savage contemporary jingle, part of which described Gladstone as 'sitting in state on a burning hot plate, between Judas Iscariot and Pilate'. In an epoch supposedly notable for its religious piety it would have been difficult to carry animosity much further.

Gladstone, of whom his most recent biographer has so well said that 'his concentrated self-absorbtion and inflexible adherence to an exalted conception of politics as an aspect of moral and religious truth made it hard for him to adjust his means to his ends',[1] had embarked upon his career foreseeing 'a grand struggle between the forces of good and evil', and he had ended, without any qualms, by identifying himself with the former and his rival with the latter. Thus in a conversation with Morley ten years after Disraeli's death, he could say: 'For all the deterioration in our public life, one man and one alone, is responsible—Disraeli. He is the grand corrupter. He it was who sowed the seed.'[2] It was scarcely surprising that his opponents should take up this challenge and reverse the proposition. Though when Disraeli made his celebrated and much parodied remark to an audience of prelates that he was 'on the side of the angels' he was not claiming a monopoly of righteousness, but emphasizing his rejection of the Darwinian theory in particular and of the materialistic and utilitarian philosophy in general.

The bitterness which pervaded English party politics by 1880 was therefore apt to be attributed by his opponents more to Gladstone's peculiar personality than to any other cause. In a letter to Balfour in this year Salisbury wrote of 'the utter distortion of perception which Gladstone's mind has suffered through the operation of party rancour'.[3] And in another after the election had taken place: 'The hurricane that has swept us away is so strange and new a phenomenon that we shall not for some time understand its real meaning. I doubt if so much enthusiasm and such a general unity of action proceeds from any sentimental opinion, or from a mere academic judgment. It seems to me to be inspired by some definite desire for change; and means business. It may disappear as rapidly as it came, or it may be the beginning of a serious war of classes. Gladstone is doing all he can to give it the latter meaning.'[4] Indeed, during this election there was much serious rioting and damage to property, as well as a very considerable number of cases of physical assault on candidates and their supporters.

But there were other wider reasons which gave both leaders alike no option but to accept their roles of 'Prince of Light' or 'Prince of Darkness', according to the fancy of the electorate.

[1] Philip Magnus: *Gladstone* (Murray, 1954), 188.
[2] Asquith: *Fifty Years of Parliament* (Cassell, 1926), I, 238.
[3] Balfour: *Chapters of Autobiography*, 130. [4] Ibid., 127.

For, the greater part of the newly enfranchised masses, being uneducated, unsophisticated and sentimental were incapable of developing anything that could be called a political opinion. Hence they were apt to find a focus for their feeling more easily in the person of an individual: to such the right or wrong of politics were represented by Gladstone or Disraeli, Randolph Churchill or Chamberlain, etc. Indeed, in 1868 and in 1874 the vote of the country was virtually a plebiscite in favour of Gladstone in the first place and of Disraeli in the second, and in 1880 we find a party leader (Gladstone) enthusiastically accepted by the majority of the country and backed as well by the whole force of a highly developed party organization—this to a degree unknown even to such powerful leaders of the past as Walpole, Chatham, Pitt and Peel.

MR. GLADSTONE. A SKETCH FROM LIFE.

The sharpening of the contest by raising it to a higher—or, rather, more pretentious—plane than ever before inexorably compelled each side to claim an absolute monopoly of virtue and infallibility in all things. This in turn resulted in a *reductio ad absurdum* of the much-vaunted Two-Party System, for it committed each party to maintaining that they were the one and only possible choice and that the return of the other inevitably meant ruin and disaster—in spite of having simultaneously to admit that the existence and activities of the other party were essential to the working of the Constitution. The rigour of party lines made it impossible for parties to co-operate over issues of national or imperial importance—such as Home Rule—or even to coalesce against a minority like the Irish Nationalists, when the latter made the conduct of Parliamentary business impossible. Party allegiance seemed to come even before patriotism: M.P.s were selected more for their obedience to the party line than for their disinterested devotion to the public interest. Even if the constituency as a whole inclined to set more store by the personal attributes of the individual their Selection Committee (those bodies had come into being in the seventies and were elected by members of the party in the constituency) would not sponsor his adoption until it had ascertained the certainty of his unswerving obedience to Gladstone or Disraeli, as the case might be.

In such circumstances it became vain for a Member of Parliament to allege reasons to his constituency for an occasional vote to be given against his party. The constituency was not concerned with the reasons, nor even with the measure in question. It sent him to Parliament to support Gladstone—or Disraeli: it did not care to know why he had failed to do so. This made nonsense of the old boast that the varieties and anomalies of the British representative system gave a chance to men of unorthodox opinions to be returned to Parliament. It now seemed that the candidate for a seat must not only hold popular opinions, but must hold these as explained and interpreted by the popular man. 'What will be the value of a party,' wrote John Bright to W. S. Caine, Radical Unionist candidate for Barrow, just after the defeat of the first Home Rule Bill in 1886, 'when its whole power is laid at the disposal of a leader from whose authority no appeal is allowed? At this moment it is notorious that scores of members of the House of Commons have voted with the Government, who, in private, have condemned the Irish Bills. Is it wise for a Liberal elector or constituency to prefer such a member, abject at the feet of a Minister, to one who takes the course dictated by his conscience and his sense of honour?'[1]

As a result of the three Reform Acts of the century the power of the House of Commons was inevitably greater in so far as the latter now represented a greater mass of opinion than before. But at the same time, the ever growing power of the party organizations and the corresponding loss of independence by individual members were reducing it to the character of a machine. The means which now existed for organizing public opinion and the rapid spread of intelligence which informed it combined to concentrate upon the House and its members a force which deprived them of independent action. The cheap party newspaper kept everyone well aware of the sayings and doings of members and put such a construction as might best suit its party purposes on the actions of the Government of the day. Every voter therefore had the opportunity of making up his mind what his member *ought* to be doing, and was also able to know what he *was* doing. For example, a glance at the press-cuttings collection of a man like Akers-Douglas reveals that there were at that time not only many more newspapers than today, especially in the provinces, but in particular a number of political scandal-sheets and gossip weeklies which specialized in minute and malicious personalities about even the most obscure occupants of the back benches—not to mention ministers.

Together with and probably as a result of this ease of communication and spread of information there had grown up a keener and more widely distributed interest in political questions. In fact, in these days before the cinema, television and the cult of sport, to the working man politics had become the one intellectual interest in life. Again as a result of this, as well as of the enfranchisement of the masses, there had grown up a deference towards the opinion of the working classes which had been not only unknown to the Whig nobles and gentry who pioneered reform, but also wholly alien to the minds even of the middle-class Radicals of earlier days. 'You never heard me,' said Cobden in 1846, 'quote the superior judgment of the working classes in any deliberation in this assembly; you never heard me cant about the superior claims of the working classes to

[1] John Newton: *W. S. Caine*, 167 (*q.* Garvin, II, 253).

arbitrate on this great question' (i.e. the Corn Laws).[1] But compare with those the words of Gladstone only thirty-two years later, in 1878: 'Did Scribes and Pharisees or did shepherds and fishermen yield the first, most and readiest converts to the Saviour and the company of his Apostles? As the barbarian, with his undeveloped organs, sees and hears at distances which the senses of the cultured state cannot overpass, and yet is utterly deficient as to fine details of sound and colour, even so it seems that in judging of the great questions of policy which appeal to the primal truths and laws of our nature, those classes may excel who, if they lack the opportunities, yet escape the subtle perils of the wealthy state.'[2] Apart from Gladstone's characteristic muddling of religion with politics the speech reveals the new factor which had entered politics and which was to become almost a religion in its own right—the dogma of the infallibility of the uninformed, the theory that ignorance many times multiplied may produce results more valuable than can be produced by the knowledge and experience of the few.

[1] Hansard, 84, 281. [2] Gladstone: *Gleanings of Past Years*, I, 201.

However strictly the thread of personal narrative be followed, biography broadens insensibly into history, and the career of a private member becomes the recognisable part of the fortunes of a nation.

WINSTON S. CHURCHILL, *Lord Randolph Churchill.*

I
THE SPELL OF DISRAELI

A COUNTY newspaper wrote at the time when Akers-Douglas presented himself for election that he 'possesses in a remarkable degree those special qualifications which are required in a county member . . . Where he is best known he is most liked. In fact he is a universal favourite.' Already, through the veil of genuine shyness and modesty, the electors could discern a character of unusual strength and integrity, as well as charm. In an election characterized by exceptional violence and bitterness on either side even an opponent could find a good word for this attractive young candidate. 'An Old Liberal' wrote to the local press deploring certain insulting personal remarks made by members of his party against Akers-Douglas and added rather patronizingly that he 'saw in Mr. Akers-Douglas the appearance and behaviour of an English gentleman; in fact his address prepossessed me in his favour as a gentleman with the making in him of a useful and rising man. I thought his ideas crude and open to much criticism politically, but withal there was talent in him, youthful, I grant, but still thoughtful . . .' Meanwhile, the Conservative press of the county was triumphantly declaring that 'the contest for the representation of East Kent has become a mere travesty' owing to the 'overwhelming ascendancy of the Conservative principles' and contrasted one of the Liberal candidate's meetings 'with only two gentlemen on the platform to support him' with the 'splendid gathering of county noblemen and gentlemen' who supported Akers-Douglas and his fellow candidate. Indeed, despite the theoretical advent of democracy, the same feudal note was sounded unabashed by most local Tory papers. Thus: 'In the country districts I soon found the good old families, such as the Derings, the Plumtres, the Bridges, the Honeywoods and the Oxendens, with their adherents, were all with Pemberton and Akers-Douglas and that . . . Mr. Davis was almost unknown', and 'the representatives of the old county families being conspicuous by their absence at Mr. Davis's various meetings'.

In the event all these confident predictions were fulfilled, for the Conservatives retained their 'overwhelming ascendancy' in the county winning 16 seats (a gain of 3) out of the county's total of 21. 'The tenant farmers have done their duty admirably,' as one paper expressed it—the terms of which remark reveal in a nutshell both the semi-feudal voting habits of the rural areas and the fact that the agricultural labourers had not yet been enfranchised. Akers-Douglas found himself at the head of the poll with even about a hundred more votes than his veteran fellow candidate, Leigh Pemberton.[1] Nevertheless it was a sign of the general Liberal reaction which had swept the country that their much derided Liberal opponent succeeded in halving the former Conservative majority. For indeed, on the national scale, one of the major political landslides of modern times had occurred, the Liberals having won 347 seats as against the Conservatives' 240 and the Irish Nationalists' 65, giving the Liberals an ostensible majority of 42 even over the other two parties combined. With these figures and Gladstone, at the height of his prestige, returned from his spurious retirement, it seemed, not only to Liberals but to Conservatives as well, as though the long spell of Liberal supremacy which had been temporarily broken six years earlier by Disraeli's historic ministry was about to be resumed with greater strength and permanence than ever. Yet appearances were deceptive and these expectations were to be falsified. In sonorous periods Sir Winston Churchill has written: 'What political prophet or philosopher, surveying the triumphant Liberal array, would have predicted that this Parliament from which so much was hoped, would be indeed the most disastrous and even fatal period in their party history? Or who could have foreseen that these dejected Conservatives in scarcely five years, with the growing

[1] Later Sir Edward Leigh Pemberton, K.C.B.; Legal Assistant Under-Secretary Home Office, 1885–94.

assent of an immense electorate, would advance to the enjoyment of twenty years of power?'[1]

Kent, however, jubilant over its own particular victories, was determined not to be dejected. A fortnight after the elections, on April 26th, 1880, a great Conservative demonstration was organized at Lenham, the village of which Akers-Douglas was squire, to celebrate the double event of the return of Sir William Hart Dyke and Sir Edward Filmer for Mid Kent and of Akers-Douglas and Leigh Pemberton for East Kent. For, though Lenham itself belonged to Mid Kent, the Divisional boundary with East Kent ran along the boundary of Akers-Douglas's property. A procession of electors headed by banners and brass bands marched to nearby Chilston Park, Akers-Douglas's home, to congratulate and cheer the four members assembled there, and after that a banquet was held at the village institute attended by the Members and some 200 persons, while the parish church bells were rung and fireworks and bonfires were lighted. In the following weeks Akers-Douglas and his fellow Kentish members attended numerous demonstrations, meetings and dinners, including a banquet at Margate to inaugurate the Beaconsfield Working Men's Association 'and to celebrate the Conservative victories in Kent', where 400 working men sat down to a gargantuan feast under a gigantic purple and yellow banner bearing the legend 'Long Live Lord Beaconsfield'.

But poor Lord Beaconsfield, old and ailing, had not long to live and had moreover received the most shattering defeat at the hands of the electorate whose strength he had been instrumental in so greatly enhancing: 'that great statesman who has just experienced in so signal a manner the ingratitude of the fickle and ignorant multitude', as a Kentish Tory paper bluntly wrote. It was the first occurrence of a phenomenon which has since—particularly on another recent and historic occasion—become painfully familiar to great national leaders. However, before the curtain fell on that astonishing career, Akers-Douglas was destined to witness the final scene. It appears more than probable that he had already met the great man as a fellow guest of Lord Abergavenny at Eridge Castle, since, as we know, he was a frequent visitor there during the period before his entry into

[1] Winston Churchill: *Lord Randolph Churchill*, p. 106 (Odhams' 1951 edition).

Parliament, when Lord Beaconsfield also often stayed there. Akers-Douglas was by nature too reticent ever to confirm the fact, but it was generally believed by his contemporaries that it was in these circumstances that he had come to the notice of the old 'Chief'and received the latter's blessing. At any rate, to the end of his life, he never disguised his profound admiration for Disraeli, and if this admiration may have been awakened by early personal contact at Eridge, it must have been immeasurably increased by a memorable event which took place just after his election. For among his papers he preserved the following brief summons:

May 8. Hughenden Manor, '80.

Dear Sir,

There will be a meeting of the Conservative Party at Bridgewater House on Wednesday the 19th inst. at three o'clock precisely, when the honor of your presence is requested by

Your faithful Servt.

Beaconsfield.

Aretas Akers-Douglas, Esq.

Though in fact it was destined to be Disraeli's last bow, his farewell to friends, followers and career, this was not the motive which had prompted him to call the meeting. As he told this rally of some 500 members of both Houses of Parliament, had the result of the elections been different he might have felt justified in seeking repose, 'but in the hour of failure he would not withdraw, but would still place at their service whatever advice his experience might enable him to afford'. As he addressed the meeting, we are told by one present, he happened to stand immediately beneath a large picture of the Madonna by Murillo. 'The colouring both of painted effigy and living figure was of the same tone; the sallow flesh tints, black hair and clothing were almost identical in both. One could almost imagine that the Virgin was spreading her hands in compassion over the fallen leader.'[1] Disaffected Tories laid aside their grievances and rallied to their old chief: former recalcitrants warmly swore allegiance anew. Looking back upon this vivid scene we have the feeling that it was in this moment that the seal was set upon the Disraelian legend which from then on was to be the mainspring

[1] Sir Herbert Maxwell: *Life and Times of W. H. Smith*, II, 36.

of the party's inspiration, bringing it back to power so soon afterwards and for so long maintaining it there. Writing to his beloved Lady Bradford beforehand, Disraeli had remarked that it would be 'a fine occasion for an asthmatic Demosthenes',[1] the humour of which remark, characteristically unsparing of himself, confirms the spontaneity of the drama when it occurred.

On this May afternoon of 1880 Disraeli exhorted his hearers to counter their immediate discouragement by thinking back to the far worse position which the party had occupied nearly fifty years earlier, after the Election of 1832. This he, more than any other man, was entitled to do, for the greater part of that which the Tory Party had achieved and had become in those intervening fifty years was his own work. The newly elected Member for East Kent, who now listened to him, was, to all appearances, the type of those who formed the backbone of the Tory Party—the country gentlemen of England. These were the people who some forty years earlier had been alienated by Sir Robert Peel's Repeal of the Corn Laws and who, against all likelihood, had found in the exotic young Jew their leader and saviour. Standing apart from them in absolutely every respect, Disraeli, with his great brains and almost feminine intuition, was able to interpret to them in practical terms the real significance of all that which they instinctively felt they represented, but could not formulate. He was enthralled and inspired to romantic expression by the glamorous aspects and wonderful potentialities of that English heritage which they, being part of, took for granted. It was not surprising if such followers laughed at the extravagances of the weird political romances which continually flowed from his pen; but it was less surprising if they entertained an immense respect for the extraordinary combination of faith, determination and practical ability which backed his idealism.

Disraeli's achievement lay not only in making himself leader of the Tory Party, which represented the interests of this proud and important section of the community, but in 'educating' (as he put it) its members towards ideas which to most of them had always appeared to be the property of the other side. His friend Lady Dorothy Nevill tells us that a contemporary wit aptly

[1] *The Letters of Disraeli to Lady Chesterfield and Lady Bradford*, edited by the Marquis of Zetland, II, 360.

described it as 'dragging an omnibus full of country gentlemen uphill.'[1] The acid test of his success came with his Reform Bill of 1867, when he carried most of them with him (though there were notable exceptions, including his future successor Lord Salisbury) by his impudent achievement in 'dishing the Whigs'; in other words cutting the ground from under the latters' feet by forestalling them in a great constitutional reform. By doing so he undoubtedly gave the Tory Party a new lease of life; but the Bill, which in its original form had sought to safeguard the balance between classes and interests, had been mangled by his opponents and, though he confidently asserted his unshakeable faith in the 'good sense of the British working man', secretly he could not but share the apprehensions expressed by his followers and opponents alike at the final result—the sudden acquisition of power by vast, uneducated, ill-informed and capricious multitudes. For the 'rule of mere numbers', as it was scathingly called by his opponents (who were themselves instrumental in bringing it about by their frustration of his own more subtle scheme), could only result in what Disraeli tersely described as 'the tyranny of one class and that the least enlightened'.[2]

The stock picture later developed in Conservative party literature of the complacent founder of 'Tory Democracy' is not only false, but ironical. For Lady Dorothy Nevill, who was a shrewd observer and knew him intimately, says quite uncompromisingly: 'It is very difficult to say what Lord Beaconsfield's real view of politics was, but my own impression is that he was deeply attached to the traditions of government by aristocracy, the romantic side of which appealed to his imagination and nature. At heart I think he feared the eventual triumph of a sort of mob rule, the coming of which it was ever his object to delay. Undoubtedly in his last years he was extremely pessimistic as to the future, having rightly or wrongly, no particular

[1] *Leaves from the Notebooks of Lady Dorothy Nevill*, edited by Ralph Nevill; 74.

[2] The Annual Register, 1887, gives the following figures for the proportion of illiterates among the electorate at the General Election of 1886.

England and Wales:	38,587 out of	2,416,272
Scotland:	4,836 out of	358,155
Ireland:	36,722 out of	194,994

confidence in the political sagacity of an English democracy, the judgement of which he thought could easily be swayed by unprincipled and specious agitators.'[1]

Moreover, when yet a further—and perfectly logical—extension of the franchise was proposed by the next Liberal Government, Disraeli flatly opposed it, declaring that 'we must remember that they [the people of England] have had a great meal to digest [namely, his own Reform Bill], and I am not quite sure that they have yet assimilated the nutrition which has been profusely supplied to them'.[2] He was also not afraid to say bluntly that 'if you establish a democracy, you must in due course reap the fruits of democracy' and to name among the latter a great increase in legislation and public expenditure and considerable loss of liberty. It is only fair to remember that in introducing his own Bill he had tried to draw a strong distinction between 'conceding popular privileges' and 'conferring democratic rights', adding that 'we do not live—and I trust it will never be the fate of this country to live—under a democracy'.[3] According to the usage of the day this was a perfectly reasonable remark—even if a pious hope—although only ten years later it would have been a solecism in every sense.

Disraeli died exactly a year after Akers-Douglas's entry into Parliament, but his influence upon the rising generation of Tories grew even stronger than it had been when he was alive. As for Gladstone his personality and his politics were the mainspring of nearly all the action of the next fifteen years. Lady St. Helier, that remarkably eclectic political hostess, has nicely drawn the distinction between their relative impacts. 'There was something superhuman in Mr. Gladstone's power and ruthlessness, and in the way in which he attempted to carry out his great schemes. To compare him with Lord Beaconsfield is impossible, and yet Lord Beaconsfield is much more than a memory—he is a religion to the party which he led . . .'[4]

[1] Op. cit., 75.

[2] Speech in House of Commons, May 13th, 1874, on Household Franchise (Counties) Bill.

[3] Speech in House of Commons March 18th, 1867, introducing Reform Bill.

[4] Lady St. Helier: *Memories of Fifty Years*, 255.

The great duel between the two titans had reached its final dramatic climax in this year 1880 under quite unforeseen circumstances. For Gladstone, who had announced his retirement from politics several years earlier, suddenly re-emerged to fight the election. Thus he was able to do so unexpectedly, still at the height of his powers and, untrammelled by statesmanly responsibilities, to give free rein to his emotional feelings on a theme which was not only ideally suited to him, but which enabled him to give full expression to his deep hatred of Disraeli. The theme, which was Disraeli's foreign policy, was easily defensible—and it was in fact ably defended by many Conservative candidates all over the country—including young Akers-Douglas, whose speeches on it were described at the time as having been the decisive factor in his election. In his first speech as a candidate he summed up the achievement of his leader in a simple but pungent phrase: 'Six years ago our influence in the Councils of Europe was nil, whilst now we have reached the proud position of holding the balance of Europe virtually in our hands.'

Indeed, despite the tendency in the last two years of his Ministry for things to go awry, Disraeli's successes in the spheres of imperial and foreign policy had been resounding—especially after the notable failure in these fields of his predecessor, Gladstone. Such moments of triumph as the purchase of the Suez Canal shares, the proclamation of the Queen as Empress of India, the 'peace with honour' at the Berlin Congress, were of a kind which is apt to remain indelible, and the memory of them undoubtedly served to cast a special glamour and a magic round his name when he was gone and when the country was once more suffering defeats and humiliations under Gladstone. 'Zeal for the greatness of England was the passion of his life', said Lord Salisbury at his death, and he went on to describe the feelings of 'affection and reverence' which the recognition of this fact had earned for him among the people of this country. Similarly, on the same occasion, in a rather poignant and almost envious phrase, Gladstone described him as 'the man who so entwined himself in the interest of the general heart'. Even in the heat of the election battle of 1880 Lord Hartington had felt moved to say to his constituents: 'It may be that Lord Beaconsfield is ambitious. I should like to know what man who has attained the position which he has attained in the political life of his country is not actuated by feelings of ambition.' But he refused to attribute 'any mean or unworthy motives' to his great opponent and declared his conviction that 'the greatness of his country' had been the sole consideration inspiring his policy.

In the domestic sphere Disraeli's achievements during his great second ministry had been no less remarkable—indeed, probably even greater, though triumph in the foreign and imperial fields, which involve national prestige and aggrandisement, invariably have a stronger and more romantic appeal than a series of 'down to earth' acts of Parliament. For, at long last, Disraeli had the opportunity to tackle those social reforms which had been neglected throughout the long reign of Liberalism and laissez-faire (with the exception of Gladstone's immediately preceding government) and which he knew to be the logical—indeed, inescapable—sequel to his own massive extension of the franchise. Thus, paradoxical, as it may seem, Disraeli, the 'Tory Saviour', became the inaugurator of the present era of collectivist or socialist legislation (by governments of all complexions). 'We are all Socialists now,' as Sir William Harcourt remarked a few years later.[1]

The wide scope of Disraeli's achievements in his great second ministry might have appeared certain to ensure him an extension of his lease of power. But there were various less obvious factors, besides the setback in foreign and imperial affairs and besides Gladstone's spectacular return and onslaught, which temporarily prevented the uninterrupted advance of the regenerate Conservatives and contributed to the great landslide of 1880. Most important among these was the fact that the concentration on foreign affairs in the latter years of the Ministry, added to Disraeli's translation to the House of Lords, led to a neglect and mismanagement of party interests. This neglect appears all the more astonishing in the light of the earlier advantage of the party in organization. One enduring service which Peel had rendered the Tory Party, before he split it,

[1] One of the first Labour members ever sent to Parliament, Alexander Macdonald, said in 1879: 'The Conservative Party have done more for the working class in five years than the Liberals have in fifty' (Buckle: *Life of Disraeli*, V, 369).

consisted, first, in fostering the formation of local Conservative Associations in order to secure the due registration and regimentation of every qualified Conservative vote, and, secondly, in the establishment of a central organization whose headquarters were the recently formed Carlton Club. In addition, whilst in opposition before 1874, Disraeli had determined upon a drastic reorganization and revitalizing of the party machine, which had become rusty and out of date since Peel's day. For this task he appointed a very able young barrister John (later Sir John) Eldon Gorst, and it was the latter's great organizing capacity which ensured the Conservative victory in 1874. But by 1880, as a result of quarrels, Gorst was no longer in charge, though he had written to Disraeli already in 1877 warning him that 'you must put a stop to that which has been the chief cause of all the mischief that has occurred—the system . . . of managing elections from the Treasury'. He went on to point out that 'the established principle of non-interference with the local leaders has in many instances been neglected: and those leaders have been constantly offended and alienated both in the distribution of patronage and in other matters'.[1] He was certain that 'unless some energetic measures are speedily adopted, our organisation whenever the election does take place, will be as inferior to that of our opponents as it had been superior in 1874'. Meanwhile, moreover, Joseph Chamberlain had perfected for the Liberals the machine which became known as the 'Caucus', whose virtue lay in being independent of the central party offices at Westminster and directly representative of the local associations in the constituencies.

The immediate issue on which, in this year 1880, Disraeli had chosen to dissolve Parliament and appeal to the country was that of Ireland. Although the unhappy condition of that country had moved his Cabinet to initiate various measures for relief, the latter were persistently obstructed by the factious spirit of the Nationalist members under their remarkable new leader Parnell. In fact their conduct threatened to make the continuance of the Parliament impossible. But the public mind in England still remained singularly unaffected by the problem. It was therefore partly in order to focus the attention of the

[1] Buckle, op. cit., VI, 519–20.

electorate upon the gravity of the problem that Disraeli issued a manifesto on the subject, in which he simultaneously announced the dissolution of Parliament, in the form of a letter to the Lord Lieutenant of Ireland, the Duke of Marlborough. In this, whilst emphasizing the seriousness of the Home Rule movement and the threat which it constituted to the solidarity of the Empire, he also hinted at complicity between the Liberal leaders and the Home Rulers. At the time, not only were these allegations indignantly denied by those concerned, but the whole subject matter of the manifesto was considered exaggerated by colleagues and opponents alike. Yet, if the manifesto was undeniably to a great extent a party manoeuvre, it cannot be said that the subject matter was exaggerated. By bringing the whole issue out into the open Disraeli forced the Nationalists to show their hand much sooner than they might otherwise have done—and therein, of course, he was sowing trouble for his immediate successors, the Liberals, through which his own party might benefit. He had accurately indicated—and in the process considerably influenced and intensified—what was to be the dominating theme of parliamentary affairs for many agitated years to come and to have the most profound effect upon the evolution of the political parties.

In a conversation with W. H. Smith at about this time Disraeli forecast 'the beginning of the disintegration of parties' over the Irish issue.[1] As a general prophecy it was completely accurate, though not as to the actual manner of the occurrence. He thought, rightly, that the Liberal government would at first try hard to avoid coercion for Ireland, but would soon be forced in self-defence to adopt it. As a result of that he thought they would alienate their Radical wing and so split the party. Indeed, the split might have come about in just this way had Hartington become Premier, as Disraeli was assuming. After his defeat he had in fact given advice to the Queen (recorded by her in a memorandum) calculated to accelerate the split which he foresaw. He had encouraged her to send for Hartington, who was 'in his heart a conservative, a gentleman, and very straightforward in his conduct', and also on the ground that the large body of 'respectable and moderate old Whigs . . . would rally round and support him, and the Radicals would be harmless'.[2]

[1] Maxwell, op. cit., II, 31. [2] Buckle, VI, 534.

But, inwardly, despite this pleasing picture, he must have known (and perhaps even calculated) that the Radical wing was now too strong to allow itself to be dominated by the Old Whigs and that consequently any attempt by the latter to impose their policy upon the former must lead to an explosion which would quite simply shatter the whole party.

The other main development upon which Disraeli was destined, in his final year, to exert an incalculable influence was the rise of the man who was shortly to present himself as his political heir. As a frequent visitor to Blenheim he had known Lord Randolph Churchill as a boy. When the latter entered Parliament as a Conservative representing the family borough of Woodstock in 1874 and conducted a spirited campaign against some of the lesser lights of his own government, Disraeli was amused and noted with admiration the brilliant signs of promise. Such puckish audacity and defiant independence reminded him of his own youthful career. When, in the beginning of the new Parliament, Lord Randolph joined with three other friends—Sir Henry Drummond Wolff, John Gorst and Arthur Balfour—in forming a sort of tiny 'shock group' of Tory free-lances known as the 'Fourth Party', Disraeli came specially to watch them from the Peers' Gallery.

This celebrated little band had really been born out of the astonishing 'Bradlaugh Affair' which had bedevilled the new government at the very outset of its reign, but their high spirits had soon led them to find fault with and to attack the Tory leadership in the House of Commons, which now reposed in the rather limp hands of Sir Stafford Northcote. Indeed, Balfour afterwards wrote: 'There would never have been a Churchill had there not also been a Northcote.'[1] For all the Conservative talent had now gone to the Lords and there was no one left on the Opposition Front Bench who was anything like a match for Gladstone—except Randolph Churchill. Disraeli himself told Wolff that had he not been convinced that Gladstone's 'retirement' was irrevocable he would have stayed in the House of Commons.

However, though he sympathized with the Fourth Party, Disraeli wished to deter them from open rebellion against their appointed leader. After visiting the great man at Hughenden,

[1] Balfour, op. cit., 140.

THE LAST VISIT OF LORD BEACONSFIELD TO THE HOUSE.

Gorst reported: 'Lord B. was in his talk anything but Goaty ['the Goat' being the Fourth Party's derisive name for Northcote]: he generally expressed great confidence in us, thought we had a brilliant future before us, and promised to help and advise us as much as he could.'[1] But he advised them, whilst

[1] Churchill, op. cit., 129–31.

remaining critical and firm towards Northcote, to defer to him generally and avoid an open breach. To Wolff he said: 'I fully appreciate your feelings and those of your friends; but you must stick to Northcote. He represents the respectability of the party. I wholly sympathize with you all, because I never was respectable myself.'[1]

The Fourth Party was naturally extremely elated to have received so charming a benediction from so mighty a source, though it cannot be said that they paid much heed to the advice in so far as their immediate course of conduct was concerned. But, though the Fourth Party itself soon disintegrated, the effect of this contact, almost on the very eve of Disraeli's death, undoubtedly had a profound effect, not only upon Lord Randolph's personal career, but also upon the development of Conservative party policy. For, as a result of it, Lord Randolph came more and more to regard himself as the political heir of Disraeli and, in that capacity, to develop to extremes the latter's policy—or rather what he considered that policy *should* have been—and to try to force this product upon the Tory party. As a result of this in turn the more orthodox Tories, who in his day, constituted the overwhelming majority of the party, tended more and more to reject Churchill's extreme conclusions and to cling closer to the safer path indicated by their ultimate leader Salisbury. Disraeli had foreseen the first part of the process. 'When they [the Conservatives] come in they will have to give him anything he chooses to ask for, and in a very short time they will have to take anything he chooses to give them',[2] he said to Sir Henry James two months before his death.

In the Bradlaugh affair, out of which the Fourth Party grew, Gladstone found himself at the very outset of his administration, paying the penalty for his involvement with the forces of extremism. Despite his known personal piety he damned himself utterly in the eyes of many Liberals, as well as all Conservatives, by personally moving the resolution allowing the atheist Charles Bradlaugh to make an affirmation instead of the customary oath. One horrified Liberal wrote a pamphlet which he sent to Akers-Douglas entitled 'A Liberal's View of the Government Atheism Affirmation Bill'. Part of this diatribe ran as follows: 'That a number of creatures in human form professing

[1] Churchill, op. cit., 129–31. [2] Ibid., 129.

belief in God Almighty . . . having banded together to bring about the public legislative celebration of dishonour and profanement of that belief and its author by special national enactment of atheism, rank and undisguised, is a matter at once shocking, abhorrent, incredible, looking like absolute jesting with a matter of such awful and supreme solemnity . . .' The author sent this pamphlet to Akers-Douglas with the comment that 'your language and attitude in the House last night deserve record in letters of gold'.

This was in May 1883, and, though not Akers-Douglas's maiden speech, was his first utterance in the House of any importance. ('We sometimes hear it said, with a sneer, that Mr Akers-Douglas's and Mr. Pemberton's voices are seldom heard in Parliament,' wrote a Kent paper, 'as if for that reason they were not doing their best for their constituency. We should rather draw the reverse inference.') But it lends some substance to the notion that Akers-Douglas had formed a fairly close association with the members of the Fourth Party—as he undoubtedly did with their leader, Lord Randolph—and probably accounts for the many jocular references in later years to his having been 'Whip to the Fourth Party' (though in fact, of course, a party of four members could not possibly need a Whip). At any rate, in one of his first speeches in the House he had identified himself with the cause on which they had chosen to take their stand and which had revealed them as an entity and, in view of Churchill's growing influence, it was probably no coincidence that it was at this very time that he received his first *official* appointment—as one of the Junior Conservative Whips. Actually it was Sir Henry Wolff, the real founder of the party, who had been the first to challenge Bradlaugh's right to make the affirmation, and he had been closely followed by Lord Randolph Churchill. Sir Stafford Northcote, always prone to be hypnotized by Gladstone's example (he had once been his secretary) and to forget he was Tory leader, had at first seconded the motion for allowing the substitution of the affirmation for the oath, and this was the reason of the four friends' hostility towards him and of their forming an opposition group within the Tory Party.

The extraordinary and interminable Bradlaugh affair, with its innumerable quasi-farcical episodes, was symptomatic of the overcharged atmosphere of the times. It blew up into such an issue between the two parties—for the whole Conservative Party soon followed the Fourth Party's lead—that it was blandly described in a pamphlet by one partisan as 'between those who were on the side of atheism, disloyalty and immorality, and those who were not'. The same astonishing over-simplification of ideas and issues, which was encouraged both by the new extreme rigour of party lines and by the lack of sophistication in the new electorate, caused Conservative pamphlets at the next election to put forward such propositions as: 'Suppose you give your vote to a Liberal, to one who proposes to follow Mr. Gladstone, then you will have . . . voted for the party which did so much to try to get men into Parliament who do not believe in God.' Or again: 'A man is known by his friends. The Liberals and Radicals were together in the late Government of Mr. Gladstone. If you vote Liberal you will therefore be supporting the Revolutionary Party, who do not believe in authority, any law, any order', etc., etc.

C. BRADLAUGH.

"HOUSE OF COMMONS' MANNER."

This kind of 'smear campaign' which sought to identify the entire Liberal Party with the solitary Bradlaugh and the abominated doctrines which he was held to represent, was almost solely inspired by Randolph Churchill. The episode was meat and drink to him, since he was from start to finish essentially a demagogue. There were certainly a number of superficial points of resemblance between him and Disraeli. There was in him something of the same daring originality, the same independence of judgment, the same love of adventure, the same capacity for leadership, the same supreme self-confidence as had characterized Disraeli forty years before. But there the resemblance ended. Despite the flippant tone of his most celebrated *bons mots*, Disraeli's brilliance was backed by profound study and a highly serious cast of mind, whereas Churchill's restless mind only mastered a subject when absolutely obliged to do so, as when he was confronted with the responsibilities of a government department. Then, admittedly, his ambition combined with his great natural intelligence achieved astonishing results. But in the main he simply allowed himself to become intoxicated by the ease and fluency with which he found himself able to propound his ill-digested ideas and by the effect they had upon uneducated audiences.

It was as the self-appointed heir to Disraeli's new-found tradition of Tory Democracy that Randolph Churchill presented himself to his compatriots. But, after exploiting the political legacy and the immense prestige of his great predecessor, he lost no time in discarding those parts of the heritage which he found uninteresting or inconvenient. In fact, despite his personal hand in inaugurating the Disraeli cult through the Primrose League, he made no bones with friends and colleagues of his suspicions regarding the genuineness of Disraeli's Tory Democracy. Needless to say, the main advantage of this course was in making himself appear as the 'true prophet' and the true innovator. His motto was, like Disraeli's, 'Trust the people', and he professed the same concern for the 'condition of the people', and the same belief in 'the ascertained and much-tried common-sense which is the peculiarity of the English people',[1] to use his own words. But he went a good deal further when he said: 'If you want to gain the confidence of the working classes, let them have a share and a large share—a real share and not a sham share—in your party Councils and in your party government.'[2]

Randolph Churchill, like so many other aristocratic revolutionaries before and after him, felt so secure in his position as to be able to afford to flatter the populace at the expense of his own class. In a public speech in 1885 he said: '"Trust the people"—I have tried to make that my motto; but I know, and will not conceal, that there are still a few in our Party who have that lesson yet to learn and who have yet to understand that the Tory Party of today is no longer identified with that small and narrow class which is connected with the ownership of land.'[3] Even more explicitly he wrote later in the same year to Lord

[1] Churchill, 231. [2] Ibid., 242. [3] Ibid., 232.

Salisbury urging 'an active progressive—I risk the word, a democratic—policy, a casting-off and a burning of those old worn out aristocratic and class garments, from which the Derby–Dizzy lot, with their following of county families, could never, or never cared to, extricate themselves.'[1] Nevertheless, say what he might, he was as inescapably a member of 'that small and narrow class' and his mentality was as much conditioned by his membership of it, as any of those of whom he spoke so slightingly. In fact his own easy entry into politics and his swift advancement to the Front Bench were at least as much due to this fact as to his own brilliant natural powers. Moreover, throughout his brief career, he more than anyone behaved as though he regarded it as giving him some kind of exclusive right to rule; for he was intolerant of opposition, often insufferably arrogant and insolent, and incapable of placating enemies or conciliating antagonists.

Although Lord Randolph had apparently accepted Lord Salisbury as his party leader after the death of Disraeli, and had even (in a letter to *The Times* of April 12th, 1883) called upon the party to 'rally round' him, he really only pretended to defer to him, inwardly somewhat looked down on him, and all the while regarded him as a rival for that coveted position. For in another letter to *The Times* only a few days earlier (March 31st) he had bluntly declared that the Conservatives were divided among themselves and without any real leader. Having scornfully rejected both Sir Stafford Northcote and Lord Cairns[2] he indicated Lord Salisbury as the only possible choice, although implying that even the latter was from 'an exaggerated idea of political loyalty' to some extent ineffective. In this connection it should be said that Lord Salisbury was indeed strictly only leader in the House of Lords and even the Queen had privately assured Northcote that she regarded him as the 'Leader of the great Conservative Party'.

The same reasons inclined Lord Salisbury, on his part, to see in Lord Randolph a rival whom it was wise to placate, but also to keep a wary eye upon. Apart from both being members of the aristocracy the two men had practically nothing else in

[1] Churchill, 415.

[2] First Earl Cairns, Lord Chancellor 1867–8 and 1874–80.

common. Where Churchill was blatant, voluble and sociable, Salisbury was aloof, reserved and unapproachable. If Churchill wooed the masses and ostensibly forswore his own class, Salisbury remained impenitently aristocratic in both manner and outlook—a fact which was very crudely and unfairly exploited by Chamberlain in his 'Radical Jo' days when he said: 'Lord Salisbury constitutes himself the spokesman of a class—of the class to which he himself belongs—"who toil not, neither do they spin . . ."'[1] Scion of a great family accustomed for centuries to a leading role in the country, wealthy and extensive landowner, powerful county magnate, it was inevitable—especially with his personal characteristics—that Salisbury should seem to embody that older type of conservatism which reached back beyond the Tory Democracy of Disraeli or the middle-class mercantilism of Peel. But actually, despite outward appearances, he was too outstanding both in intellect and in intelligence to be so glibly labelled as Chamberlain tried to suggest.

Salisbury, that is to say, was too astute a politician not to realize that, though Churchill could at times be a most embarrassing liability, he was in the main, through his immense personal influence and magnetism, one of the party's principal assets. Indeed, through these qualities Churchill became for a time not only far more in touch with public opinion than Salisbury ever could be, but also he became to some extent the actual creator of public opinion. An example of this fact is afforded by the founding in 1883 of the 'Primrose League'. Although it was actually the brain-child of Sir Henry Wolff, Lord Randolph instantly saw that such a league, modelled on the lines of the already popular and numerous 'friendly societies', would have an immense appeal for the masses—of a kind, moreover, which the existing, orthodox Conservative associations could never have. It was to be expected, therefore, that the new League should in its beginnings have been 'viewed with sour distrust by all Conservatives who were officially orthodox, virtuous and loyal', as Churchill's son and biographer afterwards expressed it.[2] Yet, within a few years, it had been taken up by the leadership of the party as a most valuable propaganda instrument, and by 1891 it had enrolled a million members. Well might Chamberlain say in a speech at this time: 'I pay the

[1] Speech at Birmingham, March 30th, 1883. [2] Churchill, 204.

greatest attention to anything he [Churchill] says because I find that what he says today his leaders say tomorrow. They follow him with halting steps, somewhat unwillingly; but they always follow him. They may not always like the prescription he makes up for them; but they always swallow it.'[1] It was the fulfilment of Disraeli's prophecy about him.

In the end, of course, they did not swallow it. But, long before that point was reached, Lord Randolph had become fully aware that, though they might relish and applaud his impudent attacks upon their adversaries, and especially upon the 'Grand Old Man' himself, all the most influential Conservatives in the House of Commons and the Carlton Club were united in their dislike, distrust and jealousy of him. Therefore, having made the formal gesture of inviting Salisbury to come forward and head the 'Tory Democratic Movement', he turned away from the leaders in Parliament and began to base his political power on his undoubted popularity in the country.

LORD R. CHURCHILL.

The New President of the Working-Man's Conservative Association—"A Horny-handed Son of Toil."

It was in conformity with this policy that Lord Randolph deliberately set to work to capture as much as he could of the Conservative Party organization. The latter at this date comprised two distinct bodies with quite distinct characteristics. On the one hand there was the 'Central Committee', a prolongation of the Committee set up and presided over by Disraeli after the electoral disaster of 1880 in order to consider methods of improving the party organization. Its members were nominees of the leader of the party—and he, not unnatur-

[1] Speech in favour of the Reform Bill, House of Commons, March 27th, 1884.

ally, kept the ultimate control of party affairs and funds in his own hands, except in so far as he delegated it to these nominees. On the other hand there was the National Union of Conservative Associations, a popular body representing the constituencies through elected delegates, which had no executive powers and only acted in an advisory capacity. The National Union was therefore the obvious object of Lord Randolph's championship and having in 1883 got himself elected to the chairmanship of their Council, he openly declared war on the Central Committee and set about wresting from it both power and finance and placing these instead in the hands of the Council of the National Union.

It was at this point that the least attached of the four original members of the Fourth Party began to sever his links with it. Not only did Arthur Balfour consider that reform of party organization was entirely outside the sphere of Fourth Party activities, as these were originally conceived, but he had a family tie and a growing political sympathy with Salisbury both of which were incompatible with the other allegiance. Moreover, as he afterwards wrote, he 'mildly resented all this talk about "Tory Democracy"—as if Tory Democracy was an invention of the Fourth Party, and in some mysterious way mixed up with the proposed changes in Conservative organization'.[1]

Another who had perhaps an even more cogent reason for ending such connection as he had had with the Fourth Party was Akers-Douglas. For, having in the previous year been appointed to be a junior Conservative Whip, he was now, in 1884, promoted to the place of second Whip, with a strong hint that he was likely to be made Chief Whip in the foreseeable future The letter which he wrote on this occasion to his old friend and adviser Sir William Hart Dyke was rather touching in the loyalty and consideration shown towards one of his friends at the very moment when his own ambitions were about to be splendidly fulfilled.

Private

House of Commons,
May 16, 1884

My dear Dyke,

I told you the other day that Sir Stafford Northcote had sent for me and had asked me to undertake the duties of Whip in the

[1] Balfour, op. cit., 157.

place of Lord Crichton[1] who wished to retire, kindly hinting at the same time that there was a possibility of my being hereafter called upon to take the place of 1st Whip. Acting on the advice of my friends I am quite prepared to accept the duties now discharged by Lord Crichton as 2nd Whip, but I feel my friend Tom Thornhill[2] may be hurt by my appointment as I know he is anxious to appear as teller during the present session in the place of Lord Crichton.

Bearing in mind the future possibility I have alluded to I am anxious to see as much of the work as I possibly can (especially with regard to Electioneering etc.) and therefore would like to be behind the scenes with Mr. Winn.[3] Under these circumstances would it be possible to arrange an amicable understanding that while taking Crichton's place I could hand over the 'telling' to Thornhill for the present session as I know he is very anxious to be entrusted with that duty.

Yours sincerely,
A.A.D.

In his obvious ability, integrity and discretion, as well as in his amiable character, the official leadership of the party had recognized the makings of an invaluable staff-officer whom it would be inept not to attach firmly to the orthodox cause as early as possible. For his part no doubt even Lord Randolph, who was no great admirer of the current whipping as conducted by Rowland Winn, was glad to press the claims of so promising a young man and to plant in a key position in the official camp one who was already a friend and ally. Actually, with his natural soundness and steadiness of character Akers-Douglas did not need overmuch persuasion to accept real responsibility and 'settle down' politically. He retained always an admiration and affectionate regard for Lord Randolph, whose confidence he had to the end, as is proved by the general tenor of their correspondence and the fact of the latter addressing to him the most momentous letter of his life.[4] Indeed it could reasonably

[1] Eldest son of Earl of Erne; M.P., Co. Fermanagh.

[2] Sir Thomas Thornhill, Bart.; M.P., West Suffolk.

[3] Rowland Winn, Chief Conservative Whip 1880–85; created Lord St. Oswald.

[4] The letter of January 1st, 1887, explaining the reasons for his resignation (see below p. 108). It is true it was addressed to Akers-Douglas in his official capacity, was quite impersonal and intended to be shown to other colleagues; but Churchill could have chosen any other colleague for the purpose.

be argued that his early association with Lord Randolph and the Fourth Party was an earnest of that progressive outlook which, on certain topics, he was to make felt when later he reached a position of influence under Salisbury. These things apart, nothing could have been more dissimilar than the characters, temperaments and careers of the two men: in fact they presented a complete antithesis. The one blatant and mercurial with a meteoric career of spectacular but brief fame; the other reserved and level, with a long, steady, successful but unspectacular record of service.

In Akers-Douglas Salisbury found a man in many ways of his own type—great landowner, county magnate, staunch Conservative—but, fortunately, though also by nature reserved, not like himself, aloof and unapproachable. Akers-Douglas was therefore for him the ideal chief-of-staff (as he was very soon to be), because whilst he understood his master's mind and way of thinking, he also understood the minds of the party rank and file and the ways in which they were likely to be affected by his master's policies and decisions, and so he could keep each in touch with the other with the minimum of friction or misunderstanding. It was small wonder therefore that he not only rapidly became indispensable to the Chief, but also won for himself a position of influence in the party councils, which, under a different type of chief, could scarcely have been so great or so unique.

II

LORD RANDOLPH RAMPS: AKERS-DOUGLAS ARRIVES

THE course which Lord Randolph Churchill proceeded to adopt as head and champion of the National Union of Conservative Associations was little calculated to recommend itself to men like Salisbury, Balfour and Akers-Douglas, for it made him appear as little better than a demagogue or an agitator with no regard for the cohesion and long-term interests of the party of which he was supposed to be a leading member. It was his aim and that of his supporters to air the grievances of the National Union at the annual conference to be held at Sheffield in July 1884. From an angry letter (dated July 27th) from him to Akers-Douglas it is clear that Sir Stafford Northcote had, after consultation with Akers-Douglas, at first tried to dissuade him from such a course in the party interest, but had later decided that it would be more politic not to interfere and had informed 'loyal' members of the Council that he would not tender any advice about the Conference's agenda. Churchill, who had been making capital out of the official leaders' anxiety and probable interference, was furious.

> . . . I have been placed in a false position by such conduct and by the language held to me on the subject both by yourself and Mr. Winn [Chief Conservative Whip]. For the future it will be impossible for me to place any reliance on information given to me from the official and recognised authorities of the party.

Having thus proclaimed that he considered himself absolved from his allegiance, Churchill, in his capacity as chairman, immediately set about tackling Salisbury regarding the aim of securing for the National Union 'its legitimate influence in the party organization'. There followed a duel of wits between the rival leaders in which Lord Salisbury, whilst pretending to be conciliatory, did his best quietly to snuff out the National Union's pretensions, and Lord Randolph attempted to force Lord Salisbury's hand by bringing the whole issue into the open and before the public. Lord Randolph had an initial success, for there sprang up a considerable popular movement in his favour, supported by *The Times*, which wrote: 'The main issue between him and the official leaders of the Opposition is whether the internal organization of the party should be for the future established on a popular and representative or on a secret and irresponsible basis.'

Despite this encouragement, however, there remained a sufficiently powerful minority against Churchill on the Council for him to decide to come to terms with Salisbury and the official leaders. Salisbury, on his side, had not been intimidated by Churchill but, as in all his other dealings with him, inclined 'to let Randolph hammer away', as Balfour put it. At the same time he was sufficiently impressed with the extent of Churchill's influence to wish also to come to terms for the sake of the party. Moreover, by this time it required little persuasion to induce the Central Committee to liquidate itself, and though there was a show of making reforms in the National Union, the latter in fact remained substantially unchanged in character and gradually faded into an obscurity from which it was destined never fully to emerge.[1] Meanwhile, the central organization of the party remained under the exclusive and direct control of the leaders, acting now only through the Whips and the staff of the Conservative Central Office.

Lord Randolph had resigned the chairmanship of the National Union as a manoeuvre at an earlier stage of the battle, but he would almost certainly have been re-elected had he so wished. However, he now dropped his ambitions in this direction altogether, readily supporting the nomination of the neutral

[1] Only two years after all this commotion Middleton was writing to Lord St. Oswald (March 29th, 1886): '. . . I quite agree with you as to the part of the National Union but I hope soon we may make it a more useful society—if it refuses to move with the time it will soon cease to exist.'

Sir Michael Hicks Beach as chairman, and of three of his erstwhile adherents—Gorst, Balfour and Akers-Douglas—as vice-chairmen. The truth was that, with a general election approaching, he realized he would no more benefit by this display of internecine strife than would the official party leaders. Moreover, earlier in the year, he had accepted the invitation of the Birmingham Conservatives to contest that citadel of organized Radicalism against its two most formidable leaders—John Bright and Joseph Chamberlain. His nervousness about the effect upon his prospects of his recent mutinous conduct is evident from a most amiable letter which he wrote to Akers-Douglas only a few days after the angry recriminations of the one already quoted about the Sheffield conference. Akers-Douglas had asked him to speak at Margate, which was in the former's constituency. He replied:

2, Connaught Place, W.
July 2nd, 1884.

My dear Akers-Douglas,

I would do almost anything to oblige you, but I am bound to say that if I was to go to Margate next week having shirked the meeting at Birmingham tonight on a plea of indisposition which I imagine takes in no one, I should be giving mortal offence to my friends at Birmingham, whom I fear I have already tried rather high. I enclose you a letter for the gentleman at Margate whose name I cannot read, written in the sense you wish . . .

Yours very sincerely,
Randolph S. Churchill.

It is a measure of his morbidly nervous constitution that of these two letters written within the space of a few days the handwriting of the earlier is so shaky with anger as to be sometimes almost illegible, whereas that of the later one is firm and clear.

If Lord Randolph was still being careful not to overreach himself, so were the party leaders. When the National Union quarrel had first shown him up in his true colours, many Tories had been in favour of an immediate show-down. But Balfour formulated the policy which evidently commended itself as much to his uncle as to himself when he wrote to the latter: 'I am inclined to think that we should avoid, as far as possible, all "rows", until R[andolph] puts himself flagrantly in the wrong by some act of party disloyalty which everybody can understand and nobody can deny. By this course we may avoid a battle altogether, but if a battle is forced upon us we shall be sure to win it.'[1]

Lord Randolph, however, did not under-estimate the strength of the forces which backed Lord Salisbury and it was for this reason that he used the latter as a stalking-horse. He pretended to defer to him and also pretended to think that Salisbury shared his own advanced views, whilst all the time underlining the fact that they were equals and rivals for the leadership. When he had seemingly supported Salisbury's leadership and invited him to come forward and head the 'New Tories', he had written in a public letter of 'a statesman who fears not to meet, and who knows how to sway, immense masses of the working classes' and who 'by all the varied influences of an ancient name can move the hearts of households'.[2] But he undoubtedly calculated that, if the description was definitely ironical when applied to Salisbury, it was also blatantly applicable to himself.

Lord Randolph also knew that, if the bulk of his own party hated his ideas, the Liberals hated them just as much—not as emanating from a self-styled Tory, but because of the excesses to which, through rivalry, they goaded their own Radical wing. Proof of this is to be had from Gladstone himself, who wrote to Hartington (November 10th, 1885): 'I wish to say something [in his election speeches] about the modern Radicalism. But I must include this, that, if it is rampant and ambitious, the two most prominent causes of its forwardness have been: (1) Tory Democracy; (2) the gradual disintegration of the Liberal aristocracy.'[3] Lord Randolph, for his part, scorned the latter category and determined to hasten its disintegration. 'The Whigs hate the New Conservatism and the Tory Democracy because it has cut the ground from under their feet; because the Tory Democracy has taken the place of the Whigs . . .'[4]

The sum of all these things may well incline us to accept Lord Rosebery's later judgment on Lord Randolph, that he was 'in the wrong party . . . his opinions, his instincts, his aims

[1] Balfour, op. cit., 164.
[2] Churchill, 199.
[3] Morley, op. cit., III, 240.
[4] Churchill, 355.

were all not merely Liberal, but Radical'.[1] In the light of this verdict it is interesting therefore to compare his policy on important issues with that of the self-professed Radicals of the days.

The foremost issue of that time was that of Irish Home Rule. Here, though their policy might at first sight have been expected to be obvious and unanimous, the Radicals were divided. Many Radicals of this time were in fact, for various reasons, great imperialists, and this ultimately led to the split in the Liberal Party and the desertion of such great Radical leaders as Chamberlain and Bright.

Lord Randolph, too, proved to be one of Home Rule's most violent opponents. It is true that for a time he was convinced that Ireland could be ruled without coercion and that on his own initiative he approached Parnell and gave a virtual pledge that the Tories would reverse the policy, in return for which Parnell promised the Irish vote to the Tories at the coming election. Despite this, however, Lord Randolph remained adamant towards the idea of legislative separation. 'The surrender to Home Rule, no matter how you disguise it, is the reverse of conservative . . .', he wrote, adding most unbecomingly, 'the Disraeli epoch of constant metamorphoses of principles and party has passed away.'[2] Moreover, he was at one with Salisbury in being strongly opposed to any co-operation between Tories and Liberals on the Irish question—although Gladstone himself, as well as some Tories, were in favour. 'Oh no, we will have nothing to do with Home Rule now,' he is reported to have said on hearing of Gladstone's intentions, 'we have got Gladstone pinned to it; we will make him expose his scheme in the House of Commons. Let him defeat us with the aid of the Parnellites, and then let us dissolve and go to the country with the cry of "The Empire in danger".'[3]

Coming from Lord Randolph this slogan was, to say the least, inappropriate; for, in the words of his son, 'Lord Randolph Churchill was never what is nowadays called an Imperialist'[4]—unlike his political antecedent Disraeli or his Radical contemporary Chamberlain. Indeed, in this connection, it is ironical

[1] Lord Rosebery: *Lord Randolph Churchill*, 117.

[2] Churchill, 419–20.

[3] A. G. Gardiner: *Life of Sir William Harcourt*, I, 550.

[4] Churchill, 487.

to find Gladstone writing in all sincerity to Hartington (November 20th, 1885) about a condition 'which you and I both think vital to the solution of the Irish problem, namely the unity of the Empire'.[1] Five years earlier he had even referred to the Irish nationalists as 'marching through rapine to the dismemberment of the Empire'. But then the trouble with Gladstone was that as soon as he had become 'converted' to it, Home Rule became with him a religion, and, therefore, his peculiar temperament made him henceforth utterly unable to appreciate either the nature and consequences of such a momentous step or the bitter accusations of his enemies.

Another issue on which Lord Randolph's attitude appeared, in the light of his professed principles, either disingenuous or at best paradoxical, was that of the Third Reform Bill, which the Gladstone Government introduced in 1884 to carry Disraeli's measure to its logical conclusion by extending household suffrage to the counties and enfranchising the agricultural labourers. Although his biographer admits that Lord Randolph later confessed that he could not be expected to look upon a measure for the extinction of the borough he represented (which the Reform would entail) 'with any very longing eye', yet he claims that he took his stand against the Bill mainly because he believed the rest of the Tory Party to be united against it.[2] Actually, what the Conservatives opposed so strongly was the separate treatment of the questions of reform and of redistribution of seats: they insisted that they were inseparable and required simultaneous treatment. Churchill later attempted to represent this argument as merely a mask for Conservative opposition to reform or change of any kind. But the argument was perfectly logical and Churchill's attempt to misrepresent it was shown to be nugatory by the Liberals' final acceptance of it. Indeed, as far as Conservative reformatory zeal went, both Gladstone and the Queen declared themselves shocked by what the latter called 'the too Radical nature'[3] of the Conservative proposals for redistribution! In any case, no Conservative now dared (since Disraeli's Bill) to attack reform in principle—and, of course, Churchill least of all. Therefore, in the beginning, when

[1] Holland: *Life of the Duke of Devonshire*, II, 92.
[2] Churchill, 263.
[3] *The Letters of Queen Victoria*, Second Series, III, 569.

he was following what he allegedly supposed to be the party line, he attacked it on more trivial grounds—the inopportuneness of the moment, the risk of a large addition to the Irish electorate. He denounced it as a Government ruse to divert attention from foreign affairs, and—this from the arch-demagogue of the day—he alleged that there was no indication of any desire for the vote among the unenfranchised masses.

Such was the stuff which Lord Randolph was propounding to a great audience of Scottish artisans in Edinburgh on December 19th, 1883, when of all people, his old comrade in arms Arthur Balfour unexpectedly, on the very platform itself, dissociated himself from all that Churchill had said against the Reform Bill. Mortifying as this experience was, it brought home to him the untenability of his position. Furthermore, his acceptance of the invitation to contest the Birmingham seat against Chamberlain and Bright, which had already influenced his conduct over the National Union struggle, now finally decided him to abandon his opposition to Reform. With the prospect of such opponents and of a large, urban, democratic constituency—instead of a small rural family borough—there was no rational alternative.

Lord Randolph's method of storming the great Radical stronghold was, however, most peculiar and casts an interesting light upon his character and his real political beliefs. Beginning with lengthy tributes to the value of the Radical contribution to English life and thought in the past, he had proceeded to disclaim any knowledge of Tory policy or any right to propound it. 'I do not know what will be the policy of the Tory party,' he told the Birmingham electors. 'I am not the least bit in the confidence of their leaders, and I must admit that I do not enjoy the high honour of their friendship . . . but I think I can tell you what their policy ought to be—and in general terms what I shall try and make it to be—if ever I should represent this powerful constituency.'[1]

On the eve of the election (November 22nd, 1885) he wrote to Akers-Douglas:

> . . . Things are in a curious state here. The best opinion seems to be that it will be very close, and my own opinion is that Bright

[1] Churchill, 227.

will win by the skin of his teeth. But after all we may get an awful licking and then we shall look very foolish.

The Caucus are straining every nerve; at the same time our party has never been so well worked before, and is quite as popular as the Brightites.

I think we shall finally decide to count on Tuesday night. We are so awfully afraid of being thought afraid.

Lord Randolph's guess was pretty accurate, for, though John Bright's devotees managed to prolong again the reign of their venerable idol, Lord Randolph came within 700 votes of ending it: a remarkable achievement in all the circumstances.

Parnell's promise to Lord Randolph that the Irish vote would be given to the Tories at the next election in the expectation of the latter reversing the coercion policy was actually fulfilled even earlier, when the Irish members voted for the Tory amendment to the Budget which brought Gladstone's five-year-old second Ministry to a sudden and inglorious end in June 1885. It was indeed the Irish Question which lay at the bottom of what at the time appeared as a most startling and unforeseen occurrence, the truth being that the Liberal party was split upon the question of the renewal of the coercion laws and that it therefore welcomed an opportunity to commit hara-kiri and pass the baby on to the Tories.

The Tories, on their side, despite the tremendous barrage of fire which they had been maintaining against the Liberal Government, were aghast at the prospect of having to assume responsibility for matters on which they were themselves divided, the more so since they were in a minority and under the provisions of the new Reform Act there could not be a general election until at least the autumn. But the Irish were exultant to see an end to the vacillating policy of the Liberals towards their country, their hopes now pinned upon the great rival party which could scarcely do worse for them and which, if Lord Randolph's pledge and other portents counted for anything, might even do a great deal for them.

When therefore the Liberal Government fell, Lord Randolph himself, who at the head of his little band had often joined forces with the Irish Nationalists against it, led their cheering and that of the other bright young Tory back-benchers, regardless of the dismay, bordering on panic, of the Tory party mandarins. The extraordinary contrast was vividly described in a contemporary newspaper report.

> No one who witnessed the scene will ever forget it, amplified, exaggerated, and rendered grotesque by Lord Randolph Churchill, waving his hat and shrieking as he stood upon his bench. Mr. Winn [Chief Conservative Whip] stood half terrified at the paper signifying the defeat of the Government of 1880; his hand trembled and his voice shook with the emotions that swayed him . . .

It is significant that already the Conservative leaders were becoming interested to know the sheep from the goats among their Liberal adversaries, for next day (June 9th, '85) Akers-Douglas wrote to Salisbury: 'Sir Richard Cross[1] tells me you are anxious to know the names of Liberals who walked out to avoid voting last night. I am sorry I cannot ascertain their names as none was seen to go out within ¼ hour of division—No member was seen in Central Lobby during division—sixteen Liberals who did not vote were in the House earlier in the evening.' Despite his inability to answer the question it is clear that the man who was to be called the 'Prince of Whips' was beginning to get his intelligence service pretty well organized.

The unexpected emergency immediately focused attention on the extremely ambiguous position of the Tory leadership. Although circumstances seemed to point to Salisbury as the man of destiny, Northcote appears to have nursed the illusion that it was to be himself, and to have been deeply mortified when he was not sent for by the Queen. Meanwhile, the fact that Hicks Beach lost no time in urging Salisbury to placate Churchill by offering him high office in any Tory government which might be formed, and the fact that Salisbury immediately acted upon the suggestion, all goes to prove the unique position which Churchill already enjoyed and the importance which these other leaders attached to giving public recognition to it.

As soon as Lord Salisbury had received and accepted the Queen's commission to form a government he offered Lord Randolph the India Office. But the latter refused because his

[1] Home Secretary, 1874–80 and 1885–6, later 1st Viscount Cross.

old bugbear, Sir Stafford Northcote, was to be Leader of the House. Obstinately resisting the entreaties of colleagues and friends, his mother and even Lady Salisbury, he refused any compromise, impudently declaring to a friend: 'He [Salisbury] can form a ministry if necessary with waiters from the Carlton Club.'[1] When Salisbury hesitated, Hicks Beach again urgently intervened declaring his conviction that Churchill's membership of the Government was 'vital to any hope of Conservative success at the General Election, for his popularity with the new electorate was greater than that of any other member of the party'.[2] If final proof of Churchill's power were needed it was provided by Salisbury capitulating to his presumptuous terms and relegating Northcote to sinecure office and a peerage, whilst the *enfant terrible* himself finally accepted the India Office, after extorting as a final condition marks of favour for two of his henchmen, Wolff and Gorst.

Meanwhile the hopes which had in the preceding year been held out to Akers-Douglas were now realized, and, at the relatively tender age of thirty-three, he found himself appointed Chief Whip with the office of Patronage Secretary to the Treasury, which gave him the rank of a junior minister in this first short ministry of Lord Salisbury. Even whilst he had been allegedly 'whipping' the Fourth Party, Akers-Douglas had begun to take the measure of the members who trooped into the lobby after the regular whips, and, when he himself became one of the latter, it was observed with surprise that he had already acquired a thorough knowledge of the individuals who had composed the House since his entry into it. Indeed, it soon became apparent to his masters that he possessed an uncanny insight into the passions, prejudices and potentialities of the motley collection of individuals who filled the back benches, intrigued and gossiped in the lobby and who, when all was said and done, *were* the party. From being a diffident and nervous candidate he had through natural ability and intelligent observation mastered his highly responsible job as well as all the niceties of parliamentary procedure, so that he had acquired not only a reputation, but an authority and a *savoir-faire* which few would have predicted when he had first entered Parliament only five years earlier. These six months of responsibility in Salisbury's

[1] Churchill, 319. [2] Ibid., 311.

first ministry (known as the 'Caretaker Government') were to be the prelude to his long and triumphant reign under the Second Salisbury Government. In them he was tried and tested and found to be the ideal Whip and the foundation was laid for the long and intimate association between chief and lieutenant which was to be a factor of the first importance in the domestic history of the next twenty years.

Here we may pause for a moment to survey through the young Whip's eyes, as it were, the theatre of his activities at this time, together with some of the actors who moved upon its stage whose names will constantly be recurring throughout the ensuing pages.

Gladstone was of course the dominating figure, whether in or out of office. There was no member who could have remembered the House without that tempestuous and tremendous presence; the massive head with the granite features, the burning eyes and the tight-lipped mouth which could open to such astonishing effect. Next to him, affording the most complete contrast, with top-hat tipped well over his eyes, would lounge in an almost recumbent posture the somnolent figure of the Marquess of Hartington. He too had become almost a permanent feature, having sat there for close on thirty years. The lethargic demeanour, the heavy almost oafish look and the rather jagged beard, which marred his otherwise essentially fine and handsome features, concealed the undoubted fact that, though limited in many respects, he was a man of strong convictions, great courage and intense public-spiritedness. T. P. O'Connor has related that a peculiarity of his speeches was that towards the ends of his sentences 'you would suddenly hear something like a prolonged wail: it was an extraordinary form of that stammer and hesitancy in speech which is characteristic of so much English oratory'.[1] He was also said to have been seen to yawn in the middle of one of his own speeches and when chaffed about it to have replied, 'Yes, wasn't it damned dull!'

Next would come another complete contrast: the 'Great Joe' Chamberlain—immaculately dressed, orchid in buttonhole, monocle set in face of studied inscrutability, yet of bird-like alertness, at this time disconcerting and affronting 'the People's

[1] T. P. O'Connor: *Memoirs of an Old Parliamentarian*, I, 185–6.

William' and the Whig Marquess alike by the extreme Radicalism of his views and speeches, though within a few months to break away for ever from the former and to find himself a comrade-in-arms with the latter—and eventually with the Tories. Also on the point of going over to the enemy was another pair who had held high office under Gladstone—Goschen and Henry James. Otherwise they had little in common. Goschen was in appearance a beetling, myopic, German professor with a mild manner but an obstinate character; his undoubted ability and value was offset in the eyes of his contemporaries by an irritating meticulousness. James was the prototype of the handsome English gentleman, bluff and kindly both in face and manner; but he was an abler advocate at the Bar than in the House of Commons.

Also on the Front Bench would be Joe's erstwhile crony, the blunt-faced, bearded, republican baronet Sir Charles Dilke, still regarded as Gladstone's most likely successor, but destined shortly to have all his hopes ruined through the machinations of a ruthless woman and to spend the remainder of a long life on the back benches. Another 'natural' successor to Gladstone, who also never became it, and a notable ornament of the House of long standing, was the gigantic, awkward and tiresome Sir William Harcourt, likewise an aristocrat (but of far more venerable descent than Dilke) who affected various Radical attitudes which came strangely from one with his patrician and haughty countenance and arrogant demeanour. Never on the Front Bench (owing to the Queen's strong objection to him) but always conspicuous by his actor's air and style of dress, and always in the thick of any intrigue, was that notorious exhibitionist Henry Labouchere ('Labby'), owner and editor of *Truth*. Not aristocratic, but immensely wealthy, he was ostensibly an advanced Radical: but above all he was a *poseur* and *farceur* and therefore takes his place rather as a sort of clown or court jester of the House.

But even those typical Victorian worthies, like John Bright and John Morley, whose solid, bourgeois virtues were so often extolled at the expense of the aristocrats and adventurers, could be and often were just as vain, arrogant and perverse as the latter. Bright, in his day the wielder of an influence greater than Gladstone's, was now long past his prime and quite out of step with the later development of Radicalism of which he had once been the foremost exponent; but his small fierce presence and leonine head still aroused feelings of awe in the House for reasons which were now but dimly comprehended. He was another who was shortly to break from Gladstone over Home Rule; although Morley, a younger man of humble origin but

H. LABOUCHERE. W. V. HARCOURT. W. E. GLADSTONE.

LABBY AND "THE MERRY OLD GENTLEMAN."
"QUIPS AND CRANKS."

great intellect and high principles (including a fervent agnosticism), was to stick to him and that cause through long years of disappointment. In fact it might be said that Morley was too intellectual and too high principled to be a really successful politician, though he undoubtedly exerted a powerful influence upon his times through his rare consistency and his intimacy with all the leading men of his day, particularly Gladstone.

In the early days of the 1880 Parliament the Conservative Front Bench could exhibit nothing comparable, not only in weight and stature but in sheer diversity and originality. The weak but worthy Sir Stafford Northcote with his goat's beard, thick glasses and kindly air of refinement; the less kindly, less refined, but equally bearded and bespectacled face of Sir Richard Cross; the honest, rather bewildered monkey-face of W. H. Smith, with the troubled but resolute eyes; Hicks Beach, dark and bearded ('Black Michael'), withdrawn and touchy. Even the rather overwhelming figure of Henry Chaplin, his monocled nutcracker face wreathed round with carefully curled quiffs and whiskers; that portly, dewlapped, heavy-lidded lawyer Sir Richard Webster, or the irresponsible, American-born Ashmead-Bartlett, who advocated a policy of fatuous jingoism for the land of his adoption and in appearance affected the style of a Confederate Colonel of the land of his birth—even these could not make up for the relative lack of weight and colour on the Tory Front Bench.

No, the focus of attention on this side of the House was at this time upon the bench below the gangway where were ensconced the four members of the Fourth Party: the dapper, dandiacal figure of Randolph Churchill with his baleful, bulging eyes, twirling his prodigious moustaches; Drummond Wolff, the stout, urbane, semitic diplomat; Gorst, the frigid, cantankerous, but ever-vigilant lawyer; Balfour, so frail and ladylike in manner and appearance, concealing (were it only known) a mailed fist in a velvet glove. This little group really set the pace of the House by their indefatigable and relentless exploitation of every opportunity which current affairs offered and of every difficulty which beset the Government. For even the Irish, with whom as fellow rebels (even if in a different cause) there existed a natural bond of sympathy, often took their lead from the Fourth Party's interventions and joined in the hue and cry after Gladstone, who at this time was still their enemy. Other excitements were periodically provided by the sudden incursions of the vast sea-monster-like form of Charles Bradlaugh attempting to take his seat and being removed struggling from the House—the man who for several years was represented by partisans on both sides as a sort of antichrist, but who later on being admitted, and still more on dying, won golden opinions from everyone for his goodness and kindness and courage.

But the most important and powerful figure in the whole House—not excepting even Gladstone—normally sat on the back benches, often even apart from his own followers. There was a truly hypnotic quality about the abnormally pale, hawk-like countenance of Charles Stewart Parnell with its dark, inscrutable eyes and apostle's beard. This extraordinary man, whose singleness of purpose had made him not only the uncrowned King of Ireland (although a Protestant landlord) but virtually the arbiter of the destinies of Britain for a whole decade, was a poor speaker and far from assiduous in his attendance at the House. He was as cold towards his devoted adherents as to his opponents—'there was always underneath an inner sneer',[1] as even the benevolent Justin M'Carthy admitted —and evidently too a surprising vulgarity and commonplaceness of mind and outlook. Moreover this apparently cold, implacable tyrant was in reality a passionate, highly-strung man, who was a prey to a continual gnawing fear of blackmail and exposure owing to his truly epic love for the wife of a colleague, Captain O'Shea.

O'Shea was one of the 'smart' Irish members—in every sense of the word—whereas the rank and file of the Nationalist Party were mostly poor and humble, though highly educated, men. Therefore, apart from the natural tendency for them to be shunned on account of their policy and behaviour, they could not afford, had they so wished, to join in the sumptuous wining and dining which was so much a part of the life of a House still dominated by the wealthy and 'high society'. One of them, T. P. O'Connor, has described how they would slip out of the House in twos and threes, going over Westminster Bridge or along Vauxhall Bridge Road to find a cheap meal and how, by contrast, their great leader would speed through the night by train and hansom to Eltham to snatch a few hours' rest and felicity with his mistress, as well as a succulent meal prepared with her own hands.[2]

Nevertheless, however drab or sordid might be the circumstances of their private lives the influence upon the course of English politics of the Irish Party and its leader is quite incalculable—a fact to which the greater part of the present narrative will bear witness. By their carefully evolved methods of deliberate and systematic obstruction they completely disjointed the easy-going parliamentary system of centuries, forcing their op-

[1] T. P. O'Connor, op. cit., I, 347.
[2] T. P. O'Connor, op. cit., passim.

1. Chilston Park, from the painting by George Arnold (*c.* 1840).

2. The Four Whips.

Lord Arthur Hill, Col. Waltond, Hon. Sidney Herbert
A. Akers-Douglas

3. A. Akers-Douglas, M.P. (*c.* 1890).

ponents drastically to re-frame the rules of procedure and to muster at all hours massive forces of their supporters for the purpose of smashing this obstruction by the 'closure'. Lord Midleton has written in his memoirs: 'The House of Commons, until 1887, when the closure was none too early invented, professed itself to be master of its own destinies. The duration of debates was uncertain; the House by summary methods shortened unwanted speeches; but a really fine effort being heard by all might and did at times sway votes. A contrast, this, to the system of the present day, by which the closure being fixed some days earlier for a certain evening at eleven, the audience is swelled in the last hour by 100 or 200 legislators, who have been attending to their business elsewhere, and may roll up to vote without having heard a word of the arguments.'[1] Of more immediate concern to the person around whose career this book is woven was the fact that the machinery of the closure, necessitating the attendance of a given—and very high—number of Government supporters, endowed the office of Whip with vastly increased importance and responsibility.

Finally, here is a contemporary vignette of the Whip himself from the *St. Stephen's Review*:

> . . . Mr. Akers-Douglas is looked upon by politicians of all grades as a coming man. His urbanity is a household word; his unobtrusiveness, considering the nature of the duties he has to perform, is wonderful, and the rapidity with which he counts the House astounding . . . He stands over six feet in height, with a lithe, active frame, and a face upon which sits a perennial smile. As he converses his vigilant eyes wander away over one's shoulder, as though on the look-out for any recalcitrant who is meditating a bolt, or a malingerer who would escape the toils. His conversation is rapid and pointed, and one feels intuitively that one is sitting at the feet of a political Gamaliel.
>
> Suddenly at a sign from one of his subordinates, he vanishes into the House with a stride that seems to take in the entire Lobby, and in a few moments the whirr of the division bell breaks in on your tympanum. Five minutes later sees the genial smiling Whip disappearing into his *sanctum sanctorum* the scorer of another victory. As an analyst of men's idiosyncrasies, how they may be expected to vote, and what dissentients will lower his majority, Mr. Akers-Douglas has no living equal, nor is it probable that any

[1] Earl of Midleton: *Records and Reactions, 1856–1939*, 56–7.

> Prime Minister had so staunch a henchman. Mr. Douglas holds very decided views on many of the subjects which are at present stirring men's minds, and although his duties in the Lobby practically preclude him from addressing the House of Commons as a body, it is well known that his powers of suasion are brought very prominently into play when dealing with waverers. Taking him altogether apart from his political position, the Chief Conservative Whip possesses a marked individuality which would have won him distinction in any walk of life. Quick to see a point and grasp it, tenacious of everything which gives dignity to the Conservative cause, a terror to the *dolce far niente* member who would fain regard the House as a comfortable lounging club, Mr. Douglas has earned for himself the regard of every true Conservative. Why we of the *St. Stephen's Review* admire him is that he is the type of ourselves, in that his public utterances show him the contemner of the mutton-headed standard of that Tory squirearchy that declines to move with the times. He is almost democratic in his ideas, and his tenantry have cause to bless the fact that they have so liberal-minded a man to deal with . . .

If Akers-Douglas owed his advancement—as was the view of the contemporary press—to some extent to the recommendation of Lord Randolph, then he in turn was responsible for recommending another key figure of this Tory epoch—Richard Middleton, the Chief Party Agent. For Middleton, an ex-naval officer—usually erroneously addressed as 'Captain' and familiarly known as 'the Skipper'—had been Conservative agent for West Kent in the two preceding years and had impressed Akers-Douglas by the exceptional energy and ability which he applied to his task. He was therefore appointed Chief Party Agent in this summer of 1885 and remained in the post till 1903, working hand in glove with the Chief Whip and with him providing Lord Salisbury with a party intelligence service upon which the latter came absolutely to rely.

With a general election already looming at the time of his appointment, Middleton lost no time in setting to work. 'We are raising a special fund for the purpose of distributing pamphlets, leaflets and etc., from house to house throughout England,' he wrote to Salisbury on July 17th, 1885, 'the men we employ for the purpose of distributing these leaflets are good Conservatives and working men who talk to any they meet on the way.' To one of his lieutenants in the provinces he sent a 'list of working men who are leading men of their trades—I think it might be well to enquire of the local men their opinions as to their fitness'. In September he reported to W. H. Smith: 'The free distribution of leaflets is giving great satisfaction and I think will prove of great service—as far as possible we are endeavouring to leave some Conservative literature at every house in England . . .' And a few days later (September 23rd) he suggests to Lord Claude Hamilton, Chairman of the Council of the National Union, that the pamphlets should be purchasable 'through any bookseller . . . the object is to reach that class of people who are willing to read the truth as published by our side but who will not use the Conservative organization for the purpose'.

Amid the growing atmosphere of party regimentation it is both surprising and refreshing to find a man occupying such a position writing with singular common-sense on the subject of the amount of directive to be given to candidates. The letter is to Lord St. Oswald the former Rowland Winn, whom Akers-Douglas had just succeeded as Chief Conservative Whip.

Private

25th Sept., 1885

Dear Lord St. Oswald,

. . . We are now publishing Campaign Notes—proof of which I forward—which will give our candidates the *facts* on various points—I do not believe much in the utility of a conference of candidates nor do I think it either wise or possible to bind candidates down too closely on domestic questions—Lord Salisbury's speech at Newport next month will sound the key note of Conservative policy but the details should be left to each candidate to settle with his own Constituency—I am sure any attempt to define too closely the relations that must exist between a candidate and his electors on each and every topic of the day would be full of danger—This is my view but of course it is *only* mine.

Yours truly,

Rich. W. Middleton.

A copy of this he sent to Akers-Douglas with the comment '. . . Of course I am only expressing my own views and if you think otherwise I will at once endeavour to arrange a meeting and etc.'

Similarly, with regard to the Bradlaugh affair, over which so many Tories had allowed themselves to become hysterical, Middleton preserved a nice sense of proportion. To one of his lieutenants he wrote (October 8th, '85):

'Mr. Almy's pamphlet. With regard to this I do not think it is suitable for distribution by the Party. It deals exclusively with Bradlaugh and in a somewhat prosy manner, too prosy for the General Public. I have sent a copy into the Church Defence Institution, who might be willing to help, and I have also sent a copy to East Finsbury where Mr. Bradlaugh is going to stand, and to Northampton [which had elected him in 1880] suggesting that if required they should be ordered direct from the Author. Outside of these places I do not think it would be of interest.'

Then again, with confident authority, he gave firm advice (October 14th, '85) to Lord St. Oswald on the delicate question of the participation of peers in elections. 'The Peers are going in for Election matters more this time than usual—Following the example of others I think you might speak, but I should advise your not actually proposing votes of confidence in any candidate but rather confining your remarks to general questions of policy.'

On the other hand, in view of the part which Goschen was so shortly to play, it is curious to find Middleton writing to his Scottish lieutenant (October 24th, '85): '. . . I am sorry to hear . . . that a feeling is springing up against opposing Goschen—the general feeling here is that he should be opposed even if only to keep him at home—He [Goschen] is doing us a lot of harm and undoing the good work which men like Lord Brabourne[1] and other converted men are doing amongst the moderate Liberals—Lord Salisbury was talking about it only the other day and expressed a hope we should find a man—I think he should be a Scotchman. If *possible* do this.'

As the General Election campaign got into its stride Akers-Douglas, too, grew in confidence and began to speak to his Chief in a corresponding tone of authority. Thus on November 5th, 1885, he wrote to Salisbury:

> I had many pressing letters urging me to bring before you the importance of making a reply to Mr. Gladstone after his first two Midlothian Speeches [in which he had guardedly, but persistently

[1] See below, p. 68.

> harped upon the Irish Home Rule theme] . . . I am very strongly of opinion that you should make another speech on the eve of the Election and that that speech should be delivered somewhere in the North . . . The reports from our Agents and Candidates improve every day and my only fear is that they are taking too sanguine a view.

For, by temperament, Lord Salisbury instinctively recoiled from that side of a Prime Minister's task which increasingly demanded direct contact with the public, as is revealed in his wry remark in a memorandum to Queen Victoria two years later: 'This duty of making political speeches is an aggravation of the labours of your Majesty's servants which we owe entirely to Mr. Gladstone.'[1]

[1] *The Letters of Queen Victoria*, Third Series, Vol. I, p. 365.

III

'POLITICS ARE IRELAND'

DURING the six months of Salisbury's 'Caretaker Government' (June 1885–January 1886) the question of Irish Home Rule increasingly filled the whole horizon and the parties frenziedly occupied themselves partly with trying to outbid each other over it and partly with reconsidering their respective attitudes to it. The Conservatives had given out hints that they were prepared to govern Ireland without exceptional legislation, and indeed, apart from Lord Randolph's unofficial exchange with Parnell, the Viceroy himself, Lord Carnarvon, had had a private interview with the Irish leader in which, so the latter alleged, he had conveyed the impression that he was prepared to go far in the direction of Irish self-government. Indeed, Carnarvon had never made any bones about his own views. 'Our best and almost only hope is to come to some fair and reasonable arrangement for Home Rule,' he had written to Salisbury in February 1885.[1] But he was an old friend and comrade in arms, and despite this clear statement of a view which he already knew to be at variance with his own, Salisbury had pressed him to accept the Viceroyalty on forming his government in June.

We know that Salisbury was 'not easy about Carnarvon'[2] when he sanctioned the interview with Parnell, having just previously made clear to him his absolute rejection of the Home Rule solution and having evidently noticed with apprehension

[1] Sir A. Hardinge: *Life of Lord Carnarvon*, III, 151.
[2] Cecil, III, 155.

W. H. SMITH. C. T. RITCHIE. R. CHURCHILL. DE WORMS. R. A. CROSS. HICKS-BEACH. H. CHAPLIN. J. MANNERS. G. HAMILTON.

NEW MEN AND OLD ATTITUDES.

PRINCIPALS OF THE NEW CONSERVATIVE COMEDY COMPANY TRYING TO LOOK AS MUCH AS POSSIBLE LIKE THE OLD PUBLIC FAVOURITES.

the different bent of the Viceroy's mind. This would naturally render his regret and mortification afterwards all the greater and account for the uncharacteristic violence of his reaction, as when he told the Queen that the Viceroy had 'acted impulsively and with little foresight'.[1] It was in fact a blunder for which he was just as much responsible as the Viceroy—although the latter generously took the onus upon himself. For Salisbury should have realized earlier that, though they had originally shared common ground in their dislike of coercion as a policy, there was a growing and vital difference of emphasis in their view of the problem—Carnarvon placing it on alleviation of the lot of the Irish and Salisbury on protection of the interests of the minorities—the landlords and the Protestants. This difference reached its logical conclusion in Carnarvon's resignation not long afterwards and in Salisbury's blunt statement to him later that 'rightly or wrongly, I have not the slightest wish to satisfy the national aspirations of Ireland'.[2]

Meanwhile, however, on the strength of appearances, the order had gone forth that all Irish votes were to be given to the Conservatives in the forthcoming General Election. The latter took place in November 1885, with the result that 334 Liberals were returned, 250 Conservatives and 86 Irish Nationalists. The earliest returns from the English Boroughs had seemed to portend a sweeping Tory victory, but the balance was redressed by the English counties, where (with the exception of Kent) the agricultural labourer expressed his gratitude for the vote by giving it to the Liberals who had endowed him with it, and by Scotland and Wales which voted almost solidly Liberal throughout. In Ireland, however, the effect of recent Tory attitudes and manoeuvres was startlingly demonstrated by the fact that not a single Liberal was returned (as against 14 in the preceding Parliament). Akers-Douglas, together with every other Conservative candidate in Kent, was returned with an ample majority. Standing for the newly-formed 'St. Augustine's Division', he beat a formidable Radical, Alfred Simmons, out of the running by 2,260 votes. From a former Conservative Whip, Sir Thomas Bateson, just created Lord Deramore, he received the following lively survey of the field.

[1] *Letters of Queen Victoria*, Third Series, I, 147.

[2] Balfour: *Chapters of Autobiography*, 195.

Belvoir Park,
Belfast
Dec. 7, '85

My Dear Douglas,

As you always told me you had selected the worst district of Kent, I was very anxious about your fate until I saw that you were safely landed. I cannot resist now writing one line to congratulate you.

With the exception of the Metropolitan Counties the other County Divisions have gone over bodily to the enemy—Lord Arthur Somerset's[1] defeat astounded me—and a carpet bagger like the Knight of Kerry[2] to run Knightly within 50 shows how demoralized the agricultural voter must be.

The present Parliament cannot fail to be a very short one—and during the interval our county magnates must cultivate the agricultural voter and bring him to a sense of his responsibilities. In Ulster we have not a single Gladstonian M.P. left—That Ruffian Dickson got his quietus in Mid Antrim last week.

With the exception of poor Sidney Herbert[3] and our friend Ridley[4] both of whom I regret much, our front bench has pulled through wonderfully.

Ever yours
Deramore.

Feeling was even more acrimonious than in 1880. 'It is no longer a question between Liberal and Conservative, but between Radicals, or rather Jacobins, and Anti-Radicals . . . wrote a Kentish newspaper, '. . . the coming struggle is not a contest between reform and reaction, but between constitutionalism and revolution.' There were again a good many cases of violence. 'Serious riots are announced from Nottingham which prevent the counting,' Akers-Douglas wrote to Salisbury in November. Writing to Lord St. Oswald (December 24th, '85) Middleton reported: 'Yesterday Shaw [local party agent] came up to see me—he reports that although doubtless in certain villages a good deal of violence was used, still he cannot

[1] Lord Henry Arthur Somerset, third son of 8th Duke of Beaufort.

[2] Sir Maurice Fitzgerald, Bart., 20th Knight of Kerry; A.D.C. to Duke of Connaught.

[3] Assistant Whip under Akers-Douglas; later 14th Earl of Pembroke.

[4] Sir Matthew White Ridley, Bart. (later 1st Viscount Ridley), Home Secretary 1895–1900.

trace anything amounting to general intimidation and moreover he learns in almost all cases the Conservatives had polled their strength before the violence began—I think the better plan to check the recurrence of such things will be to get someone who has been intimidated to summons the ringleaders of the Radical mob—this whilst being less costly than an appeal would thoroughly ventilate the matter.—If however the local authorities do not mind the expense of petition it may result in the disfranchisement of what to us seems at present an almost hopeless seat.'

For the time being the most important fact which had emerged from the elections was that 86 Irish Nationalists had become the allies—at least temporarily—of the Conservatives. 'Now the Irish Party number 86,' wrote Akers-Douglas to Salisbury, when Parliament met and the Liberals took office, 'there is the greatest difficulty in obtaining seats on the Opposition side of the House . . .' But there was another more important aspect of the matter which was that the Nationalists, though potential allies of the Conservatives, were first and foremost the puppets of Parnell—and with these 86 puppets Parnell now exactly held the balance between the two great parties, since the over-all Liberal majority was also only 86 seats. Thus, united to the Tories, Parnell could at least reduce the Liberals to impotence, whilst if he joined the Liberals he could seemingly dictate to the House of Commons. But this depended on the Liberals being united on the Irish question, which they were very far from being. Meanwhile Gladstone, with the prospect of once again being premier, knew from previous experience that by their obstructionist tactics the Irish members could make government virtually impossible. He also knew that, though he himself had now made up his mind in favour of Home Rule, he could not hope to carry all his party with him. Therefore, in view of the apparent Conservative involvement with Home Rule and its leader, he had hoped to induce that party to assume responsibility for action by the promise of Liberal support for a Conservative initiative. But Salisbury refused to discuss the matter. As Churchill had said, they had 'got Gladstone pinned to it'; let him therefore incur the responsibility, the odium and the ultimate defeat which any such measure would be sure to meet.

It is scarcely surprising if these tactics on the part of the Conservatives were considered by some as a cynical, narrowly partisan manoeuvre; moreover, the equivocal, even sly, nature of their earlier Irish policy had, as even Lord Randolph admitted afterwards, undoubtedly strengthened the Nationalists' hand and contributed to Gladstone's 'conversion'. 'The Conservative Party is national or it is nothing,' Disraeli had proudly declared, and what, it might be asked, was Home Rule if it was not a national, or even an imperial, issue of a kind which should have been the subject of bipartisan action, as Gladstone had suggested. The fact that the Conservatives represented the question as a 'national issue' *after* pinning Gladstone to it, though it was an artful and highly successful ruse, does not exculpate them morally.

The whole matter was one of considerable embarrassment to the Conservatives in after years—especially when they had finished with Parnell and were fully committed to a policy of coercion. At first Parnell had been only too willing to cover them up as when, in July 1885, he wrote a public letter denying the accusation of Herbert Gladstone that there was an 'alliance' between himself and the Conservatives 'for Parliamentary purposes and for the purposes of the General Election'. But a year later, during the election on the Home Rule issue, when he knew at last where he stood with the Tories, he flatly contradicted this statement and even declared that Carnarvon had claimed at the famous interview to be speaking 'officially'. Later on still, in a speech at Hull on December 13th, 1887, another leading Irish Nationalist, Justin M'Carthy, launched an even wider charge accusing 'Lord Salisbury and members of his cabinet' of 'intriguing with the Irish members with regard to Home Rule' and declaring that he had 'had an interview with two gentlemen who came to him as representing the Tory Party . . . one was the Tory Whip and the other Sir H. D. Wolff', at which an undertaking was given to discontinue coercion in return for the Irish vote at the election. This naturally drew vehement and indignant public denials from all concerned—Lord Salisbury, Lord Randolph Churchill, Lord St. Oswald, the former Chief Whip, Akers-Douglas, his successor, and Sir Henry Wolff; though M'Carthy's circumstantial account leaves little doubt that there had in fact been secret negotiations between the

Tory leaders and himself, as Parnell's deputy, in the summer of 1885—apart from the more celebrated interviews of Churchill and Carnarvon with Parnell. The real doubt was how far these interviews were to be considered 'official'—a point which the Tories were naturally at pains to insist upon. But of course the subject continued to dog the party; so many dubious, or at best inexplicable incidents built up into a body of evidence too damning to shake off. Indeed, the conclusion is inescapable that for mere reasons of immediate party advantage a supreme opportunity was missed of dealing with a vital question which was to confuse and bedevil English politics for another generation and which was to become so exacerbated in the process as to make it finally incapable of any solution save the very one which the Tories had declared themselves resolved to prevent.

However, taking the short-term, opportunistic view, as they had done, the Tories could scarcely have hoped for a better outcome to the tangled story. Gladstone had kept his growing plans for Home Rule strictly to himself, but as soon as the truth began to dawn upon his colleagues the inevitable disintegration of the party began. His son Herbert (who, with the noblest intentions, was instrumental in 'blowing the gaff' about his father's conversion), whilst admitting the policy of silence to have been unwise and inexpedient, claimed that for Gladstone to have proclaimed his conversion to Home Rule would have been 'bidding for Irish support' and behaving no better than the Conservatives.[1] But no such moral argument could really excuse Gladstone from having kept the entire British electorate in the dark, as well as those who shared with him the responsibility for Liberal policy, and did nothing to dispel the suspicion that he might just the same be himself committed to some secret deal with Parnell. Indeed, in fairness it must be said that Gladstone's policy was equally capable of being interpreted in terms of unscrupulous political calculation. For he cannot have been unaware that silence enabled him to retain the undivided support of his party throughout the election of 1885 in which he saw his great chance to regain power and implement his plans for Home Rule. Now, at any rate, despite the ominous signs of revolt, he doggedly resolved to go forward—alone, if he must.

[1] Viscount Gladstone: *After Thirty Years*, 285.

'His decision,' wrote Asquith in after years, 'changed the whole course of British politics during the lifetime of a generation.'[1]

Lord Randolph, with others of his party, had not been slow to perceive the opportunity which lay before them of splitting apart the incongruous amalgam of the Liberal party, but he did not realize that the process would be so automatic as to need little acceleration. Worried by the Liberal success at the recent elections, he put forward plans for an immediate coalition with the 'Whigs' by means of a greater liberalization of Conservative policy. Salisbury agreed with him in principle but felt the plum could afford to ripen a little longer on the tree. 'The extra tinge of Liberalism in our policy,' he wrote, 'will be part of the bargain when it comes, and must not be given away before that time comes. If we are too free with our cash now, we shall have no money to go to market with when the market is open.'[2]

But Lord Randolph persisted and finally drew up a monumental memorandum urging not only immediate coalition, but the adoption of an ultra-Liberal programme of reforms intended to make such a coalition more attractive to the other side. At a Cabinet Council held in December 1885, after the Elections, in order to review the whole political situation and plan further strategy, Lord Randolph pressed the claims of his memorandum. But most of the Cabinet already had their views on the subject and were disinclined for further discussion. Hicks Beach, whom he thought he had won over, spoke against it, and the whole project was abruptly dismissed. Lord Randolph was angry and mortified. On the following day, from the home of the Duke of Edinburgh, where he was staying, he wrote a letter to Akers-Douglas in which he referred to this rebuff and also to some other incident from which it would appear that Akers-Douglas was already exercising his official discipline over his old 'chief' and that the latter was anxious not to displease him—a measure of the young Chief Whip's growing authority.

[1] *Fifty Years of Parliament*, I, 129.
[2] Churchill, 412.

Private

Eastwell Park,
Ashford, Kent
Dec. 16, 1885

Dear Akers-Douglas,

... I hope I did not do wrong last night. I was not a free agent, but was carried into the room 'vi et armis', and was told you had sent for me. Hothfield[1] looked very green.

... I am desperately worried vexed and personally embarrassed by a certain decision of the Cabinet yesterday. Beach was most treacherous to me.

Yours ever
Randolph S. C.

The obvious differences which were daily growing within the Liberal party now encouraged Salisbury still more to disregard Churchill's pleas for immediate coalition and, though he knew the temporary pact between Tories and Parnellites was already dissolving, to carry on his government, meet Parliament and invite battle on a specific issue. In the short interval before Parliament met, Gladstone made a last appeal to him (through Balfour) to take the initiative in solving the Irish problem with the promise of Liberal support. It would be, he said, 'a public calamity if this great subject should fall into the lines of party conflict'.[2]

But Salisbury had by now decided not only to meet Parliament, but to force the issue by a direct challenge. On the strength of the growing restlessness and disorder in Ireland, which the controversy had now enormously aggravated, he decided to announce in the Queen's Speech the immediate introduction of a Coercion Bill. He would thus endeavour to dispel at one blow any doubts as to the relations of his government with Parnell, or as to the real sentiments of his party, and at the same time make a bid for the support of the Whigs and Moderate Liberals.

However, on the same day (January 26th, 1886) as the Government announced their intentions they were defeated on an Amendment to the Address (Jesse Collings's celebrated 'Three Acres and a Cow', urging the provision of allotments for labourers). Lord Salisbury at once resigned. But it was noteworthy that 18 Liberals, including Hartington and Goschen,

[1] Henry Tufton, 1st Lord Hothfield, Lord in Waiting to the Queen.

[2] Viscount Gladstone, op. cit., 396.

voted with the Government, and that 76, including Bright, stayed away.

Gladstone accepted the commission to form a government without hesitation, bent now solely upon bringing his plan for Home Rule to fruition with the least possible delay. But, beyond a vaguely phrased intimation about 'examining' the 'possibility' of meeting Irish aspirations, he did not take his colleagues into his confidence about the detailed plan which he had in fact already prepared. So suspicious, however, had his former colleagues already become that, nearly all the 'old guard', except Chamberlain and Trevelyan—and these joined with considerable misgivings—refused to join his government. But when, only some six weeks later, he produced his Home Rule Bill before his Cabinet, these two immediately resigned. Hartington and most of his Whig following had stood aside at the outset and the reason for the desertion of this remnant of the old aristocratic 'Grand Whiggery' scarcely needs to be explained.

Another very important Liberal had already gone a big step further. George Goschen had fallen out with Gladstone many years earlier and, since his abilities were exceptional, consequently occupied a rather unique and powerful position among the statesmen of the day. As early as the beginning of February of this year Salisbury had reported to Akers-Douglas:

Private

20, Arlington Street,
S.W.
Feb. 9, '86

My dear Douglas,

. . . Goschen came to see me today—among other things to talk of the possibility of some treaty between us to secure his friends from being opposed by us at an election if they joined us in opposing the Govt. I acknowledged the importance of coming to an understanding on the point and said I would consult you. I said it would not be worth our while unless they would break definitely with Gladstone. He admitted this: and further limited his proposal to those places, where, without a split, our chances were hopeless. Without pledging myself I gave him general hopes of an understanding.

Yours very truly,
Salisbury.

Here were the first gropings towards the creation of the Unionist Party.

G. J. GOSCHEŃ. J. CHAMBERLAIN. SIR H. JAMES. SIR G. O. TREVELYAN. MARQUIS OF HARTINGTON.

A BACK SEAT.

Meanwhile the twin kings of the Radicals, Chamberlain and Bright, were not only deeply offended by Gladstone's omission to consult them over his plans for Home Rule, but were influenced also on grounds of principle. Although Chamberlain himself had earlier proposed a form of *local* self-government for Ireland (and continued to cherish the ideal), his lifelong 'imperial' outlook was outraged at what he deemed to be a secretive attempt to 'dismember the Empire' by the proposed separation of parliaments. 'The position,' he wrote to Mrs. Jeune (later Lady St. Helier), 'is . . . a painful one for me; but I am sure I am right and will have no part or responsibility in what I believe will prove the dishonour, and perhaps the ruin, of my country.'[1] John Bright's Protestant conscience was equally appalled at the proposed desertion of loyal Ulstermen and the surrender to Catholic 'rebels and traitors'.

The latter was also an aspect which Lord Randolph had resolved to exploit. 'I decided some time ago,' he wrote to his friend the Irish Lord Justice FitzGibbon, 'that if the G.O.M. went for Home Rule, the Orange Card would be the one to play.'[2] He accordingly went over to Belfast and addressed inflammatory harangues to gigantic meetings, the gist of which was summed up in the phrase, written to a correspondent: 'Ulster will fight: Ulster will be right.'[3] At the same time he coined the term 'Unionist' for all the varying elements which opposed Home Rule, pressing more strongly than ever for immediate coalition and the 'formation of a new Party, containing all that is best in the politics of Tory, Liberal and Whig'.[4]

Although at first there was considerable mutual reserve between Tories and Whigs, as soon as the Home Rule Bill made its appearance in the House—on April 8th, 1886—passions rose so quickly and sharply that the seeming gulf began to be bridged at many points. The Conservatives now strained every nerve to present the issue as a national one, transcending party politics. Middleton wrote to Lord Iddesleigh (the former Sir Stafford Northcote) (April 19th, '86): '. . . I send you copy of a letter and petition I sent immediately after Mr. Gladstone's speech on Thursday 8th to every County and Boro in England & Wales.

[1] Lady St. Helier, op. cit., 286.
[2] Churchill, 446.
[3] Ibid., 450.
[4] Ibid., 454.

The result of this letter has been in many, I may say most cases, the arranging of non-Party meetings—In Hertfordshire I believe they intend asking the High Sheriff to convene a meeting of the County . . .' And two days later (April 21st) he wrote to him again: 'I hope this [the Hartington] section of the Liberal party may be of more active use in the future as they are getting up an organization and I am told propose starting an office in London.' To Lady Iddesleigh, who enclosed a letter from a militant partisan, he wrote (May 2nd) '. . . I quite sympathize with his feeling of enthusiasm for the safety of the Union and his anxiety to fight the matter on party grounds but after much consideration it was decided that the question at issue was of a nature that we might invite our Liberal friends to assist us and make common cause against the proposals of Mr. Gladstone and the Irish. Mr. Bullock is wrong in supposing no Conservative meetings have been held—in several parts of the Country where non-party meetings could not be got together our party have acted alone, but in the majority of cases I am glad to say Liberals and Conservatives have appeared on the same platform.'

Naturally those of the Liberals who had left Gladstone several years previously, at the first signs of his 'mania', were the most eager to proclaim the justification of their earlier action and to join in the halloo. Such an one was Lord Brabourne, a former Liberal Whip and Under Secretary of State and a neighbour of Akers-Douglas in Kent.

Hotel Royal,
S. Remo, Italie
April 15, '86

My dear Akers-Douglas,

. . . If you are organizing any demonstrations against Gladstone's separation Policy, I shall be happy to go anywhere and do anything . . . Of course I do not know what you are doing, but I am sure that we ought to do our utmost to awaken the constituencies to a real understanding of the question now before us . . . I hope things look well, and that Hartington will join with those with whom he really agrees upon main points. Considering that I left Gladstone's Party in 1880–1, when he took to my mind a new departure in Irish Policy which I thought *must* lead him to where he is now, it would be eminently satisfactory to me to see

> so many of my old Whig friends practically confessing now that I was right, if it were not for the spice of bitterness brought by the feeling that, whilst everyone gives them credit for the highest and most patriotic feelings, *I* have been reviled, abused and ostracised for five years past simply because I saw a little further ahead than they did, and could not stop with them to support and strengthen Gladstone or his march to separation. However, the thing *now* is to overthrow him, and this can only be done by vigorous and united action . . .
>
> Ever sincerely,
> Brabourne.

The supreme moment came when even those aloof politicians Salisbury and Hartington, as well as the usually cool and independent Goschen, found themselves suddenly sharing the public platform at Her Majesty's Theatre in excited denunciation of the Bill. But this first enraptured embrace of the parties was quickly realized by both to be dangerous and premature and gave way to more considered arrangements. 'There is something of a pause in London politics,' wrote the *Western Weekly News* of April 24th, 1886:

> . . . Meanwhile a separate organisation on the Liberal side against the concession of Home Rule has been set on foot. It became a necessity after the meeting at Her Majesty's. That was much too Conservative an affair to be pleasant to the Liberals who spoke at it. They seemed like captives of the bow and spear of Mr. Akers-Douglas. To avoid that dangerous appearance in future Lord Hartington and his friends have started a Liberal Unionist Society, which will manage the great movement.

Thus far the Hartingtonians had managed to put a respectable face upon their revolt and at the same time to indicate their distinctness from the Conservatives. But what of Chamberlain? He had resigned from the government for the same reason as the Hartingtonians had refused to enter it; yet, apart from that, he had literally nothing in common with them. During the election contest Lord Hartington had been the target of his invective as often as Lord Salisbury. What was even worse was that, though he still reigned over the hearts of his subjects inside his Birmingham kingdom, he had been repudiated even by his own creation—the 'Caucus'.

Seeing his ex-colleague's apparently pitiable isolation and wishing to mitigate his own isolation by winning back a figure potentially still so formidable, Gladstone offered to drop, before the Bill's Second Reading, the clause which appeared to be most obnoxious to Chamberlain—namely that relating to the exclusion of Irish members from the Imperial Parliament. But he underestimated the strength of Chamberlain's unabated self-confidence. In Chamberlain's own words: 'The disposition of Mr. Gladstone and his friends was sometimes conciliatory, sometimes the reverse, and it varied in the ratio of their hopes and fears for the success of the Bill on the Second Reading. It seems likely that they were misled by their Whips as to the state of things in the House of Commons and by Schnadhorst [organizer of the Caucus] as to the position in the country. Every time that they obtained a favourable report of probabilities they retreated from their offers and raised their terms, and at the very last moment an arrangement which had been promised was repudiated and the fate of the Bill thereby sealed.'[1] Moreover, he had written to Harcourt (April 30th): 'I do not expect any compromise or concession. I imagine we shall fight the matter out to the bitter end and break up the Liberal Party in the process. We can't help ourselves and we know whose fault it is, if that is any satisfaction.'[2] Meanwhile, Parnell's obvious interest lay in preventing Gladstone from conciliating Chamberlain by conceding a point which would have dished his (Parnell's) plans for the complete legislative separation of Ireland. 'Great excitement today,' wrote Middleton to St. Oswald (May 10th), 'and great anxiety to know if and how much the G.O.M. is going to give way to Chamberlain.'

There was an extraordinary atmosphere of intrigue and excitement during these days which has never quite been equalled in our parliamentary history either before or since, and Akers-Douglas was by the nature of his position in the very thick of it all. Some of the contemporary press cuttings which he preserved best convey the quality of those stirring times and his own exciting part in them. Thus the *Manchester Courier* of May 11th,

[1] Chamberlain's 'Memorandum', q. Garvin: *Life of Joseph Chamberlain*, II, 219.

[2] Garvin: *Life of Joseph Chamberlain*, II, 219.

1886, reporting the first day of the debate on the Second Reading:

> Mr. Gladstone certainly took the House by surprise tonight, and perhaps Mr. Chamberlain was more astonished than anyone. A Cabinet Minister informed him on Saturday night that the Government had decided to accept the chief point of his ultimatum [regarding the retention of Irish members], and this he took to be an official intimation. Acting upon this, too, Mr. Akers-Douglas yesterday afternoon got together all the members of the late Cabinet and took them down by special train to Hatfield, where they had a consultation with the Marquis of Salisbury. As a result of this conference, probably it was decided that on Mr. Gladstone announcing tonight that he would recast his Bill so as to admit of the continuance of the Irish members at Westminster, a motion for the adjournment of the debate should be put on the ground that the Bill before the House was not the same as that read a first time. But no such announcement was made, and all the House wondered.

From Chamberlain's views, as cited earlier in his own words, it can be deduced that this 'betrayal' by Gladstone was not only fully expected but also secretly desired by him, so that the proposed Conservative manoeuvre, which was designed to prevent any risk of his re-attraction into Gladstone's orbit, would have been unnecessary. This did not, however, deprive the actual dénouement on the floor of the House of its due suspense and excitement, as will be seen by the following graphic description by the parliamentary correspondent of the *Liverpool Mercury* (May 11th, 1886), which is given *in extenso* on account of the vividness of its portrayal of the men and the issues.

> Mr. Gladstone has not capitulated to Mr. Chamberlain. He has made no definite promises of any kind whatever. His Home Rule scheme stands tonight, as regards opposition, almost precisely where it stood last week. His relation towards the Radical leader is scarcely altered. His attitude towards the Whigs is not altered at all. The men who have been making lists tonight with great confidence place the Hartingtonians and the Chamberlainites in the Opposition lobby, and add to their number the names of half a dozen members who were previously doubtful. It is generally said tonight that Mr. Gladstone is rushing upon a defeat, and is prepared to surrender the reins of government to Lord Hartington. The calculations may be premature. The deduction from Mr.

Gladstone's speech that he foresees his own immediate resignation may be unsafe. I do not think there is much to support it. But it is undoubted and indubitable that his Bill and his Government stand in greater jeopardy at this moment than they have hitherto done.

It had been a bright day, and Mr. Gladstone's admirers expected a great demonstration in Downing Street. The Prime Minister drove down in an open carriage, with Mrs. Gladstone on his right hand. There had, however, been no organized Irish crowd. Much of the excitement of last month seems to have passed away, and though the Premier received a great cheer as he came out of Downing Street, there was very little evidence of popular emotion. He looked more cheerful than ever, smiled and bowed with great gratification to those who raised a shout in his honour. Throughout the night too he bore himself as one who was assured of success. When he rose in the House he began in a style youthful, rapid, and jubilant. When he concluded it was in a high strain of passionate rhetoric, full of glorious hope. The resources of civilisation are not exhausted. There are still cards to play with which Mr. Gladstone may yet win his success. As I was not among those who believed that he would begin tonight by capitulating to Mr. Chamberlain, notwithstanding the confident statements made by those who were 'in the know', I may perhaps be trusted when I say that next we shall find the Prime Minister making his final proffers.

But the story of the last three days is intensely interesting. Saturday's Cabinet did come to a decision, which was intended, at all events, to conciliate the Radicals. Mr. Chamberlain is said by his friends to have come down to the House with beaming anticipations of being given a personal triumph. He had been approached; he understood that he was to be pretty nearly the director of the situation. The news got afloat as such news will. It reached Mr. Akers-Douglas, who rushed to Hatfield with it, there to attend a sort of Conservative Cabinet Council. It reached Lord Hartington, who at once put himself in communication with the Tory lord, in order to prepare himself against a surprise. It reached Mr. Parnell, and the Irish lord is said (but I am not likely to get this officially confirmed on one side or the other) to have put his foot down sternly upon the project. He bade Mr. Gladstone choose between Mr. Chamberlain's followers and the Irish Eighty-five, and the result was that Mr. Gladstone had to fall back tonight upon hints and suggestions which were so vague that nobody who heard him quite understood his meaning.

It was a curious situation to those who knew what it involved. Mr. Chamberlain and Lord Hartington sat close together. They were in quiet communication during the progress of Mr. Gladstone's speech. Mr. Akers-Douglas sat opposite Lord Hartington. They had arranged to signal one another. The Irishmen waited expectantly. The understanding between Mr. Chamberlain and Lord Hartington was that Mr. Chamberlain was to tell Lord Hartington if he were satisfied. Had he been satisfied, Lord Hartington would have advised the front Opposition bench, and Sir Michael Hicks Beach would have moved the adjournment of the debate on the ground that the House was asked to read a second time a new measure which had not been printed, and which nobody had had time to consider. Had the Prime Minister bowed to Mr. Chamberlain and admitted the Irish members to the House of Commons, the Parnellites would, in disgust, have joined the Whigs and the Tories in insisting upon further time for consideration. Lord Hartington would have refused to move to reject an unprinted Bill, and Mr. Chamberlain would have stood out awaiting further enlightenment.

There is no denying that the Liberal Party listened coldly to Mr. Gladstone's speech . . . In the purely expository portion of his long oration the Prime Minister felt greatly affected by the chillingly critical manner of those who were behind him. Twice he turned his back upon the table, and, looking full in the face of the Whigs who sat silent upon the well-filled benches, he arraigned them face to face. But they were not generous enough to give him a response. They took no notice of the unusual position, and the orator had to turn round again to carry on his argument. When he came to explain what he meant to do, his indistinctness made it impossible for Lord Hartington, who sat immediately behind him, to follow him.

The critical moment came when the Prime Minister explained what the Government could not concede. He had never mentioned Mr. Chamberlain, and I do not think that his words can be construed into an absolute and flat rejection of Mr. Chamberlain's demands; but Mr. Chamberlain instantly took them in that sense. He had been taking notes; he was full of eager anxiety, but a frown came upon his brow when Mr. Gladstone said that he would not insist upon retaining the Irish representation at Westminster against its own desire. He gathered up his papers with an eloquent gesture, buttoning up his coat, folded his arms, as one who should say 'war to the knife'. The signal was understood on the Tory benches.

Mr. Gladstone went on to say that in order to maintain the principle that representation must go with taxation, he would admit Irishmen to Westminster when questions of Excise or Customs were being debated. He then sketched in dim outline a constitution resembling in its nature that which gives the delegations to Austro-Hungary; but before he had got thus far Mr. Chamberlain had sent a card across to Lord Hartington, and Lord Hartington had instructed his messenger to meet Mr. Akers-Douglas behind the Speaker's chair. 'Chamberlain says it won't do', was Lord Hartington's message, and the idea of moving the adjournment was abandoned. Lord Hartington prepared to move the rejection of the Bill. The Whig leader was deeply affected. Mr. Gladstone had praised him to the skies while attempting to out-flank his position. It was with difficulty that he got out the two or three words of reference to the painful nature of the action he was taking, but he did not hesitate. He was dead against the Bill.

LORD HARTINGTON'S ATTITUDE TOWARDS MR. GLADSTONE.

'Now to dinner,' was the cry when Lord Hartington had done; but for nearly an hour the lobbying went on. The Radical malcontents came out in a very ill humour. Some of them talked of being insulted. They gathered round Mr. Chamberlain to hear what he had to say. It soon became known that he intended to lead all his forces against the Bill; they began to reckon up their strength, and announced themselves presently as already 57 strong. Mr. Chamberlain himself, I believe, will make no further effort to secure a compromise. If an offer is made it must come from the Government. He will be stiffened in his resolve that his 57 had increased before the evening was out. Many Whigs, or those who were thought to be Whigs, regard Lord Hartington as not giving them a sufficient lever in the constituencies, but it is certain that Lord Hartington can count on 25 votes. If Mr. Chamberlain's men are true to him, therefore—and the 57 have given solemn pledges of support—Mr. Gladstone has got already a majority against him. His speech tonight has conciliated nobody. It has hardly the old magical influence, and not a few Liberals are alarmed at the idea of the Irishmen coming in to vote on the Budget, and who, after it may be turning out a government, will leave its successor without a parliamentary majority.

Nobody seems tonight to quite understand Mr. Gladstone's Austro-Hungarian scheme. The general impression is that the Bill is dead. Certainly the tide seems rising high above it. Tonight the Whig-Radical combination is stronger and fiercer than ever . . . The serious point in the situation for Mr. Gladstone is the almost wild temper of the Radicals. They are in the mood to reject all further advances. Those who have committed themselves irrevocably are revengeful; but if Mr. Gladstone can arrange matters with Mr. Parnell there may be a change and a great one. His tactics may be directed to that result if he can show Mr. Parnell that the rejection of the present plans will in any case leave him disappointed for years, and in certain eventualities may place Home Rule again outside practical politics, the Irish leader will probably take up again the foot which he has put down so firmly.

The debate will last at least a fortnight. It may last for three weeks. Nearly every Liberal member who intends to vote against his party will want to tell the reason why. Unfortunately for them the Ministerialists are outmatched in debate. But they also will desire to speak man for man. The Conservatives are not so anxious to orate. They maintain their policy of leaving the fight to the Liberals, but they also must have their say, and the strife of tongues is likely to be the most prolonged we have had since the repeal of the Corn Laws.

There is some difficulty, I understand, in arranging a formal bargain between the Conservatives and the Unionist Liberals to the effect that the Tory electioneering managers shall throw their electoral influence in favour of every Liberal member who votes against the Second Reading. The Tories want a 'quid pro quo'—they want to have Liberal votes for their candidates. The Hartingtonians say that that would come naturally. The Chamberlainites, however, refuse to enter into any understanding. The disorganization of parties in consequence is becoming almost comic . . .

Even in the midst of such a tense drama as this Akers-Douglas was not allowed to forget that he was Patronage Secretary as well as chief manager and organizer for the party in the House of Commons. By way of tail-piece—and anti-climax—we append the following specimen of a kind of letter which from now on he was to receive regularly in hundreds—though not always couched in quite such stately and uncompromising terms.

May 5th, '86
St. Margaret's Mansions,
Victoria Street, S.W.

Dear Mr. Akers-Douglas,

I hear that you have influence with the *Daily Telegraph* and I should be very much obliged if you would exert it to get a paragraph inserted mentioning Limerick as a candidate for the Chairmanship of Committees, and touching upon the good work he has done for so many years, especially on Private Bills and Committees.

Limerick returns from Ireland tomorrow, but writes he is most anxious this should be done as soon as possible, as it is not sufficiently known that he wishes for the appointment.

Please forgive my troubling you and believe me to be

Yours truly,
Isabelle Limerick.[1]

[1] Née de Colquhoun, wife of William, 3rd Earl of Limerick, A.D.C. and Lord-in-Waiting to Queen Victoria.

IV
THE UNIONIST ALLIANCE

AKERS-DOUGLAS was one of the chief instruments in the Conservative moves to strike a bargain with the Whigs. Therefore when Hartington convened a meeting of his followers on May 28th, 1886, to reaffirm their utmost resistance to the Home Rule Bill, he was able to harden their resolve by reading a message from the Conservative Chief Whip giving an absolute undertaking on behalf of that party not to contest at the next election the seat of any Liberal member who voted against the Bill.

As for Chamberlain, though he was as determined to kill the Bill as Gladstone was to get it passed, and though, like Gladstone, he put the realization of his aim before the welfare of the Liberal Party and was resigned to the prospect of seeing the latter fall apart, he was still not ready to do a deal with the Tories. There was one man, however, who could provide Chamberlain with a special, non-committal kind of link with 'the Right', and that was the Right's most 'leftist' member, Randolph Churchill. These two political adversaries who, in their time, had accused one another of almost every imaginable political crime had, of course, a great deal in common. 'Their moods and ways of looking at things—to some extent their methods—were not altogether dissimilar,' wrote Winston Churchill;[1] of which Asquith remarked, 'To put things more crudely, they were both born and highly trained demagogues.'[2]

At any rate, from the moment that the trend of Chamberlain's policy became clear Churchill sought to establish intimate

[1] Churchill, p. 458. [2] Asquith: *Fifty Years of Parliament*, I, 141.

relations with him, to smooth his difficult path and to stiffen his attitude to Home Rule. 'I do implore you to stick to your guns,'[1] he wrote to Chamberlain on May 29th, 1886, when he feared the latter might waver in the face of last-minute reports of Gladstone's intention to withdraw and remodel the Bill. But his anxiety proved groundless, for Chamberlain meant to stick to his guns, and, despite appearances, his position was strong. When, on June 8th, the division on the Second Reading was taken and the Home Rule Bill defeated, half the ninety-three Liberals who voted against it were Chamberlain's Radical followers.

Already on the next day he was prepared to propose a bargain with the Tories, but it was significant that he approached them through Churchill, who evidently immediately passed it on to Akers-Douglas, among whose papers it is. Possibly the cryptic reference to the 'Doctor's Champagne' was meant to convey his reluctance to be cajoled by the Tories into anything more than just doing hard business with them.

Private

40 Prince's Gardens, S.W.
June 9, '86

My dear Churchill,

My brother[2] fought Temple[3] last time. He has not publicly withdrawn his candidature but I can promise that he will not stand, if Hastings [Liberal Unionist][4] is let alone.

No one else has the slightest chance.

The Doctor's Champagne is the natural prelude to his medicine, but I would prefer to take the latter without the former.

Next to Mr. Gladstone's it is the very worst wine in London.

Yours ever,
J. Chamberlain.

Gladstone had decided to dissolve Parliament and 'go to the country' on the Home Rule issue, confident that he would carry all before him and be returned with an unequivocal mandate to pass the measure. But meanwhile there was a real fear among the Conservative leaders that, in the fluid state of parties and

[1] Garvin, II, 241.

[2] Arthur Chamberlain, Liberal Candidate for Evesham.

[3] Sir R. Temple, Bart., M.P. Evesham.

[4] Elected for East Worc. 1856; expelled from House 1892 on conviction for breach of trust.

ideas, Gladstone might somehow turn any delay to good account. Thus W. H. Smith to Akers-Douglas (June 8th, '86):

> I hear there is to be a dissolution, but I also hear . . . that Govt. proposes to take all the Supply remaining and pass some Bills, avoiding the necessity of bringing the House together in August, or of meeting before the Autumn. This would postpone the Elections for two or three weeks and give them another three months of office before they can be challenged . . .

When the dissolution was announced in the House of Commons (June 10th) Hicks Beach accordingly asked for some assurance that, in the event of the result of the elections being indecisive, Parliament would be immediately called together after their conclusion. On Gladstone giving some such assurance, Beach expressed himself satisfied—but evidently too readily and politely for the liking of Lord Randolph. For, in a letter to Akers-Douglas (June 12th) the latter wrote: 'I thought Beach made an ass of himself on Thursday. Very feeble and grovelling before the G.O.M. That is not the way to win.' Poor Beach, who was always lauding Churchill's talents and championing his claims to office and who was afterwards described as 'his oldest and truest political comrade', seems to have got little but abuse for his pains, to judge from this and an earlier letter already quoted—as well as from an astonishing outburst against him later in the same year which has been recorded by Lord George Hamilton.[1]

In the event, however, Gladstone dissolved Parliament only a fortnight after his defeat, so the Conservative fears proved groundless. Meanwhile, Lord Salisbury exerted his influence to ensure that Liberal-Unionists were not opposed by Conservatives at the coming elections. But it was not always easy—in fact often a very delicate matter—to bring the constituencies, with their local prejudice and narrow-minded outlook, into line with his policy. In a speech at Deal Akers-Douglas had emphasized his chief's wishes and had added his personal promise to do all in his power to carry them out. But there was undoubtedly some truth in the assertion of a Liberal newspaper that 'this, however, is not the unanimous view of local Tory

[1] Lord George Hamilton: *Parliamentary Reminiscences and Reflections 1886–1906*.

managers; and Mr. Akers-Douglas has reckoned without his Primrose League . . . They are clamouring for local dispensations and relaxations of the rule that the Conservative Whip has laid down; the letter of the self-denying ordinance is a burden to them.'

These difficulties are illustrated by two letters received by Akers-Douglas at this time from Lord Bath.[1] In the first (dated June 1st, '86) he wrote: '. . . We have held a small meeting of some persons of influence in the Conservative Party in West Wilts and have determined not to start a candidate of our own against Fuller [Liberal] but to support a Liberal Unionist should one come forward. Such candidate of course ought not to be started by us but should come forward independently of us . . .' But a little later (June 18th) he reported: 'The Bath people will not listen to reason, if they run Lawrie [Conservative] and drive out Wodehouse [Liberal Unionist] they destroy Weymouth's chance [his son, at Frome], will certainly lose one, possibly both seats for their city besides the harm this will do our cause everywhere by disgusting the Liberal Unionists whose help we so much require. There is a strong minority among our people in favour of Wodehouse and I am sure if strong pressure is exerted from Head Quarters it will tell, but it should be exerted at once.'

Indeed, when Salisbury found a member of his own Front Bench about to speak on behalf of a Conservative candidate who was fighting a Liberal-Unionist he called on the assistance of Akers-Douglas. The case was all the more involved and delicate since the Conservative candidate, William Nicholson, had formerly sat for the same constituency (Petersfield) as a Liberal and was now opposing Lord Wolmer, who was not only one of the Liberal-Unionist leaders, but also Salisbury's son-in-law.

20, Arlington Street, S.W.
June 13, '86

My dear Douglas,

I hear that Webster[2] is advertised to speak for Nicholson on Tuesday. Surely this can be stopped. It will have the worst possible effect on our Unionist allies.

Ever yours truly,
Salisbury.

[1] John Alexander, 4th Marquess, 1831–96, Lord Lieutenant of Wiltshire.
[2] Sir Richard Webster, Attorney-General 1886–92.

The same day he wrote again:

> I have been thinking over this Webster–Albon [?] business and it seems to me that we shall expose ourselves to terrible misconstruction if we—i.e. the front bench—individually support a Conservative in attacking a Unionist Liberal seat.
>
> It is one thing to say that we cannot impose our will on the local politicians—quite another to take part ourselves in the proceedings we profess to lament.
>
> If you see Beach would you ask him whether he does not think it would be a good rule for us to observe—that where a Conservative is attacking the seat of a Liberal who had voted in the majority [against the Home Rule Bill], the front bench should abstain from taking any part in the contest.

However, despite all these doubts and difficulties, the efforts of the Tory leaders to encourage the dissident Liberals without falling foul of their own men were rewarded beyond their wildest dreams. For as a result of the elections, the Liberal Unionists won 78 seats in the new House, whilst the Conservatives increased their own number from 250 to 316. The Gladstonian Liberals, on the other hand, dropped from 334 to 191. The Parnellites remained at their old figure. Thus, whilst no single party had an independent majority of its own, the two Unionist groups in combination exceeded the rest of the House by 118. The vote in Parliament against Home Rule for Ireland was thus overwhelmingly confirmed by the vote of the country and, without waiting for a further vote in Parliament, Gladstone resigned (July 30th).

But in the short interim between the declaration of the election results and Gladstone's decision to resign there reigned a state of confusion and uncertainty quite unprecedented in the annals of British party politics. Anxiety was shared alike by those Liberals—less determined than Chamberlain—who had forsworn their old leader and yet were still partially hypnotized by him, as well as by the Tories, who were trying to seduce them away without scaring them back to his fold. Again, among the Liberal Unionists strong motives of self-preservation further complicated their attitude. This delicate situation, and suggestions for its handling, were the subject of some revealing correspondence between Akers-Douglas and Sir Arthur

Forwood, who had represented the Ormskirk Division of Lancashire in Parliament since 1858 and was now Parliamentary and Financial Secretary to the Admiralty.

Dear Mr. Akers-Douglas,

I do not know whether you have time to read a few political reflections—anyhow I will send them. A letter from Lord Wolverton[1] was read to me this morning, written in response to an enquiry from a G.L. [Gladstonian Liberal], in which he says that the G.O.M. will not budge one jot from the establishment of a Parliament in Dublin, and the tone generally indicated an unwillingness to approach the Unionists. My friend was a Radical Unionist and evidently anxious for a modus vivendi being found with the G.O.M.

When I pressed upon him the absolute certainty of such a policy destroying every vestige of hope of a strong Government or one with any degree of permanency, his real sentiments came out, and these are their fear of Gladstone proving mischievous to them, and dangerous to the Liberal Party. Clearly the inner life of the [Liberal] Unionists is at the moment most unhappy, thro' fear of Gladstone—if he resigns all will go well but if it becomes necessary to turn him out you must reckon on their abstention and nothing more. You ask me the moral of all this, my reply is that we should secure if possible Lord Hartington's aid in office with Chamberlain's benevolent neutrality out of office. Such a conjunction will give us the solid Unionist vote, in the teeth of any threat from Gladstone, without it we shall be liable to the whim and caprice of a body of weak anxious men. At the same time I am bound to admit that, as many of the Unionists know, they could not get back, they will do nothing to bring about a dissolution, so we may hold on, but we want 400 votes to settle the Irish question. A word on the latter point, make any legislation applicable as much to one part of the Kingdom as another, whether it be criminal or remedial. Pass the Procedure Rules en bloc, these the Unionists will support.

Finally, let us earn some credit for originating and passing useful measures, such as appeal to the working classes. There are many such that can be framed that would be popular. Now a word to help you in your labours and to ease your friends. The 86 Irish and ? [sic] Radicals will always be on hand to trip you up. Would it be possible so to make us work as one man, that you might feel that at no moment had you less than 100 within call?

[1] 2nd Baron, Paymaster General in Gladstone's Ministry 1880–5.

4. Shooting Party at Eridge Castle, 1889.

Prince of Wales A. Akers-Douglas Lord Randolph Churchill Lord Abergavenny

5. A. Akers-Douglas, M.P. (*Spy* cartoon of 1885).

Could we not be formed into a sort of rota, each list pledged to stay in the House every night and all night for a given week—working week and week about,

Yours sincerely,
A. B. Forwood

Liverpool, 15 July [1886].

The following is Akers-Douglas's draft reply:

Confidential

C. P. [Chilston Park]
July 19,' 86

My dear Forwood,

. . . From all I have heard I should say the fears of your Radical Unionist friend are generally shared by his political party—The true Hartingtonians are I think a little more sound and would if necessary support us in carrying an amendment to the Speech if Gladstone does not resign.

I fear Hartington would not join us—I saw a prominent member of his party yesterday and the following were his arguments against a coalition ministry which may be worth your consideration. In the 1st place he said 'It is no doubt your wish as it certainly is ours that the new ministry about to be formed should be a strong and lasting one—one that if possible should last out Gladstone'—With that object in view it should be a purely Conservative one—'We cannot make one ourselves and Coalitions have always proved weak and shortlived. Hartington should remain outside giving you as I know he will, every possible guarantee that you shall be maintained in office not only until your Irish Bill is passed, but so long as Gladstone lives—that is if you only behave decently.

'If H. joins you he must split with Chamberlain—and can only bring you 43 votes—the voting power of Unionists being classed as follows—6 men pledged to follow either Salisbury or Hartington whichever is in power—43 followers of Hartington—21 followers of Chamberlain and 8 who mean to rejoin Gladstone at once. If Hartington remains outside he can with Chamberlain hold the whole of his 75 votes.' Then again if H. joins he will do so sorely against his own inclinations and will have to give guarantees to his Radical following that directly he has assisted to pass necessary Irish legislation he will retire. This retirement in 18 months or so will be the signal for a break-up and probably another election. The very thing we want to avoid. Then again the Lib. Unionists dread the necessary re-elections on taking office and at present have only in the Lower House 2 men of Cabinet rank—H. and James [Sir Henry James]. What they would prefer rather than a coalition is to give Lord S. a support such as we gave Palmerston from '59 to '65.

I have simply stated these arguments much as my informant stated them to me but do not vouch for the soundness of his views or his logic.

In my humble opinion every inducement should be held out to H. to join us—if necessary with lead of H. of C.—our party would not stand his being Prime Minister as has been suggested—such a proposal would be absurd when we number 317 to his 43—but I fear he will [not] agree to join us at all.

On the other hand I have every reason to believe that so much do the L.U.'s dread the return of Gladstone and the possible results of another appeal to the country in the near future—that we may count on their loyal support in all matters of importance and on their non-interference in smaller issues.

I quite agree in your views as to the necessity of passing some useful measures for the working-classes and note your proposals for keeping a roster of members in bi-weekly batches for purposes of divisions.

Yours

A. A-D.

Akers-Douglas had been taking soundings not only among the Liberal Unionists but among his own party and the results he passed on to Salisbury, reinforced by his own decided opinions. On July 17th he wrote to the Chief, '. . . I have seen Brand[1] and several other Whigs and from what I can gather from them Hartington shows no desire to or intention of coalescing. In the first place they do not desire a split with Chamberlain and secondly they persist in their view that a Tory Government would be stronger with their united support *outside* the Government. They divide the [Liberal] Unionist party as follows—6 Salisbury, 43 Hartington, 21 Chamberlain, 8 Gladstone—and fear that a coalition would drive the 29 into opposition . . . while the [Conservative] party would be ready to follow Lord Hartington in the Commons, they would I know insist as far as they could on your being Prime Minister—but I am bound to say the majority would decidedly welcome a pure Conservative Government.' '

[1] Hon. H. R. Brand, son of the former Speaker; a leading Liberal-Unionist.

But Salisbury, despite the strong views of Akers-Douglas and others, neither for the first nor the last time, was prepared and even anxious to see Hartington become Premier, himself serving under him beside other leading Liberal Unionists. But Hartington, as anticipated, firmly refused both this and any other form

LORD R. CHURCHILL.

"DEAR ME! THERE SURELY CAN'T BE ANY DIFFICULTY IN SELECTING A PRIME MINISTER!"

of collaboration inside the Government—possibly stiffened in his resolve by Chamberlain who had written to him on July 16th '. . . Of course I could not join any Coalition: it would be absurd in me, and I need not argue it. With you it is somewhat different. You might join and be perfectly consistent. But if you do you must make up your mind to cease to be, or call yourself, a Liberal. The force of circumstances will be irresistible, and you will be absorbed in the Great Constitutional Party . . .' Assuming that Hartington did not desire this, Chamberlain summed up what he thought their attitude ought to be: '. . . in that case we must all give a loyal support to the Conservatives, provided that they do not play the fool either in foreign policy or in reactionary measures at home. They might count on some years of power—after which, if Mr. Gladstone is out of the way, the Liberal Party will probably pull itself together again and I hope may be strong enough to turn them out.'[1] It is amusing—as well as a tribute to Gladstone's immense power—to note how desperately both sides tried to believe in his early demise! At any rate, Salisbury had to accept the Queen's commission to form a ministry—his second—which was therefore a purely Conservative one, backed by a composite majority in Parliament.

Salisbury said at the end of his life that Gladstone, in struggling for Home Rule, had 'awakened the slumbering genius of Imperialism'. Indeed, though the genius had been animated and fostered by Disraeli, it was not till after his death, during the particularly disastrous handling of imperial affairs under Gladstone's second ministry, that it really began to stir to life. The conception of Britain as a world power, the heart of an empire, now began for the first time to find conscious expression in the mind of the great public. It was then that Disraeli's—and consequently the Conservative Party's—part in fostering this subconscious urge, this dazzling conception, was first fully recognized, and, simultaneously, Gladstone's direct challenge to it. It is largely to this simple metamorphosis of feeling—epitomized in the struggle round the Union with Ireland—that the great electoral landslide of 1886 can be attributed. But even after the election was won the Tories felt that this aspect of the matter should be continually emphasized and hammered home.

In sending to Akers-Douglas copies of his articles in the *Quarterly Review*, Louis Jennings, journalist, M.P., and devoted ally of Churchill, wrote (October 14th, '86): '. . . you will see that I have placed before the public in a distinct shape the last and worst form of the Gladstonian policy—namely to stir up sectional strife throughout the country, setting Wales and Scotland against England and England against them, for the sake of carrying out the principle of separate Parliaments. This

[1] Holland: *Life of Duke of Devonshire*, II, 168–9.

scheme is the most reckless and wicked that any statesman has ever undertaken in this country, and I do not think the public are yet sufficiently alive to it.'

It was the fact that the imperialist issue cut right across the traditional party lines—including, especially, the Radical one—that those party lines underwent such violent change and distortion. The cases of Bright and Chamberlain are the most outstanding because of their obviously profound effect on the course of events. But Lady St. Helier has described the equally astonishing effect of the Home Rule issue upon a most uncompromising Radical and lifelong Republican who had earlier been a fervent admirer of Gladstone, but who was not a politician. Her friend Goldwin Smith had in fact been Regius Professor of Modern History at Oxford, but so strong were his feelings against monarchy, privilege and all hereditary institutions that he left England to live in the purer atmosphere of North America. In 1887, however, he was writing to her about 'the fallacies which the unscrupulous sophistry of the G.O.M. has, I fear, implanted in the minds of the masses' and suggesting it would 'be a great thing if Royalty could appear upon the scene again and draw the eyes of the people to it and away from its rival before the elections'. After declaring that 'if the patriotic understanding between Conservatives and Liberal Unionists breaks up we are done for', he ends: 'It is rather a sad "Jubilee" for the Queen, who is merely discrowned by an arch-demagogue, while her dominions are threatened with dismemberment to feed his insatiable passion for popularity.'[1]

This was the kind of feeling which played directly into the hands of the Tories and enabled them to hold power for twenty years, with only one short interruption and without having to come seriously to grips with any of the really fundamental social and constitutional problems which were the natural outcome of the recent huge forward leaps in the democratic process. For, by taking their stand on the Irish question and appealing to the awakening imperial conscience of the nation, Salisbury and the Conservatives obscured for a while the really burning issues of the times.

The price of this temporary advantage was of course that these underground fires broke out with all the more violence

[1] Lady St. Helier, op. cit., 290–1.

when the Tories were at last swept from power in 1906, remaining in their turn in the wilderness for all but twenty years, whilst Labour-supported Liberal governments indulged in orgies of socialistic reform. Not that the Tories did not carry through a number of important reforms during their long tenure of power; but these had rather the appearance of random concessions to the mood of the day than of a planned programme of reform—such as might have wrested the initiative from their opponents. The Tories gave the impression that domestic problems occupied the background in their scheme of things, whilst the conduct of foreign policy and the extension of the Empire occupied the forefront. Indeed, when their leader, Salisbury, was so patently and exclusively absorbed by the latter problems, this was bound to be little short of the truth—however much some of his associates might try, as they did, to make him alter the impression.

Akers-Douglas (who had been returned unopposed at the election) returned to the post of Patronage Secretary and Government Chief Whip which he had filled with such outstanding success in Salisbury's first short ministry of the previous year. 'I have not seen any formal announcement of your appointment as my successor,' wrote his Liberal opposite number, Arnold Morley on July 29th, 'but I take it for granted—unless you claim—as your success entitles you to do, some less arduous position than that which falls to our lot.' The next six years, during which he remained in that office, were at once the heyday of his career and the supreme test of his exceptional ability. For the circumstances under which he laboured were exceptional also. Although the Conservative government had a majority, its life depended on the dissentient Liberals, whose adherence to the Government was swayed by the dual and sometimes alternating counsels of Hartington and Chamberlain. The control of these composite forces required firmness, tempered with tact and discretion, and this was the very combination of qualities which Akers-Douglas possessed in an eminent degree. Moreover, as a contemporary afterwards wrote:

> . . . no one knew better the changing mood of the lobby, the exact value of the 'frondeur' or the extent of an intrigue. He possessed a preternatural dexterity in judging the qualifications of men for office or party service, as well as their claims for honorific recogni-

> tion. In dealing with the importunate suitor he could 'smile without art and win without a bribe'. His will was tenacious; his character strong. He compelled the attendance of ministers at the House with the insistence which he applied to private members. In all the affairs of government or party Lord Salisbury trusted him implicitly.[1]

Indeed, Salisbury, with his peculiar temperament, had far more need than most prime ministers of the services of such a lieutenant. Living as he did in an ivory tower, he had acquired no skill in party management and was not interested in doing so, so long as the 'machine' ran smoothly. And it did run smoothly; for in Richard Middleton, the Chief Party Agent, Akers-Douglas had a brilliant helpmate, and between them there grew up a combination as efficient as it was popular. For the first time the Lobby was in close relation with the constituencies, while the party leader was kept completely informed by these admirable exponents of dual control. Well might Lord Salisbury say, as he once did: 'Douglas and Middleton have never put me wrong.'[2]

'That was the classic period in Conservative electioneering,' wrote Lady Gwendolen Cecil in her biography of her father. 'Under Mr. Akers-Douglas as Whip and Captain Middleton as Chief Agent, the organization attained a completeness which could hardly have been improved upon.' She goes on to describe the almost uncanny accuracy with which Middleton could forecast the results of by-elections and how at the end of the day Salisbury would come round to Middleton's office and 'go through the last reports from the constituencies, or discuss with Whip and Agent the latest teacup-storm among some section of his supporters'. She adds: 'Apart from their efficiency, both party officials had a straightness, loyalty and simplicity of outlook which made them very pleasant to work with, and their chief's relations with them were intimately easy.'[3] Lady Gwendolen admits that there were times when the two lieutenants were sorely tried by their Chief's occasional 'epigrammatic indiscretions' on the platform which often seemed

[1] J. S. Sandars: article on A. Akers-Douglas in *Dictionary of National Biography*, 1922–30.

[2] *Studies of Yesterday, by a Privy Councillor* [J. S. Sandars], 161.

[3] Lady Gwendolen Cecil: *Life of Robert, Marquis of Salisbury*, III, 197.

to them to jeopardize at one stroke all their labours to keep the party in power. But they 'stood the shock'. 'Both . . . were gifted with a saving sense of humour which buttressed the confidence, which contact had inspired, in their chief's larger attributes for leadership. The unstinted personal loyalty which they gave him up to the end was among the most satisfying of his experiences in politics.'[1]

When Akers-Douglas became Patronage Secretary for the second time in June 1886 he was instrumental in introducing an interesting and important reform connected with that office. Under an Act of 1782, and a further one of 1839, the Patronage Secretary received an annual sum of £10,000, in four quarterly payments from the Consolidated Fund, for 'secret service', of which he was not obliged to give any account. In 1886, an agitation had begun because it was suspected that, under the security of secrecy, moneys originally intended to be used at critical times in purchasing important confidential information respecting intrigues or enterprises hostile to England had been diverted and perverted to the paying of election expenses of members of the ruling party. Actually it had become the custom to spend a large part of the money on the routine expenses of the Parliamentary Secretary's office, such as wages of messengers, also on the secretarial and travelling expenses of the Chief Whip and his personal private secretary, or in payment of the latter, on the party offices in London and elsewhere; a part, too, might be invested.[2] But there is no doubt that in a long Parliament a very large sum could accumulate, which, at least potentially, could considerably influence an election.

In July 1886, during the Home Rule Election campaign, the *Whitehall Review* made a direct accusation regarding the use of Secret Service money:

> . . . it is an open secret at electioneering headquarters that the General Election was delayed till after quarter-day purely in order that Mr. Arnold Morley, the Liberal Chief Whip, might draw a second quarter's instalment for distribution among impecunious Gladstonian candidates. Mr. Akers-Douglas drew the money down to Lady Day; and then Mr. Morley drew it down to

[1] Lady Gwendolen Cecil: *Life of Robert, Marquis of Salisbury*, III, 198.

[2] See H. J. Hanham: *Elections and Party Management: Politics in the time of Disraeli and Gladstone* (Longmans, 1960), 369–70.

Midsummer. He has now drawn it down to Michaelmas, and the whole of the money (£5000) has been spent on the elections.

And the correspondent of the *Sheffield Daily Telegraph* (August 28th, 1886) declared:

I understand that at the end of Mr. Gladstone's administration last year something like £30,000 of this secret service money had accumulated. This presumably was spent to promote the interests of Liberal and Home Rule candidates at the election.

It was said that no balance had been returned to the Exchequer for fifty years, but, at any rate, Akers-Douglas drew attention to the matter when at the end of his first tenure of the office in 1885 he handed back a surplus to the Treasury. From that time he was foremost in trying to institute some reform of a practice which at least invited the very worst suspicions, and, as a first step, sponsored a Treasury Minute to oblige repayment of any future surplus into the Exchequer. A little later he had no difficulty in persuading the then Chancellor of the Exchequer, Lord Randolph Churchill, to sponsor a Bill to amend the old Acts.

Though they were generally held to have benefited much in the recent past from the Secret Service moneys, it was obviously impossible for the Liberals to put up any serious opposition and the Bill abolishing the Secret Service money vote was accordingly passed without delay at the beginning of September 1886. It is scarcely necessary to add that, apart from the moral aspect of the matter, it was a shrewd political move on the part of the Conservatives, which did much to enhance their prestige in the country at large. In announcing the Bill for the Repeal (August 28th, 1886) Lord Randolph gave Akers-Douglas due credit for initiating it:

. . . the main credit of it will be due to my hon. friend the Parliamentary Secretary to the Treasury, who, from the day that he came into office last June, took a great interest in this question, and by measures which he induced the Treasury to adopt anticipated the Minute of the Public Accounts Committee which had been set up to make recommendations on the subject.

V
THE CLIMAX OF CHURCHILL

SINCE Lord Salisbury had decided not to repeat the experiment of combining the Foreign Office with the Premiership, Lord Iddesleigh (the former Sir Stafford Northcote) was, after two others had refused, induced to become Foreign Secretary. Salisbury had been prepared to invite Hicks Beach to resume the position of Chancellor of the Exchequer and Leader of the party in the House of Commons, which he had filled with efficiency and resourcefulness in the last Conservative government. But Beach declined because he 'felt that Lord Randolph Churchill was superior in eloquence, ability and influence to myself; that the position of Leader in name, but not in fact, would be intolerable; and that it was better for the party and the Country that the Leader in fact should be Leader also in name.'[1] At this, not only did Lord Salisbury press him all the more strongly to accept, but Lord Randolph himself showed the most becoming hesitation—which deeply impressed Beach—on account of his 'youth and inexperience'. As a condition of his acceptance he insisted upon Beach taking the Irish Secretaryship, pointing out that the latter 'could only honourably give up the Leadership by taking what was at the moment the most difficult position in the Government'.

Thus it was therefore arranged; Churchill becoming Leader of the House as well as Chancellor of the Exchequer, and Beach becoming Chief Secretary for Ireland. Lord George Hamilton,

[1] Churchill, 493.

in his *Reminiscences*,[1] stresses Beach's great self-abnegation by this act and also the 'double personal obligation' under which he placed Churchill by surrendering to him these two great offices and shouldering again the most onerous and thankless job in the Government. This lends a special interest to his account of the extraordinary personal attack which Churchill made upon Beach, in his presence, a few months later. The outburst was so unwarranted and inexplicable that Hamilton concluded it must be 'jealousy for Beach's splendid altruism which undoubtedly made him the most esteemed if not influential man in the House'. At any rate, although Churchill made a handsome apology to his friend immediately afterwards, the scene boded ill for the cohesion of the government.

LORD R. CHURCHILL

"DOESN'T PUT HIS FOOT DOWN.'

Despite the rise in his fortunes which occurred in the summer of 1886, Lord Randolph did not appear to be any more elated than did the majority of Conservatives of whom he was now the leader in the House of Commons. 'I feel awfully alone in the House of Commons,' he wrote to Hartington in September, 'and am glad to grasp an opportunity of placing things before you as I look at them'.[2] It was as if, recognizing the profound distrust of his fellow Tories and warned by that inner sense of doom and failure which always seemed to dog him, he knew that he had reached the zenith of his career. The attitude of his own party—at least in its most extreme form—may be seen in the following extract from a letter to W. H. Smith from Robert Bourke[3] (July 1886), complaining that after his long and distinguished service he had been left out of Salisbury's Government: '... I hear that all who are not personae gratae to Lord

[1] Hamilton, op. cit., 38. [2] Churchill, 510.

[3] Foreign Under Secretary, 1874–80 and 1885–6; created Baron Connemara 1887.

Randolph Churchill may in future look forward to nothing but political effacement so long as they belong to the Conservative Party. If this is so, the sooner we place ourselves under the allegiance of some other leader in the House of Commons, the better for our own self-respect and consistency.'[1] There was no mistrust, however, among the huge section of the working-class electorate which had always supported him: in fact, as if sensing his predicament, their enthusiasm for their favourite and champion naturally tended to increase in proportion to the growing dislike and distrust of his colleagues. Hence it was perhaps scarcely surprising if he himself turned his face more and more gladly towards the sycophantic mob and his back more and more defiantly upon the frowning party mandarins. Yet really the latter had cause to be grateful to him; for by the very fact of his being against them he won extra support for the Tory Party.

At any rate, Lord Randolph became increasingly reckless in his appeals to the popular fancy, until, in a celebrated speech, at Dartford on October 2nd, 1886, he formulated a programme of 'Tory Democracy' which, at least to the orthodox majority of the party, appeared indistinguishable from the Radicalism of Chamberlain and Bright. To the Liberals also it seemed incompatible with any conceivable form of Conservatism. 'It was the wolf of Radicalism in the sheepskin of Toryism,'[2] wrote Lord Rosebery in later years. Gladstone himself had denounced Churchill's brand of Tory Democracy in no uncertain terms in a letter to Lord Acton in 1885. 'Tory Democracy,' he wrote, 'is no more like the Conservative party in which I was bred, than it is like Liberalism. In fact less. It is demagogism, only a demagogism not ennobled by love and appreciation of liberty, but applied in the worst way, to put down the pacific law-respecting economic elements which ennobled the old conservatism, living upon the fomentation of angry passions, and still in secret as obstinately attached as ever to the principle of class interests.'[3]

Lord Randolph began his Dartford speech with a eulogy of the loyalty with which the Liberal Unionists had supported the

[1] Hambleden MSS.

[2] Lord Rosebery: *Lord Randolph Churchill*, 136.

[3] Morley, III, 173.

Conservative ministry and, in so doing, went out of his way to pay a handsome tribute to the work of his friend, Akers-Douglas.

> There is a cause to which success is due, and one which I should like to bring before your notice, and that is the fact that the Government have been supported by large and regular and unvarying majorities in the House of Commons, which support is due to one thing, and mainly to one thing—it is due to the indefatigable energy, to the tact, to the good humour, to the zeal, and to the knowledge of one of your members of the County of Kent—Mr. Akers-Douglas—(cheers), who has elaborated and perfected all those excellent principles and methods of party management which were inaugurated and established by another of your County members, Sir William Hart-Dyke.

Only a few days earlier (September 23rd) Salisbury had written Akers-Douglas a line, after the division on Parnell's Half Rent Bill, to congratulate him on a 'splendid bit of whipping', and on the same day, in a speech at St. Albans, had made the rare gesture of publicly acknowledging the 'self-sacrificing work' of his Whips. It was well deserved, for in a notoriously difficult season of the year, with dull business into the bargain, they had secured 'devoted and resolute attendance' and—final triumph—at the division on Parnell's Bill 'every single man in the Conservative Party in the House of Commons was either in his place or else he was paired'.

After its pleasant preliminaries, however, Lord Randolph's speech struck a chill into the hearts of the Conservative leaders. It ranged over the whole compass of affairs—domestic, foreign, financial—and coolly presented and promulgated the policy which in each case the Government should, in his opinion, adopt. Although it is with justice that his son and biographer has pointed out that 'nearly all these legislative projects have since been passed by Conservative Administrations into law', by the standards of the day it could not be considered otherwise than as a Radical policy. Although, too, Lord Randolph so innocently claimed[1] that it was 'a mere repetition of the programme of Lord Salisbury at Newport in 1885' and 'a mere reiteration and elaboration of the Queen's Speech of January

[1] In his speech to the conference of Conservative Associations at Bradford, October 26th, 1886.

last', he knew that it was—and that he had intended it to be—a great deal more than that. Certain features of the programme no doubt bore some relation to the broad lines of policy agreed upon by the Cabinet, but others definitely did not. But apart from these considerations—and, perhaps, above all—his colleagues were moved by the simple human reaction of disliking to have their hands forced.

After delivering himself of this bombshell Lord Randolph slipped away on a brief continental holiday. These trips were another great source of embarrassment to his colleagues, for his fame stood high abroad and he was in the habit of having private interviews with leading statesmen of other Great Powers, during which no one knew quite what transpired except that ever and anon evidence of indiscretion or at least of a misapprehension created emerged to embarrass the official conduct of foreign policy—of which, moreover, he was known to be a severe critic. His professed dislike of publicity and alleged attempts to preserve an incognito were treated with not a little scepticism by his colleagues. 'I see by today's *Scotsman*,' wrote Akers-Douglas to Salisbury (October 8th, '86), 'that Randolph's elaborate preparations for the preservation of a strict "incognito" have failed and that his arrival in Berlin is announced.'

If Churchill's colleagues did not immediately repudiate the Dartford programme, it was rather as the result of stupefaction than of agreement. When they had recovered, those who were already his enemies began to fight his proposals tooth and nail. But Salisbury remained patient, despite attempts to goad him against Churchill by making him feel that the latter had put him in a ridiculous position. As leader he was naturally anxious for the cohesion of his government and party; but also, despite his reputation as a die-hard, he was actually by nature far more flexible than some of his colleagues. Therefore he tried to bring the latter round on such points of Churchill's programme as he felt personally able to endorse; but his efforts were without avail. With bitterness Lord Randolph wrote to him on November 6th: 'I see the Dartford programme crumbling into pieces every day . . . I am afraid it is an idle schoolboy's dream to suppose that Tories can legislate—as I did—stupidly. They can govern and make war and increase taxation and expenditure *à merveille*, but legislation is not their province in a democratic constitution . . . I certainly have not the courage to go on struggling against cliques, as poor Dizzy did all his life . . .'[1] Incidentally the last remark does not seem quite consistent with his jibe on a previous occasion about 'the Derby-Dizzy lot with their following of county families'.

In a very wise and kindly reply to this letter Lord Salisbury stated the case for a cautious policy with admirable precision.

> The Tory party is composed of very varying elements [he wrote], and there is merely trouble and vexation of spirit in trying to make them work together. I think the 'classes and the dependents of class' are the strongest ingredients in our composition, but we have so to conduct our legislation that we shall give some satisfaction to both classes and masses. This is specially difficult with the classes—because all legislation is rather unwelcome to them, as tending to disturb a state of things with which they are satisfied. It is evident therefore that we must work at less speed and at a lower temperature than our opponents . . .[2]

Lord Randolph's accusation about the Tories' ability to 'increase taxation and increase expenditure *à merveille*' revealed another growing obsession which was to be the cause of the final rupture between him and his colleagues. Whilst few Chancellors of the Exchequer have ever entered upon their job with less knowledge of its rudiments, few have also mastered these so well and so rapidly as he did. But, having done so, he proceeded to produce a Budget which, among other controversial things, reflected his views on the need for the reduction of public expenditure by the curtailment of foreign and imperial commitments. This attitude was in conformity with his known views over the past few years as well as with all those recent public utterances by which he felt himself pledged. But, in view of the ultimate outcome, it is worth noticing that it ran counter not only to the Government's policy but also to the new imperial consciousness of the country and therefore lacked the popular appeal which he may have thought it had.

The logical result of this attitude was that Lord Randolph demanded reductions in the Army and Navy Estimates. The ministers concerned, W. H. Smith and Lord George Hamilton,

[1] Churchill, 564. [2] Ibid., 565.

felt strongly that it was rather a moment to strengthen than to reduce the Armed Services, but, being on friendlier terms with him than their colleagues and being anxious to preserve harmony in the Cabinet, they endeavoured to come to terms with him. Hamilton even consented to cut down his estimates; but Smith was adamant. This caused Churchill to explode (November 20th):

> . . . I can't go on at this rate. Whether on foreign policy or home policy or expenditure I have no influence at all. Nothing which I say is listened to. The Govt. are proceeding headlong to a smash and I won't be connected with it; the worst feature of all is this frantic departmental extravagance.[1]

This was followed soon afterwards by an offensive reference to 'your frightful extravagance at the War Office'.[2]

Of course every reason inclined the Prime Minister to back his Service Ministers; but the urgent necessity to call the bluff for good and all must have been borne in upon him by receiving from the exasperated Smith a note: 'It comes to this—is he to be *the* Government? If you are willing that he should be, I shall be delighted, but I could not go on on such conditions.'[3]

Although Churchill had thrown out these hints that he was prepared to stake his career on the outcome of the issue, when he in fact resigned and attributed his decision to this difference of opinion they were all flabbergasted. Lord George Hamilton was the first person to whom, quite casually, he communicated his decision, whilst both were on their way to Windsor to dine with the Queen on December 20th, and it was in his astonished presence, at Windsor, the same evening that Churchill penned the fatal letter to Salisbury. As the sole witness and naturally having made a desperate attempt to impress upon Churchill the disastrous nature of the step, as well as the extreme impropriety of the manner of its execution, Hamilton was in a unique position to judge of the motive involved. He felt convinced that Churchill had come to the end of his tether physically and that, driven by a blind impulse, he was seeking an immediate respite from office by any means that came to hand, rather than making some calculated political move.

But even that did not diminish the gravity of the step. 'I

[1] Hambleden MSS. [2] Ibid. [3] Cecil, III, 331.

knew then,' Hamilton wrote, 'that the whole fat was in the fire. Salisbury's patience had been very strained during the past three or four months, the whole Cabinet was groaning and creaking from the wayward and uncontrolled language of one member, and I was certain that Salisbury would be only too pleased to accept that colleague's resignation.'[1] Nevertheless, Lord Salisbury did not hurry to reply to Lord Randolph's letter. In the interval speculation was rife and the suspense tremendous. On December 22nd Lord Henry Manners, the Prime Minister's Private Secretary, wrote to Akers-Douglas: 'Up to now—4.15 p.m.—Ld. R. C. has had no answer from the Chief. But I came up from seeing Moore [Churchill's Private Secretary], and he says that there is no change in the situation at all —and that he [Churchill] is "quite determined". Moore is miserable; and has just discharged his advice, with, he says, no results whatever . . .'

In fact, on this same day (December 22nd), Salisbury had replied to Churchill saying unequivocally that in the controversy over the Estimates he felt bound, in view of the serious international situation, to take the side of the two heads of the Services, Smith and Hamilton. Churchill did not hesitate to take this as an acceptance of his resignation—though, coming from Salisbury, it was really nothing so explicit or crude. He also deeply aggravated his original offence of sending his resignation to the Premier without telling the Queen, although staying under her roof, by now—immediately—personally announcing it to *The Times* before the Queen had accepted it.

Lord Salisbury seemed to favour Hamilton's diagnosis of the case, for in a letter to Akers-Douglas of December 26th he wrote only briefly on the subject: '. . . R. C.'s conduct can only be accounted for on the theory that the work has upset his nerves—and when his nerves go, his judgment goes altogether . . .' But otherwise the first reaction of most people was the more obvious one that Churchill's overweening self-confidence and thirst for power had led him to think that he could bring Salisbury and the others to their knees by the threat of depriving them of so indispensable a colleague. This appears to have been more or less the view of Smith in the following letter written to Akers-Douglas on the day after the announcement.

[1] Hamilton, 49.

Private

Greenlands,
Henley-on-Thames.
24 Dec. 1886

My dear Douglas,

. . . I am very sorry about Churchill, but the real truth is Estimates are a pretext—not the real cause. It was really Salisbury or Churchill: and if Salisbury had gone, none of us could have remained—not even those who are disposed to go with him on Allotments and Local Government rather than with Salisbury.

He dined with Joe [Chamberlain] on Friday and that I think settled it, for after trying for two hours on Monday to beat me down, he told me, quite in a friendly way, that he should resign, and he let out frankly that his 'rapprochment' was towards Joe rather than any other politician of the present day; and unless they quarrel we shall see the two working together.

Will he take any of our men with him?

I am cordially in favour of Salisbury's intention to work with Hartington if it be possible and any personal sacrifices that be required from the present Cabinet should be offered cheerfully and ungrudgingly. With such a combination Salisbury will swallow a far more Liberal Local Government Bill and even Allotments, that I am sure of.

Yours very sincerely,
W. H. Smith.

Next day (December 25th) Smith wrote again to Akers-Douglas evidently continuing the train of thought of the above letter and implying that Salisbury's undoubted wish to collaborate with the Liberal Unionists should have reassured Churchill that the liberalization of Conservative policy was imminent in any case: 'I am glad our friends stand by us. It is insanity in R. C. It might be right for him to go if he felt he could not get on with us, but not now; nor on the grounds he chose . . .' An early report of the effect of the Chancellor's resignation in the constituencies came to Akers-Douglas from his colleague W. L. Jackson,[1] Financial Secretary at the Treasury, in a letter of December 26th: 'So far as I can gather Public Opinion in this district [Leeds] it condemns Lord Randolph's action. The members of our Party are all sorry but I find none

[1] M.P., Leeds North; Chief Secretary for Ireland, 1891–2; created Lord Allerton.

who defend Lord Randolph's action—they think it will do our Party great injury but there is no feeling against the Govt. or against Lord Salisbury . . .' Another colleague, Sir James Fergusson, the Foreign Under Secretary, ventured (December 28th) to think 'that the circumstances of the party are less affected by Churchill's retirement than the newspapers assume and tell us that Lord Salisbury considers them to be' and from conversations with leading Liberal Unionists in Scotland reported that 'they all say that the Liberal Unionists will be more rather than less disposed to support the Government'.

From these remarks it will be clear that although Lord Salisbury did not truckle to Lord Randolph at the crucial moment, he did not attempt to conceal his perturbation at what he deemed to be the almost deadly blow dealt to his Ministry.

Once again he turned towards Hartington, to seek the latter's co-operation in any way which might be acceptable to the Liberal Unionist leader and his friends—even to the extent, if necessary, of serving under him. In this attitude, however, Salisbury was by no means supported by his colleagues—or even by the Conservative Party generally. Though aware of its partial dependence on Liberal Unionist support, the party was conscious and proud of its great strength and by no means inclined to allow its leader to sell its birthright for a mess of potage.

Knowing his chief's inclination and jealous, as always, for the party's honour, Akers-Douglas had taken an early opportunity of trying to reassure him. On December 24th, he had written to him: 'I have refrained from bothering you with any letter before as to the condition of the Party but take this opportunity of mentioning that I have had a large number of letters and telegrams from your supporters in House of Commons assuring you of their loyalty and continued support, Middleton has also received many to the same effect. I am quite sure the Party is sound—even those of R.C.'s own section and several of his personal friends who I have seen have expressed their regret at the step he has taken and say they cannot defend him . . .'[1] More pungently Lord Beauchamp, the Paymaster General, wrote to Smith (December 26th): '. . . I am sorry Lord Salisbury has made such a fuss about Randolph

[1] Salisbury MSS.

Churchill's resignation. He should have filled up the place at once. It is very foolish to go again to Lord Hartington and to cry stinking fish. Lord R. Churchill carries no one with him and will not I think be able to do much harm in the country. Lord Salisbury is properly punished for having given Ld. R. C. a post for which he was never fit and thereby dislocating the proper arrangements of the Party.'[1]

When Akers-Douglas saw his chief persisting in the course which he—and others—considered unjustified by the circumstances and even rather ignoble, he began to take a very firm line—a fact which bears witness to the remarkable position of influence which he had already, in so short a time, achieved.

12 Downing Street
Dec. 30th, 1886[2]

Dear Lord Salisbury,

I have just seen Cranborne who tells me you are rather unhappy as to the advice I gave you with regard to the policy of a coalition cabinet with Hartington at its head. I have today seen several of the 'bell wethers' of the party including Dyke,[3] M'Garel Hogg,[4] Lewis[5] & Walter Long[6] and if anything the views they expressed tend to strengthen me in my opinion that such course would be highly undesirable in the interests of the party. As I told you yesterday the party are loyal to you to a man. They will gladly on your advice accept Lord Hartington as leader of the House of Commons and a Coalition containing as many of his followers as you like to take. Or they would accept Lord H. as Prime Minister provided you were in his Cabinet—but in this case I think you should call the Party together and explain the reasons which compelled you to prefer such a Coalition and ask them yourself to accept Hartington. Should you desire to take so extreme a step my objections wd be greatly removed if you could form the Coalition on Equal terms with Lord Hartington and then hand over to him the chief place. What I most fear would be the effect of your

[1] Hambleden MSS.

[2] The date on the copy is actually 'Dec. 30th, 1887', but there can be absolutely no doubt that this was a slip.

[3] Sir William Hart Dyke, Bart., see ante.

[4] Sir James (later Lord Magheramorne), M.P. Hornsey, Chairman Metropolitan Board of Works.

[5] George Pitt-Lewis, K.C., M.P., N.W. Devon.

[6] M.P. Devizes, Secretary to Local Government Board (later 1st Viscount Long of Wraxall).

resigning first and then the Queen sending for Lord H. to form a Govt. Your resignation would be taken by large members of our party as an acknowledgement that you were afraid to go on though you had 320 followers and would magnify the position of Churchill. Such a Coalition as this with Hartington at its head would be a Liberal Coalition in the eyes of many and it would offend many who now say freely that by giving you the majority at the last Election they expressed their confidence in you which confidence you wd. seem hardly to appreciate.

Believe me,

Yours faithfully,

A. Akers-Douglas.[1]

Such an extremely stern and direct admonition, amounting almost to a rebuke, must have shaken Salisbury out of his half altruistic, half pusillanimous mood, for by the time Hartington (who had fortunately been abroad during the crucial phase and had thereby avoided directly committing himself) had arrived back in London, the Coalition idea was dead—thus saving him from being placed in what might have been an extremely awkward position.

MARQUIS OF HARTINGTON.

"STARTINGTON."

On the same day as Akers-Douglas had written the above letter to Salisbury, Middleton had written to Akers-Douglas in very much the same vein, stating the problems of the moment with admirable clarity and revealing how much these two key party men were attuned to one another.

[1] A copy of this letter was preserved by Akers-Douglas in a leather-bound book together with copies of one or two other letters relating to this crisis, and it is this copy which is here reproduced. Oddly enough the original is not among Lord Salisbury's papers; but there is no indication on the copy that it was not sent and moreover the completeness of its form and the care with which it was copied makes this seem unlikely.

Stroud
30 Dec., 1886

My dear Douglas,

My letter of yesterday will have told you how anxious I am about the present crisis and consequently your letter of this morning telling me nothing definite had been settled was quite a relief to me after reading the various newspaper reports and leading articles which all more or less harp upon the blessings of a Coalition with the Lib. Unionists—I cannot help thinking this utter want of reliance in the Conservative Party by the Conservative Press is one of the evils arising out of the past coalition at the time of the late election but at the same time it is a grave cause of weakness and much to be deplored—In this matter I deny that the Press truly represents the feeling of our Party,—but allowing that it is a true representation of existing feeling it is the more reason we should strive to instil into the Party a spirit of self-reliance rather than foster the idea that our Leaders cannot govern the Country—I see some of the papers openly advocate a coalition with Lord Hartington as Prime Minister and laud Ld. Salisbury's self-abnegation in proposing such a course—You know best what the result of such a combination would be in the House, whether you could get a House always kept and whether or no it would be possible to prevent . . . [?] . . . being formed—Outside the House the effect would I fear be disastrous and although it might be possible to keep the more educated in hand, the bulk of the Party would go to pieces—Amongst the uneducated the great strength of the Liberal Party is the personality of Mr. Gladstone—amongst our Party that of Lord Salisbury—remove either of these Leaders and the solid surviving Party will gain in strength and activity. Of course the unfortunate resignation of Lord Randolph is a most serious blow to our Party inasmuch as that to a certain degree he together with Ld. Salisbury formed the rallying cry of the Conservatives—but can Ld. Hartington fill the gap?

I presume nobody dreams of introducing Chamberlain into the Coalition—he alone could influence the classes from which Ld Randolph brought us strength. You may say these are merely electioneering considerations but a strong Government must be formed through the result of an election and must continue to receive the support of the popular voice between elections—Ld. Hartington and the Whigs will give us debating power in the House but outside their influence is more likely to be a source of weakness than strength.—If it is absolutely necessary to have a coalition—a necessity I am thankful to say I do not admit—for goodness sake induce Ld Salisbury to fill the post allotted to him by the voice of the people at the late election—i.e. Prime Minister. One more consideration before closing this long letter—If our Party are to be kept together we must have *one* Commander in Chief under whom they are to fight and with whom the victory is to be shared—Who is this to be? Ld Hartington or Ld Salisbury? If the former our Party will doubtless fight; but not with the vigour of progressive Conservatism, but as soldiers of that obsolete and wishy washy Whigism which only lately we've all been thanking God is dead at last.

Excuse this awful long yarn—Before leaving London I gave strict orders that everything possible should be done to prevent foolish articles appearing against Ld. Randolph—the worst of that is I trust already over, as it can do no good and may be the cause of serious ill-feeling in the future . . .

Yours ever,
Rich[d]. W. Middleton.

Meanwhile, Akers-Douglas had been instructed to sound Goschen as to his willingness to come into the Government and fill Churchill's place.

Carlton Club
Dec. 31 1886

Dear Lord Salisbury,

I saw Goschen as you suggested and gave him an assurance that as far as the rank and file of the party went they would cordially welcome him if he decided to assist you by joining the Government . . .

In further conversation I gathered that in addition to his fears as to his reception by our party he was afraid (1) that he wd. be 'isolated' in the Cabinet and did not know whether in asking him to join he could bring a colleague say in the Upper House; and (2) that he might not be strong enough to lead and that he did not know whether Beach or Smith wd do so at all events for a time.

I told him I was not authorized to give any opinion on these points but felt sure you would do all you could to meet his wishes on both points.

Yours very faithfully,
A. A. Douglas.[1]

But Goschen was at that time without a seat in the House of Commons. Writing again on the following day Akers-Douglas

[1] Salisbury MSS.

made various suggestions for solving this problem and at the same time forwarded to Salisbury a monumental letter which he had just received from Churchill (and which will be discussed presently). The allusion to the possibility of Churchill wanting to publish it is not without humour in view of the speed with which, without that, its contents became known to the press.

Jan. 1st 1887
12 Downing Street,
S.W.

Dear Lord Salisbury,

I enclose you a letter I have received from Churchill written to me as 'Whip'—which I fancy he intends to publish—giving a new version of his reasons for leaving you and his views for the future. I have formally acknowledged it saying I had forwarded it to you as he desired in a covering letter.

I have just received your telegram announcing Goschen's views. I think his desire not to lead a wise one and one that will much facilitate his cordial reception by our party.

He does not like the look of the Liverpool seat—so, if he joins, I conclude you wish me to find him at once a safe seat.

Goschen seemed last night much in favour of a coalition with Hartington at its head and Randolph and yourself members—If everything else fails this might work and wd. prevent what I should fear in a coalition without R.C., namely his presence below the gangway.

Yours very truly,
A. A. Douglas.[1]

Goschen, meanwhile, proceeded with extreme slowness and caution in every respect, thereby making himself a sitting target for press curiosity and conjecture. Whilst deliberating he tried to hide in the country 'in view of the indiscreet pressure of the press to squeeze information out of me', as he told Akers-Douglas rather primly in an undated letter. Thence he returned to the Coburg Hotel, 'but have given no one the address so as not to be overrun by curious visitors'. 'Have you anything to say about Oxford yet?' he went on, referring to the possibility

[1] The original is in the Salisbury MSS. and is undated, but Akers-Douglas's copy bears the above date and as Churchill's letter which he enclosed also bore the date 'New Year's Day 1887', Akers-Douglas must have received this by hand the day it was written.

of a seat there for him. 'I was at Brooks's just now, but I presume you have no news yet. How extraordinary it is that nothing escapes the papers. The Pall Mall Gazette has something about Mowbray,[1] but it may be only a guess . . . The Liverpool people make out a *good* case, but not I think an absolutely safe one. They have begged me not to decline hastily, so I have given no definite answer. This is I think what you wished.' He always showed great deference towards Akers-Douglas's opinions. It will be observed, moreover, that he was not the type of man (like Churchill) to be exhilarated by the fateful position in which he suddenly found himself: he was dreadfully fussed by it and so concerned to do the right thing by everybody.

Therefore it is perhaps understandable if Lord Randolph should have overlooked a person whose reactions were so totally unlike what his own would have been in a similar situation. For Lady St. Helier (then Mrs. Jeune) who, with her husband, was an intimate friend of Lord Randolph, has recorded how they invited him to lunch on the day after the announcement of his resignation in order to try to reason with him. He acknowledged that Salisbury would be glad to be rid of him, but 'pointed out that Lord Salisbury's position . . . was a difficult one, from the impossibility of finding a successor in his office'.[2] Mrs. Jeune suggested Goschen, whom she also knew intimately and whom she knew to be ready to accept office under Salisbury, but the idea was scouted by Lord Randolph. A few weeks later, when her guess had proved to be right, he met her with the words: 'You are quite right, I forgot Goschen.' If these words, which he repeated in various forms to other people for the rest of his life, really represented the truth they certainly implied that his resignation was a carefully calculated move. On the other hand, they may—as Hamilton believed[3]—merely have been an ingenious afterthought to explain away what was really a sudden brainstorm.

But meanwhile, as we have already seen, for the benefit of his political friends and for the information of the party as a whole, Lord Randolph had written a closely reasoned memorandum

[1] Sir John Mowbray, Bart., M.P. Oxford University.

[2] Lady St. Helier: *Memories of Fifty Years*, 274–5.

[3] Hamilton, 51.

on his reasons for resignation in the form of a private letter to Akers-Douglas. Sir Winston Churchill published this letter in his biography (1906) with the comment that 'it is remarkable that this letter has never yet been published'.[1] Nevertheless, as will presently be shown, it was in fact virtually almost immediately published, in so far as it was freely circulated among colleagues who gave extracts and summaries to the press. It is clear, moreover, from a letter of Chamberlain's[2] that Lord Randolph had in any case sent a resumé to this cherished ally simultaneously with his dispatch of the original to Akers-Douglas. Meanwhile the press was almost immediately in possession of its contents, and the *Pall Mall Gazette* (January 5th, 1887) wrote: 'The letter which Lord Randolph Churchill addressed to Mr. Akers-Douglas, the Chief Whip of the Tory Party, seems to have been involved in unnecessary mystery. Paragraphs have gone the round of the papers . . . There is nothing mysterious about the letter which, although a private one, has been shown very freely to members of Parliament and others.' It then proceeded to publish an exact and complete summary of the letter.

Despite the fact of Lord Randolph's letter being addressed to the central figure of the present book, since it was in no other sense personal and since it has already been published in full in Sir Winston's biography,[3] it is not necessary to give here more than a summary with quotation of some of the salient points. The argument was simple and indeed ingenuous. Starting from the premise that 'the primary object of all government at the present time is to maintain the Union with Ireland' and that the Gladstonian Liberals, in their resolve to establish Home Rule, had a very substantial proportion of the British electorate behind them, Churchill reasoned that anything which the Conservative Government might do which became too 'unpopular' would automatically bring back Gladstone and make Home Rule certain. He then proceeded to demonstrate that Conservative policies *were* unpopular—at any rate with him: 'a foreign policy which may at any moment involve this country in a European war; a domestic policy . . . marked by stagnation

[1] Churchill, 596. [2] Ibid., 599.

[3] Ibid., 596. The original is not among Akers-Douglas's papers, having been passed on by him to Salisbury and others and never returned.

rather than progress; free expenditure, necessitating high taxation . . .' etc.

The pursuit of these policies, Churchill asserted, 'not only involved so insignificant a person as myself in a marked violation of pledges given to the public, but also to all intents and purposes the entire Conservative party in the House of Commons'. If such a course were persisted in he foresaw at the next General Election a Tory rout even more terrible than that of 1880, and, if it were to come, he would not have it said that he had borne any responsibility for it.

LORD R. CHURCHILL.

"A GLOOMY VIEW OF THE POLITICAL SITUATION."

He concluded on a lofty note: 'I seek for no re-entry into the present Government; I decline to commence any undignified or unworthy bargaining and huckstering as to the terms of reconciliation . . .'; but he would offer to serve again in any government which could give an earnest of better things. Finally he gave a promise that he would do nothing to embarrass the Prime Minister in Parliament or country, but would merely 'watch silently and sadly the progress of events'. This final grand gesture was rudely deflated by Chamberlain when he wrote to him: 'If I had been you I do not think I should have added the last paragraph. When a man says that in no case will he return a blow, he is very likely to be cuffed. However,' he added sardonically, 'I dare say Lord Salisbury will not take you too literally at your word, and will avoid any extreme test of your most Christian disposition.'[1]

Nevertheless, the Great Joe, moved partly by feelings of friendship with his exiled friend and partly by reasons of policy, chose to see in him a victim of the forces of 'reaction'. 'My sympathies are entirely with you, and I think you may rely on my

[1] January 3rd, 1887, see Churchill, 599.

cordial co-operation, if it can be of any value,' he wrote to him on the day that his resignation was announced (December 23rd).[1] Reacting from his recent revolt, Chamberlain had already begun to dream afresh of Liberal reunion, and Churchill's 'expulsion' by the 'stupid party' seemed to offer welcome evidence of the impossibility of any real form of co-operation between the two Unionist wings. On the same day at a meeting in Birmingham of the Liberal Divisional Council, he declared: 'I confess it seems to me possible—I fear it is probable—that the old Tory influences have gained the upper hand and that we may be face to face with a Tory Government whose proposals no consistent Liberal will be able to support.'[2]

On December 26th Chamberlain wrote again to Churchill emphasizing the similarity of their respective positions and rather as one outcast to another: '. . . You will have a hard time to go through. Your case will be mine almost exactly, and I can tell you it is a bitter pilgrimage which is in prospect. The party tie is the strongest sentiment in this country—stronger than patriotism or even self-interest. But it will all come right in the end for both of us. I assume that you will maintain an independent position, and in that case you will be a power that your party cannot ignore . . . in their hearts they know you are indispensable, and when they find they cannot bully you into submission they will come to your terms. Next time, however, that either you or I join a Cabinet we must be certain of our majority in it.'[3]

It was indeed to be a 'bitter pilgrimage', and, whilst it took nine years for things to 'come right' for Chamberlain, they never did for Churchill. Meanwhile the point about the 'party tie' had been expressed even more pungently by that cynical Radical-Liberal Henry Labouchere, who wrote to Churchill on the day of the announcement urging him to 'in your own interests think it over'. He went on: 'Parties just do not hang together by principles. They are gangs greedy of office. You got your lot in—there is a wide difference between this and siding in getting them out. You and Chamberlain seem to me both to make the same mistake. You ignore the power of the "machine". It has crushed many an able man . . .' Finally he added with

[1] Churchill, 586. [2] Garvin, II, 277–8.
[3] Churchill, 587.

brutal perspicacity: 'Joe is no good to you . . . You are not a Radical, in that line Joe will always cut you out.'[1]

Behind its rather lurid wording there was much wisdom and truth in this assessment of the case. For both Churchill and Chamberlain cherished at the backs of their minds the illusion that they were indispensable to their original parties and that ultimately the latter must surrender to them and take them back on their own terms But Churchill was less patient and self-controlled than the self-made Joe, and his ambition was moreover sharpened by that sense of urgency which is sometimes induced by failing health, so his anguish and desperation were the more intense and drove him to overplay his hand even more frequently and persistently than before.

[1] Churchill, 588.

VI
RECONSTRUCTION AND ATTACK

Although Hartington had not accepted Salisbury's invitation on his own behalf, he was not averse from using his influence to persuade Goschen to accept the similar offer tended to the latter from that quarter. This seeming inconsistency he justified on the grounds that, whereas Goschen's financial knowledge would be an admitted asset to the Government, his earlier quarrel with the Liberal Party deprived him of influence in and therefore of value to that party: therefore he was, so to speak, expendable. Goschen, long neglected and a most valuable man on any count, thus had a niche found for him and scope for his undoubted talents, whilst the Tory Government received a much-needed 'shot in the arm'. '. . . I have never had a more difficult choice to make,' wrote Goschen at the time, 'but I am glad now that I have acted as I have done; and I may say that Hartington *urged* it on me. The fear was that the Government would go to pieces unless it was strengthened, and the collapse of the Government might have led to the worst results. This I think was Hartington's deciding motive . . .'[1] 'I joined as a Liberal Unionist, not as a Conservative',[2] he reassured another friend; but of course it was precisely this fact, apart from his abilities, which rendered his joining so immensely valuable to the shaken Ministry.

Here we may remark that before Goschen's acceptance of Salisbury's offer had even been made public, an offer of a seat

[1] Arthur Eliot: *Life of Lord Goschen*, II, 107. [2] Ibid.

had been forthcoming. The following letter is interesting and amusing for the glimpse which it affords of the wary and almost cynical politician in the otherwise notoriously trusting and good-hearted Smith, and also for the hints that 'leaks' were not unknown at Hatfield.

Confidential

Greenlands,
Henley-on-Thames
30 Dec. 1886

My dear Douglas,

Makins[1] has just been here to say that if Salisbury wants to bring Goschen in and is in any difficulty for a Seat, he believes his Constituents would elect Goschen and he would be glad to make way.

No terms were mentioned and I of course only said it was a very generous and patriotic act or intention on his part and of a piece with Salisbury's own readiness to give way to Hartington etc. but I tell you in strict confidence.

No doubt there is something behind and you would have to settle that.

I shall write to Salisbury to say a Seat is to be had but not mention which, as it might leak out at Hatfield and that would do harm.

Yours sincerely,
W. H. Smith.

But evidently Makins's proposition—whatever it was—was unacceptable, for in the event Goschen stood for the Exchange Division of Liverpool, as Akers-Douglas had suggested. As already noted, Goschen had a high regard for the Chief Conservative Whip and wished to act in the closest concert with him, as the following letter from Middleton shows. The letter also reveals the highly delicate state of the Government's and the party's standing in the country as a result of Churchill's resignation.

12 Downing Street,
S.W.
11 January, 1887

My dear Douglas,

I have just been having a long yarn with Goschen about Liverpool—he tells me he has wired to you about the matter—He

[1] Col., later Sir William, M.P. Walthamstow.

(Goschen) is very anxious to act in accordance with your wishes and upon your advice—personally he is satisfied as to the chance being a good one—I assured him you would certainly not be opposed to his accepting and also that the Tory Party would use every exertion to secure his return. The result of that conversation is that unless he gets an unfavourable reply from you before 6 or 7 this evening he is going to accept and I feel sure it will be the best solution to the matter. Goschen was most anxious you should not learn of his taking this step through the Press and begged me to write you. Yesterday we had a good meeting at Leeds and everything went well—the feeling up there is the same as elsewhere in the country—dead in favor of Ld. Salisbury—I fear however it will not be so smooth for long unless Randolph acts like an angel—any violent demonstration in favor of the Cabinet would produce a reaction in favor of R.C . . .

Yours ever

Richd. W. Middleton.

This is matched by an appeal by Akers-Douglas in a letter to Salisbury two days later (January 13th): '. . . I hope you will complete the Gvt. as soon as possible as delay gives cause for various rumours and creates jealousies.'

Unfortunately, after all the fussing and to the dismay of all, Goschen was beaten at Liverpool by seven votes. However (although Makins repeated his offer) the situation was saved through the generosity of Lord Algernon Percy, who gave up his seat in St. George's, Westminster. Goschen's adherence was much welcomed by all the more broadminded and far-seeing elements in the Conservative Party and Government. Thus Hamilton to Smith (January 4th, '87): 'I am glad we have got Goschen. For debating and general knowledge he is superior to Hartington, and if as I hope you are to lead he will relieve you of much trouble, and be a tower of strength to you . . .'

From this it will be gathered that the vital question of who was now to lead the Unionist Party in the House of Commons had not yet been finally settled. In the ordinary way the practice had hitherto been that, when the Prime Minister was in the House of Lords, the Chancellor of the Exchequer became Leader of the House of Commons. But Goschen was still a Liberal—even if a Unionist as well—and the great majority of Unionists were Conservatives. It was therefore pretty clear that they would not work cordially except under a man of their own party. Under these peculiar circumstances 'all eyes turned upon W. H. Smith', in the words of his biographer, 'who, despite the mediocrity of his oratorical power, was felt to be the one safe man to whom the lead could be assigned.'[1] Being exceedingly modest he accepted it with much misgiving and only as a duty which he felt in honour bound to undertake.

W. H. SMITH.

"READY!"

Scarcely anyone could have afforded a more complete contrast to his flamboyant and unstable predecessor than the worthy and modest 'bookstall-man', whom Disraeli had shrewdly introduced into his cabinet in 1874. Indeed in earlier days he had been one of Lord Randolph's favourite butts—as a member of 'the Old Gang', a follower of 'the Goat', and as one of 'the lords of suburban villas . . . of pineries and vineries'. But he had filled successively the Offices of First Lord of the Admiralty, Secretary for War and Chief Secretary for Ireland (the latter

[1] Maxwell, II, 182.

for only a few weeks, but under particularly difficult circumstances), and to each he had brought the same tremendously high standards of duty and integrity. 'Old Morality' his fellow members in Parliament dubbed him; but he impressed them all profoundly by his high qualities and endeared himself to all who had to do with him by his simple kindness and goodness. In 1881 a Liberal successor at the Admiralty, Sir George Otto Trevelyan, was moved to write and thank him in the following terms: 'I have felt keenly the handsome and fair manner in which you have behaved towards me, in what was to me a very critical session, in a rather peculiar and difficult post, and I should thank you the more warmly if it were not for my conviction that your treatment of Admiralty questions is founded primarily on sincere care for the interest of the Navy . . . Public spirit seems, I suppose, a simple and natural thing to those who possess it; but the mutual relations of many generations of front benches proves party spirit in department matters to be the rule, and public spirit the exception.'[1] This may be capped by the tribute of Sir Winston Churchill in his biography of his father: 'Of all the characters with which this story deals scarcely one of them improves so much upon acquaintance as this valiant and honest man. He was the true type of what Disraeli calls "an English worthy".'[2]

It was characteristic of Smith to have a nice consideration for the feelings of his colleagues and he knew that there was another who had every reason to feel entitled to the office of Leader—Hicks Beach, its former and very successful holder in the last Salisbury ministry, who had made way for his friend Churchill and taken on the thankless Irish Office. Beach was also a man who had earned the respect of his contemporaries, as much for his integrity and courage as for his undoubted ability. But he was of an aloof and reserved disposition and many of the duties connected with the Leadership were uncongenial to him. Moreover, his uncertain temper contrasted with the even benevolence of Smith. The latter indeed seemed always a little perplexed and alarmed by Beach's somewhat *revêche* character and consequently required much reassurance as to his (Beach's) real feelings in this matter of the Leadership. In fact he evidently wrote to Beach in order to probe these for himself, for he sent

[1] Hambleden MSS. [2] Churchill, 434.

on to Akers-Douglas the letter which Beach wrote in reply (January 4th), of which the following is an extract.

> . . . With regard to the leadership, I did not go *quite* so far as to say that I would not take it on any terms or any considerations. I put most strongly before Salisbury my own reasons for objecting to take it, in any shape: and I told him it was impossible for me to take it *with* Ireland. His reply was that he *could* replace me as leader, but felt it absolutely impossible to spare me here, and that Ireland must be the first consideration. I by no means think that I am indispensable here! but that is the position; so far as I am concerned.
>
> I am very glad that you are going to lead instead of me, anyhow: and need not say, will do anything I can to ease you in the work. But you know already that that may not be much, nor for any length of time . . .

Smith was still not entirely reassured by this and wrote anxiously to Akers-Douglas the next day (January 5th) asking 'Is Beach at all huffed that he has not been pressed by Salisbury to take the lead?' Then again on the day after that he returned to the subject in a letter which also reveals other instances of his modesty and diffidence.

> *Private*
>
> War Office
> 6 Jan. 1887
>
> My dear Douglas,
>
> There are two or three matters on which we ought to meet if my nomination goes on, but I suspect Beach does not really like it.
>
> Are the mover and seconder of the Address fixed upon? Had Randolph communication with any one on the subject? If he had I should be very much inclined to take up his men.
>
> When will you and Salisbury both be in town again?
>
> Have you any idea when we shall have to go to Osborne?
>
> What is the form of invitation to the dinner given the night before the House meets?
>
> Is it the First Lord of the Treasury requests the honor etc. or simply Mr. W. H. Smith?
>
> I should prefer the simpler and plainer—but the cards will have to be printed—*if I go on.*
>
> Yours sincerely,
> W. H. Smith.

Besides himself there were others—not to mention, inevitably, his predecessor Lord Randolph—who made no bones about their lack of confidence in him. Thus Cecil Raikes, the Postmaster-General, wrote to Akers-Douglas (January 10th, '87): '. . . You will see that the attempt to conduct public business under Smith's leadership will prove a sad fiasco'. But, a few years later, even when Smith's health broke under the strain—and despite his own misgivings—they begged him to continue.

Before Parliament reassembled a very poignant event occurred which cast a further shadow over the already rather sombre opening of Salisbury's second ministry. When this ministry was first formed Lord Iddesleigh had, as already recounted, received the Foreign Office. But now that Salisbury was obliged to reconstruct his Cabinet he decided to resume that office so dear to him. He told the Queen that he proposed to offer Iddesleigh the Colonial Office, but a few days later had to tell her 'that Mr. Smith and Mr. Akers-Douglas (the Whip) thought it would be very undesirable to appoint Lord Iddesleigh to the Colonial Office, because his apparent feebleness would be talked of, and would have a bad effect in the Colonies'.[1] The Queen, who had always felt a high regard and affection for Iddesleigh, was distressed. 'She is grieved that Mr. Smith and others, who she thinks take too much a House of Commons view, should oppose his being appointed to the Colonies. It would do harm, she thinks, if he were to be *sacrificed* to M.Ps' opinions, and she greatly regrets this step . . . anything that looked like his management of Foreign Affairs being considered a failure, the Queen would consider as *very* wrong and most unjust, as well as impolite.'[2]

Actually, as Lord Salisbury was able to prove to the Queen, Iddesleigh had twice indicated that he 'would rather not resume office in any capacity'. Moreover, Smith had written to him, on hearing this, 'as an old friend will you let me say what pain it would give me if you went from us?'[3]—thus showing he could be no party to a plot to oust him altogether. In any case the 'feebleness' about which he and Akers-Douglas had been worried was his obviously fast failing health rather than his

[1] *The Letters of Queen Victoria*, Third Series, I, 251.
[2] Ibid., 252. [3] Maxwell, op. cit., II, 184.

well-known mildness of disposition. Nevertheless, by some unhappy slip, Iddesleigh first learned of his displacement from the Foreign Office through the newspapers—and this naturally pained him. However, on January 12th, he called at 10, Downing Street to make his adieux and, suddenly stricken by a heart

SIR STAFFORD NORTHCOTE.

"THE WAYS OF LIFE ARE DIFFERENT NOW."

attack, died in the presence of the Prime Minister. Lord Randolph wrote a letter of condolence to the latter, which, though betraying a twinge of compunction, had a naive and grimly ironical quality: '. . . I felt much the old Lord's death, for he had for years past gone through much bother, disappointment and probably vexation, nor can I conveniently repress the reflection *quorum pars magna fui*.'[1] Lord Salisbury was moved as he was seldom moved. His self-reproach—for far lesser injuries—was far deeper and seemed far more genuine. Thinking of 'our thirty years companionship in political life' he dwelt bitterly on 'the reflection that now, just before this sudden parting, by

[1] Churchill, 606–7.

some strange misunderstanding which it is hopeless to explain, I had I believe for the first time in my life seriously wounded his feelings. As I looked upon the dead body stretched before me, I felt that politics was a cursed profession.'[1]

The foremost problem which the Government had to tackle in the new session, which began on January 27th, 1887, was to forestall and prevent obstruction by the Irish members of the transaction of affairs in Parliament. Ten days before Parliament reassembled Smith reminded Akers-Douglas (January 17th) of a plan which had been suggested. 'Beach reminds me that it was agreed you should get our men to give notices of Bills and Motions so as to cut out the Irish Members for the Wednesdays. Has any systematic effort been made? It would be useful if a really large number could be arranged—*bona fide*.'

But, though such tactics might be of some help, much more positive measures had to be envisaged—and had in fact been prepared. A new draft reform of the Rules of Procedure—the fifth set which had been submitted since Gladstone first attempted in 1882 to deal with the growing evil—had been drawn up by the Government. The Conservative battalions were therefore enjoined to rally round the Government to see the Rules through and by a judicious piece of stage management it was planned to cheer and impress them by holding a special party meeting and making the date of it coincide with the first appearance in the House of the party's great 'conquest'—Goschen.

Private

Foreign Office.
Feb. 5, 1887

My dear Douglas,

I have discussed the matter of the meeting with the Cabinet—and they are of opinion that one should be held speedily, and for the purpose of urging the general support of the Party to the proposed rules of Procedure.

We agree that Thursday at twelve—when we hope Goschen may appear as a member of the House of Commons—would suit very well.

What do you say? If you agree pray summon the meeting at the Foreign Office.

Yours very truly,
Salisbury.

[1] Churchill, 606–7.

The Government's resort to this rather delicately planned expedient emphasized how much they felt it to be necessary at this stage to nurse their supporters. Although Akers-Douglas was now sending out his Whips to Liberal Unionists as well as to Tories proper, even some of the latter seemed to need reassurance after the Randolph Churchill affair, as appears from a letter which Akers-Douglas wrote anonymously to *The Times* (February 23rd, 1887).

To the Editor of *The Times*

Sir,

The recent differences in the Cabinet have evoked so much discussion, even in the ranks of the Conservative party, and have been the subject of so much jubilation on Separatist platforms, that I ask leave to refer in your columns to some remarks made by Lord Salisbury at the Foreign Office meeting yesterday . . . Lord Salisbury in alluding to the resignation of Lord Randolph Churchill, expressed his regret at the loss which the party had sustained by that resignation and his high sense of the noble lord's great ability. He went on to say that he hoped with confidence that the separation would only be transitory, and that ere long they would again have the advantage of Lord Randolph's services. Lord Salisbury's expressions were much cheered by the meeting . . .

I have the honour to be, Sir,
Your obedient servant—
M.P.

Thus, there must still have been a sufficiently important body of Churchill-sympathizers, outside as well as inside Parliament, to require mollifying by such definite assurances, broadcast in this rather unusual manner.

Considering the all-round delicacy of the Government's position Akers-Douglas's achievements in the sphere of 'whipping' were therefore all the more remarkable. 'The Tory members in the House live in dread of their Whips,' wrote one newspaper; 'Mr. Akers-Douglas has adopted a very faultless and comprehensive system of book-keeping. He knows to a nicety how often every one of his men have attended the House, and how often they have voted. Those who are slack are brought severely to task.' But, in the circumstances, this discipline had to be blended with considerable tact and persuasion—two qualities which in him were fortunately pre-eminent. With his lieutenants, the kindly and industrious Colonel William Walrond,[1] Lord Arthur Hill,[2] Sir Herbert Maxwell[3] and the popular and irresistible Sidney Herbert[4] ('before whom,' as a contemporary wrote, 'the aggrieved and ill-mannered bent like willows, and remained to vote')[5] he managed night after night to keep well over a hundred members dining in the House as insurance against the snap division. The precaution was essential, for there were according to a contemporary report, 'always at least a hundred Radicals and Parnellites who never leave the premises, and a score or two who never leave the House'. No wonder that, after producing an array of 106 against Parnell's Amendment to the Address, Akers-Douglas was 'congratulated on all hands' and 'received with enthusiastic ministerial cheering'.

The most striking proof of the necessity for prompt steps to reform the Rules of Procedure was provided by the fact that the passage of the first rule, establishing closure by a bare majority (subject to the discretion of the Speaker), occupied no less than thirteen nights. Moreover, as a result of this slow progress, the first was the only one of the total of fifteen rules which was persisted with and carried. It is in these circumstances that we find that irrepressible Radical, plutocrat and poseur, Henry Labouchere, urging Akers-Douglas to use his influence to prevent members from 'airing their fads' on the new Rules, in order that he, Labouchere, may be given time to move a Resolution of his own about the House of Lords in which he can express his personal animosity against some of his own party. Further on we shall see that 'Labby' was always trying to arrange private deals and bargains with his opponents through their amiable Whip, to whom he seems to have taken a strong liking. Akers-Douglas, for his part, was always amused by impudent characters,[6] but

[1] M.P. Tiverton, succeeded father as 2nd Baronet 1889. Created Baron Waleran, 1905.

[2] M.P. West Down; 2nd son of 4th Marquis of Dounshire.

[3] M.P. Co. Wigtown; 7th Baronet.

[4] M.P. Croydon; succeeded brother as 14th Earl of Pembroke, 1895.

[5] *Studies of Yesterday*, 160.

[6] Unlike his colleague George Hamilton, who wrote: 'Labouchere attracted a good deal of attention whilst an active Member of Parliament,

that is by no means to say that Labby ever got much change out of him. The following letter gives a typical instance of the involved and persistent arguments with which the older man loved to bombard his adversary and also of the final cynical twist which was so obviously intended to shock all sober, staid and lesser mortals.

24 Grosvenor Gardens,
S.W.
March 7 [1887]

Dear Akers-Douglas,

I suppose that you will get through the Govt. rules of Procedure today, and if so, I trust you will not take next Friday to air all the fads of private Members, which they have elaborated into new rules—This was not done when Mr. G. first brought in rules, and it would practically be taking the day from the M.P. who has got Friday, to give it to M.Ps who have not got it.

But even supposing that Fowler[1] or someone who has a new rule, talks out the fag-end of the Govt. rules, if you put down procedure on Friday, you will have fads discussed until 12 p.m.—Would it not in this case be better to put it down on a Govt night as Second order, and finish up in an hour.

You will be surprised at my interest in this, but that surprise will cease on perceiving that I have got Friday for a Resolution about the House of Lords—I do not suppose that I shall carry it, but I want to denounce the Rathbones and such like 'half and halfs' on our side.

I write instead of coming to the House to speak to you, as I am doctoring up a cold.

Yours truly,
H. Labouchere.

There had been considerable heart-searching and dissension as to what precise form the closure (or 'clôture', as some called

---

and he was popular in certain circles; but I frankly own that his tricks and personality were very repugnant to me, and I am certain that he would have been an intolerable nuisance to any Cabinet of which he became a member', op. cit., 207. He never did become a Cabinet Minister because the Queen would not agree to his remaining a newspaper editor whilst sitting in the Cabinet.

[1] Sir Henry Fowler, M.P. (Lib.) E. Wolverhampton; Secretary to Treasury 1886–92; President Local Government Board 1892–4; Secretary of State for India 1915–18; created Viscount Wolverhampton 1908.

it) should take. A Tory back-bencher, A. Beresford Hope, had written to Akers-Douglas some months earlier (November 7th, '86):

> . . . I am, as I believe many of the party are, much exorcised [sic] by Lord Randolph's line on the 'clôture'. I cannot and will not believe that he means 'clôture' by a bare majority. Still, he hasn't said that he does not though the enemy pertinaciously insists that he does. So, for the purpose of this letter I assume that he does and on that I must say that it would be a terrible mistake. It would be leaping from the Frying-pan into the Fire. I quite agree with his description of the horrors of the present situation, but to try to cure them by 'clôture' with a bare majority would leave us open to worse perils on a change of scene. Let the Radicals have a majority and with such a terrible weapon in their hands, they would have no difficulty in stamping out all that was most essential to our old Constitution. Besides look how we, the rank and file of the Tory party would stand. We have not forgotten, nor have our enemies either what we said about the Clôture in that autumn session [of 1882]. Things have certainly changed since then, but not so as to turn black to white and we have still some regard for our consistency. I trust you will be able to make me happy by assuring me that the 'clôture' proposed is a proportional one.

Here was evidently that rare bird a legislator of some years standing who was not yet inured to the perpetual somersaults of party politics. One wonders how he had felt about the sudden metamorphosis of his party's Irish policy! Actually, indeed, when in the autumn of 1882 Gladstone's government had sought to introduce the closure and a Conservative amendment had sought to insist upon consent by a two-thirds majority of the House, Churchill had urged his party to resist it altogether, or at least to insist on the principle of the simple majority. He had declared that proportionate majorities were utterly alien to the British Constitution ('we do not require proportionate majorities for the election of our representatives') and had expressed his surprise 'that the Tory party, or the Constitutional party, which recoils with horror from the Radical innovation of the 'clôture', should propose with eagerness, with anxiety, almost with desperation, the much greater Radical innovation of a two-thirds majority . . .' He too had warned of the shortsightedness and danger of forging an instrument which could be a considerable embarrassment to a future Tory Government. In the event the Tory amendment proposing the proportional (two-thirds) majority was defeated and closure by simple majority was established. Now, four years later, it had become desperately necessary for the Tories to reinforce the procedure, and, though this time it was they who invoked the principle of the simple majority, they nevertheless modified it by making the Speaker the judge of the necessity for applying the closure and then making the latter conditional upon a majority of 200 votes in favour. In this form it appears to have been acceptable to Churchill, as will be seen in a letter quoted on a later page.

At this juncture the Government received, as it seemed, another body-blow, for Hicks Beach, who, as Chief Secretary for Ireland, had been bravely facing the cross-fire of the Unionists on the one hand for not being drastic enough and of the Parnellites on the other for being brutal, was forced by ill-health and incipient blindness to resign (March 3rd). Moreover, the very unexpected appointment of Arthur Balfour to succeed him at first conveyed little confidence to the Unionists as a whole, for the former had only been in the Cabinet for a few months (as Secretary for Scotland) and before that had only been known as a rather lukewarm member of the Fourth Party and generally regarded as a languid dilettante. However, appearances were never more deceptive than they were in this case. For, to an unsuspectedly inflexible will he added an enviable serenity which neither lawlessness in Ireland nor abuse at Westminster could disturb.

Now that the phase of trying to outbid the Liberals for the favours of the Irish was over, and now that Gladstone had espoused Home Rule and been defeated, the Conservatives turned a very different and a grimmer countenance towards Ireland. Lord Salisbury, in a speech to the National Conservative Club (March 5th, 1887) now felt able to promulgate the definitive attitude of his party: 'It is not a question of this party or that; it is not a question of the career of statesmen or the fate of parties . . . We are engaged upon a struggle on the issue of which depends whether our existence as a great empire is to continue or not . . .'[1] 'Twenty years of resolute government'

[1] Annual Register 1887, [81–2].

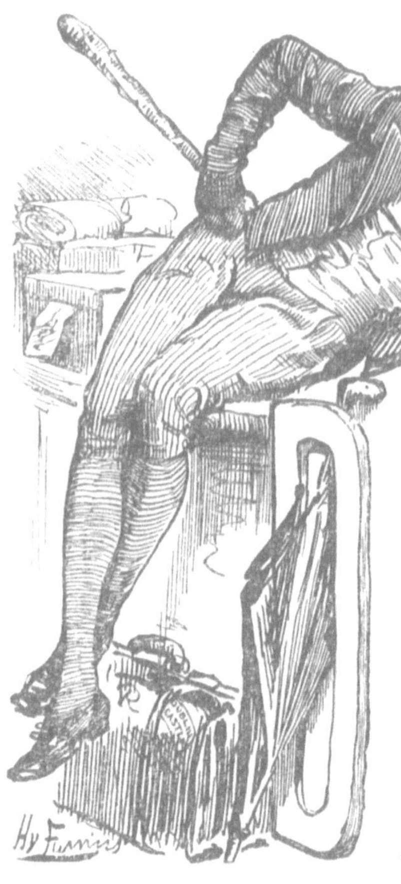

J. A. BALFOUR.

"FIRMNESS WITHOUT RASHNESS?"

became the declared Conservative policy for Ireland, and firmly and suavely, and with extraordinary success, Balfour proceeded to enforce it.

Since, in the words of Lord Salisbury, 'All the politics of the moment are summarized in the word "Ireland" ', Balfour very soon became the first man in Parliament. Lord George Hamilton has written that 'the history of the House of Commons for the next four years is really a record of Balfour's marvellous Parliamentary performances',[1] for the latter succeeded in asserting his authority in Parliament in the teeth of unresting opposition led by such giants as Gladstone and Parnell, and in implementing his policy in Ireland by breaking down lawlessness. In initiating the declared policy of coercion his first step was to introduce a new Crimes Bill—differing from its predecessors in that its provisions were permanent—and this from its introduction and through all the succeeding years of his administration was the central point of the political battlefield.

[1] Hamilton, op. cit., 62.

The session of 1887 became memorable as one of the most trying sessions ever recorded. Divisions in the House took place unceasingly and, whereas the Opposition Whips only had to keep their members together when a very special division was expected, Akers-Douglas and his colleagues had to keep a majority in the House at all times. Moreover, now they had never to let the number drop below 200, lest it be necessary to apply the 'closure', the new Procedure Rule which required this minimum of votes to carry it.

'Four nights a week the Whips are kept at their posts in the House from 4 o'clock in the afternoon till nearly three on the following morning,' wrote a contemporary press correspondent. 'Departmental business calls for their attendance at Downing Street at noon every day, and as most of them have public and private business outside Parliament to attend to the earlier hours of the morning cannot be called their own. Robust and energetic though they may be, it is too much to expect them to go through the strain of working fifteen or sixteen hours a day. If the present state of things is to be continued for any length of time it will be necessary to have two sets of Whips.'

Another paper depicted the humorous side of the business: 'Hon. gentlemen strolling in at 1 a.m. in dinner dress were held prisoners for the Navy vote, and when it was found that an all-night struggle had become imminent official messengers were sent to scour the party clubs, and even bring hon. gentlemen out of their beds. The joke of the lobby this afternoon went to the effect that very few of the younger race of Conservatives were in their beds at four and five to be called up at all. The wife of a well-known hon. and learned gentleman[1] received a telegram at eight o'clock for her husband signed "Akers-Douglas", calling for his immediate attendance at the House. The Senator had not been home. His wife rushed to the House and found her spouse in evening dress. He vowed he had been at his post despite the incriminating telegram which was shaken ominously in his face.'

Addressing a great meeting of the Primrose League at Albert Palace on April 20th, 1887, Lord Salisbury paid a personal and public tribute to the success of his lieutenant's immense labours.

[1] J. Addison, Q.C.

Two days earlier a Liberal amendment to the Crimes Bill had been defeated by a majority of 101 (315 Conservatives and 65 Liberal Unionists voting) and the second reading had been carried without a division. 'It is hard enough,' said the Marquess, 'to bring up in its integrity a whole party to vote in a great division. That great result was achieved by a prominent member of this League, to whom on all occasions we ought to pay a fitting tribute—I mean Mr. Akers-Douglas. (Cheers.) I believe I am not exaggerating when I say that the oldest man among us has never seen a more efficient Parliamentary whip. But it was a harder task still, so far advanced in the fight as this, to bring up with so little loss, and constituting so vast a majority, a combination of parties drawn from different camps, and still retaining their political individuality.'

A. AKERS-DOUGLAS.

"AN UNBROKEN FRONT."

But, despite this rigorous discipline, it was an uphill fight and there were occasions when the Government found themselves unable to deal summarily with the wanton obstruction. Thus: 'Mr. Akers-Douglas had not 200 men within call and Mr. W. H. Smith was compelled to look on disconsolately and helplessly while hour after hour stole away . . .' etc. In fact Smith was anxious. On May 13th he wrote to his daughter: '. . . The obstruction of the two Oppositions [Gladstonians and Parnellites] now united in one is beyond anything that has been seen in this House, and unless it gives way under the pressure of public opinion very drastic measures will have to be taken. Here I am again droning on, while the Irish and their allies spit and splutter and obstruct. It is desperate work, unmitigated obstruction, utterly regardless of all consequences to Parliament or the Country. We have now been 8 days over one clause, and we have not finished it yet. The country is getting very angry, and is beginning to say that Government is "deplorably weak" in not insisting on faster procedure. I got to bed at 4 this morning . . .'[1]

To Akers-Douglas he wrote at this time:

Private

3 Grosvenor Place
8 May 1887

My dear Douglas,

I think it very likely we may want to put on the closure at ½ past 6 or 7 tomorrow, and again after dinner at 10 or half past. We have been talking a good deal about obstruction and it will be necessary therefore to use all the powers we have got even at some risk of being defeated.

Perhaps you will pass the word to men to be down at the House by 6.

Yours very truly,
W. H. Smith.

[1] Maxwell, op. cit., II, 193.

VII
CRITICS AND MALCONTENTS

LORD RANDOLPH, meanwhile, having on the first day of Parliament's reassembly made a public explanation of his resignation (which added nothing new to his letters to Salisbury and Akers-Douglas), lost no time in seeking rest and change abroad—a fact which lent some substance to the theory of nervous and physical breakdown. At any rate, surveying from a distance the tumultuous scene at home, he seemed for the moment relieved to be out of it—though very far from uninterested in it.

March 20, 1887
Rome

My dear Akers-Douglas,

Many thanks for your interesting letter. I see by to-day's papers that you settled the closure numbers at two hundred, which is I think the best settlement. What a fool H. Chaplin must feel about it all when he recollects what a row he kicked up. I am afraid you will have an awful time over the Coercion Bill but it can't be helped. Gladstone's speech seems to be very artful and honied and Trevelyan is playing his (Mr. G's) game and sowing seeds of disintegration in Liberal Unionist ranks. Since I came abroad I have done nothing but bless my resolutions on economy for it has given me more than six weeks of real good time and fine warm weather. I have shuddered and shivered over the account of the cold in England.

I am very much obliged to you for getting Wainwright into the Carlton. I think I may possibly turn up in the House on Monday 28th unless the weather should be very warm and bright in Paris. Give my love to my friends.

Yours ever,
Randolph S. C.

The 'H. Chaplin' of the above was Henry Chaplin, M.P. for Sleaford, Lincs., and later first Viscount Chaplin. He had been a devoted admirer and follower of Disraeli, who had shown him marks of esteem and favour; but he had been from the very beginning hostile to Lord Randolph and his policy. The feud had begun when Chaplin, after listening to Churchill's maiden speech in 1878 had advised him, if such were his opinions, 'to lose not a moment in going over to the other side of the House'. Another clash—presumably the one referred to in the letter—occurred when Chaplin denounced the closure by a simple majority as unconstitutional and improper. What, however, brought the wrath of Chaplin—and others—still more upon Churchill on this occasion, was the latter's airy assertion that he 'regarded the Liberal Unionists as a useful kind of crutch' and 'looked forward to the time, no distant time, when the Tory Party might walk alone'.[1] If anything was calculated to 'sow the seeds of disintegration in the Liberal Unionist ranks', surely this was it. By contrast, Gladstone's 'honied speech' to which he referred in the letter had actually done no more than advise the Liberals to do nothing to 'wound or embarrass' the Liberal Unionists.

Nor could Churchill's self-esteem allow that a government which no longer included him could be capable of maintaining itself in office, especially in view of the 'mediocre' talents of his successor. Thus from Palermo he wrote to his wife (March 2nd):

> I think the Government are earning a rather second-rate kind of *succès d'estime*, but I fancy I detect signs of feebleness and inefficiency, which will become obvious when real difficulty arises. I own W. H. Smith has done better than I expected for I expected a complete breakdown; but having made that admission, his speeches read to me most commonplace, and I think before long the House and the Party will get much bored with him. I am amused at the Government surrender about my Army and Navy Estimates Committee . . . I expect the Burnley election quickened their sluggish economic impulses. The election I look upon as very significant, and as bearing out what I wrote to A. Douglas.[2] They may plod on in Parliament but they are losing their hold on the imagination and enthusiasm of the country generally. However all this is speculation . . .[3]

[1] Churchill, 612.

[2] Presumably in the semi-official letter of January 1st, 1887.

[3] Churchill, 617–18.

Soon afterwards, however, he was deigning to give Smith the benefit of his advice. On April 15th a considerable scene occurred in the House when a Conservative member, Colonel Saunderson, asserted that the Executive Committee of the Irish Land League, of which Parnell was the head, included both murderers and persons guilty of treason and that Parnell must be aware of this. Healy, one of the Irish leaders and later to be first Governor-General of the Free State, called Saunderson a 'liar' and after refusing to withdraw was named and suspended. Smith was ready to fall in with the Speaker's wish to have the suspension rescinded, for he wrote next day to Akers-Douglas: 'The Speaker is evidently anxious to bring Healy back and Saunderson is not at all unwilling to say that he did not refer to him, so that the matter may be arranged if Sexton[1] is instructed by Healy to apologize in any words which the Speaker will accept . . .' But, getting wind of Smith's intention, Lord Randolph wrote to him an immense letter, couched in the most insufferably condescending and didactic terms, strongly deprecating any such course. It is worth reproducing not only as a revelation of his peculiar arrogance but also of the sort of thing his former colleagues still had to endure from him—even in the form of well-meant advice:

Private & Confidential

Carlton Club,
April 16. 1887

My dear Smith,

The 'Scene' in the House last night was unfortunate. I should not however trouble you about it had I not understood from Plunkett[2] this morning that there was a possibility that the Speaker and you as Leader of H. of Cms. might be disposed to take a favourable view of some motion to be made on Monday to rescind the suspension of Healy.

Against such a course much may be urged. In the 1st place I don't see how the motion can come on without a most unusual departure from the rules of ordinary procedure.

[1] Thomas Sexton, M.P. South Sligo; another leading lieutenant of Parnell.

[2] Presumably the Hon. David Plunket, M.P. Dublin University; First Commissioner of Works; created Lord Rathmore.

A motion to rescind a decision of the House must be made after due notice and has no claim to precedence.

I suppose that by the general consent of the House the Leader of the House might make a motion of the above kind without notice and before the commencement of public business, but even this is most doubtful and sets up an evil precedent.

However, assuming that in some way or other the motion comes on I hope the Govt. will resist it. The authority of the Chair and the rules of orderly debate are in grave danger just now and any appearance of weakness on the part of the Speaker or the Leader of the House may entail consequences of which you cannot foresee the limit.

I see no hope of ultimate safety and success except in this, that the Chair on points of order must consider itself as infallible and the Leader of the House must take the same view . . . [follows a lengthy examination of the incident in question] . . . Please let me urge this. You have to fight two battles—one in Ireland against crime, the other in Parliament against disorder. You must win both. The loss of one entails the loss of the other. As you are firm with respect to matters in Ireland, so you should be equally firm with respect to the rigid preservation of order in the House of Commons. The return triumphant of Healy, after having called a member a liar and defied the Chair, under the pretext that Saunderson's conduct justified his conduct, would be ruinous to your position as the defender and guardian of parliamentary order. I quite understand the immense inconvenience which may result from any course which may lead to a postponement of the division on the second reading [of the Crimes Bill]. In a choice of evils it is best to choose the least and the greatest evil without doubt would be the selection of a course which establishes precedents of the worst kind and prepares the way for irretrievable disorder in the H. of Cms.

Excuse this lengthy letter. It deals with a general matter on which I feel much anxiety and I greatly prefer communicating with you beforehand to expressing any difference of opinion with you in the House itself.

Yours very sincerely,
Randolph S. C.[1]

Nevertheless, in point of fact, the matter was cleared up—and Healy's suspension rescinded—through Saunderson being induced by the Speaker to climb down.

[1] Hambleden MSS.

Soon other wholesome, if unasked for, advice was reaching the Government from another outpost of its varied empire. In July Joseph Chamberlain wrote to Akers-Douglas:

Private

40 Prince's Gardens,
S.W.
July 12th, 1887

Dear Mr. Akers-Douglas,

The enclosed extract from the letter of a trustworthy correspondent in connection with the Coventry election may interest you. He is a Radical Unionist. I think there is a great deal in what he says as to the necessity of some previous consultation between the Liberal Unionists and the Conservatives before a candidate is selected.

Yours faithfully,
J. Chamberlain.

[Extract enclosed]: We personally did everything that was possible under the circumstances. The Liberal Unionists are not free from blame, but the Tories gave them every excuse. The candidate was thoroughly unpopular and regarded as a type of all that is reactionary and objectionable in Toryism. The fact that he was a Colonel on active service is not in his favour for a working-class constituency. Mr. Woodcock the great tricycle maker would have been willing to stand as a Conservative. If he had been selected he would have won the election easily. Could not some arrangement be made with the Tory headquarters that in future Liberal Unionists should be consulted before a candidate is chosen? I do not see how we can expect common action during an election unless there is some common action in choosing a candidate.

At the top of this letter Akers-Douglas jotted '? possible try it'. The fact was that throughout this phase the Tories were too anxious to eat their cake and have it. As the immensely stronger partner they remained loth to defer to Liberal Unionist wishes in these matters, although they were eager enough to get Liberal Unionist support and speakers where Tory candidates stood in jeopardy. The latter point is illustrated in a letter written at this time (June 17th, 1887) to Akers-Douglas by Lord Winchilsea, who, until his recent succession to the peerage, had represented Spalding as a Tory and who was now trying to whip up support for the new Tory candidate, Admiral Tryon.

> I hear from Spalding they are much in want of some good speakers for next week . . . My idea is that they ought to have at least 15 or 20 speakers next week, on various days, including *Hartington* who by all means should go, and 2 or 3 others of Cabinet rank—Stanhope and George Hamilton for choice. Chaplin I believe will go—I am arranging for a letter from Jesse Collings—one from John Bright would be *most* useful if you could arrange it . . .

Therefore when the Conservative was beaten by a Gladstonian Liberal by nearly 1,000 votes it may have been because the Liberal Unionist leaders did not rise to the occasion quite so readily as Winchilsea had hoped. But even where the position was reversed and Liberal Unionist candidates were receiving the support of the local Conservative organization, they did not always relish it, since it tended to imply a dependence on and a subservience to the more powerful ally, which was naturally wounding to their self-esteem. The breezy and practical Middleton had no time for their delicate susceptibilities: in fact he drew attention to the sacrifices which the Tories were called upon to make. He wrote Akers-Douglas (July 9th, '87):

> . . . I would suggest that the Liberal Unionist members should rather welcome than otherwise any activity on the part of our organization—Without the Conservative Party being properly organized for the contest no Liberal Unionist can secure his seat at any future election. From my constant intercourse with the various constituencies I have every reason to hope that our Party are still prepared to make the same sacrifice in the future as they have done in the past by loyally supporting those Unionists who may be called upon to defend their seats, but to give such support efficiently we must keep our Party as well organized as is possible under the disadvantageous circumstances in which we are placed in such constituencies.

However, for all their show of independence and despite Chamberlain's truculence most of the Liberal Unionists knew in their hearts that they had burnt their boats and were anxious enough to maintain the alliance in being. The temporary phase, following on Churchill's resignation, of wanting to reunite the Liberal Party, had already evaporated with the breakdown of the 'Round Table Conference' which Chamberlain had sponsored in the previous January. He himself had really killed the idea when he wrote a letter which was published in a

Nonconformist newspaper, *The Baptist*, containing the blunt statement that 'thirty-two millions of people must go without much-needed legislation because three millions are disloyal, while nearly 600 members of the Imperial Parliament will be reduced to forced inactivity because some 80 delegates, representing the policy and receiving the pay of the Chicago Convention, are determined to obstruct all business until their demands have been conceded'.[1] As a matter of actual fact, Parnell had long since quarrelled with the American extremists who had formerly financed the terroristic 'Land League' and had replaced the latter by a 'National League', allegedly pledged solely to the attainment of Home Rule by constitutional means. Nevertheless, after this broadside, which in other respects gave a pretty fair estimate of the situation, the severance between Chamberlain and the bulk of the Liberal Party became final; and in the following session his association with and active support of the Government policy of Coercion made the gulf month by month wider and deeper and in the end impassable.

That Chamberlain's course should arouse bitter hostility among those that he had deserted was scarcely to be wondered at, but the length to which such feeling could run in those rumbustious days may be gauged by the following letter to Akers-Douglas from Chamberlain's devoted henchman, Jesse Collings. Particular interest attaches to it since the author of the attack which was the subject of Collings's complaint was none other than John Burns, later to be the first Labour man to enter a Cabinet (at Campbell Bannerman's invitation in 1906). The fact that there was as yet no distinct Labour Party had caused the few pioneer 'Labour' men to hitch their wagon to the Liberal Party, *faute de mieux*, and naturally, at first, to pin their hopes on 'Radical Joe'.

Private

Edgbaston,
Birmingham,
April 12/87

My dear Sir,

I think a question should be asked about speech on other side and notice drawn to the fact that a Member of Parliament Mr. O. V. Morgan was present as one of the speakers but according to

[1] q. Asquith, I, 168.

report made no protest,—This is the sort of thing that weighs with the House and with the Country more than a hundred speeches and should therefore be noticed and accentuated.

Yrs. very truly,
Jesse Collings.

Attached to the above is Collings's account of the matter:

Saturday, April 9th, Battersea, O. V. Morgan present and one of the speakers—see *Times* report 11th.

Mr. Burns: Chamberlain would not get the cane but the *ball* and the amount of ground necessary for him to own will be 6 ft. by 2 ft. Henceforth they would mete out to traitors that punishment which their treachery justified. Great sorrow was evinced at the attempts to rid the earth of the Czar. He was sorry, very sorry they did not succeed. He asked those present if they deprecated force and extreme measures, if some of them did not like the idea of Joseph Chamberlain following Lord Salisbury to Heaven by means of Chemical Parcels Post.

Burns, later so correct and even strait-laced as an administrator, was at this stage of his career a dangerous agitator. In the autumn of this year he led a demonstration of South London workers to Trafalgar Square, which culminated in an ugly riot and in his own arrest and imprisonment. In the previous year (February 1886) he had led another demonstration which had nearly caused panic by invading the heart of the West End and smashing the windows of shops and clubs and overturning carriages. Generally speaking, the immediate cause of these alarming upheavals (similar ones occurred in some other big towns in England during 1886–7) was the current depression in trade and agriculture, aggravated by the report of the Royal Commission which had been appointed to inquire into it, which had *inter alia* pronounced that wages were too high in relation to prices. But, had not the Government been so immersed in the Irish problem and so frustrated by the resistance and obstruction which their policy in this connection had brought upon them, they might have been able to discern and perhaps to remedy the profounder discontents which underlay the riots.

For these really amounted to a general and growing impatience with the social and economic conditions of the day. The only one who had sensed the urgency of this atmosphere and in his crude way had sought to come to terms with it was Lord Randolph Churchill; but, alas, the defects of his personality had prevented him from exerting an influence upon the formulation of policy.

The Liberal Unionists as a whole—though many with unconcealed reluctance—supported Balfour's Crimes Bill throughout. Furthermore, when the Government proposed to devote the whole time of the House to the Bill in order to push it through and in so doing set aside a motion relating to the Disestablishment of the Welsh Church, even Bright, the Apostle of Disestablishment and the originator of the 'Force is no remedy' dictum about Ireland, voted with the Government, as did also Chamberlain, the paramount chief of thousands of Nonconformists. But there was one occasion on which the latter's loyalty was overstrained. This was when the Government decided to proclaim the Irish National League as a 'dangerous association'. A former Tory Whip, Lord Claud Hamilton, wrote to Akers-Douglas: 'I am very glad the Govt. have proclaimed the League. By their action they will gain many strong reliable friends, whilst they will lose no one except poops of the Otto Trevelyan type.' But there was to be at any rate one surprise. Chamberlain was absolutely against the policy both in principle and on practical grounds. In his view this was 'the old confusion—extending suppression of lawless acts to war upon political opinion'[1] and, moreover, only likely to make the League 'more potent though less open'. So he went into the Lobby behind his old leader Gladstone against the 'proclamation' of the League—although Hartington and Bright voted with the Government.

The fact was Chamberlain was still dreaming of an 'alternative scheme' of modified Home Rule—without separation of Parliaments—and had hoped to carry both Hartington and Churchill with him, and through them and with them to convert the Unionist Party away from a merely repressive policy towards a constructive policy for Ireland. But neither Harting-

[1] Garvin, II, 308.

ton nor Churchill could be persuaded and in fact urged him in the interests of the Unionist alliance to refrain from putting forward any proposals of this kind in the House—and to this request he assented. This much is revealed in the letters published in Garvin's biography and explains the puzzlement of some of his contemporaries that he should have registered disapproval by so strong a step as voting with the Gladstonians, yet have adopted a conciliatory tone towards the Government beforehand. Thus Sir Archibald Orr-Ewing[1] in a letter to Akers-Douglas (August 22nd, 1887): '. . . after the Speech that Mr. Chamberlain delivered on Saturday in which he admits that the Government is best able to form an opinion on the subject, I am surprised that he announces his intention to vote with the Home Rulers.' It was indeed a nice compromise between principle and practice.

Three days after this vote Chamberlain addressed his Radical Unionist followers at Birmingham and, whilst again condemning the suppression of the National League, he took the opportunity of roundly denying the rumours of his leaving the Unionist Party and commending the promise of a more progressive policy shown by the Government in their Allotments Bill. This gesture, taken in conjunction with the warning implicit in his adverse vote on the 'proclamation', was not wasted on the Government. Acting on a happy impulse Lord Salisbury telegraphed the Queen at Balmoral proposing to send Chamberlain to the United States as Chief Commissioner for Britain in an effort to settle the current Fishery Dispute. The Queen 'highly approved' ('it is a wise measure in many ways')[2] and Chamberlain accepted without hesitation.

It was the first step on the new road which had opened before him—and before the Conservatives with whom he was to be associated: but many years were to elapse before its full significance was to become apparent to either. For, meanwhile, not only was he shaken by the loss of most of his followers through the support of Coercion, but he continued to feel privately that there was no future before the Unionist Party unless it adopted a more positive policy towards Ireland—in the sense of a 'moderate' Home Rule scheme of the kind he had earlier

[1] M.P. Co. Dumbarton 1868–92.

[2] *Queen Victoria's Letters*, Third Series, I, 347.

pressed upon Gladstone. In vain he appealed again on these lines to Hartington (September 22nd, 1887):

> . . . I decided after my last conversation with you not to put my alternative scheme forward at the present time in opposition to your wish . . . At the same time it is right that I should privately record my dissent from the policy which you have finally adopted. It is a negative policy, and, while it may do very well for the Conservatives, it will not retain any considerable number of Liberal or Radical Unionists in the country. Unless something unexpected turns up, we are certain to be extinguished at the next election . . .[1]

Meanwhile he continued to press his advice on the Conservatives, rather in the manner of a stern physician who prescribes drastic and unpalatable remedies for the patient's 'own good'; though there was no doubt that he was in a unique position to give advice where Birmingham was concerned. To Akers-Douglas he wrote at about this time emphasizing in a most pessimistic strain the practical obstacles to uniting the Unionist vote and to finding the right kind of candidate for a traditionally radical constituency:

> *Private*
>
> Highbury,
Moor Green,
Birmingham
Sept. 13, '87.
>
> Dear Mr. Akers-Douglas,
>
> I have been making further enquiries about the prospects of a bye-election in East Birmingham with the following results.
>
> The Constituency is essentially radical and the normal Liberal majority is over 1000. There is no probability of any local Tory candidate with sufficient personal popularity to overcome this majority. It would be almost impossible to get the Radical Unionists to vote for a Tory from a distance under present circumstances.
>
> On the other hand it is almost equally impossible to find a Liberal Unionist candidate who would unite the Unionist vote. The Mayor is the only man who could do this with certainty and he will not stand. We have no other local Liberal suitable and if

[1] Holland, op. cit., II, 196.

we ran a stranger like Evelyn Ashley[1] it would be difficult to get the Tory rank and file to support him.

The Tories have, as you know, only one Birmingham seat out of 7, and it would dangerously strain their patriotism to ask them to give this up to a Radical who had no personal claims on them.

It follows from all this that if there is a vacancy at any early date the Tories must be prepared to contest the seat—and *they will almost certainly lose it* although the leaders of the Liberal Unionist party may be relied on to do their best.

I think therefore that it is most undesirable that any vacancy should be created, if this can be in any way avoided.

I am,
Yours very truly,
J. Chamberlain.

As an example of the perennial touchiness of the Liberal Unionists and of the problem which it continually constituted for the Conservative leaders—not least their Chief Whip—we may here cite part of a letter of almost a year later (July 27th, 1888) from Lord Wolmer,[2] the Liberal Unionist Whip in the Commons. The latter was of course for all practical purposes a comrade-in-arms with Akers-Douglas, but ever and anon he felt obliged to step forward and remind him that the Liberal Unionists were not to be trifled with and that their support could not just be taken for granted.

> . . . At Liverpool our party are a little sore at the way they are being treated by your party. They declare that as regards some of the seats you are living in a fool's paradise, since you are relying upon the majorities obtained in 1885 which were really largely Irish. Our party are very anxious to act in cordial support and co-operation with yours, but they are distinctly hurt at their never being consulted about anything by the Conservative leaders there, and they desired me . . . to inform you distinctly that unless they were treated with more consideration and unless they got a quid pro quo they certainly would not support your sitting members in the event of an election. I really do not think there is any serious hitch there. It really means that there has been a want of tact on

[1] Rt. Hon. Evelyn Ashley, P.C.; Under Secretary of State for Colonies 1882–5; M.P. Isle of Wight.

[2] M.P. E. Hants., later as 2nd Earl of Selborne Under Secretary for Colonies 1895–1900, First Lord of Admiralty 1900–5, High Commissioner for S. Africa 1905–10.

somebody's part and as for the quid pro quo I have already your distinct assurance that if we can find a good candidate we can have the Exchange Division . . .

With the relish of the weaker party which is able to find skeletons in the cupboard of the stronger he added a parting shot:

From Manchester I pass on to you two warnings about two of your seats. You probably are aware of what I shall tell you already, but in case you are not I will let you know. (1) That at the *Gorton* Division the Londoner Mr. Hatch who has been adopted as your candidate has not the ghost of a chance and is not at all the type for a Lancashire constituency. (2) Eccles—That Egerton so entirely neglects his constituency that the Gladstonians will certainly win it unless you promptly bring out another candidate or effect a complete revolution in Egerton's behaviour.

This session of 1887, lasting unprecedentedly from January to September, became memorable as one of the most trying ever known, as much for the acrimony of its debates as for the regu-

BARON DE WORMS. COL. WALROND. AKERS-DOUGLAS.

RECORD OF THE SESSION 1887.—422.

"DEAD HEAT."

larly late hours to which they were prolonged. Moreover, the strain was further intensified by the many official and social functions connected with the Queen's Golden Jubilee. Indeed, many members and several ministers began to find it too much for them. One of those whose life was undoubtedly shortened by it (he died, like Smith, four years later) was Cecil Raikes, the Postmaster-General. The following letter from him vividly conveys the almost nightmarish quality of an M.P.'s existence at the time:

Llwnegrin,
Mold
Aug. 22, 1887.

Dear Douglas,

I have been knocking up so fast all through last week with sleeplessness after the long nights that I ran down home hoping to get some rest by two nights in fresh air. But I have not found the prescription sufficiently operative so far, and am suffering from such terrible headaches into the bargain that I am really quite unfit to come back until I can shake them off and get some sleep.

Anyhow I shall of course come back on Thursday and if I am decidedly better I will struggle up before, but I think that two or three days real rest will be the only means of pulling myself together so as to get through the interminable session.

Yrs very truly
Henry Cecil Raikes.

Smith, of course, would not have taken his duties lightly whatever the circumstances—but the latter being what they were he exerted all his will-power to overcome his fatigue, his frequent despair and his physical handicaps in order to carry out conscientiously what he felt his high post demanded of him. His biographer relates that 'unwilling to be absent from his post for even an hour, [he] began the custom of having dinner served in his private room, and continued to do so until his last session, so that he was ever at hand when wanted. The table was generally laid for six, and the party was generally made up of one or more of his colleagues in the Cabinet, Mr. Akers-Douglas, one or more of his private secretaries, and any member specially connected with the business under discussion in the House . . . After dinner, if no debate of an urgent kind was going on, Smith would, for the first time since the morning, have a quiet hour to himself, and begin his daily despatch to the Queen, to be sent off at midnight. Then came Mr. Akers-Douglas and Mr. Jackson, the Secretaries to the Treasury, to settle the order of business for the following day.'[1] Apart from these daily personal

[1] Maxwell, op. cit., II, 214.

encounters Smith was in constant communication with Akers-Douglas by letter, consulting him and confiding in him. Thus:

> Goschen came to me at the levee in great alarm about Hampshire and he said he was going to ask you to send down village lecturers to meet the Irish Members who are holding small meetings after the Spalding fashion all over the place. G. is desponding now I am afraid . . . (July 16th, '87).
>
> . . . if you have any information to give me as to the temper and feeling of your men with regard to a temporary abatement from the Judicial Rents fixed [under the Irish Land Bill] . . . I shall be very glad to see you . . . (July 17th, '87).
>
> Come to me at 3 go through the paper and see if we can do anything to expedite business (September 1st, '87).
>
> Tell me what I am to say to Lord Henry [Manners].[1] He is not by any means a pet of mine but I will do whatever you think best for the party (September 12th, '87).

As for Akers-Douglas himself, a relative wrote to him at this time: '. . . if there were a Victoria Cross for endurance you ought to have it'. However, it is pleasant to be able to record that the general respect and admiration for his unceasing efforts and for the astonishing feats performed by him and his little band of devoted Whips was expressed in a most striking manner this summer of 1887, when a banquet was given to them by 300 members of Parliament at the Crystal Palace on July 13th. In the afternoon of that day a special train and a number of horse-coaches—the leading one driven by Lord Charles Beresford, the Fourth Sea Lord—converged on Sydenham, where a veritable festival began. The opera *The Huguenots* was performed by the Covent Garden Company and in another quarter the band of the Coldstream Guards played whilst the more frivolous M.P.s sampled the 'ordinary attractions' of the Palace, 'of which tobogganing was by far the most popular'. In the evening there was an open-air ballet performance with over a hundred performers and 'thousands of fairy lights and lanterns twinkling among the trees', and finally a firework display which included a 'fire-picture' of that supremely unfiery figure, the Leader of the House, and the name of the equally modest Chief Whip in gigantic many-coloured letters.

[1] Private Secretary to Lord Salisbury 1885–8.

But it was not all bouquets and banquets. Amid the cannonades of the warring parties there reached Akers-Douglas the continual and petulant crackle of fire from the malcontents of his own party who thought the Chief Whip had neglected or thwarted their careers or interests, or that the Patronage Secretary (for he was this too) had failed to press their claims for honorific recognition. We quote the following exceptionally bitter recriminations, for they are a good specimen of their kind.

138 Piccadilly, W.
July 2, 1887

Dear Akers Douglas,

I do not think you are behaving well to me. I know that my name has been brought more than once before you in connection with some of the vacant seats, and that you have thrown cold water on the idea. You seem to require but one qualification for a candidate, and that is wealth. I have heard this very strongly commented on by more than one M.P.—I have never sought a constituency, and never shall, but I think it is very hard that when my name is brought forward, no encouragement should be given. I have worked very hard and at great sacrifice for the party, and have always been content to contest hopeless seats, and think it is rather hard to see preference continually given to those who have nothing but wealth to recommend them. There is no doubt I should have had the offer of Brixton, had you not discouraged the idea. Perhaps I may get it even yet. I hope we shall not have many reverses like Spalding.

Yrs. very truly,
Fred Milner.[1]

More in sorrow than in anger was this one:

10 Duke Street, S.W.
Aug. 12, 1887

My dear Douglas,

In accordance with your request I shall be at the House today at 5.30. I am always glad to oblige one for whom I have (if you will kindly allow me to say so) a great personal regard although I am bound to say I am not much enamoured of the party generally. I think I have been treated very shabbily. I am in my 23rd year of continuous parliamentary life during which period I have

[1] The writer has not been identified, but he was clearly neither the future Lord Milner nor yet Sir Frederick Milner, 7th Bart., P.C., G.C.V.O., who had been M.P. for the City of York from 1883 to 1885.

fought five contested elections and never received the smallest consideration although it has been well known for some years that I have been a candidate for a permanent appointment. However be this as it may I shall always be ready to do anything in my power to assist you in your arduous duties when you personally appeal to me.

Yours sincerely,
A. G. Dickson.

In the following year this Major Dickson (who was M.P. for Dover until his death in 1889), decided to aim higher than a mere 'permanent appointment' and demanded an honour. After setting out much the same arguments as before, he threw in for good measure this astonishing claim: 'Would the fact of my having last year saved the Crystal Palace—a semi-national institution opened by the Queen—from collapse be an additional argument in my favour?'

Often, of course, the Patronage Secretary was able to gratify these desires and then the grateful recipients loaded him with thanks and compliments. Rather mysteriously such an one declares:

> . . . An interview with you is likely to be under difficulties from other ears in the lobby, or in your own room. Therefore I write to thank you very sincerely and very heartily for your efforts in getting my father a peerage. Not only am I grateful to you for the trouble that you have taken, but also for the tact which you have shown in managing, under circumstances which both of us know, a touchy and delicate matter. You will not take it a fulsome compliment when I say that it is 'tact' that makes you the good head whip that you are—I will not write more—but I am not the sort of chap to forget a good turn, and in fair weather or foul hope you will count on me as a good pal in the future . . .

Then again there were those who blamed their leaders, when framing the business of the session, for not having more regard for the local problems peculiar to their own particular constituencies, thereby forcing them to choose between displeasing their constituents or defying the party Whip. Such members not unreasonably felt that they were being treated like so much cannon-fodder by the ruthless party machine in so far as they were obliged to risk their hard-won seats for the sake of some Bill on which they had not even been consulted.

14th June, '87

My dear Douglas,

Some of us (at least I can speak for myself) sit as *Conservatives* for radical divisions of large Boroughs. In many of these the Nonconformist Element is overwhelmingly strong and one point or weapon which is always brought out and used against us at Election times is that some Tory has arbitrarily and shamefully refused a site for a *Chapel.* This always tells against us and it is a favourite argument with the howling dervishes of the order! It was therefore most unfortunate that we were last night landed in the position of having *practically* to *approve* the Places of Worship (Sites) Bill!

It is to be regretted the Hon. Member for Oxford or somebody for him or somebody on behalf of the Govt. did not block this Bill and so have saved us the dilemma in which we last night found ourselves.

I had to vote against the adjournment and *so* I noticed had several on our side.

You will excuse me bringing this point strongly under your notice, but I regard it as of Great importance and I am naturally anxious not to imperil my seat which has cost me years of hard work and a very considerable expenditure in money to obtain and which also necessitates a sacrifice in time and *continuous* and *heavy cost direct* and *indirect* to keep! I could afford to be more indifferent if this were not so!

Hinc illae lacrimae

Believe me

Faithfully yours

Fred B. Grotrian.[1]

Meanwhile, the indefatigable Middleton, like the resourceful field commander he was, never relaxed his efforts to keep up the war against the enemy by every available means and to guard against surprise. To his lieutenants, the party agents throughout the country, he circulated the following order of the day:

Confidential

9th Sept. 1887

Dear Sir,

The experience gained by the late elections have shown that the only method by which we can cope with the activity of the Gladstonian Party, is by placing able and energetic volunteer workers

[1] M.P. E. Hull; Proprietor of *Hull Daily Mail* and *Hull & Lincolnshire Times.*

to reside in each parish during the period of a contest for the purpose of carefully watching the action taken by the Radical emissaries and counteracting without delay the many false statements with which they attempt to gain the votes of the labouring classes.

With this object in view I shall be very glad if you can let me have the names of any gentlemen who will be prepared to undertake the work for the good of the Party . . .

I am also anxious, if it be possible, to obtain the services of volunteer cyclists as canvassers and for general work on the day of the poll. The employment of gentlemen cyclists has been tried on a small scale at the late elections and has been found most useful and a very great saving of expense.

I shall be glad if you will give this your earliest attention so that should a bye-election be sprung upon us at any moment we may be prepared to take the field with a fair prospect of success.

Faithfully yours,

Rich[d]. W. Middleton.

It was during this autumn that the Government was once more made aware of the ever-present menace to their security represented by Randolph Churchill. The latter was always a potential rallying point for malcontents, but the particular person who appears to have plotted with him now was a rather unexpected one. But the fact was that in the few months since he had resigned the Irish Secretaryship Hicks Beach had made a startling recovery and was already chafing to be at the centre of affairs again. Feeling himself neglected by his former colleagues he appears to have made common cause with Randolph Churchill. Despite the quarrels, already described, between these two men, there was a firm friendship, and their combined abilities, as critics of the Government, might have proved extremely embarrassing. As soon as Beach had made his position clear to Smith the latter immediately wrote to Akers-Douglas.

Private

10 Downing Street,
Whitehall
28 Oct., 1887

My dear Douglas,

Beach has been staying with me for two nights and this morning before he went away he showed me a letter he had written to Lord Salisbury declining to remain in the Cabinet without office[1] but

[1] He had remained in the Cabinet when he resigned his office.

expressing his willingness to come back and take any office that may become vacant and that may be offered to him. He thinks Salisbury does not himself care to have him back, or that he could get John Manners to give up in his favor; and he is a little hurt at the coldness or indifference which has—as he thinks—been shown to him.

It came out afterwards that he (Beach) had been in correspondence with Randolph and that Randolph wants to come back and to have the War Office: and Beach suggests that, as Holland[1] threatens to give up Stanhope[2] might go back to the Colonies.

I expressed doubts of the possibility of Randolph and Salisbury sitting in the same Cabinet. Beach said he was sure he could and would, as Randolph would be quite a different man at the War Office from what he was as Chanc^r^. of the Excheq^r^. and leader. 'He would not give Salisbury any trouble' and 'he is sure he would get on very well with Goschen.'

I begged Beach not to allow any public notification of his retirement from the Cabinet to appear, and he said that for his own part he should publish nothing, but that when he spoke at Bristol next month it must be either as a Minister in Office or as an independent member.

It is clear therefore that if Beach is not on our bench he will sit beside Randolph and the two will work together availing themselves of any opportunity to make their power felt.

Salisbury in speaking of Randolph's speeches to me the other day said that he wanted to come back, and I thought Salisbury was not so strong against it as he had been.

The great question is what is best for the Union and for the Party. I told Beach it would be infinitely more agreeable to me to give up than to go on, but he did not encourage that view, he did not deny however that the position of leader would be very far indeed from being a pleasant one.

Beach spoke of the strong personal antipathy Randolph has for Stanhope and that is of course a difficulty—if there was no other, in bringing him back. Holland would like to keep the Colonies and go to the Lords, but if he cannot have both, he would prefer a Peerage to remaining in the Commons with office. He said so plainly on Wednesday.

I must talk over these things with Salisbury early next week and

[1] Sir Henry Holland, Colonial Secretary 1887–92, created Lord Kantsford, 1888.

[2] Hon. Edward Stanhope, Colonial Secretary 1886–7, Secretary for War 1887–92.

tell him what I think. I wish I could have a chat with you first . . .

My aim will be to carry our own friends with us solidly and to present as strong a Government as possible to our opponents.

Does the Party wish to have Randolph back? Will Salisbury accept him?

Yours sincerely,
W. H. Smith.

When, a little later, Salisbury offered Hicks Beach the Presidency of the Board of Trade—no other office being vacant—it may well have been partly in order to forestall the dangerous combination foreseen by Smith: although he may in any case have wished to readmit such a tried and valuable minister once the latter's health was restored. But despite his declared readiness (to Smith) to take any office offered to him, Beach delayed acceptance and kept them all on tenterhooks by continuing his flirtation with Churchill. He proposed to the latter 'that they should both sit together and work together for the rest of the Parliament'. Churchill, however, 'would not countenance this generous attempt to relieve the isolation of his position' and urged Beach to follow the path of duty. 'They need you, and besides I shall like to feel I have one friend there.'[1]

However, before Beach finally accepted the Board of Trade early in the following year there seem still to have been difficulties and misunderstandings with which Churchill was somehow connected, for on February 26th, 1888, Smith appealed to Akers-Douglas 'Will you come round here . . . Beach had a talk with Randolph last night and as a serious misconception appears to have arisen I want you to clear it up with Beach who is here . . .' Evidently the matter was cleared up, for very shortly afterwards Beach was installed at the Board of Trade, where he remained throughout the rest of the Government's term.

[1] Churchill, 676.

VIII
CHURCHILL'S FINAL FLINGS

DESPITE the new Rules of Procedure, the passing of the Crimes Bill had been so much held up by obstruction from the Irish members that Smith had been obliged to ask for the confidence of the House in taking action for which there was no precedent. Thus, when by June 10th, 1887, only four clauses had been passed, he moved a resolution that if the Bill were not reported by 10 o'clock on the 17th the Chairman would proceed to put the remaining clauses without debate. Despite some opposition Smith carried his motion by 245 votes to 93 and when the appointed time came on the 17th the debate was duly cut short by the chairman. The indignant Opposition, Gladstonian as well as Parnellite, rose and marched out of the House. The remaining fourteen clauses were then put and agreed without debate or division. This was the instrument known as the 'Guillotine' or the 'Gag'.

Two months earlier an event had taken place which, temporarily at least, undoubtedly created an atmosphere favourable to the adoption of exceptional procedure and to the passing of the Bill. *The Times* was at this time publishing a series of articles on 'Parnellism and Crime', purporting to establish the complicity of the Nationalist leaders in the long series of outrages and terrorism in Ireland. On April 18th, 1887—the date appointed for the Second Reading of the Crimes Bill—*The Times* printed in facsimile what purported to be a letter from Parnell to an anonymous correspondent apologizing for having had to denounce the Phoenix Park murders (Lord F. Cavendish, the Irish Secretary, and his secretary Burke were assassinated in Dublin's Phoenix Park in May 1882) and containing the sentence: '. . . though I regret the accident of Lord F. Cavendish's death, I cannot refuse to admit that Burke got no more than his deserts'.

The letter naturally created an immense sensation. It was just before the division was taken on the Second Reading of the Crimes Bill that Parnell rose in the House and declared it to be a 'barefaced forgery', adding that he 'would willingly have placed his own body between Lord Frederick Cavendish and the assassin's knife'. 'After a slight pause, in answer to the challenge of the House, he said that he would have done the same for Mr. Burke.'[1] But, though Gladstone and his colleagues accepted this slightly dubious disclaimer, the public at large was more sceptical. The Bill passed its Second Reading, as noted on an earlier page, by the great majority of 101 votes. A motion by Gladstone for a Select Committee to inquire into the charges and another to the effect that they constituted a breach of privilege were both negatived by the Government, and for twelve months the matter dropped.

In the summer of 1888 the whole subject was revived by an action for libel entered against *The Times* by one O'Donnell, a former member of the Irish Parliamentary Party, on the grounds that he was one of the persons affected by the imputations of the articles. The Attorney-General, Sir Richard Webster, appeared (in his unofficial capacity) as counsel for *The Times* and practically converted his defence of his clients into an indictment of Parnell. A verdict was given in favour of *The Times* on July 5th. The following day Parnell rose in the House to contradict the charges made against him by the Attorney-General and to repudiate again the facsimile letter. When *The Times* retorted that they were prepared to prove the authenticity of the letter Parnell asked the Government for a Select Committee. But Smith, in the name of the Government, refused a Select Committee on the grounds that such a body, being necessarily partisan,[2] was

[1] Annual Register for 1887, [100].

[2] Select Committees are usually constituted on a party basis, the various parties being represented on the Committee in proportion to their strength in the House.

unfitted to judge matters of such gravity and offered instead to introduce a Bill appointing a Commission with full power to inquire into the allegations.

At the time Smith declared that the Bill was offered for the acceptance of Parnell and his colleagues and that the Government were not disposed to press it if it were unacceptable. But when introducing the Bill on July 16th he revealed a significant change in the attitude of the Government by declaring that they were now resolved to proceed with it at all costs. This brought the Cabinet under suspicion of having resolved to make political capital out of the charges against their opponents. Smith was taxed with having received a visit from John Walter of *The Times* whilst the question was under consideration of the Cabinet, and frankly admitted he had done so 'as an old friend'.[1] Upon this Sir William Harcourt roundly charged the Government with having acted in collusion with *The Times*—a charge which was inevitably reinforced by the fact that the Attorney-General, Sir Richard Webster, whose duty it was to give legal advice to the Government, had also been Counsel for *The Times* in the recent trial. For, according to the custom of the time, the Law Officers of the Crown were free to take private work and Webster's Government colleagues had not been consulted or informed about the line which he had taken in this civil action. As a result of this duality of status—his official status as a public servant and his private status as a fee'd lawyer—Webster's position, once the Commission had been set up, was singularly delicate.

The proceedings of the inquiry were due to begin on October 17th, 1888; in the meantime the Government were filled with apprehensions about its many implications. From the South of France, where he was recouping his strength, Smith wrote to Akers-Douglas:

Private

Aix les Bains.
6 Sept. 1888.

My dear Douglas

... Webster has written to me to say he has come to the conclusion he ought not to appear before the Commission and Salisbury is very much distressed as he thinks it may be fatal to the

[1] Maxwell, op. cit., II, 226.

case; and especially as James[1] also has retired—for the same reason alleged by Webster—that he wants to be free to take part in any discussions that may arise in the House on the report.

I have sent Salisbury's views on to Webster and I shall probably hear from him or see him as soon as I get back . . .

If good men can be found to take Webster's place for the *Times*; and if the case will not be prejudiced by his withdrawal, I shall be glad of it as we shall be much more free on the Government bench with the Law Officers standing aside from any participation in the case before the Commission, but they are large *ifs* and I have told Webster that if Salisbury's fears are realised it will be a very serious matter indeed.

James is unfortunately at Royat and Salisbury has been talking very freely to him; all of which James has written to Hartington who has been here with the Duchess of Manchester;[2] and therefore everybody knows Salisbury's anxieties and fears which is unfortunate.

Hartington has been to see me twice and is well and cheery. He thinks James and Webster are best out of it. I was careful to avoid hinting at Webster's retirement, but he told it to me as news . . .

Yours sincerely,
W. H. Smith.

It is curious thus to find another reference to Lord Salisbury's 'indiscreetness' in speaking too freely to those around him about government affairs. What, however, is more important is the evidence which this letter provides of the fact that the head of the Government envisaged their cause as now being inextricably bound up with that of *The Times* and that, however much they might for other reasons wish the Law Officers 'out of it', if Webster was essential to proving *The Times* case then he must be kept in at all costs. Moreover, the very fact that the Attorney-General's appearance as leading Counsel for *The Times* gave the inquiry all the semblance of an impeachment or indictment of Parnell by the Government seemed from the latter's point of view to make it all the more essential that the charges should be substantiated. The Government found themselves in this clearly dangerous position partly through Webster's dual status and

[1] Sir Henry James (later Lord James of Hereford), former Liberal Attorney-General, now a leading Liberal Unionist, but not in office.

[2] Née Countess von Alten, Hartington's intimate friend for thirty years. They were married in 1892.

partly through his actual handling of the earlier case, in which he had, as an ordinary fee'd lawyer, first accepted the authenticity of the letters simply on the authority of his brief from *The Times* and then subsequently committed himself—and through his official position the Government also—to this line of indicting Parnell as a traitor and criminal.

In a further letter to Akers-Douglas of September 7th, 1888, Smith tried, not very convincingly, to sort out the problem:

> . . . There is a wide difference in my opinion between the acceptance of a brief in an ordinary action at law: and appearing as an Advocate before the Commission which we have constituted to ascertain the truth. I own to a feeling that when this Tribunal is set going it would be better if possible that all members of the Government should stand aside and take no part one way or the other in influencing the decision: but I have no feeling of that kind with reference to an ordinary legal proceeding before an Ordinary Court.

By this Smith presumably meant to imply that Webster was the one exception to the rule and should therefore participate in the proceedings. Another point which caused misgivings by laying the Government open to the suspicion of trying to make political capital, was the fact that the terms of reference of the Commission, instead of being confined to establishing the authenticity or falsity of the letters, authorized it to inquire generally into the charges and allegations made in *The Times* articles against Members of Parliament and 'other persons'. Among the strongest opponents of the proposed procedure was Lord Randolph Churchill, who, though he held his tongue in the House, drew up and submitted to Smith a closely-reasoned memorandum of protest concluding with these words: 'I do not examine the party aspects of the matter: I only remark that the fate of the Union may be determined by the abnormal proceedings of an abnormal tribunal. Prudent politicians would hesitate to go out of their way to play such high stakes as these.'[1]

Events proved such fears to be far from groundless—though for other quite unforeseen reasons the final outcome was by no means so catastrophic as that foreshadowed by Churchill. Owing to its wide terms of reference the Commission sat for 128

[1] Churchill, 706.

days and examined some 450 witnesses before the defence, consisting of Sir Charles Russell and the budding Herbert Asquith, were able to put in the witness-box the man whom they had known all along to be the forger of the letters. This man was a seedy journalist named Pigott, who after two days of agonizing cross-examination, fled the country, leaving a full confession behind him, and shot himself in Madrid. Meanwhile Parnell had gone into the box and had denied on oath the authenticity of the letters, whereupon *The Times* offered an apology and withdrew their allegations.

C. S. PARNELL.

"SIR PARNELL."

Needless to say this denouement was the cause of much chagrin, not only to *The Times*, but to the Government—and equally of much jubilation in the Irish and Liberal camps. Parnell became the hero of the hour, stayed with Gladstone at Hawarden, received the freedom of Edinburgh and accepted a gift of £3,000, publicly subscribed, towards his expenses in the affair. Undeniably the Government suffered a serious, but temporary, loss of prestige, since, although they were in no way responsible for what had occurred (except in so far as they had been dupes of *The Times*), to the man in the street the whole matter appeared to have been unequivocally settled against them.

As a matter of fact, however, apart from the question of the authenticity of the letters, it had not yet by any means been settled. For the Commission sat on till near the end of the year 1889 and only finally submitted their report in February 1890. This naturally acquitted Parnell as regards the letters, but it found him and his confederates guilty of conspiracy by a system of coercion and intimidation to promote agrarian agitation against the payment of rent and tending to incite to sedition and the commission of crime. In other words the criminality of the Land League had been proved by the huge mass of evidence which the Commission had so carefully sifted, and thus the

Government's action in proclaiming it as a criminal organization, which had excited such criticism and so many misgivings three years earlier, received its final justification. This was certainly very important for the Government, since it endorsed not only that particular action of theirs but also the whole indictment which for the last few years they had been making in Parliament, through the press and on the platform against the Nationalist Party.

Nevertheless, when the report came to be debated in Parliament (March 1890) Lord Randolph Churchill at last spoke forth the feelings which he had privately conveyed to Smith in the beginning. He said that it was 'procedure of an arbitrary and tyrannical character used against individuals who are political opponents of the Government of the day'. The fact was he felt angry and humiliated that a Tory Government should have so far demeaned itself—and played right into the hands of its enemies—by snatching at the forgeries in a wild attempt to discredit Parnell and justify the coercion policy. It was perhaps unbecoming in him—of all men—to set himself up as keeper of the party's conscience; but his argument was really quite unanswerable. For, despite the ultimate findings of the Commission, the Government had taken an enormous risk by the course which they had adopted, and they *had* been duped over the forgeries. Moreover, the fact that they knew how dangerous their course of action was is proved by their extreme anxiety to make out a case and to win it at all costs—as revealed in Smith's letter quoted above. But, as so often, Churchill overreached himself. Ending his speech on a scathing—and quite unpardonable—note he demanded: 'What has been the result of his uprootal of constitutional practice? What had been the one result? Pigott! a man, a thing, a reptile, a monster—Pigott!—the bloody rotten, ghastly foetus—Pigott! Pigott! Pigott!'[1] All the time he pointed at the Government as though Pigott had been their creature. Gladstone, meanwhile, appealing to members of the House 'as citizens—I will not say as Christians', tried to persuade them to 'record their reprobation' of 'this frightful outrage' (i.e. the false charges brought against Parnell). But his amendment was rejected and the Report was adopted by a substantial majority.

However, Parnell had brought an action for libel against *The*

[1] Churchill, 709, and Appendix IX, 827.

Times and in February 1890 the case was compromised by the payment to him of £5,000 damages. This, added to the partial revulsion of popular feeling in his favour and the marks of esteem and sympathy which he had received from his friends and supporters, vindicated his honour and certainly immensely raised the stock of the Nationalist cause. But all these favourable portents were very soon to be falsified, for in the meantime he had become involved in the O'Shea divorce case, which swiftly shattered his career, caused his deposition from the leadership of the Irish Party and led to his premature death in the following year.

For Randolph Churchill his speech in the debate on the Report of the Parnell Commission was the final step which completed the isolation that had increasingly become his lot. For, by it, he not only severed the last links which bound him to the Conservative Party, but he lost his last and most faithful personal supporter—Louis Jennings.[1]

Churchill had persuaded Jennings to move an amendment to the Government motion for adopting the Report, but then suddenly changed his mind about his own attitude and decided to 'stand altogether aloof from the Amendment', leaving Jennings in the lurch. To George Curzon,[2] Churchill's brother-in-law, who was the bearer of the message, the unfortunate Jennings expostulated: 'What will people think of him? He has himself told one of the newspaper correspondents that he intends to speak and vote for the Amendment.'[3] Then he added: 'I know what I shall think of his behaviour—first Birmingham and now *this*. You cannot doubt what my opinion will be.' When Churchill therefore launched into the outrageous tirade against the Government which has just been described, Jennings was so incensed that he rose and refused to move the amendment, at the same time repudiating Churchill's speech as being quite alien to his own views and intentions. The breach between Churchill and his faithful disciple was never repaired and—what was of more public consequence—an equally irreparable breach was caused between him and the Government and the Conservative Party generally.

[1] See ante p. 86. [2] M.P. High Wycombe; later 4th Earl Howe.
[3] Churchill (Appendix IX), 826.

Jennings had said 'First Birmingham and now *this*'. It is necessary therefore to go back a little to recount the other episode which had already overstrained the indulgence of many of his friends, and which for one of them, Chamberlain, had been definitely the 'last straw'. The fact was that, despite his safe seat at Paddington, Lord Randolph still hankered after Birmingham, which, both as a great popular constituency and as the foremost Liberal stronghold, seemed to him to offer the most complete scope for his peculiar talents. Whether or no there was really, as Churchill's supporters asserted there was, a definite compact between the local Conservative leaders in Birmingham and the Liberal Unionists that in the event of a vacancy in the Central Division he was to be invited by both wings of the Unionist Party to stand, nevertheless a personal understanding between him and Chamberlain to this effect undoubtedly subsisted.

In May 1888 John Bright, Chamberlain's fellow member at Birmingham, appeared to be so near death that an informal exchange took place between Churchill and Chamberlain, in which the latter assured Churchill of his support should he decide to stand for Bright's seat and Churchill wrote modestly that he would only consider doing so if it was 'the strong and unanimous wish of the Tories and of your party combined',[1] and emphasizing the fact that the seat rightfully belonged to the Liberal Unionists. However, Bright lived nearly another year. Incidentally, just before he died, a celebrated journalist and war-correspondent, Charles Williams, passed on to Akers-Douglas 'the suggestion that somebody should obtain from Mr. John Bright—preferably Mr. Chamberlain—a declaration of his views on the Union, and that, in case of his death, this should be placarded high and low over the country as "Last words of John Bright to British Workmen".' So far as is known this rather crude-sounding scheme, savouring of the most dubious kind of party political propaganda, never materialized, but it gives some idea of the unique position which Bright then occupied and the quasi-magic power attributed to his influence over the masses.

By the time Bright did actually die, in March 1889, Chamberlain felt quite differently about his earlier understanding

[1] Garvin, II, 437.

with Churchill. For to him Churchill's recent conduct had seemed to boil down to irresponsible attempts to injure the Government and to please the Opposition, and he no longer felt either their respective aims or respective methods to be compatible with any form of collaboration—especially if it were to be in double-harness as representatives of the great city. What this conduct was like apart from the episode already described, we can see from a letter written by Akers-Douglas to Salisbury at this time (February 5th, 1889):

> . . . I left Randolph at Monte Carlo doing his best to break the bank. I am glad to say he intends to stay abroad till the end of March—otherwise he might give us some trouble on the Address. He is very much annoyed at Arthur Balfour's success in Ireland, and is freely expressing his disapproval of the policy of the Govt. in Ireland.[1]

When John Bright's son Albert came forward to champion the Liberal Unionist cause Chamberlain therefore set himself to convince the Tory leadership that this candidate represented the only hope of maintaining the Unionist alliance and therefore should be supported even in the face of local Tory opposition.

Confidential

40 Prince's Gardens, S.W.
March 31, 1889.

Dear Mr. Akers-Douglas,

I have just received a telegram that Albert Bright is willing to stand.

I have also received information which I believe is quite trustworthy that the Gladstonians will not bring out a candidate against him although they would certainly fight anyone else.

All therefore will go well if you can manage your people and Powell Williams[2] [Liberal Unionist party manager] telegraphs that he has a letter from Rowlands [local Conservative leader] which makes it necessary that you should act without a moment's delay.

[1] Salisbury MSS.

[2] Rt. Hon. Joseph Powell Williams, P.C.; M.P. (L.U.) S. Birmingham from 1885; Vice-President Birmingham Liberal Unionist Association and subsequently Chairman of Management Committee, Central Liberal Unionist Association; Financial Secretary to War Office, 1895–1900.

Will you send for the Birmingham leaders at once and press them not to risk anything?

If they were to do anything against Bright the feeling among our people would be so strong that it would be impossible to hold the alliance together either for the Parliamentary or Municipal elections.

I congratulate you on Enfield [by-election].

Yours very truly,
J. Chamberlain.

Akers-Douglas also received a formal letter of warning from his comrade-in-arms, the Liberal Unionist Whip, Lord Wolmer.

House of Commons
April 1. 1889.

My dear Douglas,

As you are aware, rumours are in the air that the Conservative party in Central Birmingham may endeavour to run a Conservative candidate for the seat rendered vacant by the death of Mr. Bright.

This would, as you know, be a breach of the deliberate engagement between the Liberal Unionist and Conservative parties to respect each others' seats, and would, I can state as a matter of fact, do serious harm to the country in weakening that intimate alliance and complete mutual confidence between our parties, by which alone we can hope to succeed. I wish therefore to enter a formal and deliberate protest on behalf of Lord Hartington and Mr. Chamberlain against the proposal that Central Birmingham should be contested by any other candidate than a Liberal Unionist.

Believe me,
Yrs very truly
Wolmer.

Nevertheless, the Birmingham Conservatives claimed the vacant seat for Churchill, whom, despite all his recent aberrations, they had apparently continued to idolize ever since he had first contested the seat in 1885. In fact on April 2nd, 1889, an ardent deputation went up to the House of Commons and enthusiastically invited him to stand. Although he now eagerly aspired to the seat Churchill knew that, not only was Chamberlain hostile but that, through that fact, the condition which he had himself earlier declared to be essential—namely, unanimity of support from both Unionist wings—no longer existed. He therefore wavered and put himself in the hands of three persons—Hicks Beach, Hartington and Chamberlain himself. The last-named was a subtle and cruel choice, since Chamberlain, though hostile, still felt himself morally pledged by the earlier understanding to support him. However, Chamberlain neatly extricated himself. 'We unanimously advised him not to stand, although I again told him that if he did I should feel pledged to give him any support in my power.'[1]

LORD R. CHURCHILL.

"RANDOLPH MEDITATING."

The extraordinary scene in the corridors and conference rooms of the House whilst this matter hung in the balance has been graphically described in a special memorandum by Louis Jennings. This ill-used friend, trying his best (as later in the already described Parnell Report Amendment matter) to carry out what he imagined to be his friend's dearest wishes, was in similar fashion exploited, misled and finally let down. Whilst the ardent deputation from Birmingham waited at the door he was, all within a short space of time, asked first to write a valedictory address to the electors of South Paddington plus one of greeting to those of Birmingham, then informed that his friend had put his fate in the hands of—among others—his principal antagonist and finally told that he had decided not to stand for the seat after all.

Akers-Douglas, as was to be expected, was in the thick of all this and had to take the Birmingham deputation under his wing whilst these extraordinary metamorphoses succeeded one another. Matters were further complicated by the fact that for some reason Jennings was not at the time on speaking terms with Akers-Douglas and therefore refused to enter the conference room—where Churchill was trying to break the news to

[1] Joseph Chamberlain: *A Political Memoir*. Ed. C. H. D. Howard, p. 286.

the deputation—until Akers-Douglas had been called away by a division bell. When he did enter a scene of ruin confronted him. 'The deputation were very incensed and loudly declared they had been cheated, and would go back and vote for the Gladstonian candidate. R.C. tried to smooth them down, but it was quite useless . . .'[1]

It was really the end of Lord Randolph's hopes, not only at Birmingham, but altogether and evermore. Nevertheless, the fight was carried on passionately by some of the Conservative leaders in Birmingham, who absolutely refused to support Albert Bright, the Liberal Unionist candidate, even though they had been so profoundly disillusioned by Randolph Churchill. For a few days, owing to these convulsions within the Unionist ranks, it seemed as though the Gladstonians might carry the seat. In all the circumstances, Chamberlain thought it best for the time being to keep out of the struggle and out of Birmingham and to confine himself to impressing upon the Tories the necessity for putting their house in order and for close collaboration with the Liberal Unionists. A week after Churchill's withdrawal he wrote to Akers-Douglas a letter in which, whilst he gave every evidence of his desire to maintain a common front against the 'enemy', he was at pains to try to correct any Tory misapprehensions as to the extent of their power vis-à-vis his own power and that of his supporters.

40 Prince's Gardens, S.W.
April 8, '89.

Dear Mr. Akers-Douglas,

. . . The news from Birmingham is much better, and the Conservatives are beginning to come in and work both in St. Thomas' and Ladywood ward. We have an army of Liberal Unionists out and the division will be canvassed before the election.

By the bye, in calculating the Tory numbers I forgot the Irish (600 votes) who went solid for Randolph last time and are now against us. The local Conservatives enormously overrate their own strength and unnecessarily depreciate the strength of the Liberal Unionists.

I hope to convince them of this after the election.

Myddleton [sic: presumably Richard Middleton] does not wish

[1] Jennings's own account reproduced in Churchill, 687–8.

me to speak for fear of stirring up controversy with Sawyer & Co. [local Conservative leaders] My people agree to this and also to keep silence themselves on the misunderstanding, although they are wild at Rowlands' 'inaccuracy'. But they must have strong Tory support from London and they ask me to press you urgently for Hicks Beach, the Attorney-General, or Goschen.

Is it possible for any of these to go down on Tuesday?

Will you please telegraph . . . to say what you can do?

Yours very truly,
J. Chamberlain.

In the event Balfour was dispatched post-haste to exert his famous charm and persuasion upon the heated local Tories. He was so successful that nearly the whole Conservative party voted for Albert Bright on the election day (April 15th) and the Gladstonians were crushed by more than two to one. Nevertheless, despite this seeming settlement, bitterness and rancour still prevailed among the local Churchillians. Charges of bad faith were brought against Chamberlain, and, although in the beginning Lord Randolph helped to defend his friend against them, he inevitably soon found himself defending his own followers against the harsh tone which Chamberlain had adopted towards them and this led, of course, to open warfare between the two former cronies.

Chamberlain became exasperated and began not only to complain to the Tory leaders of their followers' behaviour, but to adopt a very strong and critical line with the former in all matters pertaining to the management of political affairs in his 'kingdom' of Birmingham. This was rather resented by the Tory leaders, who felt that they had already paid a pretty high price for his support. 'There seems to be a jolly old row on at Birmingham,' wrote Akers-Douglas to Schomberg McDonnell, Salisbury's Private Secretary (April 23rd, 1889), 'Joe really ought to behave well after all we have done for him—I hear from Rochester on good authority that the majority of the L.U.'s went solid against us, which also showed base ingratitude.'[1] Nevertheless, the Tories knew that they must continue to bear with him. Some months later, the question arose of a vacancy in East Birmingham, at that time held by Churchill's protégé, Henry Matthews, the Home Secretary, whom Salisbury wanted

[1] Salisbury MSS.

to get rid of. Chamberlain again poured out advice mingled with complaints to the unhappy Smith, who passed it all on to Akers-Douglas.

Private

Greenlands,
Henley on Thames,
27 Oct. 1889.

My dear Douglas,

Chamberlain is against vacating East Birmingham. He says it would be very difficult for Unionists to hold the seat. He says his friends would be loyal but that the Conservatives have no Candidate ready and that the Gladstonians have a Mr. Fulford a rich brewer with great interest in the field.

He says further that the Conservative organization in the division is bad, and that in the Town Council Elections Fulford won by a large majority last year and then he goes on to complain of the 'offensive conduct' of the Randolphian section of the Conservatives since Bright's election and he says the Gazette [*Birmingham Gazette*; Conservative organ] appears to be under their influence and a series of articles has appeared most insulting to the Liberal Unionists and others attacking Austen Chamberlain who is standing for the Town Council.

He goes on to say that Middleton being the Chairman of the Directors [of the *Gazette*] he had intended to bring the subject to our notice, but he thought he would let the elections pass over first.

He is however evidently very sore and if the Alliance is to last something must be done to remove the cause of complaint. I have sent his letter to Salisbury.

Yours very truly,
W. H. Smith.

Middleton immediately answered the charges levelled against his newspaper, at the same time naturally endorsing the leaders' views on the main point at issue. 'Chamberlain must be squared if Birmingham is to be considered safe,' he wrote to Salisbury (October 28th),[1] and the same day to Smith:

Private

Dear Mr Smith,

28 Oct. 1889

Unless we have Chamberlain's cordial cooperation it would be very dangerous to vacate any Birmingham seat . . . Chamberlain's great fear is that Lord Randolph should be invited and until that is removed difficulties will always be made.

[1] Salisbury MSS.

Regarding the 'Gazette' I have only seen one objectionable article and I at once took steps to prevent a repetition of such folly and expressed my strong disapproval of the line taken—Although Chairman of the Gazette Co. naturally the Editorial dept. is in no way under my direct supervision and I read the articles referred to with the rest of the public—I have told the editor it must be stopped.

Truly yours

Rich^d. W. Middleton.

A letter written on the same day by Salisbury's private secretary, Schomberg McDonnell, to Akers-Douglas also stressed the role of Churchill as once again the bone of contention—but revealed what was evidently the *public* reason given by Chamberlain for his objections, i.e. 'Chamberlain would be opposed to a contest taking place in Birmingham and I hear that he bases this opposition on the ground that if Randolph stood he might get beaten owing to the feeling against him among certain Conservatives.' At any rate, since the maintenance of the Unionist Alliance took precedence—even without Chamberlain's reminder to the effect—of any other consideration and since he himself was a national figure whom it was unthinkable to alienate, the Tory leaders had little choice but to placate him and to follow his advice. Accordingly, after a hastily arranged conference between Salisbury and Smith two days later, Smith wrote to Akers-Douglas:

10 Downing Street,
Whitehall.
30 Oct. 1889.

My dear Douglas,

We have decided to send Middleton down to see the great Jo and talk it out with him, and as he reports so will S. [Salisbury] act.

Will you write to Selwin Ibbetson,[1] and say our conclusion is that it would be very injurious to the Party to vacate the Seat before May or June next.

Yours very truly,

W. H. Smith.

[1] M.P. Epping; he had been promised a peerage (he eventually became Lord Rookwood), but could not for the present be given it as his was another very unsafe seat.

As a result of these negotiations a conference was held between the two wings of the Unionist Party as to the future representation of the city. Chamberlain insisted on adherence to the original compact (of 1886) whereby Liberal Unionists in constituencies held by them before the election of 1886 were promised the fullest Conservative support. No settlement being reached, the conference unanimously agreed to refer the question to the arbitration of Lord Salisbury and Lord Hartington. A year elapsed before these statesmen published their award, but, when they did, it fully supported Chamberlain's contention and, although Hartington earnestly advised that the Liberal Unionists in Birmingham should not insist upon the strict letter of their rights, Chamberlain remained adamant about retaining the six out of seven seats in the city which they then had. Not till eight years later—by which time Chamberlain had at last taken the plunge and joined the Government—were the Tories allowed an additional seat in Birmingham.

JOSEPH CHAMBERLAIN.

"JUST IN TIME."

The 'Birmingham Affair', which marked the final severance of Lord Randolph from the Tory Party and from his 'companion in exile', Chamberlain, also marked the beginning of the latter's final alignment with the Tory Party and the end of his own exile and isolation. Churchill, who had once seemed to be the obvious bridge between 'Radical Jo' and the Tories, was now quite clearly revealed as having been the main obstacle to this rapprochement. For Churchill, who was really steadily moving—in all except, ostensibly, the Irish question—towards the Liberal camp, did not perceive that the very pain and violence of Chamberlain's break from his old party rendered his new allegiances all the more vital to the recovery of his self-esteem. And here we may observe that the Irish question was to Churchill, for all his protestations, merely a pawn in the game, as is so clearly revealed in his opportunistic and cynical handling of the theme—the meeting with Parnell, the 'pinning' of Gladstone, 'playing the Orange card', etc. Later, when he had broken with Salisbury's Government, as shown in a letter already quoted, he turned definitely against their policy in Ireland. By contrast Chamberlain's attitude to the question was quite clearly the result of earnest reflection and deep conviction and had its logical place in the Imperialism of which he was to become the foremost apostle. Chamberlain was therefore genuinely concerned to preserve and cement the Unionist alliance with the Tories, which Churchill, who had been discarded by the latter, liked to speak of disparagingly as a 'crutch'. Again, whilst Chamberlain was careful to tender advice and criticism to the Government as far as possible through private channels, Churchill lashed out at them publicly and heedlessly —though he usually injured himself more than them in the process.

It took Birmingham nearly two years to recover from Churchill's intervention there, and then (January 1891), for the first time since the Liberal disruption, Liberal Unionists and Conservatives held a joint meeting there. Later the same year final peace was consecrated at a great Conservative rally during which Chamberlain sat beside Lord Salisbury and proposed the toast of the 'Unionist Cause'. He then described the process by which he found himself in that situation—the hopes once held that the rupture with Gladstone would be only temporary and the prospect of ultimate reunion. But—'if I refer to that now it is to say that since then the gulf has widened and deepened. Now I neither look for nor desire reunion.'[1]

[1] Garvin, II, 443.

IX
TORY ATTITUDES TO REFORM

However much Chamberlain might agree with the Conservatives on the need for preserving the union with Ireland he never departed from his original principle that the Government's policy there should not be negative—that is, merely repressive without offering any prospects of some degree of eventual *local* self-government. Actually, Balfour was already working out some such scheme, but it was never easy for the Government to expedite progressive policies which might be deemed by the Irish landlords to affect their status, when they depended to a great extent on the support of the latter and of those who sympathized with them. It was, indeed, the same story with the English county magnates and gentry when it came to the Government's County Councils Act. For this was but a part of the perennial problem of the Conservative leaders: to please the widely differing elements which composed their party—not only in regard to Ireland, but in regard to home affairs also. As a result their policy *was* always in danger of being negative—in the one case as in the other. Above all they were at this time so absorbed with the immediate task of coping with the turbulence of the Irish both in Ireland and at Westminster that the longer-term aspects of policy and the more fundamental but none the less pressing reforms which the advent of democracy made inevitable could at first only receive their intermittent attention.

Indeed, despite the new Procedure Rules and the spectacular

efforts of Akers-Douglas and his Whips there was partial parliamentary paralysis until the O'Shea divorce case broke the spell in 1890, and, except for the County Councils Act of 1888, the bulk of projected Tory reforms had perforce to wait. Of this phase Lady Gwendolen Cecil has written with her usual succinctness: 'Opposition tactics prevented questions upon which at that stage it might have been difficult to induce Liberal Unionists and Conservatives to vote together from being ever brought to the test of a division, while the perpetual harping upon Irish grievances concentrated attention exclusively upon one subject on which their cooperation was certain.'[1] From the point of view of the immediate advantage of the Government and its chief this was by no means an unsatisfactory state of affairs, partly because it kept in being the alliance on which their life depended and partly because it continually underlined the imperial theme which engaged Lord Salisbury's interest and absorbed his energy to a greater extent than anything else.

Here we begin to touch upon the seeming paradox about this great man. He had too much intelligence and too much conscience not to sense the current dissatisfaction with existing social and economic conditions; at the same time he was far too shrewd a politician not to realize that a positive and progressive policy was essential to ensure the future prospects of his party. Yet, with one or two notable exceptions where his personal convictions were deeply involved, he was temperamentally disinclined to take any positive action in these matters—unless he was strongly pressed to do so, as was sometimes the case. He had much greater faith in the merits of sound administration than in the making of new laws. Moreover, his philosophy had been evolved by an outstanding brain through years of study and reflection and he had a calm confidence in it. But this philosophy did not necessarily include ideas which others might hold to be 'natural', humane or popular. We find this exemplified in that rather shattering remark about Ireland, that 'rightly or wrongly he had not the slightest wish to satisfy its national aspirations'. So with social reforms in England: he was essentially far more 'open-minded' than most of his colleagues and he regarded these problems with his habitual detachment; but if

[1] Cecil, IV, 146.

their claims did not survive the keen scrutiny of his powerful intellect, no other considerations were likely to influence him in their favour. His genuinely Christian and moral outlook was unblurred by the least trace of sentiment. This ruthless thinking gave him an immense strength; though for a practical politician who must deal with human passions and emotions it had its obvious drawbacks.

But not even Salisbury could afford to ignore entirely the trend of the times; still less could he reverse the process by which Disraeli had geared the Tory Party to that trend. In the beginning he had indeed been a bitter critic of Disraeli's and had resigned office over the latter's Reform Bill, which had set the whole process in motion. But he could not fail to see afterwards the inevitability of such a course if the party was to be able to survive and to compete for power. He was not prepared, like his rival, Randolph Churchill, to press the process on to its most logical—or illogical—conclusions; but he was prepared to accept it philosophically so far as it had gone. 'Our absolute sovereign is the people of this country; and it is they and they alone who can bring a remedy to the mischief that is going on,' he said at the time of the Russian crisis of 1885. 'If they do not interfere, no one can interfere. You have to form a government from many points of view purely democratic and you must take it with the incidents that naturally adhere to it . . .'[1] The words had the same resigned and melancholy ring as those of Disraeli, the initiator of the process: 'If you establish a democracy, you must in due course reap the fruits of a democracy.'

Nevertheless, we believe that a false impression of Salisbury's character is given when it is said by a Conservative historian that he 'dreaded the rising tide of democracy and the swelling menace of socialism',[2] or when a Left-wing historian speaks of his 'fear of democracy and belief in the virtue of resisting for resisting's sake'.[3] For instance, however 'conservative' his general approach to the great problems of his time, his exceptionally honest and logical mind instinctively refused to allow basically sound and good motives to be obscured and smeared by meaningless party labels. Thus, when he—of all people—was accused

[1] Hansard, May 12th, 1885.

[2] F. J. C. Hearnshaw: *Conservatism in England*, 236.

[3] A. J. P. Taylor: *From Napoleon to Stalin*, 121.

by Lord Wemyss of 'Socialism' for introducing (in 1885) a modest Bill to secure better housing conditions for the working class, he retorted: '. . . do not imagine that by merely affixing to it the reproach of socialism you can seriously affect the progress of any great legislative movement, or destroy those high arguments which are derived from the noblest principles of philanthropy and religion.'[1] And he also declared that 'the main commandment of the gospel preached by my noble friend is: "Thou shalt not use the public resources to benefit the poor." '[2]

Truly, he was not in the least 'democratic' in any usual sense of the word, except that he headed a government of democratic form. He was every bit as class-conscious, in the sense of accepting his high place in Society, as the other men of his time with whom he consorted, and also he devoutly believed that *noblesse oblige*. But here it may be observed, as further proof of his astuteness, that he also possessed a keen and critical insight into the motives and methods of his own class. As he had once explained to Churchill he had, as chief policy-maker, to maintain some sort of balance between the 'classes' and the 'masses', and he knew the former to be dangerous and wily if their interests were threatened. 'I do not mean that the "classes" will join issue with you on one of the measures which hits them hard, and beat you on that. That is not the way they fight. They will select some other matter on which they can appeal to prejudice, and on which they think the masses will be indifferent; and on this they will upset you.'[3] Indeed, had he possessed the same insight into the mind of the masses as he undoubtedly did into that of his own class he would have been the nonpareil among Prime Ministers. As it was 'he did not know or come sufficiently into contact with influences, movements and aspirations of classes other than his own'.[4]

Nor, for that matter, did he sufficiently trouble to acquaint himself with the personalities and feelings of the rank and file of his own party—especially those who happened to sit in the Lower House. 'Lord S. does not understand the value of the H. of C. nor the feelings of the Constituencies,' complained Sir

[1] Cecil, III, 83. [2] Ibid., 82.
[3] Churchill, 565. [4] Hamilton, 253.

Algernon Borthwick[1] to Akers-Douglas (August 15th, 1892), and the *Pall Mall Gazette* (November 3rd, 1893) wrote:

> Lord Salisbury shares Mr. Goschen's dislike to mixing with the party at large, and his ignorance of the *personnel* of the House of Commons has sometimes produced unpleasantness, as when he refused an interview to a member of Parliament who he afterwards made a baronet, because he didn't know who he was. There is a well-known story, which, if not true, is *ben trovato* that Lord Salisbury was walking across the Horse Guards Parade with Mr. Akers-Douglas when a gentleman passed and just raised his hat. 'Douglas,' said the Chief, blandly, 'pray who is that fresh-looking young man?' 'That, Lord Salisbury,' answered the Whip, 'is a member of your Government—Walter Long, the Parliamentary Secretary to the Local Government Board.' Again, Lord Salisbury has been begged to show himself at the Carlton, but he has always answered that if he did he would only get into a corner between Sir William Blank and Sir Henry Asterisk, and never escape.

The above story is indeed almost on a par with the well-known ones of his whispering an inquiry at his own dinner table as to the identity of W. H. Smith when the latter was a member of his Government and of his gravely greeting his own son in the grounds of Hatfield House as an important but unrecognized guest.

It was, in fact, mainly due to those of his colleagues and associates with wider contacts and a deeper insight into public opinion—men like Smith, Hamilton, Akers-Douglas and Middleton—that the topics which became the subjects of his legislation ever came within Salisbury's purview. Moreover, his natural predilection for and intense preoccupation with the field of foreign and imperial politics inevitably inclined him to neglect the domestic field until and unless its claims were pressed upon him by his colleagues. Since, too, he preferred to delegate the management of the party, for which he had neither inclination nor talent, it is not surprising that some of these colleagues—notably Akers-Douglas—achieved positions of

[1] M.P. South Kensington, Proprietor of *Morning Post*; later 1st Baron Glenesk.

importance to which they could never have aspired under any other Prime Minister.

Meanwhile, throughout the period of Lord Salisbury's ascendency the Labour Movement was gradually getting under way. In the beginning it was almost entirely a trade union movement and Salisbury had followed the line laid down by Disraeli of justifying the formation of trade unions and of admitting their right to strike—and strike they did with a vengeance: in 1888 there were more than 500 strikes. Moreover, the movement was in its inception motivated by religious principles and philanthropic considerations with which he had every sympathy. It was in 1874 that the trade unions had first made a bid for direct representation in Parliament, and of the thirteen so-called 'Labour' members which they nominated at the General Election of that year, two were elected. One of them, it will be remembered, had later paid a remarkable tribute to Disraeli's social legislation during his great six years' ministry. Nevertheless, the few more who were elected to subsequent parliaments, though bearing the Labour label, acted with the Liberals and were reckoned among their number.

Yet, owing to Disraeli and to the success of the Conservative Working-Men's Clubs which had been founded under his auspices, the Conservatives could still count on a large section of the working-class vote; and since there was as yet no separate Labour Party the idea did not sound so strange in the 'eighties as it would to modern ears, of attempting to sponsor 'Conservative Labour' candidates. In fact, just before the fall of Gladstone's second ministry in 1885, Akers-Douglas made a report to Salisbury on the subject.

April 3, 1885.
Chilston Park,
Maidstone.

Dear Lord Salisbury,

There was a meeting on Wednesday last of the London Workmen's Association. The Chairman Mr. George Potter announced that the Association was in a position to guarantee to any bona fide working man a sum equal to the returning officer's expenses should they seek election in any Constituency as labour representatives.

My informant who was present tells me that . . . the grant would be made to any applicant provided (1) he was a bona fide working man of the wage earning class (2) that he could show that he had some prospect of success and that he had the support of some local organization (3) that subject to foregoing provisions the grant would be as freely given to Conservative working men as to Radical.

There are several places where we have a fair chance of winning with such candidates and we may as well get some of this grant if we can.

I don't however like to move in the matter until I know what y^r^. views and those of Sir Stafford are on the subject of Labour representation.

Yours very truly,
A. A. Douglas.[1]

Lord Salisbury's reply is further proof of his complete open-mindedness about subjects on which he was so often alleged to be intractable and reactionary.

Private

Hatfield House,
Hatfield,
Herts
April 3, '85

My dear Douglas,

As far as I am concerned, my vote is entirely in favour of Conservative Labour Candidates, wherever they have a good chance of winning the seat. My impression is that on most questions you will find them voting much straighter than some more cultured persons.

Yours very truly,
Salisbury.

Sir Stafford Northcote, ridiculed by Lord Randolph Churchill as the epitome of all that was most retrograde and unimaginative, also backed the idea and in a letter to Akers-Douglas suggested a way of implementing it.

[1] Salisbury MSS.

Private

30, St. James's Place,
S.W.
April 5, 1885

My dear Douglas,

I should be very glad to see two or three Conservative Working-Men in Parliament; and perhaps it might be well to run a candidate in connection with the London Workmen's Association. I suppose we should not appear in the matter at all, but that the selected candidate would go to the Association, prove himself to be a bona fide working-man, show that he has a reasonable expectation of support, and ask for the guarantee.

If they give it without more ado, I do not see any danger in the course: but we must take care that our man is not held to have contracted any obligation (moral or pecuniary) to the Association which would hamper his freedom of action when elected. I don't know much of the Association or its workings.

I should like to talk to you on the subject.

Yours very faithfully,
Stafford H. Northcote.

The warning contained in the second paragraph of this letter was an echo of some remarkably prophetic words of his at Edinburgh in the previous year. Describing the dangers of adhering to the 'principle of mere numbers' by continual extensions of the franchise and of weakening the structure of the Constitution he forecast the coming of a 'bureaucratic despotism'. 'You will have the trades-unions developing their power, carrying on not only that which is legitimate and desirable—namely the consideration of the proper interests of their own trades—but carrying on political business, and also interfering to overrule the elected representatives of the people.'[1]

The whole subject of the relationship between conservatism and the working classes was discussed carefully and critically three years later in an interesting letter from Middleton to a member of the Council of the National Union of Conservative Associations named Cropley.

[1] Andrew Lang: *Life of Sir Stafford Northcote, First Earl of Iddesleigh*, II, 219–20.

25th June 1888

Dear Mr. Cropley,

I am much obliged for your letter re Conservatism and the working classes. It is a matter in which I take the deepest interest, as being one of the most difficult problems which the Conservative Party has to solve.

The difficulty principally arises from the fact of the Conservative working men outside the Trades Unions not being an organized solid body. Whenever patronage or distinction is conferred it is considered as applicable only to the individual instead of being a compliment to the entire class as it certainly would be if the individuals we had to deal with were representative of any actual organization.

With regard to your remark that you make as to our working class supporters not being placed on Royal Commissions, I think you may remember that Mr. Drummond and Mr. Birtwhistle, both good Conservatives, were on the Royal Commission on the Depression of Trade. Also that Mr. Dumphreys contested a seat for us and that all three of these gentlemen were elected Honorary Life Members of the Constitutional Club.

The chiefs of the Party are without doubt most anxious to do all in their power to show the working classes that they are deeply interested in their welfare and that they wish as much as the Radicals, to give them their due share of recognition. If in the place of the three gentlemen I mentioned three members of any solid organization, like the Trades Union could have been selected, the reality of that desire could have been impressed upon the working classes but, as I stated previously, as the matter stands anything we may do is only looked upon as an individual compliment.

Again the question of Conservative working men in Parliament.

I am most anxious, and I am sure the Leaders of the Party are also, that we should have representative working men sitting on our benches in the House of Commons, but it would be a farce and do more harm than good if a working man was selected by the Conservative Party and run with Conservative money. To take the justly independent position in the House which the working classes should take, it is most important that the working class M.P. should be representative of, and that his candidature should be forwarded by an organized body amongst the working classes themselves.

With regard to the question of Protection and Free Trade, I am glad to say at present there is room for both lines of thought in the Conservative Party and the former is a question that must come from the masses before legislation could be successfully introduced.

I am very glad to see you have joined the Council of the National Union, where you will be able to advocate your views and they will be sure to receive careful earnest consideration.

Faithfully yours

Rich[d] W. Middleton.

It is often stated or implied in students' manuals that such progressive legislation as the Salisbury governments carried out in these years was almost solely in response to pressure from their Liberal Unionist allies. But the above instances will show that this is very much of an over-simplification of the case. Undeniably it was necessary from time to time to make certain gestures likely to win the approval and secure the adherence of certain Liberal Unionist leaders—notably Chamberlain: but apart from that there is abundant evidence that the Tories were firmly resolved not to abrogate their undoubted rights of majority. The conclusion therefore is that by far the greater part of the initiative for their forward policy came from inside their own ranks. Nor was this so improbable. They were not all hidebound reactionaries, nor yet impenitent aristocrats. For instance there was the self-made man Smith of whom Lord George Hamilton wrote that 'he knew, felt and assimilated all that was best in the progressive movements of the day . . . His common sense and perception (amounting to genius) rarely, if ever, failed him in his diagnosis of the agitation of the moment.'[1] Even Hamilton himself was accounted one of the more liberal spirits in the Government, being, among other things, one of Randolph Churchill's oldest friends—despite their occasional rows.

For Churchill's enormous influence in his day had been of two opposite kinds. In the first place there was no doubt that by the time he left the Government he had by his behaviour to a great extent discredited 'Tory Democracy' in the eyes of a large section of the party and that he had also given the die-hards an excellent excuse for resisting all 'change' more strongly than ever. On the other hand he retained a number of individual

[1] Hamilton, 253.

friends, both among the leaders and the rank and file, who, though they might deplore his tantrums and demagogic excesses, still agreed with him either on specific points or on general lines. It is clear, for instance, that Akers-Douglas not only retained Churchill's confidence to the end, but, despite the fact of being the arch-dispenser of the official party line, never shed the outlook which had prompted him in his early days to associate himself with the Fourth Party. References to him in the contemporary press often touched upon his 'progressive' outlook, exemplified by his favouring Women's Suffrage, by his abolition of the Secret Service money and—despite his being a great landowner and a magistrate and a tithe-owner—by his attitude to the Local Government and Tithe Bills.

With regard to these last-named measures it completes the picture of Salisbury's varied character and outlook to find that he was among their foremost supporters. Their natural opponents were unfortunately the leading element in his own party—namely, the country gentry, who envisaged the material foundations of their local prestige and influence in the counties being undermined, even destroyed. Salisbury's attitude to their scarcely unnatural reactions appeared unbecoming in one who, however much more enlightened and more responsible he might be, was after all the natural leader and figurehead of their class. 'A sense of their unutterable wrongs will suddenly burst upon them,'[1] he wrote scathingly; and 'to say you have dethroned the squirearchy when they have in fact no throne left to sit upon is hard upon the squirearchy'. The fact was he was too great a magnate, territorially as well as politically, to be able to sympathize with the natural preoccupations of their smaller spheres. This contemptuous attitude was of more serious consequence, however, when, referring later to the omission of parish councils from his local government scheme, he carelessly suggested that the rural population preferred 'a circus or something of that kind'. It illustrates only too well that insensitiveness which was the counterpart of his cold, clear thinking.

The Tithe question was one of the few domestic problems about which Salisbury felt strongly enough to wish to take remedial action. This was because he was a devout churchman and the problem affected the welfare of the clergy.

[1] Cecil, IV, 148.

Akers-Douglas shared his viewpoint, and, though himself a tithe-owner, told Kentish farmers that he 'had long desired to see the incidence of the tithe altered from the occupier to the owner'. He was in a good position to judge of the necessity for reform, since Kent was, next to Wales, the main centre of Tithe agitation, owing to the 'extraordinary tithe' levied on hop-gardens. To alleviate the latter burden the Government passed an Act in 1886, but shortly afterwards events made them feel that the whole Tithe question needed general reform and they drafted a more comprehensive Bill to transfer the responsibility for payment of tithes from occupier to owner. The object was not only to ease the burdens of agricultural tenants as a class at the expense of their landlords during the current agricultural depression, but also to ease the position of the clergy vis-à-vis their parishioners, especially in those cases where the former were themselves the tithe-owners. Again, nonconformists had not unnaturally been among the principal resisters of tithes, which to them were simply contributions to a Church to which they did not belong. Yet, partly owing to the factious opposition of their own die-hards and partly to the general obstruction of the Irish members, the Government were unable to get through any Bill till 1891.

Meanwhile, anti-tithe agitation was becoming so serious that the Government made various attempts to introduce any temporary measures on which they could obtain a modicum of agreement and support. Thus Smith wrote to the Liberal-Unionist leader:

Private

10, Downing Street,
Whitehall.
7 Aug. 1887.

My dear Hartington,

I am pressed very strongly to do something with the Tithe Bill before the Session closes by many of our friends who are apprehensive of very serious mischief during the coming winter if an attempt is not made to deal with the evil.

It is suggested that the Bill should be limited to effect the transfer of the incidence of the charge from the occupier to the owner . . .

The Bill to be for two years only and a Royal Commission to be appointed forthwith to enquire into the operation of the Tithe Commutation Act of 1836 generally.

Would you and your men support a proposal of this kind—It would cut the Bill down very much, and it would be in the nature of a truce rather than a settlement: but breathing time is required.

Yours very sincerely
W. H. Smith.[1]

Salisbury, meanwhile, was becoming exasperated with the attitude of his fellow landowners.

Private

August 9, 87.

My dear Smith,

The landlords had better not talk about revaluation: honesty is their best game just now.

It is evident the people are putting about that we are giving up the Tithes Bill—not on account of the difficulty of time—but because some of our own landowners oppose it. It would be very desirable if possible to dissipate this error.

Yours very truly
Salisbury.[2]

But by the beginning of the following year he was himself reduced to trying to find a formula acceptable to the landowners. On January 13th, 1888, he sent Smith the outlines of a scheme, prefacing it thus:

In view of the serious opposition with which we are threatened, it occurred to me that considerable relief might be given to the clergy without any burden on the landowner or the occupier by the following provisions . . . Pray think over this as I think it would be simpler and easier to push through the House than the bill of last year.[3]

Smith later received an assurance that the main body of the Opposition would not stand in the way of legislation on this question when Gladstone wrote to him (July 27th, 1888):

You are I think aware of my general disposition with regard to the Tithe Bill and I agree with you in thinking it in no sense a party measure. And I should be sorry under any circumstances to take any steps which would prejudice a settlement . . .[4]

[1] Hambleden MSS. [2] Ibid. [3] Ibid. [4] Ibid.

About the attitude of the Liberal Unionist allies there seemed to be a little doubt, however, for Smith wrote to Akers-Douglas (July 26th, 1888):

> Can you rely on the Liberal Unionists to support us in the Tithe Bill? Will you run round to Chamberlain in the morning and find out if he will stand by us on this—or make his men stay away. I cannot help feeling that if we fail to pass this Bill we shall disgust our own friends and discredit ourselves.

But for the time being, nothing came of all these efforts, and later that year (August 17th, 1888) the Archbishop of Canterbury wrote to Smith: 'The *distress* of the clergy increases—The *legal* difficulties are greater than those due to violence. And may I add that unless it is made compulsory on Rate-collectors to give information as to *who owns land*, the transference of the obligation to owners will be of little service. The Clergy cannot ascertain them, and the Collectors are the only officials who know them.'[1]

Despite the opposition within the Tory Party the actual delay in making any progress with a suitable measure was due almost entirely to the tactics of the Irish. Hence, as soon as the O'Shea divorce case had broken their obstructive power—that is, in December 1890—the Tithe Rent Recovery Bill was introduced, embodying the main principle of transferring the obligation on to the shoulders of the owners, and was passed into law in the following year. So the agitation was allayed for the next thirty years, until, after the First World War, occupying tenants in large numbers became owners in their turn and thus came face to face with the old bugbear once again.

The Local Government Act of 1888 extended representative Local Government from the towns (where it had been established in 1835) to the counties by the establishment of County Councils to take over most of the work previously discharged by nominated magistrates. It was an overdue reform, since local administration had fallen into a chaotic condition through the piecemeal legislation of the last fifty years creating ever new administrative functions and new authorities to perform them. It was estimated that by 1888 there were no fewer than 27,069

[1] Hambleden MSS.

independent local authorities taxing the English ratepayer, and taxing him by eighteen different kinds of rates.[1] Nevertheless, as already observed, it was inevitable that the proposed reform should appear to the die-hard wing of the Tories as a threat to the traditional influence of the squirearchy, and that consequently they should strongly oppose it.

Although he was both a squire and a magistrate, Akers-Douglas supported the Bill. He was therefore in a singularly strong position for defending the measure as well as for reassuring its critics. With characteristic diplomacy he paid tribute to the merits of the old system and the men who had worked it at the same time as he stressed the advantages of the new. He told a meeting in his constituency in January 1889 that he 'did not think that any of them could complain of the efficiency with which they had been served in the past, and he felt quite certain that they would not get their affairs more cheaply, faithfully and judiciously managed in the future'. He added that 'he was glad to see they were recognizing that fact in that they were electing in so many cases those who had faithfully served them in the past'. In fact, it was true here, as in the case of so many other apparently revolutionary reforms that—at least at the outset—the same class of people came forward and were chosen to serve in the same capacity as before—if under a new guise—simply because they were the best fitted by education and experience to do so. Meanwhile, due homage had been paid to the elective principle and also, indubitably, a great alleviation of local taxation resulted from the new system. 'In Kent alone,' Akers-Douglas declared, 'under the Local Government Bill, the relief to local taxation would amount to a sum of £79,640 a year.'

However, these—the Tithe Act and the Local Government Act—were but two of the reforms introduced by Salisbury's Government. For, despite the unavoidable delay due to Irish obstruction and despite Lord Salisbury's general disinclination towards new legislation, the fact remains that a number of other notable and progressive measures were passed under the sway of this prototype of Conservatism. There was that by which elementary education—already compulsory—was made universally free, another by which the government of London was

[1] Sir J. A. R. Marriott: *Modern England, 1885–1945*, 40.

reorganized and entrusted to a London County Council; there was a new Factory Act, enforcing sanitary conditions in factories, forbidding the employment of children under eleven and reducing the working hours for women. There was also a new Employers' Liability Act, extending the scope of Gladstone's earlier Bill, a Shop Hours Act and a Small Agricultural Holdings Act.

But if the Conservative leaders knew that they were irrevocably committed to reforms and progressive legislation that is not to say that some of them did not still have the darkest forebodings about the ultimate implications of the course upon which they were embarked. Smith, for instance, might advocate progressive policies both from the point of view of party expediency and because he was a genuinely benevolent and philanthropic person, but he was under no illusions as to the spirit in which a high proportion of his contemporaries approached these matters—and that spirit appalled him. In a letter to Salisbury (February 3rd, 1889) he wrote: 'The extension of the suffrage has brought us face to face with the most grave possibilities. It has made the extreme Radicals masters of the Liberal party, and men support a policy now from which they would have shrunk with horror ten years ago. There is also this strange uncertainty in the English mind to be taken into account. Men who are strictly honest in their transactions with their neighbours have come to regard Parliament as an instrument by which a transfer of rights and property may equitably be made from the few to the many; and there is yet another feature of the present day which is disgusting, and that is, that familiarity with crimes against property, or a class which is not their class, gradually deprives these crimes of the nature of crimes in the eyes of the multitude, and even seems to create a sympathy for them.'[1]

In his reply Lord Salisbury wrote: 'I agree in all you say as to the gravity of our present condition. We are in a state of bloodless civil war. No common principles, no respect for common institutions or traditions, unite the various groups of politicians who are struggling for power. To loot somebody or something is the common object, under a thick varnish of pious

[1] Maxwell, II, 239.

phrases. So that our lines are not cast in pleasant places.'[1] Even allowing for party bias and for the usual human tendency to grouse about the evils of the times, there was an unpleasant element of truth in this summing up by the two statesmen. But there was little they could do about it; indeed—such is the tragic irony of party politics—they knew that as the moving belt of political development quickened its pace they must themselves to some extent contribute to the process which they deplored in order to maintain their foothold and their party's claim to govern.

The key to the matter was this: so long as the dominant and controlling element in both the traditional parties was drawn from essentially the same class there could be no really deep ideological gulf between them, however much one party might try to win popular support by professing progressive views and the other play on the conservative instinct which is always inherent in varying forms and degrees in all classes. But as soon as the growth and spread of radical or socialistic doctrines began to coincide with the growth of the power of those sections of the community who for varying reasons were most susceptible to them, then a real ideological gulf began to appear between the parties.

[1] Hambleden MSS.

X

THE STRICKEN LEADER

As the 'eighties drew to a close, the careers of three outstanding statesmen, who, in totally different ways, had given the decade so much of its peculiar flavour, were drawing to a close also; those of Smith, Parnell and Churchill. Each was nearing the end of his physical resources before his time through overwork and strain—but Smith, the finest and least self-seeking of them, was probably the only one who actually prayed for release through death. Intensely honourable as he was, he was continually torn between doubts as to whether it was more right to stick to his post to the bitter end or to relinquish it lest his failing powers should become an embarrassment to the Government. Everyone, from the Queen downwards, vied with one another to reassure him as to the immense value which was placed upon his services and the universal esteem and affection in which he was held, and, of course, when thus pressed, he agreed without demur to carry on. Nevertheless, by the end of 1888 his health had suffered so severely that he was obliged to take a brief respite from his work and go abroad. On the point of leaving he penned a characteristically kind and thoughtful message for those he was leaving in the 'front line'.

3, Grosvenor Place,
London, S.W.
14 Dec. 1888.

My dear Douglas,

I am afraid I did not today say goodbye for the present to my colleagues and friends on the bench to whom I owe so much. I do not like to go away from them while serious work remains to be done, but I cannot help it.

You know well enough how much I value your help and next to you I value and rely on Jackson.

Pray make it clear to him that I am really very sorry I could not thank him today as warmly as I should have wished for all his good work. I could not have wished to have had a better man. He has done his work admirably for the Government and for the Country—and the whole crew are as fine a lot of fellows as any Treasury Captain could wish to man his Ship with.

I hope you will pull through all right and I am sure it will not be the Whips' fault if you don't.

Yours very truly,
W. H. Smith.

Indeed, as Financial Secretary of the Treasury, the main work of getting the financial proposals of the Government through the House devolved on Jackson and owing to Irish obstruction he was peculiarly important at this time and had to be almost constantly in the House.

While Smith was away Goschen was acting Leader and had to handle the difficult situation which had recently developed over the question of sending an expeditionary force to the Sudan to the relief of the Red Sea port of Suakin. This situation had been brought to a head by Lord Randolph Churchill—who had always held very strong views about the futility of the British commitment in the Sudan—and who, by springing a motion for the adjournment of the House (on December 1st, 1888) when the Government were quite unprepared, was not surprisingly suspected of having tried to contrive their downfall. However, under Goschen's leadership the Government extricated themselves successfully from the momentary predicament, shortly afterwards carrying out a swift and highly successful operation at Suakin. From Paris Smith sent felicitations and encouragement.

Hotel Bristol,
Paris
Dec. 16, 1888

My dear Douglas,

Very many thanks for your letter which has greatly rejoiced me. I did not like coming away at all but you are getting on admirably —and Goschen seems to have shown the best possible skill, tact and good feeling in dealing with Suakim [sic] and Randolph Churchill yesterday. I hope he will be as successful tomorrow . . .

Yours very truly
W. H. Smith.

Another letter a few days later is again expressive of his unaffected kindness and consideration towards his friends and associates—as well as of his good-humoured tolerance even towards the importunate and stupid.

Monte Carlo
Dec. 22, 1888

My dear Douglas,

The Messenger has brought me your letter of Wednesday and as I hope you are now clear for the present at least of all further bother in the House itself—whatever troubles there may be outside of it—I write just one line to wish you rest and a quiet and happy Christmas at home. No man deserves it more, and I should think no man knows how to enjoy it better with his family.

Govan[1] is unlucky and Colchester if it should be vacant again will amount almost to a sorrow: but neither of these are misfortunes of our own making, and these latter are the only real cause for depression. There is an average in all human affairs, and it is certain it will redress the run against us.

As to little Gent Davis[2] who Maude[3] tells me asks for money or the Hundreds give him the Hundreds by all means. And now good go with you and all yours.

Shake off all care and enjoy the peace and happiness you thoroughly deserve with our united kindest regards believe me

Yours very sincerely,
W. H. Smith.

On December 31st he wrote again: '. . . You have done well since I have been away—better perhaps than if I had been present and by all accounts Goschen was a great success.' Only some ten days later, however, he was distressed to hear that his two valued lieutenants, Akers-Douglas and Jackson, had also fallen ill under the strain of recent affairs, and he immediately

[1] A recent by-election in which a former Tory seat was lost to the Liberals.

[2] R. Gent-Davis, M.P. for Kennington Division of Lambeth.

[3] C. J. Maude, Private Secretary to Smith, and at one time also to Akers-Douglas; became Assistant Paymaster-General in 1892.

wrote pressing them both to come out to Monte Carlo and take over his rooms there, which he was about to vacate. This offer was accepted with alacrity by both of them.

Smith meanwhile returned to face the highly disconcerting dénouement of the Parnell Forgeries affair and the anxiety of this again told heavily upon his precarious health. It was at this time that he wrote to Salisbury that pessimistic letter (of February 3rd, 1889) about the general condition of British politics, a part of which has been quoted above and at the end of which he offered 'to give place to another leader, as a simple matter of duty for the good of the country'.[1] Salisbury's reply, a part of which has also been already quoted, contained the warming phrase: 'But if you had heard the general expression of consternation with which the apparent failure of your health was watched by the principal men of the party, you would have had no doubt that in their judgment your retirement from the lead in the House of Commons would be one of the heaviest blows that could befall it.'[2] Nevertheless, to an intimate friend Smith wrote (February 24th): 'I have just entered in a sense on my New Year of anxious work and responsibility . . . I have never felt myself strong enough for the work I have to do . . .' And again he discussed his doubts about his true duty, ending: 'He [God] will take me out of my work when I am no longer required, and then will come rest.'[3] A month later he was writing to another close friend that he was 'very weary', though resolved to carry on 'until my rest comes', adding pathetically: 'I hope it is not wrong to long for it.'[4] Though his friends were already beginning to become alarmed that he might break down altogether, he continued to receive every kind of encouragement and various marks of esteem and affection from many quarters, and these undoubtedly helped enormously to sustain him.

The actual business of Parliament during this Session was 'very dreary', as Smith described it in a letter to a friend and it increased his despondency about the general trend of politics—'a very poor kind of acting or make-believe . . . an enormous waste of power and vital strength, which might conceivably be

[1] Maxwell, II, 239–40.
[2] Hambleden MSS.
[3] Maxwell, II, 249–50.
[4] Ibid.

applied to better uses in the interests of the country'.[1] That summer, as soon as he could he boarded his yacht *Pandora* and sought solitude and repose cruising round the north of Scotland, Orkney and Shetland. Even then he kept in constant touch with Akers-Douglas by letter and telegraph, discussing every problem and topic in the day to day business of the Government. 'I am a good deal fresher than I was,' he concluded one such letter, 'but I am an old man.' In point of fact he was only sixty-four.

The problem of Ireland still brooded over everything. Balfour was now working out the details of his Land Purchase Bill, which he introduced in the following year. Of this the Duke of Rutland[2] wrote to Smith (July 24th, 1889)

> I am very despondent about the future of Ireland, and cannot look upon the anticipated purchase of its soil by the existing race of tenants with complacency. If the process could be reversed and the landlords be enabled to buy out the tenants I should have more hope: but the bowl has been set trundling in one direction, and must, I suppose, trundle till it stops—and drops.[3]

However, once again, Irish obstruction was responsible for preventing the passage of the Bill—even one with, from the Irish point of view, such good intentions. Meanwhile, ceaseless efforts were made to break their power by any means that could be devised. Thus we find Schomberg McDonnell, Salisbury's Private Secretary, writing to Akers-Douglas (September 10th, 1889) about a scheme which had been submitted to the premier by the party's chief agent for Scotland, MacLeod, 'by which a sum of £30,000 is to be raised from Scotchmen to fight Irish members in their own constituencies and so keep them at home'.

By this time the Government had reached that age where they were beginning to lose an unpleasant number of by-elections—largely owing to the extreme difficulty of managing the local Liberal Unionists in certain constituencies, despite the general pact.

[1] Maxwell, II, 256.

[2] The 'Lord John Manners' who had been Disraeli's lifelong friend and colleague; succeeded his brother as 7th Duke in 1888.

[3] Hambleden MSS.

Greenlands,
Henley-on-Thames.
9 Oct. 1889

My dear Douglas,

We *are* unlucky in these fights but as we have not ourselves made a mess of it, we must cheer up and hope for better times. I get quite hopeless sometimes about the local Liberal Unionists.

Only yesterday I was asked seriously if Hartington and Chamberlain were going to form a party of amalgamation and I said that personally I should only be too glad as it would give me a chance of escape, but that I could not see that any change of the kind would make Unionists stronger numerically in the House of Commons than they are now.

Will you be about London towards the end of the month. I shall want to know what you think of Purchase, Local Government and University Education—Ireland—, before the Cabinets decide on the programme for the Session . . .

I have just had the Elgin return. It is bad but I did not expect much.

Can we have elegant extracts of the addresses and speeches of these new [Gladstonian] men in order to see what it is they have pledged themselves to and what their party is going in for . . .?

Yours sincerely,
W. H. Smith.

A few days later (October 12th) he wrote again about another pending by-election: 'It won't do to lose another seat or greatly reduce the majority . . . If the [General] Election could be taken promptly and we could win by the old figures, it might do something to raise the spirits of our friends, but by-elections are a bad business for any Government.'

There is another letter of this period which is interesting on account of the later fame of the subject of it—Alfred (later Viscount) Milner—and also because it marks the turning point in that great imperialist's career.

Private

10, Downing Street,
Whitehall.
17th October, 1889

My dear Douglas,

Goschen and Welby[1] are pressing me to offer Milner, Goschen's Private Sec., a seat on the Board of Customs or Inland Revenue on the ground of his great ability.

[1] Permanent Secretary to the Treasury.

He is a clever fellow without doubt and has been very useful to Goschen, but will it do to give him a post which has generally been bestowed as a reward for great party services. I am a little doubtful.

Yours sincerely,
W. H. Smith.

I shall speak to Salisbury about it before deciding but an 'immediate' answer is pressed for as Milner has an offer from Egypt.

Smith's answer must evidently have been a refusal, since Milner in fact went to Egypt as Director General of Accounts and thus began his rapid rise to fame in the African sphere.

During the remaining weeks of the year Smith was in almost daily communication with Akers-Douglas regarding appointments in the various government departments, the selection of parliamentary candidates, the arrangement of business for the next session, etc., etc., his still vigorous mind scrupulously examining and weighing each matter and passing it on for the opinion of his trusted lieutenant. At the outset of the new year 1890 he snatched another holiday on his yacht *Pandora*, but even then the flow of letters and telegrams never ceased. The highly damaging effect upon the Government of the exposure of Pigott's forgeries, the continuing run of adverse by-election results and the prospect of the coming session all caused him considerable anxiety—though he did not allow himself to panic. The following gives a good idea of the wide range and the chatty style of these letters:

Pandora, R.Y.S.,
Messina.
Jan. 24, 1890.

My dear Douglas,

I am afraid I have had to trouble you with one or two telegrams within the last day or two, but thought it better to push the business on a little. Our elections are a great bore, but they are not of our own making and if we do the best we can we must not get down-hearted because the chapter of accidents is against us.

As to the New York Herald and the general election—no doubt the wish was father to the thought: but I am afraid we shall have to face trouble during the coming Session. Our programme is not a pleasant one if we wish to have smooth water. E. Ashley[1] for Carlisle would be madness. E. Noel[2] would be a better man but the Scotch politicians are a hopeless lot.

Have you seen much of Goschen during the last fortnight? I suppose not as you have not mentioned it . . .

I am sorry you have been seedy. Everybody has if that is any comfort, excepting the women and they don't seem to have suffered. I am returning earlier, intending weather permitting to cross by the 5.30 boat from Calais on Saturday the 1st. Would it not do you good to run across to Calais to meet me? The double blow in the Channel might freshen you up and we might probably arrange that it would not be necessary for you to come up to town on Monday or Tuesday to see me . . .

Whether you meet me or not take care to get 'fit' for your work. Don't grind away if you are still seedy.

It is simply throwing yourself away.

Yours very sincerely,
W. H. Smith.

Smith's allusion to their programme not being a pleasant one presumably referred to the Local Taxation and Licensing Bills which did in fact stir up a prodigious amount of agitation in the country and on both sides of the House, and on one occasion brought the Government perilously near defeat. Moreover, shortly after the opening of the new Session came the debate on the Report of the Parnell Commission, in which, as already described, Lord Randolph Churchill far outdid the Opposition in his savage onslaught on the Government and was disowned by his staunchest ally, Louis Jennings. In the division which followed the majority of the Government was only 62, thus showing, despite their large majority on paper, how dependent they were on Liberal Unionist votes. Moreover, added to recent by-election results, it bore witness to the damaging effect of the Special Commission upon their reputation.

Smith, as Leader of the House, had to bear the brunt in defending the course taken by the Government in appointing the Commission, and he felt acutely the imputations made as to the motives of that policy. As a result his health deteriorated again.

[1] Rt. Hon. Evelyn Ashley, former Liberal Under-Secretary of State for Colonies; now Liberal Unionist.

[2] Hon. Ernest Noel, M.P. Dumfries Burghs 1874–86.

At the Whitsuntide recess he again took to his yacht to recuperate. But from Plymouth, on May 30th, 1890, he wrote to Akers-Douglas: 'I am afraid I shall not put in an appearance at the House on Monday. The truth is I am not much "forrader" and it may be wiser to hold on until it is really necessary that I sh^d be present as is the case with the Cabinet on Tuesday.' Next day he wrote to the same effect to Salisbury, adding: 'If I am not fit, I should not like to stay on while another man has all the labour and the responsibility. It would not be fair to him, to you, or to my other colleagues.'[1]

However, he carried on—until a serious warning from his doctor induced him in August to go to La Bourboule in France (where incidentally Lord and Lady Salisbury already were) for another rest cure. 'I wish I had not got the bother of the journey before me,' he wrote to Akers-Douglas (August 15th, 1890), 'I had infinitely rather go home and sleep.' But when he got there his spirits revived and he wrote again: 'Can I persuade you to join the Yacht at Venice . . . for a three weeks cruise in the Adriatic. Fitz[2] and his wife are coming and we intend to leave dull care behind and be as jolly as a whole crew of sandboys. Pray give me the great pleasure and send me a wire . . .'

A few days later he sent Akers-Douglas an amusing sketch of life at La Bourboule. In the same letter he referred to the problem of Sir John Gorst, to whom the party had once owed much and who was now becoming a thorn in their side through his spiteful complaints of neglect.

La Bourboule
August 21, 1890

My dear Douglas,

All's well that ends well and I am very glad you and all our friends are free at last.

I hope to hear in a day or two that you will join us at Venice. This place is an extraordinary mixture—very few English and of the French two classes only—those who are intent on spending and those who feed on them. Prices are higher than at Monte Carlo and the Salisburys amuse me by grumbling at them.

As to Gorst I would not on any account do him any harm, but I promised to speak to Salisbury about him and I should therefore

[1] Maxwell, II, 272.

[2] Penrose FitzGerald, M.P. Cambridge.

like to have your views before we part,—as we shall do I suppose in a fortnight. Gorst spoke regretfully of having allowed the Governorship of Bombay to slip—and it occurred to me but I did not say anything about it that Madras is in reserve . . .

Stormy weather about us but we get fine days. It is however a curious life—hardly worth living.

Ever yours sincerely,
W. H. Smith.

Gorst's is the typical case of the potentially valuable man whose 'awkwardness' at last proves insurmountable. Though he had rendered signal service to the party in his early days it is observable that even so indulgent a leader as Disraeli had been unable to retain him. For a time he found an outlet for his resentment against the official leadership in the Fourth Party and it was in fact at the insistence of Lord Randolph that he was made Solicitor General in Lord Salisbury's 'Caretaker' government. But his claims to this post were really too slender and when Salisbury formed his second ministry he was not invited to resume it, but relegated to the Under-Secretaryship for India. He then sank back into that sort of 'Banquo' role in which we now see him.

The sequel to the Gorst story is perhaps worth recounting even at the cost of slightly anticipating the main story. Nothing came of the Madras governorship and when, a year later, the office of Postmaster-General became vacant, Goschen wrote to Akers-Douglas (September 5th, 1891): '. . . if Jackson declines, Gorst I think should have the post; notwithstanding his drawbacks. Ridley would be better, but it is difficult to pass Gorst over . . .' Nevertheless, in the event, Fergusson, at that time Under Secretary for Foreign Affairs, was appointed to the post. Apart from his other drawbacks, Gorst's earlier association with Randolph Churchill evidently rendered him suspect to the die-hard wing of the party, while Fergusson was if anything too much identified with the latter, to judge from some remarks of Schomberg McDonnell in a letter to Akers-Douglas (September 16th, 1891),

. . . The press will not take it [Fergusson's appointment] well—nor will the public: but I know that the Chief dreads much offending the extreme Right in the declining years of a Parliament, and I believe that if he had appointed Gorst 'rightaway' many of the old boys would be very sick. I must try and square the 'Times' and 'Telegraph' over Fergusson. The 'Standard' of course I shall not attempt to touch. Gorst himself will be very nasty, I suppose . . .

But Gorst had already made it comparatively easy for Salisbury to pass him over. He had written to Akers-Douglas (September 4th, 1891) a lengthy recrimination referring to the 'self-denying position assigned to me . . . after I have served the party in and out of Parliament for more than 25 years . . . I am still an Under Secretary and the holder of a seat which is looked upon as a bar to further advancement . . .', etc., etc. Finally Smith reported:

Confidential

Walmer Castle,
Deal.
17 Sept. 1891

My dear Douglas,

Salisbury has sent me a copy of correspondence he has had with Gorst which removes all doubt in my mind that it would have been dangerous to 'endorse' him at the present moment for promotion.

Gorst writes to Salisbury that he understands the Gov. have intervened to prevent his selection at Cambridge on the ground that he ought to hold on to the critical seat of Chatham.

Salisbury replies that he has not had any communication with any Cambridge man as to his candidature and disdains any interference on the part of the Gov. and he then in a most kind way asks him to think over the effect on his own career of the independent attitude he has assumed.

Gorst's reply puts an end to the possibility of promotion.

Yours sincerely,
W. H. Smith.

The unpleasant Gorst affair provides a fitting introduction to the subject of similar 'difficult cases', of which at this time there appear to have been more than the usual number. For the problems connected with rewarding those who deserved well of the party and with pacifying those who considered they had been neglected or badly treated necessarily loomed very large in Akers-Douglas's official life—and, moreover, they often afford such fascinating glimpses into the less edifying corners of the mind of the 'political animal'.

Thus, Akers-Douglas writes to Salisbury (June 11th, '89) about a certain Conservative candidate for Cardiganshire, who 'has repeatedly pressed his claims for a Baronetcy promised him' —allegedly by Lord Iddesleigh. He had recently called on Akers-Douglas

> to ask me to get some further acknowledgments of his claim from you and threatened in the event of a refusal to make himself generally disagreeable . . . He now writes to say he intends to publish the correspondence between himself and Lord Iddesleigh unless I can obtain an answer for him this week which will be sufficiently encouraging to warrant his continuing his candidature in Cardiganshire . . . I have no doubt in his present vindictive frame of mind he will carry out his threat while we could bring sufficient pressure, if you wished it, to bear on him to keep quiet and to continue to hope . . .[1]

In the course of a surprising amount of correspondence between Akers-Douglas, Salisbury, McDonnell and Middleton, Salisbury remarked that it was very probable that Iddesleigh *had* actually given some sort of promise! Had this not been so the reply might well have been something on the lines of the Duke of Wellington's 'Publish and be damned!'

Poor Smith, ill and overworked as he was, was also sometimes the recipient of fantastic ultimatums: but even so his habitual calmness and humour did not desert him. 'I had a very mad letter from Atkinson[2] the other day,' he wrote to Akers-Douglas (December 20th, 1890), 'asking me if he was to resign at once or go on for two years taking six months sick leave each year. He wants to go to the H. of Lords, to become a Privy Councillor or a Baronet:—"a Knighthood he will not accept". My answer will be to hold on and take sick leave—unless you are anxious to make a vacancy at Boston!'

A less desperate and more insinuating proposition came from an obscure Tory back-bencher and was forwarded by Akers-Douglas to McDonnell (November 27th, '91). This gentleman declared that

> judging from the Times political articles, and from what one hears on every side, the coming General Election will probably be anything but a quiet walk-over for the Conservatives. It appears

[1] Salisbury MSS.

[2] Henry Farmer-Atkinson, M.P. Boston, 1886–92.

therefore that it wd. hardly be politic to look coldly on any offers of assistance, be they personal or otherwise, that may be made. As I have before stated I am wishful to be created a Baronet, and tho' to persons placed in the high position occupied by Lord Salisbury this may seem to be but a sorry ambition, still to me it wd. be an advance in the social scale, and one which I am prepared to make sacrifices to obtain.[1]

He then declared that he felt himself unfitted for Parliamentary life, but claimed he could make himself useful to the party by financially assisting 'suitable and clever candidates' or by subscribing to party funds. In a covering note Akers-Douglas says he has 'told him straight I could hold out no hope until those who had long laboured for the party and bled for it had been considered'.

Another note passed up to the Prime Minister stated that a certain titled person 'has been invited to stand for Exchange Div[n] of Liverpool: will only do so if promised a Privy Councillorship'. To which Salisbury simply replied: 'It is impossible to make such a bargain. S.'[2] In answer to a request from another quarter for a 'life peerage', he wrote: 'Life Peerages are likely to be creatures of the imagination for sometime to come. S.'[3]

Then there was the delicate problem involved in rewarding Liberal Unionists without pushing Conservatives out of their places in the queue. On this McDonnell had his usual admirably trenchant views.

Foreign Office.
16th April 1890.

My dear Douglas,

Wolmer [Liberal Unionist Whip] is again on the war path. He writes that he has spoken and written to you similarly as to me on the extreme desirability of

1. Knighthood for G . . . of Hartlepool
2. G.C.B. for H . . . A . . .

I must let the Chief see his letter as he asks me to do so. I propose to remark upon it that it is a strong measure to gain two honours in the same county and in the same year, and that I know Londonderry[4] intends to ask for honours for Conservatives [in Ireland] before the General Election and will be grievously annoyed

[1] Salisbury MSS. [2] Ibid. [3] Ibid.
[4] 6th Marquess; Viceroy of Ireland 1886–9.

if he does not get them. That the whole question had better wait till the dissolution is near.

G . . . is said to be long in the purse; But we shall not benefit by that. And while Honours for MPs have been steadily refused to Conservatives until the end of the Parliament, it hardly seems fair to make an exception for L.Us.

Wolmer also presses S . . . for a KCMG. I don't think myself that he would be content with anything less than a Baronetcy. And if you gave that D . . . C . . . would want the 'bloody hand' too . . . I will tell the Chief of your wish to transfer him [S . . .] to Southampton. It might be worth while to promise him the KCMG at the next election if he will go there. Then if he seemed to expect a Baronetcy it would not be too high a price to pay for his translation from Greenock.

Sorry to bother you; but I want to get the ground cleared before the annual agitation begins on the approach of the Queen's Birthday.

Do my remarks represent your views?

Yours,
Schomberg McDonnell.[1]

On this Akers-Douglas wrote: 'I quite agree with your views —why should not L-Us in Parliament wait.' Later that year (December 25th, '90) he wrote to McDonnell on the subject of the relative significance of awards of Orders as against awards of hereditary honours. '. . . I have always drawn a distinction between Orders and Peerages and Baronetcies. The former I take it are always given presumably for special services, the latter generally for Political service . . . In the present Parliament we have adorned with ribbons Sir Chas. Hall, Sir John Colomb, Sir Roper Lethbridge and Sir G. Baden Powell and there has been no mutiny . . .'

To round off this study it would be hard to find a better specimen of the brazen and minatory approach than the following letter from a well-known American-born parliamentary swashbuckler who held minor office in Salisbury's second ministry.

Private
Confidential

Aug. 9. '95.

My dear Douglas,

As the leaders have thrown me over after 17 years of the hardest possible work for the party—work by the bye which has been most

[1] Salisbury MSS.

effective for them and most worthless for myself—the least they can do is to give me some of the honours that are lavished upon people who do not do the twentieth part of my work. A Baronetcy would benefit my son, and a Privy Councillorship would be an acknowledgment of my own work.

I ask you to get these recognitions for me, and 'tis the last thing I shall *ask* the Party leaders for myself.

Yours sincerely
E. Ashmead-Bartlett.

In a memo to Salisbury McDonnell wrote: 'I have told Douglas that I do not see how your Lordship can possibly do anything in the shape of honours for Ashmead Bartlett. He is at his old games: L[d] Rothschild tells me he offered a City man a Knighthood for a good big sum.'[1]

[1] Salisbury MSS.

ASHMEAD-BARTLETT.

EXTINCTION OF EYE.

Effect of Proposed Scheme of Redistribution on Ashmead-Bartlett.

XI

CLOSE OF A CHAPTER

DURING the summer recess of 1890 Opposition speakers had been regaling their audiences with animated forecasts of the fate which lay in wait in the coming session for a Government discredited through the Parnell forgeries, and, as already shown, Ministerialists themselves looked forward with little equanimity to what promised to be a time of difficulty and possible disaster. But, by the time Parliament met on November 25th, all this was changed. For Captain O'Shea, formerly a Parnellite member of Parliament, had brought his divorce suit against his wife, naming Parnell as co-respondent.

Actually, to say that O'Shea was a 'Parnellite' member is to represent the matter in the light in which it first appeared to the world in general—namely, treachery on the part of the Irish leader towards one of his colleagues. In fact, of course, O'Shea was loathed by Parnell, as well as by the whole Irish Party, having blackmailed Parnell into securing his election for Galway and having constantly refused to take the pledge renouncing offers of office under the Crown which every other Parnellite had taken. Apart from this the first instinct of Gladstonians and Parnellites alike was to assume that the affair formed part of another vile conspiracy, akin to that of the forged letters, designed to destroy Parnell's character and wreck the cause of Home Rule. But then to their utter dismay Parnell had offered no defence and allowed judgment to be given against him.

The Commission had branded the organization of which Parnell was head as a criminal conspiracy and convicted it of outrage and crime, but this to the 'Nonconformist conscience', which swayed so great a part of the Liberal Party, was as nothing compared to his implication in a divorce case. After receiving intelligence of this attitude Gladstone immediately wrote a diplomatic letter to Parnell suggesting his temporary withdrawal from the scene. But the imperious Parnell was not taking orders from Gladstone and even impugned his sincerity in regard to Home Rule. By his ferocity, resource and vigour he managed to retain the allegiance of a part of his party; but an even larger part, under the influence of the combined attitudes of Gladstone, the Nonconformists and the Roman Catholic bishops, detached itself after a terrible struggle with Parnell and set itself up under the leadership of Justin M'Carthy (December 6th, 1890). There were now therefore two distinct and mutually antagonistic wings of the old united Home Rule Party. Naturally this appeared at first sight to be an exceptional opportunity for the Unionists to exploit. Thus, immediately after definite news of the schism, Smith wrote to Akers-Douglas:

Private

10, Downing Street,
Whitehall.
9 Dec. 1890.

My dear Douglas,

Will you get hold of Arthur Hill[1] and consider with him and any other of our friends what course we should take at the Election now proceeding in Kilkenny and in any other that may occur in Ireland. Is it sound policy to run a Unionist as against the Parnellite and his anti-Parnellite Competitor? I rather incline to the view that we ought to try our strength if we have any.

Yours sincerely,
W. H. Smith.

Meanwhile the war-whoops of the average Tory—especially those without ministerial responsibility—were quite uninhibited —besides showing a wonderful forgetfulness, or disregard, of the not so distant days when their own party had bargained for the Irish vote. The following is a letter from Sir William Grantham, Judge of the Queen's Bench Division and former M.P. for Croydon. He was probably the last of the 'political judges'—and was constantly in trouble on this account.[2]

[1] Lord Arthur Hill, Asssistant Conservative Whip (see above).

[2] Notably in 1906 and 1911. See *Dictionary of National Biography*.

Judge's Lodging,
Winchester
Dec. 14th [1890]

My dear Douglas,

Well, was I far wrong in telling you that if O'Shea was kept to his guns the Pigott defeat and disgrace would be wiped out and the Government would make the biggest score of their reign of power and that this O'Shea v. Parnell trial would be the biggest blow Gladstone had ever received. I hope though that our fellows will sit tight and not destroy the effect of this internecine strife by giving the G.O.M. or his friends a handle. Whatever we do we must not pat Parnell on the back or we shall throw all the nonconformist and religious influence stronger than ever into the Gladstone camp.

Our line must be 'we always told you so, that he was a scoundrel and a blackguard' and now that the Irish having shown their preference for a convicted liar and adulterer to the promised assistance of the leader of the Liberal Party, is there an honest Liberal who will not now acknowledge that our views of Home Rule were correct and that Mr. Gladstone knowing Parnell's character as he admittedly did prior to 1885 simply sold his party and his *country* for Mr. Parnell's 85 votes and so vote for a Government that has saved you this disgrace.

faithfully yours,
Wm. Grantham.

The remark about O'Shea being 'kept to his guns' is strange and almost seems to suggest that he had been instigated by some agent of the Tory party to launch the proceedings when he did; so also is that about the Irish 'having shown their preference' for Parnell rather than Gladstone—for, if all of them had, there would have been no occasion for any split in the Irish Party! With regard to the first remark, however, we know that O'Shea himself offered to Balfour in veiled terms the opportunity to exploit Parnell's private affairs for the benefit of the Unionists a year before the divorce came into court; but it seems certain that Balfour did not do so.[1] Also that O'Shea confided in Chamberlain, which led to rumours that the latter had instigated the divorce suit and financed it: but again the evidence adduced by Garvin seems conclusively to dispose of this theory.[2] Therefore

[1] See Blanche Dugdale: *Arthur James Balfour*, I, 182–3.

[2] Garvin, II, 397 et seq.

Grantham's remark may be presumed to be only an echo of such rumours.

The Liberal Unionists too were naturally keen to exploit this climax of the very matter which had engendered their own rather forlorn existence as a separate entity. Those of them who had owed much to Gladstone in the past—like Sir Henry James, once his Attorney General—were especially to the fore, seeking to justify their desertion and to stifle the last whisperings of guilt or conscience in the clangour of a sort of Roman triumph.

41 Cadogan Square,
S.W.
Dec. 19, 1890

My dear Akers-Douglas,

I have no doubt you and your people are alive to the position of affairs in the country—but I have received so many enthusiastic letters during the last few days that I am moved by the idea that it only wants some energy to secure an enormous number of recruits to the Unionist ranks.

The country is much moved against Home Rule but we must not let the occasion pass.

I am quite sure that from Jany. 1st to 22nd [date of opening of next session] every hour ought to be utilized in emphasizing the position. In every village there ought to be a meeting—at which a most enthusiastic and triumphant tone should be assured.

We are working away with our Liberal Unionists—but we are few and scattered.

Do make your Head-quarter men move your local men either in co-operation with us or separately to set to work all along the line to trample these Gladstonians under foot. We shall never have such another chance.

Yours
Henry James.

Akers-Douglas passed these suggestions on to Smith, but they were quite alien to the latter's grave and cautious outlook. He wrote back (December 23rd):

. . . As to Henry James—I should be very unwilling to ask my Colleagues to engage in a Campaign between this and the 22nd. I think we should be more likely to do ourselves harm than good by any exhibition of over-eagerness to triumph over Gladstonians. It would possibly turn people back again. Let the paid lecturers go to work if you please. Pegging away with little meetings of 50 or 100 is open to none of the objections which attach to a triumphal 'I told you so' which Henry James wants *us* to sing . . .

Parnell himself was at any rate able to inflict far greater discomfiture than anyone else upon the Gladstonians by the 'revelations' about his negotiations with Gladstone which he now took a savage relish in letting loose. He was also able to inflict more direct blows upon his late allies. The Government were bent upon passing in this session two important Bills which had been held up in the previous one—the Tithes Bill and the Irish Land Purchase Bill. Both Bills had been expected to arouse a considerable degree of antagonism, but the confusion in Opposition ranks rendered their passing comparatively simple. Moreover, when the Land Purchase Bill had been introduced in the previous summer Parnell had felt constrained to join Gladstone in opposing it, but he now took the opportunity to accentuate his divorce from him by leading his little band of personal supporters into the Government lobby.

Incidentally, speculation about the progress of this Bill drew from Labouchere one of his incredibly involved, laboriously humorous and brazenly dictatorial epistles—all crammed on to the back of a postcard. It is only interesting as a particularly good specimen of the style of this inveterate yet singularly inept intriguer.

Private

5, Old Palace Yard,
S.W.
Tuesday [No date]

Dear Akers-Douglas,

I have to go to Stowmarket today, but this is the exact case with the L.P. [Land Purchase] Bill—the Radicals and our Organization want to make it a feature—J. Morley is really in favour of the Bill—Harcourt is strongly against—the Irish sections want to cut each other out—the discussion therefore will go on for a long time —If your Chief wants to bring it to an end, let him take all days, and announce that he will give no holidays until it is through Committee—to do this, however, it is obvious that he must take Wed. the 13th—He never promised to hold that day sacred to women—he distinctly said that 'if the exigencies, etc., etc.'—the day before the holidays is the worst day we could have for a vote on women's suffrage—the fanatics will stay, the opponents to the measure will go home, and leave it to others to oppose—the Govt. is pledged against the measure—On our 'one vote' motion, they said that under no circumstances would they open the franchise question—this is applicable to geese as well as to ganders.

Yours truly,
H. Labouchere.

This letter was forwarded by Akers-Douglas to Schomberg McDonnell who in turn passed it to his master, Lord Salisbury, 'as an illustration of the fright the Radicals are in about women's Suffrage'. Salisbury's marginal comment was terse: 'I am afraid our people have sold the pass. S.'

The dramatic events which had almost overnight transformed the whole political situation were summarized by Akers-Douglas in a speech to constituents at Whitstable on Jan. 17th, 1891.

> We were enabled to carry through all their stages the remedial measures which Mr. Balfour thought necessary to relieve the distress in Ireland. We were enabled to do so chiefly by the fact that the whole attention of Parliament and the country was centred on the wrangles of the Parnellite Party. Is it not worth our while considering that, if this difference had not arisen, and had Home Rule been carried in 1886, you would have had at the present moment at the head of affairs in Ireland in all probability that man of whom Mr. Gladstone said that it is absolutely impossible for a man of honour to work with.

He then alluded to the divorce case and reminded his hearers that, despite this, at first Parnell had been unanimously re-elected leader by the Irish Party and that English Radical members had been declaring that the affair could have no bearing on his eligibility:

> . . . I ask you to consider this fact that during the past four years, although Mr. Parnell had not then been convicted of a breach of the Seventh Commandment, he had committed breaches of the other Commandments. If Mr. Parnell was perfectly fit to be the leader of a party when he had broken or connived at the breaking of the Sixth or Eighth Commandments he was still thought a fit and proper person to lead a great cause to victory; but as soon as he had broken a Commandment which caused a sentimental feeling to arise which would affect the votes in this country, they saw that it was time enough to depose him.

The fact was that Parnell, in his desperate determination not to give up the leadership, had skilfully dodged Gladstone's fateful communication, although Gladstone had specially charged both John Morley and Justin M'Carthy with the job of intercepting him before the Irish Members held their annual election of their leader. Parnell eluded Morley and his men in the corridors of the House and got to the Committee room where the Irish were gathered for the election. By then M'Carthy seems to have lost his nerve and therefore completely failed to convey Gladstone's attitude to Parnell—or anyone else—so that the Irish, in blissful ignorance, re-elected Parnell as their leader.

When, later, Gladstone's letter was published and the majority of the Irish revolted against Parnell because of its implications and because of the somewhat delayed reaction of their own bishops, M'Carthy took on the leadership of these anti-Parnellite dissidents, on the sole ground that he had been Vice-Chairman under Parnell. Otherwise the ugly passions and recriminations which consumed and divided his compatriots and colleagues were not at all to the liking of this gentle and highly cultured man. Thus, when soon afterwards the question arose of choosing members from among the parties for a Royal Commission on Labour (which Salisbury set up as a result of the recent grave series of strikes) M'Carthy pressed the claims of an Irish candidate, who, being among Parnell's less bitter critics, he seems to have felt would in some sense personify the continuity of the Parnell tradition and thus represent both the factions which had since emerged. This was Michael Davitt, who, although he had now declared against Parnell, had been with the latter one of the founders of the Land League and had been included with him in the 'Parnellism and Crime' allegations: he had also served several prison sentences for treason and sedition.

When considering the question of Irish representation on the Commission, Smith had written to Akers-Douglas: 'May I leave Parnell out of the question and take M'Carthy's nominee?' But when M'Carthy's nominee turned out to be Davitt he was appalled. 'Cranborne writes me today,' he wrote to the Duke of Rutland (April 4th, 1891), 'to say that he has seen it stated in the papers that Michael Davitt had been placed on the Royal Commission on Labour. I wrote at once to say there was no truth in the story. Justin M'Carthy who has been at Cannes wrote and telegraphed asking that he (Davitt) might be put upon it to represent the late Parnell party, but I telegraphed in reply that it was impossible . . .'[1] And to Akers-Douglas he wrote (April 2nd): 'I am afraid Davitt is impossible and Justin M'Carthy ought to see that the prejudice his name would create will make a bad start for the Commission.' Nevertheless, when the names of the members of the Commission were announced in the House a week later, M'Carthy tried to move the adjournment of the House to call attention to the Government's refusal to nominate Davitt, but even of his own following only twenty-nine supported him. This was a measure of the bitterness of the internecine struggle, for Davitt was known to have sent a conciliatory message to Parnell during the Kilkenny by-election in the previous December.[2]

Amid the ferment the long-delayed Land Purchase Bill—whereby the Treasury undertook to advance to the Irish tenant the money necessary to purchase his holding whenever the landlord was willing—quietly passed into law. Viewing this achievement against the sombre background of Lecky's *History of Ireland*, Smith's friend, the Duke of Rutland, wrote to him (April 8th, 1891): 'I am reading Lecky's last volumes. Good Heavens! What a record of imbecility, vacillation, stupidity and insincerity on the part of the rulers they display! Looking back on such a past I am not disposed to take a very hopeful view of the future, to which our principal contribution will be, I suppose, so many millions worth of peasant proprietors, many of whom are now engaged in breaking one another's heads. I see no salvation in that direction.'[3]

At all events, Parnell's withdrawal of his support from the official Opposition caused an almost comical confusion in the ranks of the latter. Bills were introduced and Estimates agreed to with a swiftness and smoothness which seemed almost uncanny after the years of continuous struggling and fighting. It was as well for Smith, for whom ill-health was from now on to be a constant companion. The lengthening shadows, indeed, seemed now to cause some of the bitterest political foes to draw

[1] Maxwell, II, 307.
[2] See T. P. O'Connor, *Memoirs of an Old Parliamentarian*, II, 289.
[3] Hambleden MSS.

together. Thus on March 28th, 1891, Smith wrote to Akers-Douglas: '. . . Harcourt asks me to dinner on April 15th to meet Gladstone and I am very much inclined to go. Would it frighten our friends?' And three months later he observed in a letter to another friend: 'Gladstone seems more kindly in his personal relations than I have ever known him but he is physically much weaker, and the least exertion knocks him over.'[1]

G. J. GOSCHEN.

"OH, WHAT A SURPRISE!"

About this time Smith had a brush with Goschen, who disapproved of the Government's Free Education Bill and, in introducing his Budget, complained that the scheme would absorb the whole of the surplus which he had in hand and which he had hoped would enable him to 'alleviate the burden which compulsory education has in recent years imposed on the poorer portions of the people'. In flatly declaring that the Government's mind was made up, Smith showed that he resented the tone. The incident drew from Salisbury a pleasant letter in his lighter vein.

[1] Maxwell, II, 306.

Private

8 March '91

My dear Smith,

You see the disadvantage of a good character.

When I say a bitter thing, people only say it's a bad habit I've got, and draw no inferences from it.

But when *you* say a bitter thing, there is a general explosion.

Poor Goschen! He is too sensitive for this world—especially when he has got a chill on the liver. I am afraid he will insist on sweeping away our Education project for this year—as a kind of expiation for your joke.

Ever yours truly,
Salisbury.[1]

In the April of this year the Lord Wardenship of the Cinque Ports became vacant through the death of Lord Granville. Salisbury's genial and lively Private Secretary, Schomberg McDonnell, wrote to Akers-Douglas:

Private

Foreign Office
2nd April 1891

My dear Douglas,

Poor old Granville! I am sorry for him; but it cannot be denied that this Garter and Wardenship will be most opportune. I do not for a moment suppose that the Chief will be in any hurry about filling up either post: he knows your views. What a rush there will be for the Cinque Ports!

I, like you, should like to see the Chief annex them himself: but I should doubt his doing so. All the houseless Ministers—Harry Chaplin, Halsbury, Knutsford, et hoc genus omne will surely have a try for it . . .

Ever yours,
Schomberg K. McDonnell.

Actually the Lord Wardenship was no office of profit for a needy minister, as many people—like McDonnell—were inclined to think. On the contrary, owing to the heavy expenses of running Walmer Castle, it was a considerable financial liability. Salisbury discovered this and, without mincing his

[1] Hambleden MSS.

words about that aspect of the matter, proceeded to offer it to Smith:

May 1, '91

My dear Smith,

On Hamilton's refusing the Cinque Ports on the ground of expense—it became evident that I had made a mistake in thinking it should be reserved as an assistance to a poor man. It is a white elephant of the whitest kind.

I consequently asked the Queen whether she did not think you ought to be asked to take it. It is a semi-naval position—and you have been since 1876 always exceedingly popular with naval people: and I think the Dover people would feel complimented at the Leader of the House of Commons taking it.

I enclose the Queen's answer.

Will you take it.

Yours very truly,
Salisbury.

The Queen's letter read:

Windsor Castle
May 1, '91.

The Queen highly approves of Mr. Smith's being offered the Office of Lord Warden of the Cinque Ports.

No one deserves it more than he does.[1]

In all these circumstances Smith accepted, partly attracted too by the prospect of being able occasionally to recoup his strength beside the sea which he loved so much. Not many days had gone by before he was being badgered by functionaries connected with his new post. Automatically he turned to Akers-Douglas.

10 Downing Street,
Whitehall
7 May 1891

My dear Douglas,

If you don't object I shall constitute you my Prime Minister in regard to my new functions.

I suppose I am not Lord Warden until a Patent has passed the Great Seal. Is that not so?

Then I cannot do any act in that capacity until I produce the

[1] Hambleden MSS.

requisite authority—and I should propose to answer both Gentlemen that I cannot name a day until I am constituted Lord Warden.

I feel inclined to say I should be glad to see Knocker [Registrar of the Cinque Ports] in London if he is up on other business—but as regards Stringer I think I can wait until I am full fledged.

Your sincerely,

W. H. Smith.

The same day he wrote again, having heard that Akers-Douglas was ill. 'Whatever may be the condition of other men don't attempt to leave your house until the doctor is quite satisfied you can do so with perfect safety. It would be madness for you to do so. Although I am not in the House I am keeping watch over matters and you need have no fear they will go right enough . . .' Akers-Douglas may well have been feeling a little uneasy, for also on that same day he had received a letter from Lord Limerick containing this passage: '. . . Lady Salisbury was talking freely at the [Queen's] Drawing Room about the reports of a dissolution, and saying that "they" were quite against it.'

Akers-Douglas was on his mettle just now. A kind of chain reaction of ill-health and fatigue beginning with Smith, passing to himself and then on to other colleagues and even back-benchers, had set in and was threatening the very existence of the Government. One day about this time they even suffered an inexplicable defeat in the House, which was naturally peculiarly galling to such a consummate Whip as all now acknowledged him to be. On this unfortunate episode the Duke of Rutland wrote the following revealing comment to Smith:

A day or two after it I heard from one of the supporters that he and others stayed away from their weariness of the House and its perpetual sittings, and this opens up to view other dangers likely to arise from attempting legislation for such a subject as Assisted Education late in the Session. Too great a strain will have been placed on private members, and the result will be that while those among them who take a lead, and really care for Parliamentary life, may remain to the end, others, less ambitious, and less devoted to St. Stephens will go away and the Government will run a great risk of being left in the lurch.[1]

[1] Hambleden MSS.

But just at this rather dispiriting juncture, Akers-Douglas received a great public token of confidence and esteem through the initiative of his Chief.

May 22, '91

My dear Douglas,

I have taken the liberty of submitting to the Queen that you should be made a Privy Councillor without asking your leave. I did so, because I had considerable doubt whether I should have got your leave. But I feel it to be essential that we should not seem in the eyes of the Party to be insensible to the enormous services you have rendered us—at the cost of an amount of labour which few men have equalled. So I trust you will forgive me for having taken you by surprise.

Believe me,
Yours very truly,
Salisbury.

In spite of this early intimation the actual gazetting of the honour a week later seems to have caused Akers-Douglas to feel —or to feign—surprise.

Chilston Park
May 30 [1891]

Dear Lord Salisbury,

To my great surprise I saw my name in the Birthday Gazette this morning. Will you allow me to tender to you my grateful thanks for having recommended Her Majesty to confer this honour upon me.

I had looked forward to a Privy Councillorship in the distant future after further years of service; but had not directly or indirectly sought any reward for my present short service.

Your recognition of my services is therefore the more acceptable and I trust I may be able in the future to show my gratitude.

Yours very truly,
A. Akers-Douglas.[1]

Perhaps the most gratifying and most touching of all the letters of congratulation which he received at this time came from a devoted friend and admirer outside Parliament—the eminent surgeon Sir William Dalby.

[1] Salisbury MSS.

May 31, 1891

Red Lodge,
Englefield Green,
Surrey

My dear Douglas,

I was very much gratified to see the recognition which Lord Salisbury had given to whom everybody agrees has been the best Whip this generation has seen. The supreme advantage of being young will give you some more years of useful work and power (this latter is the thing most prized by mortals) before you consent to take a seat in the House next to the one in which you will have spent *so* much of your life—Then if I am alive I shall be getting old and useless and perhaps a bore, but still life enough and heart enough to write again and say how everything good that happens to you is never too good or good enough in the eyes of yours always

W. B. Dalby.

You are now I hope well and fit again.

This year (1891) the Government passed their Free Education Bill. Opposition to it came not only from the die-hard wing of the Tories but also from the extreme individualist Liberals (such as Goschen) and those Nonconformists who feared the 'assisted' free schools would draw pupils away from their own 'voluntary' fee-paying schools. Explaining the Government's scheme in the House on June 8th Sir William Hart Dyke emphasized their desire 'not to interfere with existing arrangements more than might be absolutely necessary'. For, though the majority of elementary schools would now become entirely free, the denominational school would still remain voluntary and would also benefit by a grant up to ten shillings per child. Thus, though the more expensive Nonconformist schools might be 'put out of business', the schools of the less wealthy communities—such as the Roman Catholics—would be subsidized up to that figure, whilst remaining free from State control.

The Government's tactics appear to have been, roughly speaking, to stand back and let the Liberal and Radical opponents of the Bill show themselves up in the light of anti-progressives. The handling of the measure was discussed in a letter which Smith wrote to Akers-Douglas immediately before the introduction of the Bill, and which reveals the former in the rather unfamiliar role of wily and scheming politician. The

Lord Harrowby referred to was a Low Churchman who had been Vice-President of the Council on Education under Disraeli and more recently Lord Privy Seal. Howorth, M.P. for Salford South, was the leading Conservative opponent of the Bill. Sexton, a Catholic, was a former lieutenant of Parnell, who had been foremost in deposing him. Labouchere ('Labby') had recently become leader of the advanced Radicals, known as 'Jacobins'.

Private

3 Grosvenor Place,
London, S.W.
6 June 1891

My dear Douglas,

Dear old Harrowby who is in a highly nervous state about the Education question, writes to me from Schwalbach that we should dissuade any of our friends who may be disposed to bless the Education scheme from doing so in too pronounced a tone on Dyke's speech—leaving the Radicals to curse as much as they like. Some support will of course be necessary but a little of Howorth's tincture will probably be more healthy than too much syrup.

How can we get hold of the Romans? The Bill must be an enormous boon to them and they must wish to pass it at once I should think—but Sexton as Labby's tool may make it impossible. Is not Sexton to some extent under Priestly influence? Can it be brought to bear?

Think these things over and speak to me before I go down to the House on Monday.

Yours sincerely,
W. H. Smith.

Shortly after this Smith was laid low with a sharp attack of gout and 'only got to the Cabinet with difficulty', as he wrote to Akers-Douglas. Then, although he was just well enough to go to Hatfield on July 11th, to meet the German Emperor, everyone was shocked by his ghastly appearance on this occasion. Directly afterwards he was taken to his London house, where he lay acutely ill for several weeks. Nevertheless he still kept his hand on the reins. Only a few days after his collapse his daughter wrote to Akers-Douglas: 'My Father asks me to write and ask you to be kind enough to look in and see him on your way to the Treasury this morning, if you do not mind paying him a visit in his bedroom. He is much better, and both he and we are quite in good spirits at the way he has responded to the rest and treatment, and we are grateful to you for making it easy for him to be quiet.'

Late in August he was allowed to go to Walmer Castle, his new official residence—not so much because it was this as in the hope of the sea-air restoring him. From here too, amid the beloved sounds of the waves and the sea-birds, he still kept watch over the affairs of State and party and issued his directions to his Chief Whip. For example, when, during the summer recess, the Conservatives lost a by-election at Walsall to a Radical and then another by-election supervened at Lewisham, Smith felt that, it being the summer holiday season, it would pay even to 'whip' the Conservative electors. Thus he wrote to Akers-Douglas (August 23rd): '. . . I think if you have the addresses of the absentees or any of them you might telegraph in your own name or in mine from Downing Street to any place in the three kingdoms urgently entreating them to return for the day and vote, adding that if the Conservative Electors who are absent do abstain from voting the result must be disastrous . . .' Possibly as a result of some such step the Unionist candidate was returned.

This was practically the last personal letter which Akers-Douglas received from Smith, for the latter was now feeling so weak that he conveyed his messages and instructions through his trusted Private Secretary, J. L. Pattisson. His one wish now was to get aboard his yacht and so persistent was he that elaborate steps were taken to realize. it. On September 10th Pattisson wrote:

> As to the Chief himself I cannot report any real progress—on some days he seems better—then the gout reappears in another place and his temperature goes up, and the R.M. (Resident Medico) looks scared. Today he is brighter again and if the weather holds we may perhaps put him on board Pandora for a few hours steaming tomorrow. We have been rehearsing getting him on board—putting the R.M. in his chair and going through the whole performance—the first trial nearly sent the R.M. into the sea at the hoisting into the yacht—But now we can do it like clockwork . . .

Next day Smith himself was conveyed on board without mishap and spent several hours cruising in the Channel. Thereafter, whenever the weather was favourable, these excursions were repeated and 'one day to his great delight he was accompanied on his cruise by Mr. Jackson and Mr. Akers-Douglas, the two Secretaries to the Treasury, who were deeply moved with sympathy for the condition of their beloved chief'.[1]

The general atmosphere of anxiety about Smith and about the forthcoming session (together with an interesting sidelight on the party's reactions to Goschen as temporary leader) is conveyed in a letter to Akers-Douglas from Sir William Hart Dyke, his mentor at the outset of his career and now Vice-President of the Committee of Council on Education. It also shows that Akers-Douglas himself had suffered quite a serious, if temporary, breakdown in health. The death of Raikes, the Postmaster-General (here referred to) on August 24th, at the early age of fifty-two, 'from prostration and collapse due primarily to the pressure of official duties'[2] must have provided a timely shock and warning to his colleagues.

Private

Baron Hill,
Beaumaris,
N. Wales
[No date]

My dear Douglas,

Your letter has some bad news and I am more sorry than I can say about Smith and I hoped he was really mending. It all looks like a rough session and those of us who are left will have to bounce a bit to keep things together—I am fearful about Goschen as he is all for No. 1 and so hypercritical if any of us attempt to speak. The fact is the muzzling on our bench has been overdone rather. Gorst will I fear throw up Chatham as you say. Robertson[3] richly deserves promotion: but I fear we shall have a squeak for his seat. Are you the new P.M.G.? I hope so as I want a Telegraph Pole stuck up at Kingsdown, and you will I know let me have it. It is quite on the cards that we have an upset on the Continent before the General Election.—Now as to yourself. Go to Woodhall Spa by all means. It will set you up completely—21 days will do you—write to Dr. Williams, Woodhall Spa, Lincoln, and mention my name and tell him to engage rooms for you at Victoria Hotel—see

[1] Maxwell, II, 317. [2] Annual Register 1891, 177.

[3] M.P. Buteshire; Lord Advocate 1888–91; created Baron Robertson of Forteviot, 1899.

him the night you arrive, and begin to soak in Bromide the next morning—Oc. 1st is not a bit too late. I return home on Monday and am going to arrange some meetings.

Yours ever sincerely,
W. H. Dyke.

For a short time Smith seemed to revive under the nautical régime. But on September 13th Akers-Douglas wrote to Schomberg McDonnell: '. . . Smith is not getting on at all—I have been to see him every week since the House rose and can see no improvement. He is quite helpless and can do no business and the doctors are still very anxious about him.'[1] Schomberg McDonnell wrote back (September 15th): 'The Chief [Salisbury] refuses at present to contemplate the choice of a successor feeling no doubt that it is of no use to anticipate the inevitable day when he must do so . . .' But on October 6th Smith's condition suddenly deteriorated very seriously—and on the same day he died.

One of Akers-Douglas's closest friends and associates, Lord Dartmouth (who as Lord Lewisham had been one of the Junior Whips until succeeding to his father's peerage two months earlier), wrote to him on hearing the news:

Patshull,
Wolverhampton
8.10.91

My dear Bob,[2]

I hardly know what to say to you. This crushing blow seems to have taken all the life and heart out of me, so what must you feel, who were always with him. I can't bear to think of it. I had such a kind letter from him written on Friday, before going out for his last trip, he said then he was as weak as a child, but I never dreamt there was any real cause for anxiety. I suppose you knew he was in a critical state. It is the first thing that has really made me rejoice that I have done with the House of Commons . . . It is a terrible calamity.

Yours ever,
Dartmouth.

In a speech to constituents at Deal shortly afterwards Akers-Douglas said: 'He was certainly loved by his colleagues, trusted

[1] Salisbury MSS.

[2] The nickname used by Akers-Douglas's most intimate political friends. It was derived from 'Bob Acres' in Sheridan's *Rivals*.

by his followers and respected by his political opponents. By his great and unswerving sense of duty, by his transparent honesty and by his perpetual courtesy, he had endeared himself to every man in the House. I cannot say how much I personally feel his loss, and I am sure you will realise that no man who had worked for him for five years as I had done could do otherwise than feel the enormous loss which the country has sustained.' Akers-Douglas was also the chief organizer of a great memorial service held at Westminster Abbey (the burial had taken place at Smith's country home at Hambleden). 'I hear your Abbey Service was most impressive,' wrote Pattison, '. . . the Queen and Gladstone have written really splendid letters [to Mrs. Smith].'

On the very same day as Smith, and even more unexpectedly, Parnell died at Brighton. In the few months since his deposition from the leadership he had fought unceasingly like a lion at bay. In Ireland by-elections had been fought between the conflicting factions—Parnellites and Anti-Parnellites—with a sickening ferocity; but the tide was running too strongly now against him who had once been called the uncrowned king of Ireland, and he was beaten again and again. The tremendous strain and the bitter emotions wore down his already weakened constitution. He had married Mrs. O'Shea in June, as soon as the decree nisi became absolute, and it was to her that he returned to die.

The coincidence of their deaths was the only thing the two statesmen had in common; but their passing, which also coincided with the decline and gradual retirement of Lord Randolph Churchill and the translation of Hartington to the House of Lords as Duke of Devonshire, seemed to mark the closing of a chapter in the seething history of Victorian party politics. But the game must go on; and already on the next day those who were left behind were busy peering into the future and speculating upon the new situation created by these events. Thus Sidney Herbert, Akers-Douglas's dearest and closest lieutenant:

Baron's Court,
Ireland
Oct. 7th 1891

My dear Bob,

Your telegram [about Smith's death] reached me last night. It is a terrible blow to us as a Party, and will I fear cause terrible complications. I am very, very sorry about it. He was such a kind, good man, and so thoroughly straightforward, and we shall miss him much both personally and politically . . .

We have just heard the news of Parnell's death, which again, I fear, will militate against us by bringing the Irish together again. If we lose Manchester [by-election][1] on the top of these losses, our men will begin to get uneasy and want the Chief to dissolve.

The Irish papers say that Goschen is to lead the House. Why not send Ritchie[2] to Ireland, make Arthur [Balfour] First Lord & Leader, with leisure to help Ritchie with his bills, etc! I fear that our boys will kick at Goschen.

What with Cambridge University[3] and the Strand[4] [by-election] you will have your hands full. What a nuisance it is that we have no eminent and desirable men out of the House who want to come in.

Yours ever,
Sidney Herbert.

[1] Manchester, N.E. Sir James Fergusson's seat, which, by the rule then prevailing, he had to vacate on accepting office as P.M.G. and stand for re-election. But he *was* re-elected.

[2] President of Local Government Board. Chancellor of Exchequer 1902–3. Created Baron Ritchie, 1905.

[3] Seat vacant through death of Raikes, former P.M.G.

[4] Smith's seat.

XII

A DYING PARLIAMENT

WHO was to succeed Smith as Leader of the House of Commons? It was generally felt that there were three excellent and pretty equal candidates—Beach, Goschen and Balfour. But on closer examination there were seen to be certain objections to the first two and certain outweighing advantages attaching to the last named. Again, however, any such appointment involved the equally vital office of Chief Secretary for Ireland. Could Balfour hold both offices—and, if not, failing Beach, should the latter go to Jackson, for so long Akers-Douglas's yoke-fellow at the Treasury?

Lord Wolmer, the Liberal Unionist Whip, wrote to Akers-Douglas within a few days of Smith's death (October 12th, '91):

> . . . as to the question of future leadership I have no hesitation in giving you my *private* and personal view—A.J.B. [Balfour] is the right man. But can he remain Chief Sec. and lead the House, I don't see why not. I don't think Arthur should chuck the Chief Sec. before the dissolution; so if it is decided that he can't remain Chief Sec. and lead, you must make some temporary arrangement, and for that you have got Beach all ready to your hand.
>
> I *like* Goschen; but I don't think that he makes a good leader, letting alone the trifling detail that I don't believe your boys would have him.

The next day Jackson wrote—also backing Balfour for the leadership but opposing any temporary arrangements. He realized the difficulties which the present uncertainty made for Akers-Douglas in his position as Chief Whip.

Allerton Hall,
Leeds
Oct. 13.1891

My dear Douglas,

There is no doubt that *you* ought to be put in a position to know who should be put forward as Leader in the House without delay. The first question is are you to have a man put in temporarily or one who is to be tried permanently. From the party point of view, in view of a General Election, the advantages of a permanent leader being now selected are I think very great and I incline to think you had better make up your mind to select your permanent man. The choice I think lies between Beach & Balfour, the former would do very well for the House but the latter would carry the Country better. Goschen is very valuable in his present position but I doubt his success as a leader of the House, his defect of sight places him at a disadvantage and he would not at present be looked on as the leader of the Conservative party. On the whole my view is that you had better jump the fence and select Balfour. Details must be settled after and they must be made to fit.

Yours truly,
W. L. Jackson.

Akers-Douglas had evidently asked his close friend, Walter Long, Parliamentary Secretary to the Local Government Board, for his personal opinion on the whole question and especially if, in the first place, Beach were likely to consider the post of Leader. Long gave him a most emphatic reply on both points, including a succinct analysis of Balfour's qualities—and defects. This is particularly interesting in view of Long's highly critical attitude towards Balfour some fifteen years later, when the latter was Prime Minister.

My dear Bob, 14.10.91

. . . First as to my conversation with Beach—of course this part is solely meant for you—Quite at the end of the Session—about the very last day he and I were discussing the situation—on the presumption that there was *then* little or no chance of our poor old Leader coming back—Beach himself dismissed contemptuously the idea of Goschen—and I asked him if he would be persuaded to take the place if it seemed desirable not to move Arthur—his reply was distinct and most decided—he said nothing would induce him, that he could not possibly stand it—and when I said 'Supposing there is any difficulty'—he interrupted me and said—There can be no difficulty or doubt—Balfour is clearly the only man possible and he has every necessary quality and must be the Leader. I feel sure these are his views now.

Now for my own opinions which are of course of far less value but you ask for them and shall have them. I cannot say how important I think it is that Arthur should be made Leader—he is the man for the post in every way—we want not only a man with his ability, courage and determination, but also one who will inspire our Party all through the country with courage and awake their *sentiment*. All this and more Arthur can do—his only fault, if fault it can be called,—is a sort of indolence and a strong contempt for popularity—but his sense of duty is strong enough to overcome all this—and if he is now made Leader he will realise the necessity of doing his utmost and of rousing himself. If any man now living can lead us to victory and keep us together that man is Arthur—surely the fact that he is Ld. S's nephew will not be allowed to interfere? The idea seems too preposterous and ridiculous.

As to Ireland—surely Jackson can do that or if you don't choose to move him you can find somebody. Forgive the length of this but I feel very strongly on the subject. We cannot afford to give away a point in the game: we can win with a good Leader—with a bad one we shall, I firmly believe, go to pieces—I shall look very anxiously for the announcement. I think so much depends on the decision.

I am off to Ireland for a fortnight . . . of course I shall not mention to anybody that I have heard from you or written to you on the subject.

You have my full sympathy in the anxious and critical labours which are upon you—I am thankful we have someone so clear-headed and strong as yourself in your place.

Ever yours,

Walter H. Long.

From Ireland two days later Long wrote again to Akers-Douglas giving him an interesting on-the-spot appraisal of the situation created by Parnell's death—and incidentally propounding a most Macchiavellian scheme by which the Tory Party might take advantage of it.

Humewood,

Kiltegan

16.10.91

My dear Bob,

I hope the report in the papers as to Arthur & Jackson is correct and that they will both accept. I think it wd be impossible to do better. Ritchie[1] had just left here when I arrived—I hear he made himself most agreeable—especially to the ladies! he created the decided impression that he would like to be Chief Secretary and the Irishmen here all say they wd. like him! but I think Jackson's appointment will commend itself to them—the report has been so far very well received.

I travelled down from Dublin with Carew[2]—he talked very freely about the situation: told me reconciliation between Parnellites and anti-Parnellites is not to be thought of for a moment, that they mean to fight Cork[3]—but they think in a stand-up fight the Priests will beat them unless the Cork Unionists vote for the Parnellite—and he says if they are beaten one proposal which finds a good deal of favour is that they shall all resign in a body. They will do nothing towards electing a Leader till they meet Parliament 'if', he added, 'we ever do.' How would it be not to run a Unionist but to quietly support the Parnellite—our object is to maintain the Union and this seems just now the best way. All agree in deploring the idea of an Election next year and say 'Why not wait till July '93.'

I tell you all this as I hear it and for what it is worth of which you are a far better judge than I can be . . .

Yours ever
Walter H. Long.

Parnell's funeral made a great impression and there is a general feeling, growing in strength even among our side that he is a loss—Carew said he was a Conservative force. W.

There is a sublime irony in Long's light-hearted chatter—especially the postscript. Had all the blood and sweat of the last five and a half years of ceaseless and gruelling warfare against Parnell and all he stood for—with their coercive and repressive measures and the lengthy and perilous involvement in the Parnell Commission—had this rigorous policy which had bred so much hatred and dissension and brought statesmen on either side to early graves all along been a mistaken one? In any case 'quietly supporting' a Parnellite candidate seems a pretty desperate, short-sighted and undignified course for 'maintaining the Union'.

[1] President of Local Government Board and Long's chief.

[2] James L. Carew, former M.P. North Kildare; defeated after split in Irish Party; stood as a Parnellite in 1892 and again in 1895.

[3] Parnell's constituency.

Meanwhile, Salisbury had reached the same conclusion as most of his colleagues regarding the Leadership of the House of Commons. But he was far from enthusiastic about it. 'There is no help for it,' he wrote to Lady Salisbury (October 14th, '91)—'Arthur must take it. Beach was possible: Goschen is not. But I think it is bad for Arthur, and I do not feel certain how the experiment will end.'[1] To the Queen also he wrote (October 15th) that 'circumstances are concurring to make Mr. Balfour an inevitable choice, though the objections to it from many points of view are considerable'.[2]

Though the objections to Goschen for the post had always been the greatest for the obvious reason that he was still a self-professed Liberal Unionist while the parliamentary majority was overwhelmingly Conservative, yet it is strange to find that this sensible and sensitive man felt that his claims were valid enough to justify pursuit. Akers-Douglas wrote to Salisbury, October 16th, 1891:

> . . . I saw Goschen yesterday and urged him to follow Beach's lead in publicly stating what he had told me privately, viz: that no jealousy existed between himself and Balfour and that he would serve under the latter if desired.
>
> He demurred to this at the time but I see by the papers today that he practically did so after all . . .
>
> Has it occurred to you that Goschen's disappointment might be lessened by being appointed to the Cinque Ports?[3]

Salisbury followed this up with a very kindly and tactful letter (October 17th) to Goschen in which he told the latter that '. . . the upshot of the matter is that you possess all the qualities required for a House of Commons leader at this juncture, *except one*: that you are not a member of the political party which furnishes much the largest portion of the Unionist phalanx.'[4] Evidently Akers-Douglas had been sent to follow up this diplomatic intimation by securing a final and unconditional surrender, for in his reply to Salisbury (October 19th) Goschen wrote:

> . . . I quite understand the reasons that have induced you (shall I say compelled you almost) to arrive at this decision. You will have

[1] Cecil, IV, 219. [2] *Letters of Queen Victoria*, Third Series, Vol. II, 77.
[3] Salisbury MSS. [4] Elliot: *Life of Lord Goschen*, II, 187.

gathered from what Akers-Douglas will have told you, how entirely I acquiesce. Indeed I have felt myself during the last Session, especially when I was acting for Smith, that there was a growing uneasiness on the part of the Conservatives that I should be drifting into the leadership. I have attributed this to more motives than one; but whatever may have been the cause, I have been quite convinced lately that Balfour was the man, who should at a most important moment be able to command the enthusiastic support of all Unionists. I have the greatest confidence in his success and no one will desire it for him more than I do . . .[1]

Before finally taking his decision Salisbury had felt that political expediency as well as courtesy required that he should consult the leader of the Unionist wing—Hartington. The latter could scarcely deny the cogency of the Tory argument, so the way was now entirely clear for Balfour. The question only remained to settle once for all matter of his successor at the Irish Office, and, if this was to be Jackson, to find a suitable successor for the latter.

To Schomberg McDonnell Akers-Douglas wrote:

Private

12 Downing Street,
S.W.
[No date]

My dear Pom,

I am delighted to see the official announcement of Arthur's appointment as First Lord of the Treasury. I hardly expected it could have been carried out so soon and conclude Hartington made no difficulty at his interview with the Chief . . .

There is a letter . . . from Jackson who seems to think that Ritchie shd. be Arthur's successor. Personally I think Jackson much the abler and sounder man as he has the advantage that he knows Ireland and has been associated with Arthur on so much of his work.

There is an objection to both Ritchie and Jackson which you will no doubt have thought of viz: social position of their ladies in respect of entertainments at the Chief Secretary's Lodge—but this is a minor consideration.

Would the Chief put Jackson in Cabinet? I conclude not at first. So that Arthur can have a greater hold on policy.

I do not know what we are going to do for a successor to Jacky

[1] Elliot: *Life of Lord Goschen*, II, 188.

at the Treasury—His office is really one of the most important in the Government and a good man there is essential to the smooth working of the House . . .

Yrs. ever
A. A-Douglas.[1]

The same subject arises in a letter from Salisbury to Akers-Douglas, from which it also appears that the Chief had adopted the latter's suggestion of a consolation prize for Goschen and, having met with refusal, was preparing to hawk it to any other deserving Liberal Unionist.

Private

Oct. 22, '91

My dear Douglas,

Goschen will not take the Cinque Ports. I think of offering them to Dufferin.[2] It ought to be a Lib. Un. to stop scandalous mouths. What do you say?

I do not see much prospect of our agreeing over Fin. Sec. to the Treasury. Do you think it possible that Matt Ridley[3] would come back to it? Is there any way of ascertaining privately? I got rather snubbed by him when once I offered him an office which was not equal to his merits; and I rather dread repeating the experience.

Yours very truly,
Salisbury.

Balfour's work in Ireland had been so effective and that country was now so comparatively quiescent that it was felt that what was now needed was a good, solid man of business to consolidate his achievement. Jackson was such a man, and he accordingly became the new Chief Secretary. Balfour himself was understandably sorry to leave the field in which he had been so successful, and—it was said, more surprisingly—even the Irish as a whole, who had first ridiculed him as an effete lounger and then reviled him as a butcher and tyrant, were quite sorry to see him go. He had hoped to crown his work by a large measure of Local Government, but the scheme caused so much consternation among the more hidebound members of his own party that he was obliged to drop it. He did, however, have the satisfaction of seeing his successor pass his Irish Education Bill.

[1] Salisbury MSS.

[2] 1st Marquess of; former Viceroy of India.

[3] Sir Matthew Ridley, 5th Baronet (later 1st Viscount Ridley); Financial Secretary Treasury 1885–6.

The prospect of assuming the leadership of the Commons elated Balfour no more than it did his 'Uncle Robert'. It had been offered to him by the latter in most forbidding terms: 'I do not think it wholly for your comfort and advantage. It will make you a target for very jealous and exacting criticism. But I do not think you can avoid or refuse it as matters stand.'[1] He replied: '. . . the prospect is not exactly exhilarating:—a (temporarily) waning cause and a dying Parliament: but even if I were disposed, which I think I may say I am not, to look at the question from a personal point of view, I am too much of a fatalist to trouble myself about possibilities when the matter seems so clearly marked out . . .'[2]

Most people, however, looked forward to the advent of Balfour as Leader with the deepest satisfaction and confidence. Such an one was the mature and experienced Sir William Hart Dyke, who wrote the following lively letter about the affairs of the moment. Among these latter was the candidature of W. H. Smith's son, Frederick, for his father's old constituency, the Strand. Despite Dyke's remarks on the subject he was in fact elected by a majority of 3,006 votes over his Gladstonian opponent.

Lullingstone
Oct. 31 [1891]

My dear Douglas,

. . . Smith Jnr. speaks rather well and has money but as to his winning that seat, he is just as likely to be returned for the Mount of Olives—you want more of a rough and tumble sort of a candidate there. Why does that wretched Hinckes[3] resign? these are the men who will pivot us at the next Election. Have you been to Woodhall for a cure? I have sciatica and can't sit on a horse without groaning with pain. My people here are in good form and I am having rattling good Meetings—3 next week such is life. I am very keen as I think Arthur Balfour's leadership is going to do great things for us. We want a personality in the Commons to rally round, and now we have got him. Forgive all this jaw.

Yrs. ever sincerely,
W. H. Dyke.

[1] Blanche Dugdale; op. cit., I, 203. [2] Ibid., 204.

[3] M.P. Leek Division of Staffordshire 1886–92; he did not in fact resign at this time.

It was indeed a 'dying Parliament', this Parliament of 1886, when Balfour took up his new duties, for it met for its last session in February 1892 and was prorogued in July. But even during these six months a certain doubt about Balfour's fitness for his new position had time to grow. His casualness and nonchalance —so amusing and so powerful an asset when dealing with the factious Irish Members—shocked a House accustomed to the conscientiousness and self-abnegation of a Smith. The lynx-eyed diarist Henry Lucy noted that 'Mr. Balfour regards his duty from a different point of view, lounging in when questions are almost over, and then delegating to his colleagues the task of answering those personally addressed to him' and that when, coming in thus one night, he was hailed with ironical cheers from the Irish, instead of thunderous counter-cheers from the Ministerialists, there was silence on that side. 'Small errors of conduct', he comments sagely, 'are sometimes more fatal to success in high places than are breaches of the Decalogue.'[1] Thus, again, this contemporary report of a crucial debate: 'The clock was striking four as Mr. Balfour, with many a gentle smile, entered the chamber, and dropped, with simulated languor, into his place.'

His new role was in every way different from his earlier one and he was unable to adapt his technique to it. He was in fact really 'miscast', as Salisbury had foreseen. For example, in this brief pre-election session he introduced his Irish Local Government Bill, which has already been referred to. He felt pledged to it through references to it which he had made in platform speeches in the previous summer, but his mode of introducing it to the House now was so academic as to appear apathetic or even cynical—and this was really as much the cause of its being dropped as the prejudices aroused by its substance. The House was seeing a side of him which had been temporarily obscured by his brilliant achievements of administration in the Irish field —the remote, often seemingly complacent and insensitive philosopher—true scion of the House of Cecil.

Meanwhile, just as striking a change had taken place in the leadership of the Liberal Unionist Party, for through the death of the old Duke of Devonshire the familiar, somnolent figure of Lord Hartington had been translated to 'another place' and,

[1] Henry W. Lucy: *A Diary of the Salisbury Parliament, 1886–92*, 459.

in his stead, as leader now of the whole Liberal Unionist phalanx in the Commons, sat the alert and sinewy Chamberlain. The succession of the latter seemed just as inevitable as that of Balfour, but it had been agreed to with even greater doubts and heart-searchings. For, despite a serious diminution of his followers in the House through a sequence of unlucky by-elections, he immediately made it unequivocally clear that he had no intention of compromising over his principles and views. Addressing a meeting of his party on February 8th, 1891, he asserted 'the importance of maintaining in all respects the Liberal principles which we had not deserted when we left Mr. Gladstone on the Home Rule question'.[1] 'This statement,' writes Garvin, 'administered to the larger part of his following a very bitter pill. It had to be swallowed.'[2] For all the recent adverse by-elections, though they reduced the numbers of the party which he led in Parliament, seemed to underline the necessity for the progressive Unionism which he himself had so consistently preached.

His position was thus summed up by Henry Lucy: 'Mr. Chamberlain's personality is so strong, his ability so conspicuous, and his generalship so brilliant, that his influence accumulates though his party decays.'[3] Moreover, in spite of his apparently impenitent Radicalism, his whole attitude towards the Conservative Party had undergone a signal change, as had become clear when he had declared in a speech at Carmarthen in the previous autumn (October 13th, 1891): 'Lord Salisbury's Government has done more for the solid improvement of the masses of the population than any Government has done before in the present century in a similar period.' It was on a par with the 'Labour' member's tribute to Disraeli's great ministry. A few days later at Sunderland (October 21st) he had aroused the undying resentment of his former Radical colleagues, by criticizing the Gladstone Government of 1880–5 (of which he had himself been a member) and by describing Gladstone as 'incompetent, if not unsympathetic, in the treatment of social questions' and having 'left the Conservatives to pass Factory Acts, Mines Regulations, Artisans' Dwellings Acts, Allotment Acts

[1] Joseph Chamberlain: *A Political Memoir, 1880–92* (Ed. C. H. D. Howard), 307.

[2] Garvin, II, 528–9. [3] Henry W. Lucy, op. cit., 403.

and to give free education'. No wonder Salisbury had viewed the continuing struggle between Conservatives and Liberal Unionists in the very heart of Joe's 'kingdom' with dismay and had written to Akers-Douglas (October 21st, '91): 'I hope those idiotic people [local Conservatives] at Birmingham won't make a quarrel with Chamberlain over my body. Is it any use my sending them a message?'

Invested with his new authority as Liberal Unionist Leader, Chamberlain did his utmost to spur the Tory leaders to make this final Session of the first Unionist Parliament a fruitful and spectacular one. He had wanted to see a good Irish Local Government Bill placed on the Statute-book, but he was disappointed by Balfour's half-hearted effort. He also set great store by the Small Holdings Bill, but, though he had wanted compulsory powers to be given to local authorities, when he saw that the Tories were adamant on the point, he joined them in speaking against compulsion rather than lose the measure. So that though he set himself up as a goad to the Tories and emphasized continually his independence of their philosophy, he yet made it clear that he was resolved to give his full support to the Government when it came to the crux.

With the approach of summer, however, it became increasingly clear that the Parliament of 1886 was moribund and could not be kept together much longer. Chamberlain was most anxious to defer dissolution till the autumn to allow time for some solid symbols of Unionist good faith—such as, especially, the Irish Local Government Bill—to be passed into law and to influence the outcome of the impending election.

On May 25th, 1892, a conference was held at Devonshire House between the leaders of both Unionist parties—Salisbury and Balfour, Devonshire and Chamberlain. The Whips of both wings were present and stated their views—Akers-Douglas for the Conservatives and Wolmer for the Liberal Unionists. Middleton, as Chief Conservative Party Agent, was also present. Chamberlain pressed his argument about pushing through the Irish Local Government Bill and declared his conviction that 'the tide was rising in our favour in the country'.[1] But both the Whips and the Agent held that 'it might ebb at any moment';[2] that there is always a risk of trouble at the end of a

[1] Garvin, II, 538–9. [2] Ibid.

session, when the members cannot be brought to attend regularly—that it would be impossible to carry the Local Government Bill if even half a dozen Gladstonians or Irish obstructed it.'[1] Finally, they said that the vast majority of the local agents were in favour of June and that 'steam could not be kept up much longer'.[2] Chamberlain therefore found himself in a minority of one and June was fixed upon for the dissolution.

Meanwhile Labouchere was inundating Akers-Douglas, who on such occasions was always his chosen vessel, with all kinds of detailed and elaborate suggestions about the timing of the impending dissolution and proposing bargains between the parties for the disposal of outstanding business. The Government's Irish Education Bill was a special source of irritation to the Radicals, since the majority of the Irish approved of it, and so 'Labby' would have liked to do a deal over it.

5, Old Palace Yard,
S.W.
May 20 [1892]

Dear Akers-Douglas,

J. Morley says that he cannot understand how the Irish Education Bill can in any way benefit your Party, and says that he was perfectly astounded at the announcement to-day that it was to be passed. For various reasons do what we may to expedite it, there will be considerable time, he fears, wasted on it.

Our Front Bench was in a state of excitement because it had heard that Balfour had told Lady Jeune that the I. Local Govt. Bill was to be passed.

Yours truly,
H. Labouchere.

Two days later (May 24th) he returned to the charge:

... If you drop the Irish Education Bill, and if you can announce the Dissolution indirectly, and give us a private assurance, the matter can be worked, with the Dissolution at the end of June or before. As our sages are rubbing their hands at your getting the Education difficulty out of our way, it seems to me that from the Party view, it cannot be of any advantage to you—but the reverse ...

[1] Garvin, II, 538–9. [2] Ibid.

and again in a further letter the same day:

> The Irish are divided about an immediate dissolution—some against to get the money in . . . Almost all of our men are individually for a speedy election . . . There is a decided feeling for a vote on account until Nov.—the House organizing itself and then adjourning until the middle of October. You will gain no time by going on at once—for a dozen or two of our men will stick to it.

Indeed, the question of the Dissolution, the timing and the manner of it, appeared to exercise the Opposition—and especially their leader—even more than it did the Government. Another, particularly sardonic letter from Labouchere revealed not only this, but also the fact that Gladstone had begun to become something of a burden to his colleagues.

> *Private*
>
> 5, Old Palace Yard,
> S.W.
> May 22 [1892]
>
> Dear Akers-Douglas,
>
> I was dining yesterday with Mr. G. and after dinner, I told him what you and your Chief had said to me about the Dissolution.
>
> He considers that it is a constitutional innovation to carry over the Estimates to a new Parliament. On this subject he made an interesting Speech of a quarter of an hour, in which he reminded me that, some days ago, I had actually said in the House, that this Govt. is one of Precedent, and was only satisfied when I told him (I had forgotten the observation, if ever made) that I meant it ironically. But he finally agreed not to protest against this unconstitutional course, altho he reserved the right to 'remark on it' in this Parliament or the next. I suggested the next.
>
> Then he wanted to know why Balfour would not state openly intentions on Thursday, and said that I ought to urge this on you as constitutional. I suggested that possibly the Queen, or possibly Lord Salisbury, had not quite assented. In a second speech, he scouted the idea of either having a right to express an opinion on the subject, as it is well known that the matter only concerns Ministers in the House of Commons.
>
> He delivered a third speech on my suggesting that it would save time to take the vote on account on Thursday for three months. This is very unconstitutional. Why? I could not make out.
>
> The outcome of all was that he agreed 'for this time only', not

to pester us with constitutional theories, but to help in any way to finish up the Session.

Arnold Morley's[1] stock in trade is a profound belief that no Tory is to be trusted, so he explained that we might be falling into a trap. After an essay on 'Philosophic Doubt'[2] from Mr. G., he concluded that we might in this case trust you.

He then asked, when all your business could be finished, with our doing our best to expedite it. We went through the business, dividing it between days, and made out that, with no Whitsuntide holidays except for the Derby, it might easily be got through, including the Appropriation Bill, by the 17th or 18th of June . . .

I think that you need have no fear of a Cabinet with Mr. G. at the head, ever doing any business. He lives in the past and in the 'Constitution', and he will deliver so many essays on the Constitution to his colleagues that there will be no time for anything else.

Yours truly,
H. Labouchere.

Finally, writing on the eve of the General Election (June 20th, '92), he wanted to argue with Akers-Douglas about the choice of the actual polling day. Having worked out an elaborate way of ordering things so that it would fall on a Saturday, he ended characteristically: 'From all that I can gather, it is very doubtful whether we should gain in London by this for the Jews would vote in the East End, and the tradesmen would—as they always do—vote in the morning just before or after their breakfast. My object is a purely selfish one—It is to get the bore of the Election over before Sunday.'

It was at about this time that Labby had declared in a speech that 'in some things Judas appears advantageously with Mr. Chamberlain'. The latter's lasting resentment is evidenced by the incident of some seven years later related by Sir Winston Churchill:

. . . We passed an old man seated upright in a chair on his lawn at the brink of the river. Lady St. Helier said, 'Look, there is Labouchere.' 'A bundle of old rags' was Chamberlain's comment as he turned his head away from his venomous political opponent. I was struck by the expression of disdain and dislike which passed swiftly but with intentness across his face. I realized as by a lightning flash how deadly were the hatreds my agreeable, courteous,

[1] Liberal Chief Whip.

[2] The title of an early work by Balfour.

vivacious companion had contracted and repaid in his quarrel with the Liberal Party and Mr. Gladstone.[1]

Everyone of whichever party felt that the coming elections were going to be a very close-run thing. Middleton 'thought it *possible* they [the Unionists] might have a majority on a June or July election'.[2] Chamberlain thought they might have one on a September election; but as things stood he saw no certainty anywhere. 'Lord Salisbury saw Mr. Chamberlain last night who is a shrewd political observer,' wrote the Prime Minister to the Queen (June 3rd, '92).[3] 'He said he had never known an occasion when the future was so impenetrable. Any kind of surprise in any direction was on the cards.'

J. CHAMBERLAIN.

"10 TO 1 ON URGENCY!"

Nevertheless, Chamberlain spared no effort to make the surprise be of the right kind for the Unionist cause. Since it was a foregone conclusion that Gladstone, if returned, would attempt another Home Rule measure, he played the 'Orange Card' (as Randolph Churchill had earlier termed it) for all he was worth with the English Nonconformists and at the same time appealed to the working classes with a Radical social programme which he blandly claimed was only likely to be realized by a Unionist Government—Gladstone being too obsessed with Home Rule to bother with social reform.

Incidentally the latter argument was not as specious as it may at first appear, since Gladstone, being of the old individualist, *laissez-faire* school of Liberalism, had never been enamoured of Social Reform. This was a fact which had enabled Disraeli to seize the magic slogan for his revived and re-educated Tory

[1] Winston Churchill: *Great Contemporaries*, 73. [2] Garvin, II, 539.
[3] *Letters of Queen Victoria*, Third Series, Vol. II, 123.

Party. In the already quoted letter of 1885 to Lord Acton in which Gladstone denounced Tory Democracy as 'demagogism', he also declared that 'the Liberalism of today is better . . . yet far from being good. Its pet idea is what they call construction,—that is to say, taking into the hands of the State the business of the individual man. Both the one and the other have much to estrange me, and have had for many, many years.'[1]

Be this as it may, to Lord Salisbury, his ally's electoral promises and arguments, however well-intentioned and to some extent logical, were more than a little embarrassing. He therefore had to beg Chamberlain, in Garvin's words, 'to remember the susceptibilities of his allies and not to suggest too strenuously that the Conservative Party had become an agency for accomplishing his old Radical purposes'.[2] In a most gentle letter (June 22nd, '91) he alluded to 'the particular corn in the Tory foot which I want you to spare'. i.e. '. . . if you say that they have given in on all the points on which you differed from them in 1885—you give them an uncomfortable feeling that they have deserted their colours and changed their coats'.[3] After that Chamberlain confined himself more to the Home Rule issue.

As we have seen, Salisbury always had his eye on the delicate balance which he felt the Tory Party should maintain between the interests of the 'classes' and the 'masses'—though he tended to treat with irritable scorn what he regarded as the groundless phobias of certain sections of the former. According to his biographer he used to say at this time that though he himself had approved such progressive measures as the Local Government and Free Education Acts 'he looked upon them as electioneeringly damaging for the discontent which they had engendered among the old established Tories in the country: "You may say that they cannot vote against you, but they won't trouble to vote for you, and you'll find it out at the polls." He attributed the loss of this election [1892] as a whole largely to that cause.'[4]

Until nearly the end the Gladstonians had been counting on a majority of about 100 seats; but there were definite signs that Chamberlain's tireless campaign, especially in regard to Ulster, was making its mark upon the electorate. Old Lord Cranbrook noted in his diary (January 30th): '. . . If I may judge from

[1] Morley, III, 173.
[2] Garvin, II, 545.
[3] Ibid.
[4] Cecil, IV, 401–2.

what I hear, the experts on either side are very satisfied and it is said that Akers-Douglas, a good authority, rather inclined to an adverse majority of 28 or 30. After my experience of 1880 I shall be surprised at nothing, but I do not lose hope.'[1]

Akers-Douglas's forecast turned out to be fairly near the mark, for in the result the Gladstonian-cum-Irish Nationalist majority was 40. Moreover, the English constituencies, as distinct from Scotland and Wales, returned Unionists in a majority of 71, so that it was said that the scales had only been turned by the 'Celtic fringe'. Gladstone's own majority at Midlothian dropped from 4,000 to 690. The real triumph of the elections was scored by Chamberlain, who retained his seat at Birmingham West by a majority of over 4,000—the largest he had ever had—while throughout his area Unionists won by immense majorities and gained 3 or more seats from the Gladstonians. At the end of the election in the Counties of Warwick, Worcester and Stafford they held 30 seats out of 39. Akers-Douglas, as in 1886, was again returned unopposed—'seeing that there is practically no Radical organization in the division, it is not to be wondered at', as a Kent paper observed.

The truth was that though the usual desire for change at any price after six years of one Government had just succeeded in making itself felt, nevertheless Gladstone had outlived the time when he could bind the electorate with a spell. Moreover, while Home Rule had become his monomania, with the majority of the population it was already a declining interest. In their 'Newcastle Programme' his party tried to cover those other questions which already loomed larger and which had been pushed into the background by the Home Rule issue, but Gladstone no longer wanted to know anything about these and scarcely troubled to pretend that he did. 'Everything now depends upon the extent of our men's attendance at the House,' wrote Sir Henry James to Akers-Douglas (July 18th). 'If they will only be assiduous and constant in attending Divisions we can wear the Gladstonians down in six months. We ought to stir up everybody to think of nothing else but defeating Mr. G.—and this they cannot do unless they will make some sacrifices of time and convenience. I will answer for our small force of 44 . . . I am full of fight all round.'

[1] A. E. Gathorne Hardy: *Gathorne Hardy, First Earl of Cranbrook*, II, 331.

The actual state of the parties in the new Parliament was:

Gladstonians	269	Conservatives	269
Labour	5	Liberal Unionists	46
Irish Nat.	81		
	355		315

The two main adversaries were therefore exactly even and in view of the composite nature of the majority opposing him (even the Nationalists were divided into Parnellites and anti-Parnellites) and the lack of clarity about its combined intentions, Salisbury resolved to meet Parliament. 'On second thoughts,' he wrote to Akers-Douglas (July 24th), 'I think I will *not* send out a summons to the Peers. The form always used contains a statement that important business is coming forward: which is grossly and manifestly false. The same reasoning of course does not apply to the House of Commons.'

When Parliament met the Opposition naturally moved an Amendment to the Address on the grounds of want of confidence. Chamberlain in one of his most brilliant speeches pointed out that they (the Opposition) were going into office without a word of explanation as to what they would do when they got there. Everyone knew of course that what they would do would be to introduce a new Home Rule Bill, but, as in 1886, Gladstone would not consent to acquaint his colleagues with the details of the scheme beforehand. Ironically, the mover of the Amendment was Asquith, who was known to have pressed inconveniently for such details. Chamberlain was able to point, too, to the known disagreement between the Liberal leaders and John Redmond, leader of the Irish, and to the fact that the latter, holding the balance as they did, could make nonsense of Gladstone's nominal majority.

For all this, however, the Liberal–Irish combination carried their no-confidence vote by their full 40 majority, and Salisbury had to make way for Gladstone who, at the age of 83, took office for the fourth time.

A most amusing comment on the downfall of the great ministry appeared in the Christmas (1892) number of *Truth*—the paper founded, owned and edited by Labouchere. The best part of this consisted in an extremely witty cartoon, parodying a well-known picture of the scene after the Battle of Inkerman, where Lord Salisbury appeared as the Commander-in-Chief reviewing the exhausted and wounded remnant of the Guards (the Tory Front Bench), while Akers-Douglas, still jaunty, but with a bandaged head, was the Sergeant reading the roll-call. The familiar and extremely unmilitary countenances of Balfour, Goschen, Webster and others are pitifully woebegone and are rendered all the more ludicrous by their huge bearskins, rifles and other military trappings. In the accompanying verses Labby was able to get in another jab at 'Judas' Chamberlain:

All your Tories, need I tell you? as they neared the crucial day,
Were cocksure—at least they said so—they'd be victors in the fray.
If two met, and one was doubtful, then the other straightaway cried,
'You forget the Liberal traitors, bribed to fight upon our side.
If alone, we should be beaten, but with Judas's good aid,
We are bound to win the battle, so you needn't be afraid.'

Well, you know what 'twas that happened, how, in spite of brag and
    boast,
Your great Leader and his army overthrew the Tory host.
But you did not see as I did, what ensued when all was lost,
And the Marquis met his forces to learn what defeat had cost . . .

'Form up,' the Marquis cried, 'my men!'
  (His mirth scarce neath control)
'Form up! and Akers-Douglas then
  Shall call the muster-roll.'
And as the Sergeant with his book
  Went slowly down the line,
Their leader thus, with sneering look,
  Addressed his veterans fine:—

'Well, well,' he cried, 'the fight is done,
  And one good look at you
Shows plainly you've defeated been,
  And pretty badly too;
And yet it's clear you all incline
  To form "the Roll-Call's" famous line.

'Now why is this? What makes you hit
  Upon this fatuous plan?
The Guards you're imitating *won*
  The day at Inkerman.
But you——'
                  They hoarsely cried 'And we
  Have won a Moral Victoree!'

The Marquis laughed, 'He! he, Ha! ha!'
  In tones supremely mocking;
'For Moral Victors, then,' he said,
  'You do, indeed, look shocking.
Does poor old Goschen's face, e.g.,
  Suggest a Moral Victoree?

'Saint Webster, he seems somewhat glum,
  De Worms[1] is even glummer,
And Matthews—well, he doesn't look
  Quite like an overcomer;
My nephew, too, d'you think that *he*
  Suspects a Moral Victoree?

'There's Ritchie, he seems killed outright
  And I've no tears to spare him,
He was a Rad at heart like Gorst,
  And I could never bear him.
But though he's fallen I don't see
  That helps your Moral Victoree.

'And look at Stanhope—seemingly
  His grief he cannot stifle;
And Plunkett, not too cheery, eh,
  A-leaning on his rifle;
These two I think would scarce agree
  You've won a Moral Victoree.

'At any rate, we'll wait a bit,
  Say till next Quarter-day,
And when you find you've *nil* to draw
  For perquisites and pay—
I wonder if you'll still tell me
  You've won a Moral Victoree? . . .'

[1] Baron de Worms. Late Under Secretary of State for Colonies.

XIII
IN OPPOSITION

As his admirably impartial daughter and biographer did not hesitate to remark, Lord Salisbury's platform effusions were often a source of considerable embarrassment—and irritation—to his colleagues.[1] Thus on May 12th, 1892, in a speech at Hastings at a conference of the National Union of Conservative Associations he launched into an argument about the damaging effect upon British trade of the 'brazen wall of protection' which foreign countries were raising round their shores and hinted that in self-defence Britain might be compelled to adopt the same course. This seeming threat to the doctrine of Free Trade (which for the last sixty years had prevailed almost without question in Britain) shook his contemporaries and raised the old spectre of 'dear bread'. Sir William Harcourt, in a speech shortly afterwards, maliciously added to the Tories' discomfiture by describing Salisbury as being 'a terrible trial to his friends' and added that after each of his speeches there was a sheaf of letters from the private secretaries explaining that the Prime Minister had never said what everyone understood him to say, and that at all events, if he said it he did not mean it.

One of Salisbury's own colleagues who bore witness to the truth of Harcourt's tilt was Walter Long, late Secretary to the Local Government Board, who considered that he owed the loss of his seat (Devizes) in the election entirely to the

[1] See ante p. 89–90 and Cecil, III, 198.

above 'indiscretion' of his Chief. He wrote wryly to Akers-Douglas:

Rood Ashton,
Trowbridge
July 11. '92.

My dear Bob,

A bad blow for me and quite unexpected till that last week when they produced their dear bread cry and quoted L^{d}. S's Hastings speech: there is no doubt I owe my defeat *entirely* to that speech: the labourers are an ignorant lot and swallowed it whole. —I enjoyed my time with you all very much and shall now look on. My people of course want me to stand again but I cannot, it is too expensive and too much hard work—over 90 villages—a district 30 miles by 40 and but 6 resident Squires over the whole—so I shall make, or rather have made, my bow. If at any time I can be of any use you know you can command my services such as they are—Let me thank you with all my heart for many kindnesses and congratulate you upon the way you have done your work. We owe you and your 'boys' more than we can hope to express.

Won't the 'Chief' chuckle at the defeat of the 'Nihilist'—little dreaming that he has caused it himself? You may be sure that when I think of his splendid services at the F.O. etc. I don't owe him any grudge for this personal knock. The G.O.M. will be in a tight place and you will be able to do with him as you like—poor, old chap, they are all on to him.

Don't reply.

Of course I feel this jib as it is severing a very old connection—but it can't be helped.

St. John[1] had that sneak Gorst well.

Ever yours,
Walter H. Long.

However, despite the valedictory vein in which this letter was written, Long was returned to Parliament again in the following year (for Liverpool—West Derby Division) and continued a highly successful political career, culminating in his being First Lord of the Admiralty, 1919–21, while he very nearly succeeded Balfour as Party leader in 1911.

Meanwhile Akers-Douglas continued in his old post—only

[1] St. John Brodrick (later Earl of Midleton), M.P. S.W. Surrey, Financial Secretary to War Office (1886–92) Secretary of State for War (1900–3) and for India (1903–5).

6. The Home Rule Card Game.

Churchill Salisbury Parnell Gladstone Chamberlain

7. Reading the Queen's Speech, I. Ministerial dinner given by the Rt. Hon. W. H. Smith, M.P., as Leader

1. Sir Edward Clarke, M.P., Solicitor General; 2. Rt. Hon. David Plunket, M.P., Office of Works; 3. Rt. Hon. D. H. Madden, M.P., Atty. Genl. Ireland; 4. Mr. Walter Long, M.P., Local Govt. Board (Absent); 5. Rt. Hon. W. Hart Dyke, M.P., Education Dept.; 6. Mr. E. Ashmead Bartlett, M.P., Admiralty (Absent); 7. Viscount Lewisham, M.P., Royal Household; 8. Rt. Hon. H. C. Raikes, M.P., Post Master General; 9. Rt. Hon. E. Stanhope, M.P., Secy. for War; 10. Sir W. Walrond, Bart., M.P., Treasury; 11. Hon. W. St. J. Brodrick, M.P., War Office; 12. Hon. Sidney Herbert, M.P., Treasury; 13. Mr. Forrest Fulton, M.P., Seconder of Address; 14. Mr. C. J. Maude, Private Secretary; 15. Colonel Kenyon Slaney, M.P., Mover of Address; 16. Rt. Hon. Sir J. Gorst, M.P., India Office; 17. Rt. Hon. Baron H. de Worms, M.P., Colonial Office; 18. Rt. Hon. W. H. Smith, M.P., First Lord of Treasury; 19. Mr. A. B. Forwood, M.P., Secretary to Admiralty; 20. Rt. Hon. Sir M. Hicks Beach, Bart., M.P., Board of Trade; 21. Rt. Hon. Lord George Hamilton, M.P., First Lord Admiralty; 22. Lord Burghley, M.P., Royal Household; 23. Rt. Hon. G. J. Goschen, M.P., Chancellor of Exchequer.

8. Reading the Queen's Speech, II. Ministerial dinner given by the Rt. Hon. W. H. Smith, M.P., as Leader of the House of Commons on the eve of the opening of Parliament, 3 Grosvenor Place,

1. Rt. Hon. Sir James Fergusson, Bart., M.P., Foreign Office; 2. Sir Herbert Maxwell, Bart., M.P., Treasury; 3. Mr. C. B. Stuart Wortley, M.P., Home Office; 4. Rt. Hon. W. L. Jackson, M.P., Financial Secy. Treasury; 5. Rt. Hon. Lord Arthur Hill, M.P., Royal Household; 6. Mr. A. Ákers-Douglas, M.P., Par. Secy. Treasury; 7. Mr. J. Luard Pattisson, Private Secretary; 8. Sir Richard Webster, M.P., Attorney General; 9. Rt. Hon. A. J. Balfour, M.P., Chief Secy. Ireland; 10. Rt. Hon. H. Chaplin, M.P., Prest. Bd. of Agriculture; 11. Rt. Hon. P. J. Robertson, M.P., Lord Advocate; 12. Rt. Hon. Lord George Hamilton, M.P., First Lord Admy.; 13. Rt. Hon. Sir W. T. Marriott, M.P., Judge Adv. Genl.; 14. Rt. Hon. W. H. Smith, M.P., First Lord of Treasury; 15. Rt. Hon. A. Peel, M.P., The Speaker (Absent); 16. Colonel Kenyon Slaney, M.P., Mover of Address; 17. Rt. Hon. C. T. Ritchie, M.P., Prest. Local Govt. Board; 18. Mr. Forrest Fulton, M.P., Seconder of Address; 19. Rt. Hon. Henry Matthews, M.P., Home Secretary.

9. 'The Roll-Call', *Truth* cartoon 1892.

Salisbury Akers-Douglas Webster Goschen Matthews Chaplin Balfour
Ritchie

10. Lord Salisbury. *Spy* cartoon of *c.* 1895.

11. Rt. Hon. A. Akers-Douglas, M.P., from the painting by A. S. Cope, 1910.

now as Chief Opposition Whip. The man, however, who had been his opposite number throughout the last Parliament, Arnold Morley, gave place to another.

> I may tell you [he wrote to Akers-Douglas (Aug. 15th, '92)] that I am not going on in my present post, and I am glad to take this opportunity of saying how satisfactory to me have been our relations during the past 6½ years. I know of no one else who could have filled your position, with whom I could have worked more harmoniously or with less friction.

The new Liberal Chief Whip was the buoyant and bearded Edward Marjoribanks, later as Lord Tweedmouth to become First Lord of the Admiralty (1905) and Lord President of the Council (1908). Harcourt became Chancellor of the Exchequer, Rosebery Foreign Secretary (with Edward Grey as Under Secretary), Asquith Home Secretary and John Morley Irish Secretary.

As was generally anticipated, Gladstone lost no time in appointing a small cabinet committee to work out a new Home Rule Bill, and in the meantime the operation of the Crimes Act in Ireland was suspended by proclamation. But the novelty of the Home Rule issue had worn off since its first appearance six and a half years earlier and in those years everything for and against had been said and re-said *ad nauseam.* Moreover, if Gladstone had been secretive about his plans on the first occasion, he was still exasperatingly possessive and unbending about them now.

> We said the other day [wrote a newspaper at this time] that Mr. Gladstone's great lack was the possession of such a Whip as Mr. Akers-Douglas, who is in touch with everybody and who is very frank in expressing his opinions. Perhaps we are wrong. Mr. Gladstone's great lack is in these his later days any readiness, or even capacity, to accept new lights on the question which preoccupies his mind; and no others interest him at all. His whole party at the present moment is in commotion, but he even resents the efforts of his colleagues to sound the depth of the channel through which he would have to pass.

Meanwhile, the metamorphosis of Hartington into the Duke of Devonshire and the consequent succession of Chamberlain to the leadership of the Liberal Unionists had caused Goschen to re-examine his position. After consulting Devonshire, who sympathized with his difficult position ('. . . in confidence I think that Chamberlain . . . will be more at ease when he knows of your decision'[1]), he resolved upon formally joining the Conservative Party.

Private

Seacox Heath,
Hawkhurst
11.1.93

My dear Akers-Douglas,

The time has come when I have resolved to take the step which you and I have sometimes discussed, viz: to join the Carlton. In this New Parliament I must either take my seat with the Conservatives or the Liberal Unionists, and I am quite clear as to my wish to continue to act with my late colleagues and—with the late Whips. Will you therefore take the necessary steps or at all events let me know how these matters are generally managed.

I have written to Hartington to tell him what I propose to do.

I hope you are flourishing and prepared for vigorous action. Soon after Balfour comes, we ought to meet. Hartington writes to me that Chamberlain is full of fight and James in high spirits.

Believe me,
Yours very sincerely,
George J. Goschen.

Akers-Douglas, having conveyed the news of the final capitulation of this citadel in their midst to Salisbury, the latter wrote back from France: '. . . Of course, I shall be delighted to propose Goschen at the Carlton. I think he is quite right to belong to it . . . The Government seem to keep their secret very well—which may mean there is none to keep . . .' And Balfour wrote:

> . . . Certainly put down S. and me as proposing and seconding Goschen. He is quite right to join the Carlton . . . I have heard from Joe. Very cheerful. Has settled provisionally with Hartington on an amendment to the Address—but is apparently afraid to commit it to the post—so I shall not know what it is till Sat. week when I come to town . . .

Not till February 1893, did Gladstone disclose the new Home Rule Bill to the House of Commons. Its discussion occupied the

[1] Elliot, II, 197.

House for eighty sittings spaced over six months, but withal in a peculiar atmosphere of unreality, since not only was there little new to be said on matters of principle, but it was generally recognized that however far the Bill might get in the Commons it would receive short shrift in the Lords. In fact the Liberals, in Asquith's phrase, were 'ploughing the sands'. Moreover, under the new Bill it was proposed to do that which in 1886 Gladstone had declared to be impossible, namely to keep Irish members to the number of 80 at Westminster while refusing them the right of voting on questions exclusively British.

This 'in and out' scheme, as it was called, was not surprisingly torn to shreds in the Commons, yet the Bill which ultimately went to the Lords contained the equally illogical provision that the 80 Irish Members should be retained at Westminster for all purposes. Thus British affairs, including the choice and control of a British Government, would have been placed at the mercy of the Irish representatives, who themselves would be in no way responsible to the British electorate, while Britain could have no control over Irish affairs or legislation. Expressed in the more demagogic language of Chamberlain 'the interests of Great Britain were to be controlled by delegates nominated by priests, elected by illiterates, subsidized by the enemies of their country'.[1] Indeed, it was really altogether Chamberlain's session, for the desperate shifts to which the Government had to have recourse in the matter of Irish representation afforded wonderful scope for his brilliant powers of debate.

During the Committee stage of the Home Rule Bill (May 1893) there was a rumpus about the slackness in attendance on the part of some of the Unionist members—despite the five-line Whips issued by Akers-Douglas—resulting in deceptively large majorities for the Government. With their usual dexterity—and, of course, high motives—the press (especially the pro-Unionist organs) managed to work up a general feeling of alarm and despondency.

> It begins to be evident that there is something wrong with the party discipline of the Unionists [wrote the *Daily Graphic* (May 19th, '93)] The normal Gladstonian majority is only forty-three; but in a number of divisions in Committee on points to which

[1] Asquith: *Fifty Years of Parliament*, I, 208.

> Unionists attach, and ought to attach, a high importance, they have been victorious by majorities running well into the fifties and sixties. It is not surprising, under the circumstances, that Home Rulers profess to draw the inference that their opponents are disheartened and disorganized, and conscious that they are fighting a losing battle. Of course the inference has no warrant; the Unionist party was never in better heart than it is today; but at the same time the opportunity of drawing such damaging inferences ought not to be given. It is freely reported that a certain number of Conservative members have ignored five-line whips without giving Mr. Akers-Douglas any explanation of their absence.

And the *St. James's Gazette* of the same date declared that 'it is the figures of the divisions that go out to the world and . . . this is how the civilized world is deceived. And that is why Mr. Akers-Douglas must put his foot down smartly after Whitsuntide and let his followers know that shirking at this crisis cannot be tolerated.'

The Times, however, even went so far as to publish a 'black list' of members who were absent from divisions on the Home Rule Bill, which caused considerable feeling among the Unionists, who complained it was grossly unfair, since it took no account of 'pairs'. 'Besides,' wrote the *Bradford Observer* (May 30th), adding fuel to the fire, 'there are some gentlemen who will not be intimidated by this means into constant attendance at the House, and one or two have told Mr. Akers-Douglas so quite plainly . . . One gentleman in this position has gone so far as to resign his seat.' The same paper wrote next day: 'I hear that the Tory Whips have privately appealed to *The Times* and other Tory journals to publish no more black lists of defaulting members. Mr. Akers-Douglas is regarded as responsible for the publication of the list last week. I believe that he had nothing to do with it, but has been overwhelmed with reproaches . . .', etc., etc.

Actually Akers-Douglas had written to Salisbury:

> Carlton Club
> May 19 [1893]
>
> Dear Lord Salisbury,
>
> The papers are complaining loudly at the attendance of our party in the division lobbies—and I understand that Buckle[1] is

[1] Editor of *The Times*.

going to pillory some of our men in an article in the Times—I have urged him through McDonnell not to do so, as I am sure the policy is a bad one. They don't mind being damned collectively but will deeply resent being named.

There are really only two or three malingerers—and some have shaky seats where it will be unwise to weaken them by showing bad attendance.

As a matter of fact the daily attendance has been excellent—better even than during the last Parliament.

The fault I have most to complain of is that while the men come here every day and are in force from 5 to 7 and from 10.30 to 12 they are apt to run away to dinner sometimes unpaired and if paired to come back 20 minutes after their pair has expired. It is fair to say that pairs are very hard to obtain—while we have 310 men most of whom are on the look out for dinners their 350 for pairing purposes is reduced to 240 by subtracting the 80 Irish and 25 Government men and the Labour men who decline to pair . . .

The chief reason of the larger majorities is really to be found in the attendances of some 6 or 7 men a night at meetings in the country, who go unpaired rather than throw over their engagements. I do not see how to keep up the majorities to normal for the amendments of minor importance unless we stop all our meetings in the country—and maintain the same conspiracy of silence as our opponents. This I think would be a pity as our accounts from the Country are most encouraging . . .

Yours truly,
A. Akers-Douglas.[1]

But Lord Salisbury's cold, logical mind was in any case totally unaffected by what he evidently considered as a groundless and rather hysterical commotion.

Private

May 20, '93.

My dear Douglas,

Many thanks for your letter and the list. I agree with you in regretting Buckle's attack. Indeed I am unable to see what it is that excites his and Mudford's[2] apprehensions. You are as hopelessly beaten when you divide 40 as when you divide 60 less than your adversary. Where are we injured by the larger majorities? The only possible injury that can be suggested is that electors who are becoming Unionist in the constituencies will return to their

[1] Salisbury MSS. [2] Editor of The *Standard*.

separatist ideas, on seeing that a score of our men have failed to attend, on a set of divisions where they could not possibly have affected the issue by attending.

I cannot find out that anybody has seen or heard of any individual elector, who is endowed with this peculiar constitution of mind. I believe the whole cry to be insane, merely indicating that a certain number of people have been made excited and nervous by the fighting.

Ever yours truly,
Salisbury.

Nevertheless, by the time Parliament reassembled after the Whitsuntide recess, the press were claiming that their campaign had already borne fruit. *The Morning Post* (May 31st, '93) announced that Akers-Douglas had 'taken up the matter with the same vigour that he exercised when the party was in power and he has now got all the members of the party well in hand . . . delinquents have been privately written to or remonstrated with, and the party machine is now articulated to a nicety . . .' 'All pairs for social engagements are to be peremptorily forbidden, and none will be recognized unless sanctioned by the Whips. In short Mr. Akers-Douglas intends to insist upon the discipline of a martinet and any show of rebellion will be promptly dealt with.' The same day the *Pall Mall Gazette* also congratulated him on his success: 'The reduction of the Government majority from the normal figure of forty to twenty-one is the direct result of the reorganization of the party machinery . . .'

But of course there had really been no such upheaval as a 'reorganization of the party machinery'. The whole episode was a nice example of the magnification and distortion of an insignificant symptom into a sort of 'scandal' by a press claiming, as usual, to be carrying out a patriotic if painful duty and ending by creating a troubled but entirely imaginary situation.

After his unfortunate intervention in the debate on the Report of the Parnell Commission in March 1890 Lord Randolph Churchill had lost interest in the House of Commons, attending seldom and never speaking. The following year he went to South Africa, returning only in the early part of 1892 when the General Election was clearly impending. Naturally there was considerable curiosity—and anxiety—among the Tory ranks as to what his future line was going to be. When the South Paddington Conservative Association inquired whether he proposed to stand again and 'whether he would support the general policy of the Conservative Party',[1] his equivocal reply that he would stand and that he would 'give to the Tory Party the same support which I have given to it since the year 1874'[2] did not do much to dispel anxiety. However, in the event, he only made one quite orthodox speech and was returned unopposed.

Lord Randolph now began tentatively to reappear in the House, where he was very kindly received on all sides and urged by the Tory leaders to sit again on the Front Bench. But, alas, despite this happy atmosphere of friendliness and reconciliation, his reappearance in their midst made all too clear to his friends the terrible change which a ghastly disease was wreaking on him. The first real indication came when he rose to speak on the occasion of the introduction of the Home Rule Bill. His son and biographer has poignantly described how incredible it seemed to the crowded House that 'this bald and bearded man' with shaking hands, white face and tremulous voice could be the same as the brilliant, audacious and irresistible young leader of a few years earlier. But a week later he recovered his confidence, for the *Birmingham Gazette* (April 19th, '93) reported:

> Lord Randolph came down to the House early to start the debate on Home Rule. His colleagues began to drop in after him, and with several of them, notably Lord George Hamilton, Mr. Edward Stanhope and Mr. Akers-Douglas he held animated and mirthful conversation. Mr. Balfour was the last to arrive, Lord Randolph being already on his legs when the Opposition leader hurried into the place kept for him, which was next to where the orator stood at his desk to destroy the Bill. Lord Randolph was not in the slashing, but in the statesmans-like mood. He had evidently made a critical analysis of the Bill, and the fruits of his research formed a magnificent contribution to the debate. Although a closely-reasoned argument, the speech was not without sparkle and brilliant outbursts . . .

Throughout this period, Lord Randolph was in constant correspondence with his old crony Lord Justice FitzGibbon, who,

[1] Churchill, 738. [2] Ibid.

in his biographer's words, 'Kept him supplied with an inexhaustible stream of fact and fancy upon the Irish Bill.'[1] One of the provisions of the Bill debarred Trinity College, Dublin, from sending a member to the proposed new Legislative Assembly and Lord Randolph in a speech on the Second Reading had bitterly complained of this and other great secular institutions being 'left at the mercy of the Irish Parliament'. Thus, a few days later, in the midst of the continuing debate, when Edward Carson, the brilliant young member for Dublin University, was answering the speech of the Irish leader, Thomas Sexton, Akers-Douglas received a frantic note in shaky writing:

April 20, 1893
50, Grosvenor Square,
W.

Dear Akers-Douglas,

Give the enclosed to Carson and ask him to look at it before he speaks. It is very important and from FitzGibbon. It is also important for Carson to clear up that Trinity College matter.

Yours ever,
Randolph S. C.

On top of this Akers-Douglas scribbled the reply: 'Too late—but he has dealt very well with it.'

Throughout the remainder of the session he increased his political activities both inside and outside the House to the tempo of former years—though these activities were seldom accompanied with the same success, indeed often with failure. The realization of his failing powers roused him to immense exertions. During May and June he addressed no fewer than ten important meetings and—great and final triumph—he got himself adopted as Conservative candidate for the Central Division of Bradford. The conquest of this great northern commercial centre was a burning ambition on a par with his old longings for Birmingham. To gather his rapidly failing strength for a great campaign in this exciting new field he left England before the close of the Session to do a cure at Kissingen and Gastein. From the latter place he wrote on August 27th, 1893, to Akers-Douglas:

. . . I do hope my friends have not been vexed with me for having been away in all these difficult businesses since the end of July.

[1] Churchill, 748.

It was absolutely necessary that I should go or I should have been no use to the party in the autumn. But I own to the greatest sympathy with you and yr. colleagues and Arthur in this most unseasonable and unreasonable extension of Parliamentary work and am really sorry I have not been able to give more efficient assistance. I hope you have managed to pick up health fairly well. Hereford[1] was noble and indicates that my prediction made long ago and constantly since that the result of an Election would be 'as in 1886 only better' is sure to come true.

After his return from Germany, Lord Randolph plunged into a tremendous campaign, making speeches up and down the country, 'but the crowds who were drawn by the old glamour of his name departed sorrowful and shuddering at the spectacle of a dying man, and those who loved him were consumed with embarrassment and grief'.[2] Again he had to seek rest abroad. At Christmas that year he repeated for the last time an old and loved routine by going to join his old friend FitzGibbon at Howth in Ireland for the latter's regular Christmas party of 'wise and merry Irishmen'. Just before leaving the Continent to keep this appointment he wrote what was apparently his last letter to Akers-Douglas. The writing is painfully shaky, but the brain is still clear.

Dec. 19, 1893
Le Nid,
Monte Carlo

Dear Akers,

I shall be back in London on Xmas day and shall leave for Ireland (the Howth party) on the 26th. I will be in regular attendance from the 3rd January till the end of Session.

We have had fine weather here on the whole and I think the place and the climate and the rest has done me much good. I have hardly any engagements for speaking and really think I have done enough in that way for some time. You must be worn out all of you, and I should advise making an effort to bring to a close the

[1] The Gladstonian member for Hereford, Grenfell, resigned his seat in protest against the clause in the Home Rule Bill which retained the Irish members at Westminster with full powers over all British affairs yet with no responsibility to the British electorate. At the ensuing by-election the Unionist candidate was returned.

[2] Churchill, 760.

Session in the last days of January. I understand from Morley[1] that we might get the whole of February for a holiday. Morley is very low about everything. He has quite come round to the opinion that I expressed to him at Howth last year that 1894 would be a bad year for them and that the dissolution would take place in that year. He does not see how they can go on till 1895 in view of the awful block of business which will confront the Govt. in June. He is also dissatisfied with Ireland. He is abused by the Irish for carrying out the law—and he has no high opinion of the Irish Party. I have had much talk with him.

I am very anxious about Accrington by-election, nor can I make up my mind if it would be good or bad to win or lose it. If we won it, we might precipitate a dissolution which I don't want till July—But still we ought to win it—I told Rothschild to wire me result. Arthur Balfour has been making 2 or 3 brilliant speeches. Goschen has recanted bimetallism. He said the other day on the India Loans Bill that 'why he could not rally himself to "bimetallism" was to be found in the difficulty of reconciling the claims of creditors and debtors.' That of course is a hopeless problem and I read what he said about it with the greatest pleasure. Morley has gone to Cannes, will go to Ireland before settling down in London and will be over day and night at Howth. I have not been near the rooms; walking and driving as much as possible have been my occupations. Give my love to Arthur and to the gallant band who assist you. Kinloch[2] asked me to extend my pair to end of January—but I wrote to him that I could not do it.

Yours ever,

Randolph S. C.

Lord Randolph struggled on, though his illness was gaining on him by rapid strides and it was not till the following June that he consented to yield to the doctor's orders of complete rest. Then he set off on a round-the-world trip with his wife, but had to cut it short after a few months and return to England with mind and body disintegrating. He lingered for another month at his mother's house and then died on January 24th, 1895.

Meanwhile, after a debate extending over twelve days the Second Reading of the Home Rule Bill was carried by a

[1] John Morley—then Chief Secretary for Ireland.

[2] Sir John Kinloch, Bart.; M.P. E. Div. Co. Perth.

majority of 43 in April 1893. It was not read a third time until September 1st, when it was carried by 301 votes to 267. Only a week later, after four nights of debate, the Lords rejected it by 419 to 41. Gladstone now wanted to dissolve Parliament and appeal to the country on the single issue of Lords versus Commons, but to his immense chagrin was overborne by his colleagues.

After this the next big item on the Government's agenda was the Parish Councils Bill. The majority of Conservatives were not disposed to obstruct this Bill. Their attitude could be summed up in the words used by Akers-Douglas in a speech in his constituency (although it must be admitted that the opening gambit faintly recalled Lord Salisbury's unfortunate gaffe on the same subject a few years earlier). 'Although sceptical as to the attraction of parochial meetings in the evenings, he saw no dreadful revolution in the plan', but 'safeguards must be introduced into the Bill to secure that money should not be voted entirely by people who did not pay rates at the expense of those who did'. A small body of the Conservative opposition, however, were determined to discuss the Bill at great length and in much detail and did in fact move countless amendments. The Government therefore were driven to have frequent recourse to the closure procedure (the 'Gag')—the instrument forged by their predecessors. It is amusing to observe from the following letter from the late Irish Chief Secretary the Unionists' scornful reaction when the weapon was used against themselves.

Allerton Hall,
Leeds
Dec. 30 1893

My dear Douglas,

. . . I hope the old man [Gladstone] will move the 'Gag'. I don't see that it signifies anything except that the course pursued by the Govt. is and has been one continued system of unbusiness-like coercion. The conduct of the bill leads me to doubt whether they want to pass it—they would rather have the Lords to put the blame on and I presume they know that the rejection or rather considerable amendment is certain to a bill not discussed as to all its clauses in the Commons.

I have reason to think that the Govt. is very tired and if I were 'negociating', I should insist on hard terms from the Govt. for any help to them.

Of course you know that the Govt. did seriously consider and enquire as to hanging up or carrying over . . .

Yours v. truly,
W. L. Jackson.

Sure enough, the Lords whittled down the Bill to a shadow of its original self (January 1894). Meanwhile the Government received another severe blow over the Employers' Liability Bill, when an amendment, proposed by one of their supporters and intended to mitigate the already extensive amendments to the Bill by the Lords, was only carried by two votes. The scene on this occasion was described by the *Birmingham Gazette* (February 14th, '93).

> . . . When the figures were read out in tremulous tones by Mr. Cobb [mover of the amendment] while Mr. Akers-Douglas stood by him smiling down to his boots, there went up such a Unionist cheer as seldom is heard in Parliament . . . Meanwhile, from Mr. Gladstone downwards, the Ministerialists presented the appearance of baffled, crushed and saddened men. The Premier looked awful; his face was almost ghastly. Well might he feel ill, for it was the death-blow of his Government. The Cabinet may rally a bit, but no ministry lives on a majority of two . . .

Not surprisingly the Bill was subsequently abandoned by the Government. Indeed, as a result of these humiliations, Gladstone—though he had already decided upon final retirement owing to his increasing infirmity—again urged upon his colleagues that there should be an immediate dissolution and an appeal to the Country on the Lords v. Commons issue. But, being again overborne by his colleagues and being in disagreement with them upon other issues as well, he determined to lose no time in carrying out his resolve to resign. In his last speech in the House of Commons on March 1st, 1894, he announced the Government's reluctant acceptance of the changes made by the Lords in the Parish Councils Bill, but he ended with words which were virtually a call to battle against the Upper House.

In view of this there was some irony in the fact that Gladstone was succeeded in the premiership by a peer—Lord Rosebery. Nevertheless, though this particular choice was made by the Queen, who did not even consult Gladstone, the latter's own choice would still have been a peer, namely Lord Spencer. The man who at first sight would have appeared to be the obvious successor, Sir William Harcourt, was strongly opposed in that capacity by his colleagues; but he knew that he was essential to any Liberal government and he accordingly made his own terms for serving under Lord Rosebery. He agreed to remain Chancellor of the Exchequer with the Leadership of the House of Commons on condition that he saw all Foreign Office papers, had some control over patronage and was free to act on occasion without consulting the Premier.

Harcourt's conditions may not appear quite so extravagant when we consider that both the Premier and the Foreign Secretary, who was Lord Kimberley, were in the Lords and that consequently a far greater responsibility than usual fell on the shoulders of the Leader of the House of Commons. Nevertheless, given the extremely difficult character of Harcourt and the diffidence of Rosebery, it was from the first a most uneasy—and, indeed, hopeless—arrangement. Other personal jealousies and political differences seethed within this Cabinet, so that, taken in conjunction with their small and precarious majority in the House of Commons and their hopeless minority in the Lords, the prospect of such a government enduring, let alone achieving anything, was infinitesimal. They were dependent on the support of the Irish members, and these were themselves now divided into two factions of uncertain behaviour. Moreover, Marjoribanks, who had proved a most efficient Chief Whip, had now become a peer and had been succeeded in that office by the rather inexperienced Tom Ellis. Thus for instance we read in a newspaper report of May 5th, 1894, that 'the smallness of the Government majority on the second reading of the Registration Bill yesterday was due partly to Parnellite abstentions and partly to the failure of the Treasury and Anti-Parnellite Whips to bring up the whole of their forces'.

The one and only—but considerable—claim to fame of the Rosebery Ministry was the Budget of 1894, which was, of course, the handiwork of Harcourt. The outstanding feature of this Budget was a revolution in the Death Duties which put land for the first time on the same footing as other kinds of property. When both Houses of Parliament were still mainly composed of landowners the outcry was naturally tremendous. Yet it was not without some hesitation—and indeed considerable misgivings among some of them—that the Tory Opposition decided to give battle on the issue.

> They are not sure that the Government would not cheerfully go out of office on the Budget, and they know that this would be the worst possible thing for the Unionist Party [wrote the London correspondent of the *Leeds Mercury* (May 8th, '94)]. Under no conditions are they eager for a general election at the present moment, but if they are to throw out the Government, they are anxious that it should be over something else than the Budget, which, however unpopular it may be with the landed classes and the liquor interest,[1] is assuredly acceptable to the country at large.

Nevertheless, it was decided to divide against the Second Reading of the Budget Bill (May 11th, '94) and in the event, mainly through Akers-Douglas's energetic whipping, the decision was justified, for the Government majority was reduced to 14 and its weakness thus further exposed. A newspaper commented next day:

> A majority of fourteen was a fall such as had never been dreamt of. It may easily be explained away, but the effect of it still remains. It has indeed changed the whole political situation. More than anything else the smallness of the majority was due to the lukewarmness of the Radicals . . . Six or seven Nationalists and half-a-dozen Radicals abstained because they do not care for the Government Bill [i.e. the beer and spirit duty part]. In addition to these the Redmondites all abstained. Thus some twenty-two votes were lost . . . while on the other side the splendid whipping of Mr. Akers-Douglas brought nearly every man into the division lobby.

This was the first hint of the imminent and complete defection of the 'Redmondites' which was to be one of the final blows to the Government. It now looked, as the *Pall Mall Gazette* (May 25th, '94) put it, 'as though the chief difficulty of the Unionists' will be to save the Government from a defeat which may be premature and inopportune'.

However, in the subsequent debates and divisions on the Budget Bill, though the struggle was fierce and prolonged and many amendments were moved, the Government held its own

[1] Apart from the Death Duties reform, the duty on beer and spirits was to be increased.

and obtained more adequate majorities. At its Third Reading on July 17th an amendment by Sir John Lubbock[1] for the rejection of the Bill was defeated by 283 to 263. It passed the House of Lords without a division, though naturally not without vigorous protests. Indeed, they would scarcely have rejected it owing to the time-honoured tradition regarding 'money bills'.

On August 21st, just before Parliament was prorogued, there was another more serious revolt on the part of all the Irish Nationalists, plus a few Radicals, over a vote on salaries and expenses for officers of the Crown in the House of Lords, because, in the words of one of them (Dillon) 'during the evening we had seen Mr. Akers-Douglas cross the House and enter into conversation with the Government Whips; and from this we naturally concluded that the Government were making an arrangement with their enemies behind the backs of their supporters, and were throwing over their own allies.'

In this singularly inauspicious atmosphere the administration limped along. The arrangements made between Rosebery and Harcourt for linking up the team never really came into being—indeed Asquith has asserted that during the greater part of 1894 the two leaders were 'barely on speaking terms'.[2] And, in a remarkable letter to Lord Spencer, who had tried to appeal to his better instincts, Harcourt wrote (September 21st '94): '... As you know, I am not a supporter of the present Government. I have a great personal regard for all of you, and contemplate your proceedings with an impartial curiosity and a benevolent neutrality ...'[3] This from the Leader of the House and Chancellor of the Exchequer!

Scarcely surprising, then, that with the opening of the new session in January 1895 there began to be talk of a dissolution and a general election, for the Parnellites under Redmond now definitely went over to the Opposition and Rosebery threatened to resign on grounds of not being sufficiently defended or supported by his colleagues.

[1] M.P. London University; Chairman of L.C.C.; later 1st Baron Avebury.
[2] Asquith, op. cit., I, 224. [3] Gardiner, II, 307.

XIV
THE ALLIANCE IN THE BALANCE

MEANWHILE efforts were being made to fuse together more closely the elements of the Unionist alliance with a view to forming, as soon as their turn came, a joint administration with a common policy. Thus in January 1895, just before the new session opened, the press observed 'that Mr. Chamberlain joined with Mr. Balfour in the Saturday to Monday visit to Lord Salisbury at Hatfield' and that 'after the visit the result of the deliberations of the three leaders was communicated to Mr. Akers-Douglas'.

Conditions, however, were still very far from favourable for the realization of such an ideal. There was still considerable mistrust of Chamberlain among the Tories—and not only among the older die-hards—and in the Midlands in particular there was a good deal of jealousy of Chamberlain's great personal prestige, as well as of what was rather naturally considered to be the over-representation of Liberal Unionism in those parts. None of this was lost upon the alert intelligence of the 'Great Joe', needless to say, and it made him all the more determined only to join a Unionist administration on his own terms.

The attitude of the Tories towards their great ally—even within a few months of his becoming their most important minister—is well illustrated by the following letter from Lord George Hamilton (at this time Chairman of the London School Board), which refers to the municipal elections which were held at the end of October 1894.

Private

Wortly Hall,
Sheffield
Oct. 10, '94

My dear Douglas,

I should certainly prefer that another and not Joe should initiate our campaign against the Progressives in London, but I do not attach as much importance to this as you do. Nor is it easy to now accomplish it. Joe is a V.P. [Vice-President] of the Society.[1] Arthur Balfour is not, and the Society is largely Joe's child, whose knowledge of municipal affairs is unrivalled.

Unless he kicks over the traces I do not think any harm will be done. I . . . shall early next week come to London for good to work this machine as I feel the General Election may be considerably affected by our success or failure in London municipal affairs. It will, as you can see, be difficult to get Balfour in, even if he was willing to speak, before the 16th Nov: he speaks at Newcastle and Sunderland on the 11th and 15th and if between now and then we have any reason to believe Joe is going to play pranks on the 16th, Arthur could forestall him up North . . .

Believe me yours very truly,
George Hamilton.

But, just before the Rosebery Government finally tottered to its fall, such a crisis in the relationship between the Tories and their ally arose as threatened to wreck all hopes of a joint administration. The trouble had its origin in the rather inconsiderately timed resignation of the Speaker. The latter, Arthur Wellesley Peel,[2] was a son of the great Sir Robert and was an old adherent of Gladstone, but in the twelve tumultuous years that he had occupied the Chair he had shown such remarkable coolness, firmness and impartiality that he had earned the respect of everyone in the House. However, since the Chair had now been occupied uninterruptedly by Liberals for the last sixty years, the Conservatives not unnaturally felt it was time one of their own side held the post.

Ironically, though there was a Liberal Unionist—Leonard Courtney[3]—in the field, whom the Liberal Government would

[1] The 'London Municipal Society', which was the Conservative-Liberal label for L.C.C. Elections.

[2] Later 1st Viscount Peel.

[3] M.P. Cornwall, Bodmin Division; former Under Secretary Home Office; later 1st Viscount Courtney.

have been glad to accept for the Chair, he was quite unacceptable to his own party—and particularly to its leader, Chamberlain. The trouble between the latter and the Tories arose therefore, not out of this, but out of the seat left vacant by Speaker Peel's resignation. This seat was 'Warwick and Leamington', which the Liberal Unionists considered to be theirs. They therefore nominated for it Peel's son, George. Though actually endorsed by Balfour in a public letter—but without the approval of either Akers-Douglas or Middleton—the choice produced a revolt among the local Conservatives, who put up a candidate of their own.

A surge of pent-up feeling among the Midland Conservatives broke loose against Chamberlain, who, on his side, was both astonished and furious. He was disparaged by the *Standard*, at that time the official Conservative organ in London, and attacked and insulted by many lesser papers. Moreover, the tension was heightened by another quarrel concerning the 'rights' to the seat at Hythe which was becoming vacant through the retirement of Sir Edward Watkin. This railway king appears to have been a sort of Vicar of Bray, having asked for the Conservative Whip in 1880 and then sat with and spoken for the Liberals whilst they enjoyed power, later still posing as a Liberal Unionist after the Liberal debacle in 1886. But Lord Radnor, in a letter to Akers-Douglas (April 4th, '95) asserted that Watkin had resigned from the Liberal Unionists in 1888 and that 'No one knew what his politics were excepting that he would vote for anyone or anything to get support for his Channel. Tunnel'. At any rate, Akers-Douglas was adamant in insisting that, despite all, Sir Edward's original affiliation decided the issue—thereby, of course, further infuriating Chamberlain.

Indeed, so disgusted and discouraged did Chamberlain become at this moment that he was tempted to give up his political career for good. This much is clear from correspondence with his wife, quoted by Garvin,[1] and from a reference in a letter from Balfour quoted below. Several other interesting letters from Akers-Douglas's post-bag refer to these interlocking and anxious problems of the candidature for the Speakership, the candidature for Warwick and Leamington and the rage and

[1] Garvin, II, 623–4.

despair of the Great Joe. Here is one from a prominent Tory backbencher (later a Minister), R. W. Hanbury.[1]

Hotel Metropole,
London
March 9, 1895

My dear Douglas,

I am sorry that this demon influenza has got hold of you too—though I hope it will not be for long—especially as this affair of the Speakership may come to a crisis any day now. I cannot help thinking that the Speaker himself is creating an unnecessary difficulty for us by resigning now without seeing this Parliament out. Anyhow we ought not to let ourselves suffer from it—a party who have not had a Speaker for 60 years. Whether they choose C. Bannerman[2] or Arnold Morley[3] or anybody else, the special circumstances of his election—that it is made only a few months before we may fairly expect to be in a majority, that we have not had a Conservative Speaker for so many years, and that we behaved generously—perhaps too generously—in re-electing Brand in 1874—all these I think justify us in declining to tie our hands for any future Parliament.

The danger is that they may nominate Courtney and then of course we should be in difficulty—solely of course on account of the Liberal Unionists—for according to our ideas he is hardly the right type of man for Speaker—and perhaps not even according to theirs—but the temptation to choose a Speaker from among their own small band would be very great if they saw their chance . . .

Yours sincerely,
R. W. Hanbury.

P.S. You know what I think about your own claims over anybody else if you care for the post—and I candidly believe that there is a general opinion in that direction on our side. If the Radicals nominate an actual Cabinet Minister the argument against you as Whip would be very much weakened.

The above postscript was crossed out in alarm by Akers-Douglas with the remark: 'This won't do at all.' But the idea

[1] M.P. Preston; Financial Secretary to Treasury 1895–1900; President of Board of Agriculture 1900–3.

[2] Sir Henry Campbell-Bannerman, P.C., G.C.B.; M.P. Stirling District; Secretary of State for War 1892–5; Prime Minister 1905–8.

[3] Late Liberal Chief Whip; see ante.

was not actually so new, because nearly a year earlier the *Bradford Observer* had written: '. . . Should the Conservatives be in power the selection [for the Speakership] would be between Mr. Jackson and Mr. Akers-Douglas.'

Meanwhile Labouchere had as usual been scheming and, as a result, proposed to Akers-Douglas a bargain, characteristically elaborate and founded upon the most serpentine calculations.

Private

5, Old Palace Yard,
S.W.
March 23 [1895]

Dear Akers-Douglas,

'Joe', Dilke[1] tells me, has got it into his head that some of the Cons. want to pitch him and his Liberal Unionists over, and this coupled with the Leamington quarrel, may lead him to do anything—You probably know more about this than I do.

We both object to that God Almighty prig Courtney. Now there is no use proposing to you anything to arrive at a common end which is not to your interest—What you want is that the field should be open to Ridley[2] in the next Parliament.

Here then is my proposal—that Gully[3] should be elected without a contest and that on getting up to thank, he should state that he does not intend to stand next time—he would have to state this so that it would be known before—to all your ardent belligerants [sic]. He would have been given a Judgeship already—indeed Herschell[4] promised it to him, but he is the only Lib. who can hold Carlisle. He told me that he quite understood that if elected now he would not be re-elected again, and that in this case he would go back to the Bar and 'perhaps they will make me a Judge' —In fact the swagger of the Chair tempts him.

You would gain Carlisle. If you are in a muddle with the Lib. Unionists this would put an end to that source of difficulty. We should have got rid of Courtney.

But, you would have to promise me that if you [the Conservatives] come in, you will give Gully the Judgeship. He would not know it from me, but he would know it. This would be only

[1] Sir Charles Dilke, Bart., P.C.; M.P. Forest of Dean; President Local Government Board, 1882–5.

[2] Sir Matthew White Ridley, Bart., P.C.; M.P. (see ante).

[3] William Court Gully, Q.C.; M.P. (L.) Carlisle; Speaker 1895–1905; created 1st Viscount Selby.

[4] 1st Baron Herschell; Lord Chancellor 1886 and 1892–5.

reasonable. There would be no pension. He is leader of the Northern Circuit and anyone would think this a fair arrangement, though of course it would not be known to anyone that there had been a promise.

I am not absolutely certain that he would consent, and should not say anything to him, unless you agree.

Directly you do, you could tell our lot that you accept Gully for this Parliament, so soon as I have got the agreement from him not to stand again.

Don't write, but I shall see you in the House on Monday. Evidently if the beast got in, you would have endless trouble to get him out next Parliament.

Yours truly,
H. Labouchere.

Meanwhile, the Conservatives remained obdurate in their opposition to the candidature of George Peel, thereby hardening the resolve of the Liberal Unionists against any form of compromise. Worse still, by offensive personal attacks on Chamberlain they were jeopardizing the whole delicate relationship with the latter and his party. This is the background to a letter to Akers-Douglas from Powell Williams, Chairman of the Management Committee of the Central Liberal Unionist Association and M.P. for South Birmingham

Private

6, Great George Street,
Westminster, S.W.
11 April, 1895

Dear Akers-Douglas,

I see in the *Times* of today, with much concern, that there was a renewal last night at the Conservative Club at Leamington, of the recent offensive attacks upon Mr. Chamberlain. I am daily receiving representations as to the mischief which is being caused throughout the Liberal Unionist ranks by these attacks, and by the course which is being taken by your party at Leamington. The case is, in my opinion, extremely serious, not only as it affects Mr. Chamberlain, but also in its influence upon the Liberal Unionist party generally. My present object, however, is to say that, in face of this kind of treatment, it has, in my belief, become most difficult, if not quite impossible, to entertain any idea of withdrawing Peel, and that, therefore, I must ask you not to act upon the suggestion which I made to you the other day as being a last resort in case all other methods of restoring peace failed. I will write to Mr. Chamberlain on the matter, but at present, I strongly think that Peel must go to the poll—win or lose.

Do you not think now that the case calls for the early presence in Leamington of a very influential member of your party, and for some plain *public* speaking?

I am very sorry to bother you in this time of holiday. I only do so because I know how grave the matter has become.

Yours very truly,
J. Powell Williams.

On receiving this Akers-Douglas wrote to Salisbury (April 12th, '95):

> . . . I am sorry to say the Warwick and Leamington business still blocks the way: and the situation is rendered the more difficult by attacks on Chamberlain, both on the platform at Leamington and in the press in London, which are as unanswerable as they are offensive: and which are unfortunately much taken to heart by the man against whom they are directed . . . Powell Williams admitted that Peel's chances were hopeless and was anxious for any modus vivendi. However he writes to me today that in the face of a renewed personal attack on Chamberlain at Leamington he won't negociate and that Peel must go on 'win or lose'.[1]

But the Conservatives—and Akers-Douglas in particular—were loth to surrender their claim. For, however much they were ready and even anxious to placate Chamberlain with sympathy and flattery, they were still as obstinately determined as ever that he should not extend his physical empire by a single seat if possible. Their dual motive is revealed in the following characteristic, mildly sardonic letter from Balfour, who, having been always on good terms with Chamberlain, once again (as in 1889) found himself expected to pour oil on the troubled waters.

Dictated
Private

Ryes,
April 13th 1895

My dear Akers,

I must see what I can do to induce Joe to withdraw Peel at Leamington. I agree with you that it is the best solution.

[1] Salisbury MSS.

I have just received a most dolorous letter from Henry James, in which he dwells at great length upon Joe's feelings about the present crisis. He says Mrs. Joe is doing her best to make him leave politics. This I think not impossible, though peculiarly unfortunate. He (James) wants me at my approaching Meeting to denounce the newspaper attacks upon Joe, which I see no objection to doing.—He also asks whether there is not some means by which the Tory members of the House of Commons can shew their appreciation of Chamberlain's services! Unless they subscribe for a piece of plate ['silver' deleted], I really do not quite know how this excellent object is to be attained! They can hardly cheer him more loudly than they do at present. He quotes Bonsor[1] as asserting that there are only two Members—Howorth and another—who are hostile to Joe. I fear this is rather a sanguine view of the state of affairs, but I am, nevertheless, confident that, on the whole, the Party are sound.

Excellent golf! and excellent weather!

Yours ever,
Arthur James Balfour.

Two days later (April 15th) he writes again:

. . . I think it would be bad diplomacy to attempt to deal with the Compact [i.e. between Conservatives and L.U's] until our L.U. friends are a little more smoothed down about Warwick and Leamington. It is possible, of course, that all this is being done to make us feel their importance. I rather think however that there is a great deal of genuine soreness at the bottom of it.

This characteristically cool appraisal of a highly dangerous situation was matched by that of his uncle, Salisbury. An attempt was made to reach a compromise at Leamington by substituting another Liberal Unionist, Alfred Lyttelton,[2] for George Peel; but this was at first unsuccessful. Salisbury's remarks upon this in a letter to Akers-Douglas, were as devastating as were some of those which he added about Chamberlain. Moreover, his almost pathological detachment—even in a matter so vital to his own and his party's future—could scarcely be better

[1] Sir Henry Cosmo Orme Bonsor, 1st Baronet; M.P. N.E. Surrey 1885–1900.

[2] Rt. Hon. Alfred Lyttelton, P.C., Q.C.; Recorder of Oxford 1895–1903; M.P. Warwick and Leamington 1895–1906; Secretary of State for Colonies 1903–5.

illustrated than by his remark about not reading the *Standard* and therefore being unable to judge the merits of the case.

Private

La Bastide,
Beaulieu,
Alpes Maritimes
April 16, '95.

My dear Douglas,

I am not altogether sorry that the scheme of substituting Lyttelton for Peel has broken down. I think you would have been much tried by Lyttelton if he had come in. He is only a Courtney with better manners and great personal popularity.

I am very sorry to hear of Chamberlain's irritation. It is unworthy of him to take notice of what our newspapers say—I am unable to judge of the justice of his complaints, as I hardly ever read the *Standard*; but he ought to know that we are in no way responsible. I think some of our people are ungrateful to him: but after all his policy has been very peculiar. To sit upon the fence for nine years is an unprecedented achievement: but he can hardly complain because we will not hold his legs to prevent him tumbling upon either side.

Henry James writes to me suggesting some kind of public testimonial of our esteem. Personally I am quite willing to take any part in such a testimonial that may be assigned to me. But I cannot help feeling that anything like a round robin would break down.

Ever yours truly,
Salisbury.

Certainly nothing could be fairer—in its rather airy fashion—than the attitude of these great Conservative kinsmen: but they did not comprehend the genuine state of desperation at which their ally had by this time arrived and which had made him bent upon forcing the issue to the limit. For Chamberlain now wrote to the Duke of Devonshire a most determined letter in which he averred: '. . . I have nothing to gain by remaining in public life—I would not give a brass button to fill any office that is likely to be within my reach . . .', adding further on:

If any considerable number of Conservatives believe that they are strong enough to stand alone and can do without the Liberal 'crutch', as poor Randolph phrased it, I am ready to be thrown aside and to let them try the experiment.

> On the other hand if they still want our assistance they must pay the price they have hitherto willingly paid. There is no room for further concession and they will find it bad economy to haggle over the terms of the bargain . . .[1]

His toughness won the day. The Conservative leaders called their more unruly followers to heel. George Peel retired from the scene in the cause of peace, but the seat remained Liberal Unionist, Alfred Lyttelton being cordially elected by both sections of the Unionist Party. Meanwhile both Salisbury and Balfour went out of their way to pay public tributes of the handsomest kind to Chamberlain's services to the Unionist cause, and, recognizing these to be sincere—as, for all their irony, the above letters indicate they were—Chamberlain responded with his usual magnanimity. On May 22nd, at a Liberal Unionist demonstration, he made a public declaration of Unionist solidarity, ending: 'All we want now is the opportunity of appealing to the verdict of the British people.' A month later this opportunity came with the fall of the Rosebery Government.

As regards the Speakership, though Courtney was strongly backed and pressed by Harcourt, he declined to stand for the post 'on the ground that he would not have the support of his Unionist colleagues, especially of Chamberlain'[2]—so the Conservatives need not have been afraid on this score after all. The latter therefore put forward Sir Matthew White Ridley (as Labby had said they would) as their candidate, while the Liberals, now equally resolved to have a candidate of their own, concentrated on Gully, 'who knows nothing and whom nobody knows',[3] as Harcourt wrote to Rosebery. There was thus a sharp party struggle—which both sides had expressed a desire to avoid—and in the end Gully was elected by only 11 votes (April 10th, '95).

The Conservative leadership held strong views on the subject, however, and, declining to regard the Speaker as a sacrosanct figure, pressed on with plans to get Gully out. (He had not been elected with Conservative consent, as Labouchere had suggested, and consequently there was no question of the bargain under which he was to have foregone re-election in return

[1] Holland, II, 267–8. [2] Gardiner, II, 354. [3] Ibid., 356.

for a judgeship.) Thus, barely a month later (May 7th), Akers-Douglas wrote the following letter, published in the press, to the Conservative and Unionist candidate for Carlisle, the seat held by the new Speaker.

> Many thanks for your letter telling me of the resolution of your local committee in Carlisle, in which they declare their intention of contesting the Seat at the next election. I have taken counsel with those who have a right to express an opinion on the subject, and you may be assured that there is no reason, based either on precedent or on the particular circumstances connected with the present Speaker's election, which should deprive the constituency of the right to be represented in Parliament by a member sharing their political views. I hope, therefore, that no change will take place either in the policy of our party in Carlisle or in the energy with which they will carry on the contest.

This action drew a grave rebuke from the Liberal press, which, whilst admitting that there was 'nothing either in the constitution or in ordinary party usage to prevent them driving Mr. Gully from the House of Commons and from the post of signal honour to which its members here called him', declared that 'it will be an ill day for politics in this country if partisans forget the honour that is due to distinguished service, if they overlook respect for themselves which means respect for their opponents, and that neighbourliness in political conflict which prevents the party system degenerating into something resembling a free fight at a fair'.

But these were not the sort of arguments that were likely to carry the least weight with the Chief Conservative Whip. For, whilst being undoubtedly popular with both sides of the House by reason of his courtesy and affability, he nevertheless viewed the eternal party war with a realism and even ruthlessness which left no room for the dangerous incursions of sentiment or misplaced chivalry. Had he not done so, moreover, there is little doubt that he would never have become the great lieutenant that he was.

After the resignation of Rosebery's Government and the return to power of the Unionists, when by custom the Speaker resigned and by custom would be automatically re-elected, Akers-Douglas returned to the charge. He wrote to Lord Salisbury

(July 26th, '95) to say that Conservative opinion was still strongly against Gully and in favour of Ridley and

> . . . (1) that it is all important that we should have in the Chair a friendly Speaker and that Gully is likely to lean to the other side. (2) That Gully did use his social position to further the interests of the late Government in making his receptions the hunting ground of the '80 Club'—(3) that Labouchere put him forward originally and would unduly influence him in future while Mrs. Labby would 'run' Mrs. Gully and manage her social functions as she notoriously did this year.[1]

Salisbury was equally perturbed, foreseeing with dismay a situation where the Speakership would become as of right vested in the Liberal Party.

> Hatfield House,
> Hatfield,
> Herts.
> July 27, 95
>
> My dear Douglas,
>
> I am very glad to hear your request as I am entirely of your way of thinking. There is one consideration which does not seem to have been dwelt on sufficiently—and that is this practice of Speakers' resignations. Ever since John Russell carried the Chair by storm in 1835, every Speaker has resigned at a moment when his party was in a majority: and consequently each successive Speaker has been a Liberal. Abercromby, Lefevre, Denison, Brand, Peel—they all observed the same rule. If Lefevre, Denison and Peel had waited for a twelvemonth their resignations would have fallen to Tory Governments to deal with.
>
> Now if every Liberal Speaker resigns to a Liberal majority: and the rule is laid down that a Speaker once elected must not be disturbed—it follows mathematically that the Speakership belongs permanently to the Liberal party. But if Gully is re-elected the rule will in effect have been laid down that a Speaker once elected can never be disturbed. For you never will have a stronger case than this—an incompetent and unknown man forced into the Chair by a petty majority in the face of an electoral defeat known to be impending.
>
> I hope your view will prevail.
>
> Ever yours truly,
> Salisbury.

[1] Salisbury MSS.

Actually Salisbury's crushing assessment of Gully appears to have been unmerited, for though the latter undoubtedly was little known to the House (in which his attendance had been fitful) and was totally inexperienced in the beginning, we are told by so staunch a Tory as Lord George Hamilton that he 'gradually got control of the House and by his lucid and businesslike rulings he greatly accelerated the discharge of public business . . . it was a quieter House during his Speakership than that over which his predecessor presided.'[1]

Just at this time, when Akers-Douglas's own long reign as Chief Whip was fast coming to an end, he lost one of his oldest and ablest lieutenants, Sidney Herbert—'one of the best-tempered, best mannered and most popular men in the House of Commons'[2]—who, by the death of his brother succeeded to the earldom of Pembroke. The two men had been the closest friends throughout their parliamentary association and Herbert now wrote:

Villa Bromeis,
Bad Nauheim
May 5th, 1895

My dear Bob,

So many thanks for your kind letter. I feel more than I can write or say on the parting from the old life, and the thought that I can no longer work with you and Willie Walrond and the other boys with whom I have been associated for so many years. I can hardly realise that that life is over for me, but I do know that these last 10 years, full of work and anxieties as they have been, have yet been full also of pleasure and good fellowship, and the recollection of them will be always present to my mind. We may not be together so much in future, old chap, but I feel that neither of us will forget each other, and that pals we are and pals we shall remain to the end . . . Best love to all my friends in the old room. I have done nothing yet about Croydon [his constituency], but I suppose I must eventually write an address . . .

Yours ever,
Sidney Herbert.

The question appears to have been immediately raised—whether at the sole instigation of Akers-Douglas is not clear—as to whether Herbert should continue to sit in the House of

[1] Hamilton, 248. [2] *Irish Times*, May 4th, 1895.

Commons at least until it was certain that a posthumous son would not be born to his brother's wife. For, were that to happen, and if he had already applied for the Chiltern Hundreds, he would have lost his seat in the House of Commons to no avail. At any rate, on the same day as Herbert wrote the above to Akers-Douglas, Sir Richard Webster, the Attorney-General, wrote to the latter as follows:

Confidential

2 Pump Court,
Temple, E.C.
5 May, 1895

Dear Douglas,

I have carefully considered the question of Sidney Herbert sitting. In my opinion whatever may be the view taken as to his strict legal position, it would be contrary to all precedent and practice for him to sit. In such case I believe the practice has been invariable that the Member who will (failing posthumous issue) succeed applies for the Chiltern Hundreds. And this on principle would appear to be the right course because should no child be born, Herbert is a Peer from the date of his brother's death. As regards penalty the question is one of more difficulty. Rigby[1] I believe was of opinion as A.G. that the Statute 6 Anne Cap. 41 section 28 applies. I have my doubts about it, but whatever the true view be, quite apart from penalty I think he ought not to sit. The Committee of last year were I believe divided upon the question whether a Peer sitting is liable to a penalty.

Very truly yours,
Richard Webster.

However, in the end Herbert preferred the risk of an heir being born to the risk of being penalized for staying in the House of Commons. But, even when he applied for the Chiltern Hundreds, there was another commotion about the style by which he had signed himself in so doing.

Malwood,
Lyndhurst
Sunday, May 19th, 95

Dear Akers-Douglas,

I wrote to 'Sidney' '*eo nomine*' to say I would grant him the Chilterns though he signed '*Pembroke*'. The Clerks at the table maintain that the writ should go out in the name of 'Sidney

[1] Rt. Hon. Sir John Rigby, Q.C., Attorney-General 1894.

Herbert' as his H. of C. name . . . as there is no *official* knowledge that he is 'Pembroke'. I am not sure they are not right. I have not yet made out the *formal appointment* till the question of title is decided so please do not move the Writ till I see you and the matter is settled.

Hang their Peers and their Peerages!

Yrs. truly,
W. V. Harcourt.

The final fling of egalitarian bravado came, needless to say, from the descendant of one of the most ancient and illustrious

SIR WM. HARCOURT.

"THE MORNING'S REFLECTIONS."

families in the kingdom, almost every one of whose scions had borne titles ranging from knight to earl—including the writer himself, whose son, incidentally, was to refound the family peerage.

The fall of the Rosebery Government came suddenly and, to some extent, unexpectedly on an amendment to the Army Estimates. Asquith says that 'it was a "snap" division, which had been carefully engineered, and there is little doubt that the

Government could, if they had been so minded, have had the decision reversed'.[1] But other accounts by no means endorse his verdict. Sir Henry James, for instance, described it as 'a very strange affair' and noted:

> . . . On the Monday preceding . . . Austen Chamberlain spoke to me confidentially, asking me to promise him that in any event I wd. be in the House on the coming Friday, as a Division would be taken under very favourable circumstances. The same request was made to all Liberal Unionist Members, and we were all accounted for—by presence or pairing—when the Division came. The Conservatives, however, made no whip for the Division, and Akers-Douglas even gave permission to their members to leave the House during the afternoon. But the military men and the Liberal Unionists remained, and by them the majority was obtained.[2]

Certainly the contemporary press accounts of the occasion suggest that it took the Conservatives as much by surprise as the Government. Thus the *Daily Telegraph* (June 22nd, '95):

> The paper [with the division figures] was bandied backwards and forwards between the Ministerial and the Opposition tellers, the latter of whom were slow to realise the victory which their party had won. It was not till the record of the division had been twice placed in the hands of Mr. Akers-Douglas that he announced its result to the House . . .

But Asquith does admit what was plain for all to see—that the Government 'had had enough of living from hand to mouth',[3] so much so that for the first and last time both Harcourt and Rosebery were in cordial agreement for an immediate resignation—even in face of the prevailing wish of the rest of the Cabinet for a dissolution.

The Queen immediately sent for Lord Salisbury, and three days later he kissed hands as Prime Minister for the third time: but not before he had held several conferences with the Liberal Unionist leaders and had been able to assure himself of their co-operation in his new ministry. His final acceptance, of course, depended on this, and consequently it was not possible to

[1] Asquith, op. cit., I, 232.
[2] Lord Askwith: *Lord James of Hereford*, 238.
[3] Asquith, op. cit., II, 232.

inform the House of the final outcome at exactly the time expected. Harcourt, as Leader, with characteristic truculence refused to keep the House waiting for the promised telegram from Salisbury, but afterwards wrote the following note in reply to a protest from Akers-Douglas:

Treasury Chambers,
Whitehall, S.W.
26 June, 95

Dear Akers-Douglas,

Thanks for your note—I was surprised to learn that complaints had been made that I did not *temporarily* adjourn the House yesterday. If I had had the opportunity of seeing you I should have explained to you that I could not keep the representatives of the people cooling their heels for an indefinite period—As a fact the telegram from Windsor did not reach Rosebery till 6.10.

I am sure that after the many transactions we have had together you will not suspect me of desiring to interpose any unnecessary obstacles to the arrangements you desire.

Yours sincly.
W. H. Harcourt.

Despite the rather ignominious end of their opponents, in view of the fluid state of parties as well as the technical point that Salisbury had been defeated in 1892 on a vote of confidence, the Unionist leaders were disinclined to accept the responsibilities of office without an immediate appeal to the country. When the House mustered on the day after Salisbury's acceptance of office (June 26th, '95), Akers-Douglas—still as Chief Whip of the party now returned to power and in temporary default of a leader of the House—was very much the man in charge. Chaffingly he was interrogated by the irrepressible Labouchere:

Will the right honourable gentleman the member for one of the divisions of Kent, in whose hands the conduct of public business practically is, tell us what will be the course of procedure . . .? What we want to know is when the General Election will come on (loud cheers and laughter). We are burning with the desire to go to our Constituents (cheers and laughter). And we should like as practical men to know something about dates . . . etc. etc.

When the House had finished holding its sides Akers-Douglas replied that the Government were anxious for the election to take place 'at the earliest possible moment'. He then proceeded to move the Writs for the seats made vacant by the appointment of the new Ministers—it being necessary at that time for a Member accepting office under the Crown to vacate his seat and submit himself for re-election. The first of these was Balfour, who, as First Lord of the Treasury, was again to lead the House, and after him came Chamberlain, who was to be Secretary of State for the Colonies. The ensuing scene was described by the *Daily News* (June 27th, '95):

> At the mention of Mr. Chamberlain's name a cheer loyally raised by the Conservatives was met by an outburst of ironical applause, to which the Irish members ominously lent a fiercer note. One cried aloud 'Judas!' and there might have been a scene had the Speaker not judiciously refrained from hearing the interruption . . . Altogether this was a very dramatic incident—the issuing of Mr. Chamberlain's writ by a Tory Whip.

Speculation was naturally rife as to what lay in store for Akers-Douglas himself, who at forty-three was still a young man as ministers go, but clearly was marked out for promotion. The Lord Presidency of the Council, with a peerage, said some; others that he could not be spared from his present great role of Patronage Secretary and Chief Whip. In the meantime he remained, as we have seen, in his old capacity—in fact during these few days whilst the new Ministers were being formally re-elected he was virtual Leader of the House. Then, his caretaker duties over, he was appointed on July 2nd to be First Commissioner of Works with a seat in the Cabinet. Though he gave up his old duties regretfully and his going was deeply mourned by his party, he had had twelve solid years of the most arduous work that Parliament can provide and he knew that no man can indefinitely bear such prolonged strain without impairing his health and efficiency.

Nevertheless, as the *Morning Post* (July 31st) wrote:

> It would be a great mistake to suppose that Mr. Akers-Douglas has ceased to manage the party organization because he has become First Commissioner of Works. Although Sir William Walrond is now Chief Whip . . . Mr. Akers-Douglas is still the party

'boss', just as Lord Tweedmouth[1] continued to manage the Radical party after he became Lord Privy Seal. The truth is that Mr. Akers-Douglas has a knowledge of *le dessous des cartes* which makes him indispensable, at all events for a time, until Sir William Walrond is educated in the mysteries of the post.

The last remark was perhaps a little hard on his successor, since Walrond had been with Akers-Douglas, as his invaluable and most confidential aide, ever since the latter's assumption of the Chief Whipship in 1885.

Parliament was dissolved on July 8th and at the ensuing General Election the fairest dreams of the Unionists were realized, since they obtained a majority of 152 over all other parties combined. 411 Unionists—340 Conservatives and 71 Liberal Unionists—were returned against 177 Liberals and 82 Irish Nationalists. Akers-Douglas was again returned unopposed. Before he took up his new post he received the following letter from Alfred Austin, who had long been his neighbour in Kent and who was in the following year to become Poet Laureate.[2]

Swinford Old Manor,
Ashford, Kent
July 4, 1895

Dear Akers-Douglas,

I send you my heartiest congratulations, on your well-earned promotion to higher honours. I do not know whether your new post will be as congenial to you as your old one; but I have no doubt the Party will continue to have the benefit of that branch of your talents which caused me to say—do you remember?—when you first entered Parliament, 'you are a born Whip'. Much as I rejoice in the handsome recognition you have received I should not congratulate you on it if I did not feel that it is richly deserved.

Believe me,
Yours very sincerely,
Alfred Austin.

[1] As Edward Marjoribanks was Chief Liberal Whip 1892–4; see ante.

[2] Described in *The Autobiography of Margot Asquith* (II, 19) as 'One of the late Lord Salisbury's rather cynical appointments'.

XV
'ÉMINENCE GRISE'

THE year 1895 constitutes a great dividing line in Akers-Douglas's career, for of a sudden he was swept out of the maelstrom of the ceaseless party struggle, in which he had spent nearly the whole of his parliamentary life, into the comparatively quiet backwater of a department of state. From being the commander-in-the-field of his party's forces, constrained continually to gauge the strength and temper of his own men as well as of his opponents and to be ready to take instant action or give prompt advice, he now found himself the temporary head of a 'going concern' run by quiet and efficient permanent officials concerned with long-term projects and slowly evolving plans. Yet, as foretold by the press and others at the time, there was not so complete a severance with his old job as appearances might have led to suppose. In fact he remained for the rest of his active political life—whatever his official post might be—the *éminence grise* of the party, whose rich fund of experience his colleagues and successors continually tapped in all matters of party management, official procedure or Parliamentary practice.

Nevertheless, it would be foolish to ignore the fact that his finest hour was over or to minimize the shock which every Chief Whip receives on passing from the centre of affairs to the perimeter—and from which few recover. A Whip's work is so all-absorbing and of such a day-to-day and detailed character that he has no time to form the habit of taking his stance upon the great political issues of the day—nor is he called upon to do so. Consequently, upon being promoted to be a Minister of State, in which capacity he may be required to formulate or interpret his party's policy on major issues, he is liable to find himself severely handicapped; nor is he accustomed to the limelight and the public controversy which such occasions involve. For these reasons—as well as because they lack administrative experience—ex-Whips are usually appointed to minor Ministries. But, at least in the last respect, Akers-Douglas was an exception, because he was a born administrator. Indeed, he belonged to a group of Ministers who had been recruited not because they were politicians, but because they were felt to be potentially good administrators: others in this group were Lord George Hamilton, Edward Stanhope, St. John Brodrick, Walter Long, Arnold Forster, Gerald Balfour, Lords Knutsford, Balfour of Burleigh and Cawdor. Most of these men took little interest in issues beyond those that concerned them directly, had no following in the country and little in Parliament, but were first-rate men in the Cabinet and careful administrators in their departments. In other words they were well-suited to get on with leaders of the stamp of Salisbury and Balfour, but had little in common with the new and more 'professional' type of leader like Bonar Law—or with more thrusting and self-advertising colleagues like Joseph and Austen Chamberlain, both of whom were at certain moments runners-up for the Unionist leadership. Had it been in their nature to publicize themselves more, like the figures just mentioned, some of these men might have risen to greater heights; but, being for the most part men who were born to an assured position and a tradition of service, they did not aspire to do more than become competent heads of such ministries as might be entrusted to their care or equally admirable chairmen of Cabinet Committees and Royal Commissions.

Since we are primarily concerned in this study with the party political aspects of Akers-Douglas's career it would be inappropriate to undertake a close examination of his work and achievements during his long sojourn at the Office of Works—important though these were in their own way. It was a time of transition and innovation in civic development as well as in social life and thus he became responsible for matters ranging from the building of a whole new crop of Government offices[1]

[1] Some of the major constructional works of his reign included the widening of Parliament Street, erection of the new War Office and Local

to the question of admitting motor-cars and bicyclists to the Royal Parks. There also fell within his term the first Coronation that had taken place for over sixty years, the elaborate ceremonial of which, having thus passed beyond the ken of living memories, had to be painfully unearthed from the records of the past. However, he brought to bear on all those multifarious tasks the same energy, common-sense and shrewdness as had made him so successful in the livelier sphere of party politics. He was interested in the work, which was in some ways not unlike that involved in the management of his extensive estates—and he was considered, it may be added, a model landlord. In other words, it very soon became clear that added to his other talents he was a first-rate administrator.

Scarcely was he installed in his new office than he began to experience a new line in badgering and complaints—not about lack of recognition or the quest for honours, but the 'insanitary condition of the House'! Thus on August 20th, 1895, he found himself being asked 'Whether he was aware that during the earlier part of the afternoon there was a most horrible smell from the drains near the bar of the House and whether he would inquire into the cause of it and endeavour to put a stop to a state of things which is not uncommon in this House, and which is very prejudicial to the health of Hon. Members.'

On the quasi-comic side of his new office there remain among his papers one or two 'gems' which incidentally indicate how the lesser members of the Royal Family at this time still considered Cabinet Ministers to be as much at their beck and call as at that of the Sovereign herself. In November 1896 the ancient Duke of Cambridge, first cousin of the Queen, who had only the year before been gently removed from the post of Commander-in-Chief which he had held for the past forty years, bombarded the new First Commissioner of Works with protests against the drilling of Volunteers in Richmond Park (of which he was Chief Ranger) and more especially about that new scourge, Bicyclists, who were represented as some newly

---

Government Board offices, the completion of the Victoria and Albert Museum and Royal College of Science, the restoration and opening of Kensington Palace and the installation of the Wallace Collection in Manchester Square.

discovered and terrifyingly barbarous tribe. Whilst giving his own strong views on this 'most singular condition of things' and exhorting Akers-Douglas to 'put a stop to such proceedings', he enclosed the following incredible letter from his brother-in-law, the Duke of Teck, the father of Queen Mary.

White Lodge,
Richmond Park
Nov. 2nd 1896

Dearest Brother-in-Law,

It will interest you to hear of the doings of the Bicyclists in Richmond Park.

Already on Saturday last in the afternoon, when Mary,[1] May [2] and I went out for a drive, the Roads were greatly crowded with 'Bikes', on returning from Wimbledon about 6 o'c—by the private gate, the Park was so crowded with them, that it made it very difficult to drive.

But we had a very curious experience yesterday, Sunday. About 2000 to 3000 Bicycles thronged the Roads of the Park, not as if guided by sensible, thoughtful people, but by Maniacs, Persons in a state of madness. They went in a pace like lightening [sic], looking neither right nor left, on they went meeting each other as if they wished to annihilate each other. Many groups, actually abreast, of from 10 or 20 or more, formed of Roughs and others apparently of members of Bicycle Clubs, who *charged* up and down the Road, regardless of anyone else, but thinking of their own fun or better said frenzy.

Even Ladies seemed to have lost their Heads and tho' their expression was one of fear, passed in the terrible crowd like furies.

I cannot conceive that not hundreds of People were killed or maimed. All foot passengers fled on the Grass and the Carriages had to do the same. The *poor 5* of Park-keepers were no doubt in the same [?] plight as any of the Public on foot, and Policemen there were none in the Park. We returned yesterday from Church, but Mary and May could of course not risk getting out of the Carriage in order to walk home, as we always do on Sundays. I got out close to White Lodge to watch the going on. I felt amazed at *thickly massed* People on Bicycles, actually covering every inch of the Road, giving me the impression that Men and Women raving mad were let loose to haunt the Park.

What I write is not exaggerated, all what I saw was to me like a

[1] His wife, Mary Adelaide, daughter of 1st Duke of Cambridge.

[2] His daughter, later Queen Mary.

bad Dream. If tracks must be made in the Park, unless the Roads are to become useless for Carriages and foot Passengers, what can be done and it is most likely that those tracks will spoil the Park in looks.

Yr. most affectionate and devoted
Francis.

A few months later a further urgent appeal reached the harassed First Commissioner from the Duchess of Teck.

White Lodge,
Richmond Park,
Surrey
April 6th, 1897

Dear Mr. Akers-Douglas,

I must again appeal to your kindness to remove an evil which I foresee will become a most terrible nuisance as the warm weather comes on. The Bicyclists have taken, especially on Saturdays and Sundays, when their number is *legion*! to rest against our palings (alas! none too strong!) and refresh the *inner man*, leaving sad traces in the way of *orange* peel and greasy paper. To add to this, their loud conversation is not edifying and they can hear all we say in the garden, when sitting out with our guests. To remedy this could you put up an inexpensive iron or wire fencing (not too high) to run along the road and exclude the public from the strip of grass immediately outside our palings? If this could be done by Easter Monday, on which day the Bank Holiday Folk muster in great force, it would add considerably to the obligation.

Pray believe me,
Dear Mr. Akers-Douglas,
Very sincerely yours
Mary Adelaide.

Close on the heels of the bicycle nightmare came that of the motor-car—and here the Queen herself stepped in. On June 24th, 1900, Lord Linlithgow, Lord Chamberlain of the Household, wrote to Akers-Douglas in a surprisingly acid tone that 'the Queen refuses to drive in the Park if motors are allowed to enter it in the afternoon. Of course this settles the matter as none of us would wish our convenience to be considered where H.M's pleasure is concerned.'

The Boer War, which had broken out in the autumn of 1899, opened—in keeping with our national tradition—disastrously for England. Attempting to forestall the initial Boer offensive with a small British force, General Sir George White had been compelled to fall back on Ladysmith, where he was besieged for four months. Other disasters followed in quick succession. Sir Redvers Buller had arrived in South Africa early in November to take over the chief command, but had made the fatal mistake of dividing his forces into three columns. One under Lord Methuen had been detailed for the relief of Kimberley. After three successful but costly engagements at Belmont, Enslin and Modder River, Methuen was defeated with heavy losses at Magersfontein—the Highland Brigade marching straight into a wire entanglement in the dark (December 11th, '99). A second column under General Gatacre was heavily repulsed in a night attack at Stormberg (December 16th); whilst Buller himself, in an obstinate attempt to relieve Ladysmith by a direct frontal attack, sustained a terrible defeat at Colenso (December 15th).

Balfour had meanwhile, in a series of speeches, drawn upon himself the wrath of both press and public by some curiously unfortunate yet highly characteristic references to these calamitous events and to the Government's share of responsibility for them. He had referred to the 'unhappy entanglement of Ladysmith' as having upset the original plan of campaign; declared he did not 'feel the need so far as my colleagues and I are concerned of any apology whatever' and flatly asserted that 'there have been no great reverses in this war'. Such remarks, whatever their strictly logical justification, were obviously singularly ill-attuned to the prevailing temper of the public, which was rapidly becoming one of bewilderment, alarm and anger. It was nearly half a century since the English had been involved in a major war and in the meantime they had been nurtured on a diet of rapidly expanding and boastful imperialism. As Balfour's biographer says: 'Nothing sets in better perspective the gulf that separates our own times from those of the Boer War than the almost hysterical reactions of the national mind to unwonted misfortunes.'[1] Referring in the same place to the speeches which Balfour made at this time in answer to the current criticisms of the preparations for and conduct of the war, she adds that these 'illustrate Balfour's weak point as a political

[1] Dugdale: op. cit., I, 303.

leader, namely the uncertainty of his instinct for gauging the popular mind, or persuading it to follow his own'.

In the circumstances it was not surprising that an agitation arose for a Parliamentary inquiry into the conduct of the war and on this Balfour wrote to Akers-Douglas:

Private
Dictated
My dear Akers,

Whittinghame
Jan. 14th 1900

... I have no objection to enquiries except that they waste the time of Departments, and do no good. But I quite agree with you that probably an enquiry will be insisted upon, and we should shew no reluctance to grant it. It is worth, however, considering beforehand into what enquiry is to be made—guns? preparations? selection of generals? orders given to Generals? War Office organization? Intelligence Department? These are the matters that have been chiefly criticised, though very much in the vague.—For my own part I hope the opportunity will be taken of doing a good deal for the Army in various ways, but my personal suspicion is that the enquiry desired would diminish rather than increase the prospects of such a result.

I am wretched about Methuen. As you know, Wolseley[1] wanted to supersede him after Modder River, and *we* were all clear that he should be superseded after Magersfontein. But Buller foiled us.

Yours ever,
Arthur James Balfour.

Meanwhile, the Prime Minister, Lord Salisbury, though in principle quite agreeable to the idea of an inquiry, saw insuperable practical difficulties to carrying it out.

Foreign Office,
Jan. 16, 1900

My dear Douglas,

... I have been in favour of an enquiry ever since White was shut up in Ladysmith. I should be glad if the enquiry could take place at once: but I fear that it would be impossible, because, while the war lasts, many of the main witnesses would be in South Africa, and others would be too much engaged here to have time for appearance before a Committee.

[1] Field Marshal Viscount Wolseley, Commander-in-Chief of the Army, 1892 to November 1900.

I think the best way would be that Arthur and I on the first night should state in our speeches that the Government were quite willing to assent to an enquiry if asked for—but that it might not be possible to hold it, until many of the people who would be the principal witnesses should be at liberty to attend it.

I remember what a sorry figure the Crimean Committee cut, having as its principal military witness—Ashley Ponsonby.

Yours very truly,
Salisbury.

Though a member of the Cabinet, Akers-Douglas himself must have entertained rather mixed feelings on the whole subject since his second son, George, was sending home from these very battlefields letters which left little room for doubt as to the efficiency with which the war was being conducted. Sir Almeric Fitzroy, Clerk of the Privy Council, notes that he travelled to Osborne in company with Akers-Douglas on January 11th, 1900.

On the way down Douglas gave us some most interesting letters from his son in the Argyll & Sutherland Highlanders, whose experiences at Modder River and Magersfontein were unique in their variety and sensational character. Everything that one hears from the seat of war points to the utter muddle that prevailed during the former battle, which should have resulted in their crushing defeat; and the second and more serious enterprise, whatever may have been the merits of the design, was paralysed by the disaster that overtook the Highland Brigade in five minutes from the commencement of the action. Douglas's boy was overwhelmed in the rush to the rear, and carried insensible to the ambulance, where he lay for three hours. On recovering consciousness, he realised that he was still unwounded, and joined the firing line in time to be of some service in rallying the remnants of the Brigade. Nothing, he said, could equal his rage and despair at that moment; and indeed the incident must have burnt itself into the recollection of all who saw it.[1]

Akers-Douglas also passed his son's letters to the Queen and, returning them, Sir Arthur Bigge, her private secretary, wrote to him (January 13th, 1900):

The Queen has had these letters read to her and was deeply interested in them. H.M. thanks you for them and I am to ask

[1] Sir Almeric Fitzroy: *Memoirs*, I, 30.

whether you could have them copied for H.M., leaving out whatever parts you think fit. I imagine that probably the Queen would like to shew the accounts to some of her family—and therefore perhaps she feels you might prefer to suppress certain passages—but don't cut about too much what are most interesting and graphic accounts!

Shortly afterwards George Akers-Douglas was wounded at Paardeberg and the Queen wrote the following note of sympathy to his father in her own hand.

Windsor Castle
Feb. 23, 1900

The Queen thanks Mr. Akers-Douglas sincerely for his letter. She was very grieved to hear of his son's being wounded and felt so much for him and Mrs. A. Douglas.—She remembers so well his telling her all about his son's departure when he came to Balmoral. The Queen earnestly hopes he will continue to receive good accounts of him.

In the new year of the new century the war underwent a complete transformation in the capable hands of Lords Roberts and Kitchener and since by midsummer peace appeared to be already in sight the Government, though they had another year in hand, resolved to take advantage of this happy turn of events and hold an immediate general election. As the established seers of the party, Akers-Douglas and Middleton now came into their own, and once again their forecast was singularly accurate. To Balfour the former wrote:

Sep. 19, 1900

My dear Arthur,

Now that the Election is to be taken this month and the writs go out next week you may like to know what my forecast is, after discussing the question at length with Middleton.

We begin the fight with a Parliamentary majority of 128.

Naturally we stand to lose—For we have to defend a lengthened position and have very much fewer opportunities of attack than our opponents.

The War feeling is not nearly so acute now as in July. It exists chiefly in the Metropolis and larger towns especially in the North—in dockyard towns and Military centres—and affects in a very small degree country seats.

Our great effort has been, and must be, to keep the war in the foreground—theirs to ignore it and to substitute 'doles for landlords' and Old Age pensions.

Roughly speaking we shall gain in Scotland, Lancashire and the north generally—hold our own in the South and Metropolis but lose in Wales and in Counties distant from great centres of population.

Local and domestic quarrels and unpopular members will cause loss in certain individual seats quite apart from the issue before the Country.

[Follows a list of seats likely to be lost for above and other reasons and also of seats likely to be gained]

I am quite confident of a majority of 100 and hope with luck we may have one of over 120.

In any case it will be a great performance considering past precedents which show that since 1865 no Government has succeeded itself.

Yrs. sincerely,
A. Akers-Douglas.

The hope was amply fulfilled, for the Unionists were returned with a majority of 134—a gain of 6 seats. Moreover, the gain in votes throughout the country was 90,000, and, as Akers-Douglas had predicted, the gains were particularly marked in Scotland and the North of England, whilst a definite decline in seats, as in votes, was noticeable in Wales. At any rate, though many seats were uncontested (Akers-Douglas's was one) and though a singular apathy seems to have prevailed throughout, nevertheless the final result could not but be interpreted as a substantial vote of confidence in the Government.

Later that year (1900) Akers-Douglas received a remarkable tribute to his influence, experience and reputation for diplomacy in being charged with a highly delicate mission. It had been increasingly clear to his family and doctors that the doubling of the parts of Prime Minister and Foreign Secretary by Lord Salisbury was now too much for him—though unfortunately less clear to Salisbury himself. Also, though the Queen realized that he ought to relinquish the Foreign Office, she was afraid that by initiating the suggestion she might wound his feelings and make him think she had lost confidence in him. On a covering slip to some of the correspondence in which he was involved over this matter, Akers-Douglas showed plainly that he did not relish his task by writing:

> As to changes in Govt. 1900—especially as to Ld. Salisbury's position as Prime Minister and Foreign Secretary . . . Ld. Salisbury ultimately agreed to give up Foreign Office—I was negociator, and was successful: but it was a difficult and unpleasant mission.
>
> A. A-D.

The heavy correspondence and intricate manoeuvres involved in this affair afford a striking example not only of the influence wielded by the Queen in all affairs of State right up to the last days of her life and reign but of the great deference shown towards her personal likes and dislikes. At the same time the great position achieved by Lord Salisbury as a national symbol, whom it was almost unthinkable to displace or even to lessen in any way, becomes abundantly clear.

The opening move was made by Balfour, who sent to Akers-Douglas, who was at the time minister in attendance at Balmoral, a careful letter intended to acquaint the Queen gently with the general feeling. In a covering note he wrote:

> *Dictated*
> *Private*
>
> Whittinghame,
> Prestonkirk, N.B.
> Oct. 18th 1900
>
> My dear Akers,
>
> The accompanying letter to you expresses my views in a form in which you might, if you thought fit, shew them to Bigge, and if Bigge and you thought fit, even to the Queen. But this I leave to your judgment.
>
> Yours ever
> A. J. B.

The enclosed letter read:

> *Dictated*
>
> Whittinghame,
> Prestonkirk,
> Oct. 18th 1900
>
> My dear Douglas,
>
> I do very earnestly hope that the Queen will not insist upon Lord S. keeping *both* offices. It requires no Doctor to convince his

family that the work, whenever it gets really serious, is too much for him. I have twice had to take the Foreign Office, and three times, if I remember rightly, he has been obliged to go abroad at rather critical moments in our national affairs. He is over 70, and not a specially strong man. If the Queen desires (as I am sure She does) to keep him as Prime Minister, I feel sure She would be well advised not to insist on his being also Foreign Minister.

Lord James[1] may be right in thinking that public opinion on the Continent would view with dismay Lord Salisbury's retirement from office: but this is only because they fear that the control of our foreign policy would thereby fall into the hands of Chamberlain, whom, for some reason or other, they have chosen to erect into a political bogey. I do not believe they would be the least alarmed at an arrangement which left Lord Salisbury Prime Minister, and put the conduct of Foreign Office details into the hands of Lord Lansdowne.[2]

Yours very sincerely,
Arthur James Balfour.

The same day Akers-Douglas had written to Balfour:

Confidential

Balmoral Castle
18 Oct. 1900

My dear Arthur,

The Queen sent for me yesterday afternoon, and told me she had heard from Bigge the chief features of Lord Salisbury's proposals for the reconstruction of the Government, and desired me to telegraph to Lord Salisbury to say that, while she was anxious not to trouble him to come here, she wished to discuss with him the proposed changes. Further, she wished to know if the matter was urgent, or could wait until her return to Windsor on 8th November.

The Queen, as far as I can gather, is now quite prepared to approve, but is in some difficulty re Foreign Office, and seems to think she has been placed in a very awkward position. Bigge has told her that Lord Salisbury, while suggesting the change at the Foreign Office, would be prepared to stay on if the Queen wished him to do so. Thus the Queen thinks that the responsibility of asking Lord Salisbury to give up the Foreign Office will rest on her,

[1] The former Sir Henry James, created in 1895 Lord James of Hereford, was one whose opinion the Queen greatly valued.

[2] Henry, 5th Marquess; Secretary of State for War, 1895–1900.

and she shrinks from having to ask him to go. Her own feelings evidently are, that Lord Salisbury cannot without injury to his health undertake again the double office, and should therefore be relieved of the Foreign Office. She has no objection I think to Lansdowne at Foreign Office, though she had rather thought of Pauncefote;[1] and the proposed change is indeed more attractive to her by thought of Cranborne[2] as Under secretary . . .

Yours sincerely,
A. Akers-Douglas.[3]

Also on the same day Akers-Douglas had taken it upon himself to write the following letter to Salisbury, in which he tried to intimate to the latter something of the Queen's feelings; but it is noticeable that when he came to the crucial point about Salisbury himself, he did not say much to induce the latter to drop that equivocal attitude which was causing all the bother.

Balmoral Castle
8 Oct. 1900

Dear Lord Salisbury,

The Queen sent for me yesterday afternoon and said that Sir A. Bigge had told her of certain proposed changes in the Govt. which you had in view and which you desired she should consider.

She told me of the proposed change at the W[ar]O[ffice] and asked me what were the relative positions and service in Parliament of Brodrick[4] and Wyndham.[5] I said that, while I of course would give her frankly as I was bound to do my opinion upon any such point, I wished her to understand that, beyond one or two points which you had mentioned to me on Saturday, I was not sure of what your intentions were, nor was I authorized by you to discuss even the proposed changes you and Arthur have mentioned to me.

The Queen then said that she had not made out from Bigge whether there was any immediate hurry for her decision and

[1] Sir Julian Pauncefote, Ambassador to U.S.A. 1893–9, created 1st Baron Pauncefote, 1899.

[2] Lord Salisbury's son and heir, Under-Secretary for Foreign Affairs 1900–3.

[3] There is no copy of this letter in Akers-Douglas papers. The above version is reproduced from *Queen Victoria's Letters*, Third Series, III, 606.

[4] Rt. Hon. W. St. John Brodrick, at this time Under Secretary for Foreign Affairs; later 9th Viscount and 1st Earl of Midleton.

[5] Rt. Hon. George Wyndham, Under Secretary for War 1898–1900, Chief Secretary for Ireland 1900–5.

whether you wished her to consider your proposals and discuss them with you on her return—and further desired me to ascertain this from you by telegram.

She is very anxious not to bring you down to this Arctic region —unless absolutely necessary.

She also told me of possible changes at F.O. and Admiralty. With regard to these she is in great perplexity but said that your proposed change [i.e. his relinquishing the Foreign Office] wd. be rendered more agreeable if Cranborne were to be Under Secretary—and further asked me whether I thought you had considered the possibility of Pauncefote, (who had so long worked under you at F.O. as S[ecretary] of S[tate]. She did not fancy B[alfour] of B[urleigh] at Admiralty, but was more alarmed at prospects of Beach at Home Office.

After the Council today she told me that she thought there would be no objections to yr. Admiralty and W.O. proposals; but she hoped you would not rob her of Lord James![1]

Blandly ignoring the central and burning question concerning his own position, Salisbury wired back:

The difficulty is that two offices in question are the Admiralty and the War Office. Mr. Goschen has actually resigned and Lansdowne has intimated his intention of doing so. Both offices are consequently to a great extent paralysed—With two wars in progress this is rather awkward. The Queen is exceedingly kind in trying to spare me, but I shall not be the worse for the journey. If she will allow me I will arrive Balmoral on Tuesday morning.

Meanwhile, Akers-Douglas had shown Balfour's letter to the Queen and, as a result, now had the satisfaction of at least knowing that she had been convinced by it. But the principal figure in the drama still eluded them and, moreover, if he appeared at Balmoral before a firm undertaking had been extracted from him, there was always a danger that the Queen might weaken. There was therefore nothing for it but for Akers-Douglas to rush down and force a surrender before the venerable Premier started northwards. Thus he wrote to Balfour:

Balmoral Castle
Oct. 19th 1900

My dear Arthur,

Your letter came just at the right moment, was exactly what was wanted, and I think has quite settled the matter.

[1] From a draft in the Akers-Douglas papers.

The Queen has always been convinced that Lord S. ought not to go on with his F.O. work—She was for the moment a bit upset and unsettled by James's advice—but told me yesterday she knew we were right, and would support our view.

Her only difficulty now is that she fears Lord S. may himself suggest that he should stay at F.O. and she shrinks from the task of telling him *she* thinks he ought to go.

She has just told me she wishes me to go to Hatfield on my way South with some messages to Lord S, which she will give me tomorrow before I start. I do not at all relish the job as I fear Lord S. may resent it, but the Queen insists.

Lord S. comes here Tuesday—most elaborate preparations are being made for his comfort and the warmest rooms being prepared for him. I had hoped he would not have come until you were here or had been with the Queen, but I think your letter has answered the purpose.

As I told you yesterday the Queen suggested that changes sh[d]. be held over till her return: but Ld. S answered at once that he wished to come Tuesday.

The Queen was most anxious he shd. not take the risk of the journey; but feels apart from her desire to discuss the changes in view she ought to see him before any reconstruction is announced —even if only for public form's sake.

I shall leave this tomorrow afternoon about 3 for 113 Mount Street where I shall dress and breakfast Sunday morning & then go down as quietly as I can to Hatfield for an hour hoping I may be able to evade the keen sight of the press detectives.

Yrs. ever
A. A. D.

Just before he started south Akers-Douglas evidently thought he ought to find out from Bigge exactly what message Lord Salisbury had originally sent to the Queen about his own position. It will be clear from this that Salisbury had indeed placed her in a very awkward position. Bigge's memo ran:

The message which I received from Lord Salisbury on the 13th inst. for the Queen was: That his Drs. advocated less work: that outside opinion rather favoured a separation of the duties of P.M. & F.O. but that he felt he had quite the strength to go on in both offices: But that he was ready to do whatever is most agreeable to the Queen and is in her own judgment most beneficial to the public service.

I conveyed the message in a letter which H.M. received on Sunday, 14th.

A.B.
20.10.00

However, the delicate mission was completely successful and the sequel to these intricate and agonizing negotiations is to be found in the following draft telegram from Akers-Douglas to the Queen.

> Mr. Douglas presents his humble duty to yr. Majesty and begs to say that he saw Lord Salisbury today and understood that Ld. S. himself wishes relief from his present double office and further that his family strongly desire that for health's sake he should not again undertake both the F.O. and Premiership. Mr. Douglas was glad to hear from Lord S. that he proposed to submit the name of the new S. of State for F. Affairs in the usual course—thus relieving Your Majesty from having to express any desire that he should relinquish the Foreign Office. Lord Salisbury is well and feels no difficulty in undertaking the journey to Balmoral.

Accordingly Lord Salisbury handed over the Foreign Office to Lord Lansdowne; 'but I said that it must be on the strict understanding that he [Lansdowne] must be entirely under his personal supervision,' wrote the Queen, '. . . and that no telegram or dispatch should be sent without first being submitted to him.'[1] Lansdowne in turn handed over the War Office to St. John Brodrick. Lord Selborne succeeded Goschen at the Admiralty. Ritchie, who had done good work at the Board of Trade became Home Secretary in the place of Sir Matthew White Ridley. George Wyndham became Chief Secretary for Ireland. Finally, Salisbury, while retaining the Premiership, became Lord Privy Seal in succession to Lord Cross, who thus brought to an end a political career of more than forty years. Cross was a great favourite of the Queen, whose insistence had led to his inclusion in every Conservative and Unionist Cabinet since 1874.

Bigge, in returning to Akers-Douglas the Balfour letter which had set the ball rolling in the above affair, added some rather waggish comments about certain of the Cabinet changes.

[1] *Letters of Queen Victoria*, Third Series, III, 611.

Private

Balmoral Castle
3 Nov. 1900

My dear Douglas,

In accordance with the Queen's suggestion, I return the enclosed letter to you from Mr. A. B.

I wonder what you think of the progress of the Cabinet making.

Being a narrow-minded Northumbrian I can't help feeling that dear old M[atthew] R[idley] has been a bit hardly treated—and I gather that tho' he says nothing, he shares this feeling and that the H.O. regret his going.

I remember what you said about the North of England.

The transfer of its vote to the Govt. is surely one of the most striking of the G. Election 'phenomena', and in recognition you remove 2 Northern representatives, Cross and Ridley, from the Cabinet—and move up Ritchie.

I gather that the dispossessed Privy Seal did not at all wish to send in his cap and jacket but that old M[atthew]R[idley] did it with a good grace tho' disliking it none the less. However H.M. says she will ask the former to stay here occasionally!!

But we hear whispers that difficult tho' it may be to remove a *cross* still more serious is the business of getting rid of a chaplain![1]

And yet some people make light of the ritual question!

Yrs. ever
Arthur Bigge.

When it was all settled Salisbury wrote to Akers-Douglas, in the latter's capacity as First Commissioner of Works, the following characteristic note.

Hatfield House,
Hatfield,
Herts.
Nov. 3, 1900

My dear Douglas,

I think it will cause least inconvenience if I am housed at F.O. —supposing always that Lansdowne will consent. I only want one room—any Secretaries can remain where they are now—and if place is wanted for anyone who wants to see me to wait in, the waiting room in actual use will be quite sufficient. But before you do it obtain Lansdowne's consent personally; for the F.O. Staff, who are very cliquish, will prevent it if they can.

Ever yours truly,
Salisbury.

[1] A reference to Rt. Hon. Henry Chaplin (later 1st Viscount Chaplin), President of Local Government Board, 1895–1900.

After these extremely arduous and serious negotiations Akers-Douglas evidently thought to divert the Queen by sending her a press-cutting referring to some amusing exchange in the House. But the Queen had never been easy to amuse at the best of times—and these were not the best of times, for they were almost the last days of her life. Sir Frederick Ponsonby[1] reported (November 9th, 1900): 'I gave it to Mrs. Grant[2] to read to H.M. but "we" were not quite certain we liked it and have not alluded to it since. Arthur Balfour has been here but I don't think the Queen made any reference to his witty reply in the House.'

[1] Assistant Private Secretary to the Queen, later created Baron Sysonby.
[2] The Hon. Mrs. (Victoria) Grant; Lady-in-Waiting.

XVI
ARMY EDUCATION AND HOME OFFICE

THE war in South Africa having focused attention on deficiencies in the Army and military training the Government hastened, even while it was still in progress, to show readiness to initiate improvements. Thus the newly appointed Minister for War, St. John Brodrick, produced a scheme for the reorganization of the Army with special emphasis on the provision of a Field Force ready for immediate despatch overseas; but he was moved from the War Office (through the machinations of Lord Esher) before he had time to develop it. Meanwhile Akers-Douglas, who had shown considerable interest in the subject and had spoken on several occasions to his constituents on the 'lessons of the war', was in April 1901 appointed chairman of a Committee set up by Brodrick to report on Military Education and Officers Training. It was in this capacity that he received the following letter from Lord Roberts, at this time Commander-in-Chief and the hero of the hour. The letter is interesting partly for those views which foreshadow the breakdown of the old, rigid distinctions between the functions of the various arms of the Forces which the rapid decline of the formal conception of warfare has imposed and partly for the glimpses which it affords of the state of affairs on the South African war-front, given by the very man who was more qualified than anyone else to judge of it.

Queen Hotel,
Harrogate
29th August, 1901

Dear Mr. Akers-Douglas,

I am most anxious to have a talk with you before you finish your Report on the education and training of young men who are destined for Military Service, for I am concerned to hear from Sir Ian Hamilton that you propose to recommend that the Cadets at Woolwich should be separated, those intended for the Garrison Artillery being educated at Woolwich, and those for Horse and Field Artillery at Sandhurst.

To my mind this would be a fatal mistake.

There is very little, if any, difference required in the primary education of Artillery Officers whether they are to join the mounted or the non-mounted branch . . .

After young officers join the regiment their work becomes somewhat different, but not to a great extent, and in an emergency, such as the Mutiny in India or the present war, they may be called upon to do the work for which they may not be specially trained. For instance, during the Mutiny, I, with several other Horse Artillery men, had to man the breaching batteries at Delhi, and throughout the present war Garrison Artillerymen have been obliged to do Horse & Field Artillery duty with Ammunition columns, etc. . . .

The war in South Africa has taught us (what has been the custom in India for quite a century) that heavy guns must be used in the field, and not confined to the defence of positions. It follows, therefore, that Horse, Field and Garrison Artillery must be mixed up on service, and not kept as two distinct units . . .

Besides discussing the Woolwich–Sandhurst question, in which as you may imagine I am intensely interested, I should like to hear what you propose to do in regard to getting more capable young fellows to enter the Cavalry than has hitherto been the case. The following facts will bring home to you how essential it is there should be considerable improvement in this respect.

When the war in South Africa broke out three brigades of Cavalry were despatched. This was in October and November 1899. Shortly after I landed at Cape Town in January 1900, I found it necessary to remove one of the Brigade Commanders, and early in February I had to carry out the same painful duty in regard to the Commander of the Second Brigade. The third Brigade was in Natal, the Commander proved to be of little use, and shortly after he came under my direct orders I had to send him home.

The three officers who took the places of the deposed Commanders were almost as incapable and they in their turn had to be ordered home.

It was much the same with the regimental Commanders. Irrespective of the Household Cavalry, there were 17 regiments with me in South Africa; the Commanders of 11 of these had to be removed, and only one or two of the remaining 6 were really fit to be at the head of a Cavalry regiment . . .

Yours very truly,

Roberts.

Another member of the Committee was Dr. Edmond Warre, the Headmaster of Eton, who was worried about the great width of the field which the enquiry had to cover and wrote (June 23rd, '01): '. . . The enquiry is being rather labyrinthine and the threads will become more and more difficult to pick up unless we adopt method.' He added: 'I was up at Oxford on Thursday and had a very interesting discussion with the Provost of Queen's and the Master of Balliol upon the possibilities of the Universities in the matter of Military Education. I am sure that with their goodwill much might be effected. Especially as regards the scientific Branches and Military Science properly so-called . . .'

Next year Brodrick wrote:

War Office

March 20 [1902]

My dear Douglas,

I am reading your report with greatest interest but wait to comment till I've got through it.

I just wanted to ask whether instead of being engulfed by Ritchie or A.J.B. at the King's Birthday dinner you would not like to stray into my fold with the soldiers.

Being Coronation Year I am making my dinner specially large and am asking, besides the recognized Field Marshals, etc., some of those who have helped us at W.O.

You have done so much and your name will be so inseparably connected with Army Education that I think I have a claim on you and so venture at least the chance.

Yours ever,

St. John Brodrick.

The Report, when published soon afterwards, caused a sensation—perhaps even more because it emanated from and was sponsored by such an impeccably Conservative source than on account of the disgraceful nature of some of its revelations. In fact the Radical press, whilst seizing eagerly upon the matter, could not withhold a modicum of admiration for the courage of the Tory chairman. It was thus summarized by the *Birmingham Gazette* (May 22nd, '02):

> It is a conscientious document, which speaks the truth fearlessly. It is a scathing condemnation of the entire system of army education, which is to be entirely remodelled, both as regards the entrance examinations, the courses at Woolwich and Sandhurst, and the after-education of the officers. Sandhurst is unequivocally condemned, but both Woolwich and Sandhurst are to be retained, subject to sweeping alterations.

This account was amplified with great relish by the Manchester *Daily Despatch* (May 22nd, '02), under the heading 'Yet Another Scandal'.

> To make out such a case as this evidence is adduced which will astonish anybody who has not passed that time of life which makes surprise at anything impossible. Dealing with the Sandhurst School the Committee say that every evil, down to personal uncleanliness, is rampant. The thing which is most foreign from the Sandhurst curriculum is military education in any useful form. The primary causes of so many 'regrettable incidents' in South Africa are revealed in a somewhat startling fashion. We are told that many Cavalry officers cannot write a decent letter, and that their reports while scouting have been confused and have led whole regiments into trouble. The cavalry has been more exclusively the monopoly of the rich than any other arm of the British Military Service . . .
>
> It is made bitterly apparent that the British Army has hitherto existed less as a national than as a social institution. The passing strangeness of these revelations is less a matter of surprise than the singular fact that a Committee largely composed of service members of the House should have the temerity honestly to expose them. The report 'seeks to ensure real military education and promotion by merit alone, and not by influence and interest in high quarters, especially of women, to which some of the witnesses testify'. The fact of this very radical pronouncement is not a new thing to us. The novelty of the report lies in the emphatic stand taken by the Committee. They remark 'that it is possible to get either money or brains', and they confidently recommend the

> latter. It is an ugly reflection that lives and limbs of sons of British mothers have been confided to the gilded dandies who have been trained (?) under the conditions exposed by this inquiry. It is suggested by a contemporary that 'it is a wonder our officers have done so well', considering the circumstances. At all events it is no wonder they have done so badly. The recommendation that promotion should in future depend upon merit alone is by inference an admission that in the past it has depended on anything else . . .

On July 17th, in the House of Lords, the Government accepted at the instance of Lord Monkswell,[1] a resolution declaring that the earliest possible steps should be taken with a view to remedy the state of things disclosed in the Report of the War Office Committee on Military Education. Moreover, the Report seemed to be emphasized by disorders which occurred at Sandhurst during the summer, when Lord Roberts intervened to order the rustication of twenty-nine cadets who could not prove an alibi on the occasion of the last of a series of mysterious fires at the Academy, and also dismissed the Commandant.

Writing to Colonel Sir Edward Ward[2] nearly three years later (February 13th, '05) Akers-Douglas remarked that 'nearly all our recommendations have been carried out—so far as the Academy went at all events'.

Meanwhile, rapidly failing health had brought about the complete and final resignation of Lord Salisbury (July 11th, '02). He was succeeded as Prime Minister almost inevitably by his nephew Arthur Balfour, who had now led the House for ten years. There was no major reconstruction of the Cabinet, but Sir Michael Hicks Beach insisted on retiring from the Chancellorship of the Exchequer together with a chief whom, in his daughter's words, 'he had loved and trusted only second to Disraeli'.[3] The new Chancellor was Ritchie, who was moved up from the Home Office, and the new Home Secretary was Akers-Douglas.[4] 'Although it is against my own interests,' wrote

[1] 2nd Baron, Under Secretary for War, 1895 (Liberal).

[2] Permanent Under Secretary, War Office, 1901–14.

[3] Lady Victoria Hicks Beach: *Life of Sir M. Hicks Beach*, II, 174.

[4] It is suggested by J. S. Sandars in *Studies of Yesterday, by a Privy Councillor* (p. 162) that he could, had he wished, have aspired to be Chancellor of the Exchequer, but this seems an unlikely post for him and there is no other corroboration.

Schomberg McDonnell (Aug. 1st, '02), who after Salisbury's retirement had become Secretary to the Commissioners of Works, 'I do most certainly hope that you will take the Home Office: there must be a strong man there: and there is nobody in the Cabinet so capable as yourself of doing the business.'

The post provided excellent scope for just the qualities of capable administration, sound judgment and discretion that Akers-Douglas possessed in so marked a degree. But his contribution to the Government amounted to something more than that. As Balfour's biographer has written: 'Mr. Akers-Douglas, the Home Secretary, was one of those colleagues whom all Prime Ministers cherish, steady, wise, vastly experienced as an ex-Whip; he was a standby throughout.'[1]

From the strictly departmental angle the principal monument to his brief tenure of office is probably the Aliens Act. The Bill which Akers-Douglas introduced in March 1904 was based on the recommendations of a Royal Commission of the previous year, but he felt strongly in favour of the proposals and fought hard to secure their placing on the Statute Book. It empowered the Home Secretary to make regulations requiring the master of any ship to furnish a return of his alien passengers and authorized officers of the Home Office to require information from any alien immigrant as to his character, antecedents and proposed place of residence. When necessary, aliens were to be prevented from landing, or only permitted to land on conditions. The background to the measure can be given in the words of *The Times* (May 31st, '04):

> The measure is directed against two kinds of 'undesirables' now flocking to England—the criminal or quasi-criminal class, and persons likely to become a charge upon the public funds, or having no visible or probable means of support . . . We exported last year nearly 150,000 natives of these islands; presumably a large percentage of the emigrants being the best brains and muscle of the country. The influx of 14,000 foreigners was a poor set-off both as to quantity and quality. Such are the conditions of emigration from Russia and Poland that there is no assurance that we get the strong, the stout-hearted, the enterprising. We send out the vigorous, and their place is taken by the feeble, some of whom bring us only rags, dirt and strange uncivic habits.

[1] Dugdale, I, 336.

The Bill was ostensibly opposed by the 'Lib–Lab.' Opposition as being unworkable and also as being contrary to the spirit of liberty and to the ancient British tradition of giving asylum to political and religious refugees. But this high-minded attitude could not stand up to a very close examination. For instance, although Radicals posed as the champions of the British working man and although the latter's livelihood was undeniably threatened by the continual incursion of Russian and Polish Jews, they yet were natural allies of the interlopers also, who had emigrated or fled not only because of being Jews, but usually because of being revolutionaries or radicals as well. Thus, by refusing a reasonable measure of redress for doctrinaire reasons, they were really betraying the interests of the British working man and at the same time greatly increasing the risk of a general anti-Semitic trend which was liable to rebound against the old-established Jewish community in London.

Nevertheless, so successful were the Opposition—headed by the young and still irresponsible Winston Churchill (aided by the equally young and irresponsible Herbert Samuel)[1]—in obstructing and 'talking the Bill to death' that Akers-Douglas felt reluctantly compelled to move the withdrawal of the Bill (July '04). But the frivolity of these young hopefuls was made manifest when they turned round to rend the Government for dropping the Bill which they themselves had announced their determination to destroy. They even had the effrontery to vote for keeping it alive—but of course amended out of all semblance of its original self.

However, in the following year Akers-Douglas introduced a new Bill—in some respects less drastic but perhaps more workable than its predecessor—and this was ultimately passed just before the fall of Balfour's Government. The Bill forbade the landing of immigrants at any but eight important ports and then gave power to exclude any likely to prove incapable of supporting themselves, suffering from a contagious or 'loathsome' disease or mentally afflicted and such as might have been convicted of crime equivalent to felony in their own country. Another important measure for which Akers-Douglas was responsible during his tenure of the Home Office was a Penal

[1] Achieved office in following year as Parliamentary Under Secretary, Home Department; later Viscount Samuel.

Servitude Bill, designed to prevent judges from being deterred from imposing long sentences on habitual criminals by enabling a proportion of the sentence to be served under conditions less harsh than those of regular penal servitude, and in which some attempt at reform and training could be made.

Two *causes célèbres* also fell within his Home Secretaryship. The first of these concerned 'Colonel' Arthur Lynch, an Irishman who had raised and led an Irish Brigade to fight on the side of the Boers in South Africa. In 1901, with the backing of the Nationalist Party, Lynch was elected M.P. for Co. Galway. The Government responded by issuing a warrant for his arrest on a charge of high treason. Lynch nevertheless determined to take his seat in the House and on landing in England was immediately arrested. He spent eight months in prison while evidence was being collected in South Africa and was finally brought to trial in January 1903 before the Lord Chief Justice, Lord Alverstone.[1] After a three days' trial, on January 23rd, he was found guilty of high treason and sentenced to death. However, there was a strong feeling in several influential quarters that execution would be unjust, as well as politically inexpedient, since there were some grounds for believing that before the conclusion of peace in South Africa Roberts and Kitchener had given promises that there would be no prosecutions for treason.

The following letter reached the Home Secretary a few days after the sentence from the Duke of Argyll:[2]

Kensington
Jan. 26, 1903

My dear Akers-Douglas,

I trust there is no intention to carry out the death sentence in the case of 'Colonel' Lynch. I have no liking for Rebels, but the hanging of a man who has joined the Boers against us wd. be to take the only method by which sympathy might be aroused for him and his comrades who fought in open war.

Yrs. truly
Argyll.

[1] The former Sir Richard Webster, Attorney General 1886–92 and 1895–1900.

[2] 9th Duke, husband of Princess Louise; former Governor-General of Canada, and one-time M.P. for South Manchester.

But Akers-Douglas had in fact already recommended the commutation of Lynch's sentence to one of penal servitude for life. Lord Knollys, the King's Private Secretary, wrote (Jan. 27th) that the King 'quite approves of what you intend doing in the matter. He thinks however that what is intended should be announced to the Public as soon as possible.' To this Akers-Douglas replied: 'The commutation to P.S. for life is now public property. To make any announcement as to the term for which he may be held to serve would be contrary to practice, and most embarrassing.'

Not long afterwards Akers-Douglas received advice from his Permanent Secretary at the Home Office, Sir Kenelm Digby, tending to the further tempering of the severity of the sentence.

Home Office,
Whitehall
March 1st [1903]

Dear Mr. Akers-Douglas,

I have seen Ruggles Brise[1] as to Lynch. He (personally) feels rather strongly that a treason or political prisoner should have a different treatment to the ordinary felon or misdemeanant. It may not be necessary to consider this at present at all events in Lynch's case—at all events it would be better to do this in conversation.

As regards such matters as allowing his wife to pay him a visit, giving him extra facilities as regards books, etc.—he sees no reason at all why this should not be done quietly. Similar treatment was given to Michael Davitt and justified by Sir W. Harcourt in the H. of C. and is in accordance with the recommendations of the Devon Commission. I should myself personally be strongly in favour of allowing his wife to pay him a visit and which I understand is the immediate question.

Very truly yrs.
Kenelm E. Digby.

This policy was evidently adopted, for in the following month we find Mrs. Lynch writing to thank the Home Secretary in a very ingratiating letter, showing a rather startling concern for his health and private affairs.

[1] Sir E. Ruggles-Brise, K.C.B.; Chairman of the Prison Commission.

14 Alfred Road,
Acton, W.
25/4/03

Right Honourable Aretas Akers-Douglas

Dear Sir,

I have formally acknowledged to the Home Office, the permit I received to visit my husband, but I feel I must personally thank you for the extra favour therein granted, as I am sure they are due to your kind influence . . .

I hope you will not think it intrusion on my part when I say how very deeply I sympathize with you and your family in your recent sad bereavement.[1]

At the same time I am gratified to learn that your own health is nearly restored.

Yours faithfully,
Annie Lynch.

In July the King intervened again in the case and Knollys wrote:

Confidential

Buckingham Palace
16 July, 1903

My dear Douglas,

The King has told me to ask you confidentially whether you think it would be a good thing, in view of H.M's visit to Ireland, if Lynch were liberated or an announcement made that his sentense of imprisonment would be shortened. The King does not make the suggestion on the ground of *expediency*, but because he thinks it might be a graceful act to adopt one of the two courses mentioned on the occasion of his State visit to Ireland, and of his first one there since his accession.

Yrs. sincerely,
Knollys.

But Akers-Douglas pointed out that Lynch's offence had not been in any way connected with Ireland and that therefore it would be invidious to single him out for special grace from among others—such as South Africans—guilty of taking up arms against the Crown in South Africa. Knollys reported that the King 'at once saw the force of your arguments, and withdraws his suggestion'.

[1] His sister had just died.

A few months later Mrs. Lynch evidently approached the Duke of Norfolk, who seems to have been under a small obligation to her brother, for some special favour for her husband, for the Duke sent on her letter to Akers-Douglas (September 20th, '03) saying:

> . . . I really do not know anything of the question but Mrs. Lynch's brother gave me very prompt and efficient assistance when I had an accident in S. Africa and she came to see me about her Husband. I have been told that you regarded the case as one in which some amelioration would be just . . .

But the King himself was, in every sense, Lynch's most powerful advocate. In December he had received direct appeals from a mutual friend, Sir Thomas Lipton, and also from the Irish Nationalist, Michael Davitt, and he began to press the Home Secretary for a remission of sentence. As a result Akers-Douglas wrote the following letter to the Lord Chief Justice:

> *Confidential*
>
> Dec. 26th, 1903
>
> My dear Alverstone,
>
> . . . I am being pressed both by the King on the one hand and by some of my colleagues in the Cabinet on the other to remit the remainder of Lynch's sentence or at all events to let him out on license.
>
> You will remember that the King was anxious to make the Royal visit to Ireland last summer an excuse for Lynch's release—I successfully resisted the idea pointing out (1) that Lynch had not been convicted of any Irish political or agrarian offence, but of taking up arms against the King in South Africa (2) that less than 6 months had elapsed since the sentence (3) that he ought not to be treated differently to those sentenced for similar offence in South Africa.
>
> Though I made no bargain with the King there was some general understanding that Lynch's case should be treated on lines laid down by your Commission[1] in South Africa, i.e. that his imprisonment should be measured by a moderate standard of punishment which might be properly applied having regard to

[1] The Lord Chief Justice and Mr. Justice Bigham had gone to South Africa at the conclusion of peace in the previous year and revised sentences passed during the war.

the fact that the war had ended and peace had been re-established and there was no longer any necessity for exemplary or preventative punishment.—I then pointed out that I thought Lynch ought to serve at all events the revised average term served by prisoners convicted in South Africa for similar offence.

On looking at the Schedule to the Report of your Commission it appears 1½ years is about the average term actually served under the amnesty mentioned below.

Lynch will shortly have served a year since his sentence and was in prison some 8 months previously which might be taken into consideration. Further, I understand that the authorities in S. Africa have since your visit to South Africa proclaimed a general amnesty and that now there are no prisoners in S. Africa convicted of high treason.

If it should be decided to release him I would rather do so at some convenient date in January. His case is sure to be raised in Parliament probably on the Address and I do not want, if a release is decided on, to appear to give way to Nationalist clamour. I prefer to advise the King—off my own bat—to exercise his prerogative or else to resist definitely all idea of immediate release.

The Prime Minister has asked me to circulate a memo to the Cabinet on the subject. Excuse my troubling you in the holiday season and asking for your assistance and advice—

Yours very sincerely,

A. Akers-Douglas.

Soon afterwards Akers-Douglas wrote to Knollys outlining the position for the benefit of the King (January 20th, '04):

. . . I may add that the Irish Govt. seem anxious that he should be released as considerable feeling exists in that country at his continued detention and the Judges who tried the case—though they are disposed in their judicial capacity to take a serious view and consider that nothing less than 3 or 4 years would be an adequate punishment for the crime—recognize readily that if the matter be looked at from the point of view of Royal Grace or even of general policy it may be proper to release him.

Before advising the King as to any exercise of the prerogative, as the matter involves a question of general policy, I propose to consult my colleagues at the Cabinet on Saturday.[1]

[1] He had a Memorandum printed for their consideration, a copy of which is among his papers.

> But I should be glad if you would mention the matter privately to His Majesty and unless I hear that he has a contrary view I should propose to make a submission on the subject on Saturday afternoon.

Knollys wrote back next day: 'The King quite approves of the release of Lynch, but he strongly urges that it should take place before the meeting of Parliament.'

As a result Lynch was released—but only on licence. For the sequel we are dependent upon Sir Sidney Lee's account in his biography of the King, from which the latter's attitude does not emerge very clearly. 'The King,' he says, '. . . was inclined to a more liberal act of clemency. But when Mr. Lynch wrote to the King asking for his full freedom the King was reluctant to interfere, and the Home Secretary granted a conditional pardon, which set the Irishman free with some restrictions.'[1] In July 1906—by which time Akers-Douglas had been succeeded at the Home Office by Herbert Gladstone—Lynch again sought relief from all his disabilities; but the King was opposed to any further immediate action, though hinting that after a reasonable interval he might be prepared to change his mind. Thus a year later he finally concurred in the grant of a free pardon.[2]

The other celebrated—and most peculiar—case which began in Akers-Douglas's Home Secretaryship was that of George Edalji. The latter was a young solicitor, the son of a Parsee Anglican vicar, who had been sentenced at the Staffordshire Quarter Sessions in October 1903 to seven years penal servitude on conviction of wounding a horse. There had been numerous horrible mutilations of animals in the locality, but when these continued after Edalji's imprisonment suspicions of a miscarriage of justice arose. After careful examination of the case Akers-Douglas, as Home Secretary, decided in October 1905 to reduce the sentence to one of three years, thereafter releasing Edalji on licence. But meanwhile a public agitation about the case had been started, on the one hand by Labouchere in *Truth* and on the other by Sir Arthur Conan Doyle in the *Daily Telegraph*. By this time Herbert Gladstone had become Home

[1] Sir Sidney Lee: *King Edward VII*, II, 40–1.

[2] Lynch subsequently sat for West Clare as a Nationalist from 1909 to 1922. He joined the British Army in World War I, becoming a colonel in 1918.

Secretary and he was reluctantly compelled to appoint an official Special Commission of Inquiry. But before that it was necessary to discover from his predecessor what had caused the latter to reduce the sentence in the first place. Thus the Permanent Under Secretary, Sir Mackenzie Chalmers, wrote to Akers-Douglas:

Home Office,
Whitehall,
S.W.
5 Jany. 1907

My dear Aretas,

We understand that Conan Doyle is taking up the Edalji case, and is going to write a series of articles in the Sherlock Holmes style.

My recollection is that you submitted the papers to Lord Dunedin (at that time Ld. Advocate) and that he agreed with the rest of us that there was no ground for interference though the case had some unsatisfactory features. I can't find any memo of his in the file. Did he give you any written opinion, or did he go sufficiently into the case to enable H.O. to ask him if he gave an opinion?

Of course it would strengthen the H.O. position if Ld. Dunedin could be quoted, but it is no use writing to him till I know how far you went into case with him before deciding it.

Yrs. ever
M. D. Chalmers.

And the Home Secretary, Herbert Gladstone, wrote:

Private

Feb. 8 '07
Home Office,
Whitehall,
S.W.

My dear Douglas,

The recrudescence of the anon. letters on the Edalji case and the ferment in the public mind over it made it necessary for me to submit all the papers to L.C. [Lord Chief Justice]. He has come to the decided view that an inquiry should be held, and the Govt. has agreed to this. There is a good deal to say and perhaps it would be better to have a talk about it. The position of course is that I am now asked to give E. a free pardon. On the evidence at present before us I cannot do that. On the other hand I have never been free from doubt and misgiving, and these later anon. letters and C. Doyle's theory as to the guilty parties which he has given me confidentially and wh. of course he has to keep absolutely private, have strengthened these doubts materially.

I have asked Romer[1] ex L.J. to be Chairman, but I have not heard from him yet. Of course it will be in no sense an inquiry into H.O. action. Our opinions may be right or wrong but there is no question about any omission or blunder as in the Beck case.[2] The papers would all be submitted to the Committee, and any further informn. or evidence wh. they required would be obtained if possible.

Sincerely yrs.
H. J. Gladstone.

The Commission reported that there were indeed unsatisfactory features about the trial and conviction, but that the Home Office would not have been warranted in interfering with it. On the strength of this the Home Secretary advised the King to grant a Free Pardon (May 14th, '07). To this the King heartily agreed; but, the Commissioners having expressed the view that Edalji had largely brought his troubles on himself, the Home Secretary refused to grant him any compensation.

King Edward, as will be gathered from the above instances, was keenly interested in the Royal Prerogative of Mercy—as indeed he was interested in the maintenance or rehabilitation of all ancient royal prerogatives. But the actual exercise of the prerogative of mercy, however justifiable by precedent and laudable in intention, was, under modern conditions, obviously full of dangers for the very Majesty of the Crown which it should have enhanced. Therefore, when asked to submit a memorandum on the subject, Akers-Douglas, in the words of Sir Sidney Lee, 'wisely pointed out to the King . . . that in the interest of the monarchy it was necessary for the Home Secretary to bear the brunt of the public and parliamentary criticism, and that no opening should be given for involving the King's name in these discussions'.[3]

In writing to the King on this occasion he did not mince his words, as will be seen from the copy here reproduced.

[1] Rt. Hon. Sir Robert Romer, a Lord Justice of Appeal 1899–1906.

[2] The case of Adolph Beck, sentenced in 1896 to seven years penal servitude, had come up for inquiry before a Committee in 1904. The latter's criticisms of the Home Office were still fresh in the public mind.

[3] Sir Sidney Lee, op. cit., II, 39.

Balmoral Castle
[Sept. 26 1903]

Mr. Secretary Akers-Douglas with his humble duty begs leave to enclose a Memorandum which he has prepared at Your Majesty's desire on the Royal Prerogative of Mercy—or rather on the constitutional practice as to the exercise of the prerogative.

Mr. Douglas thinks it is most important that the practice of the last 80 years at any rate, should not be departed from. He would particularly emphasize the three following points.

(1) There are from 5000 to 6000 petitions every year against convictions and sentences. If Your Majesty is to deal personally with any of them, you ought to deal personally with all. It would be invidious to pick and choose.

(2) If Your Majesty is to deal with death sentences your attention must be available at all times from sentence to final decision. The practice of the S[ecretary] of S[tate] is to deal not only on the evidence at the trial: but on evidence which accumulates until the last moment.

(3) The power of reprieve involves the power, and duty to refuse to reprieve. This latter power is sometimes bitterly attacked, and public opinion is lashed up by an unscrupulous partisan press. For instance the Radical Press took up Lipski's case[1]—in Mr. Secretary Matthews's[2] time—and if my memory serves me Mr. Stead[3] in one of his papers said, 'So an innocent man is to be sent to the gallows to gratify the wounded vanity of the Home Secretary.'[4] Such cases may always arise from time to time—and it must be borne in mind that 'yellow journalism' is on the increase. It would be intolerable that Your Majesty's name should be dragged into the mire to serve the temporary purposes of some wretched newspaper.

Again suppose a man of good position is reprieved strictly according to the traditional exercise of the prerogative (say great temptation and sudden passion) a section of the Press would not hesitate to attribute it to personal influence and raise the cry of 'one law for the rich and another for the poor'. It is in Mr. Douglas's opinion the Home Secretary's duty to bear the brunt of such attacks, and to defend himself if necessary in Parliament.

[1] A Polish Jew convicted of murder on clear but circumstantial evidence.

[2] Rt. Hon. Henry Matthews, Home Secretary 1886–92; created Viscount Llandaff.

[3] W. T. Stead, Editor of *Pall Mall Gazette* 1883–9; sentenced to three months in 1885 in connection with the 'Maiden Tribute' case.

[4] Lipski having signed a confession on the eve of his execution, Stead next day headed his leading article: 'All's well that ends well'!

Apart from his natural interest in his own constitutional rights, King Edward was, for all his exacting nature and occasionally severe manner, a man of an extremely humane disposition. This is evidenced in the following communication from Knollys to Akers-Douglas about a certain case (August 9th, '05).

> H. M. . . . desires me to let you know that he feels very strongly that Miss Doughty's sentence should be substantially reduced, and that he thinks it merciful she should be informed of the reduction as soon as you are able to do so.

As for Queen Alexandra, she was not only extremely tender-hearted, but also embarrassingly impulsive and unpractical. Thus her Private Secretary, Sydney Smith, would write to Akers-Douglas (February 3rd, '03):

> The Queen is distressed at seeing that two women are to be hung tomorrow—and she has had an appeal also for their lives—could you send me a line to show the Queen that it is not possible to do anything as she seemed interested in their case.

Or again (February 6th, '04):

> The Queen has been receiving a great number of letters from unemployed in London and East-End. H.M. has been rather moved by some of the stories told and was most anxious for me to write to the Lord Mayor and say she would be willing to put herself at the head of any movement or Fund for this purpose. I have not written and I do not intend doing so. It is a very ticklish question, I always think, and H.M. by doing this might do more harm than good . . .

On each occasion Akers-Douglas wrote letters which were shown to the Queen and succeeded in restraining her from making these very human but ill-considered gestures.

XVII
THE CABINET CRISIS OF 1903

THE succession in the premiership of Balfour to Salisbury was so smooth, and had for long seemed so inevitable, that it caused little stir, apart from the general feeling that an epoch had come to an end with the disappearance of the great figure who had so long dominated both the international and the British scene. It is true that—apart from his great qualities—as Leader of the House of Commons Balfour had had obvious shortcomings and that these were about to be manifested still more clearly in his tenure of the premiership. But, with the possible exception of Hicks Beach—and he wished to retire with his old chief—the strongest men in Lord Salisbury's Cabinet belonged to the Liberal Unionist wing of the coalition and it seemed far from likely in 1902 that the Conservative Party would have accepted a Liberal Unionist premier. Even in 1911 they would not have Joseph Chamberlain's son, Austen, as their leader.

Nevertheless, scarcely a year after Balfour's succession Joseph Chamberlain began to eclipse him. For, returning from a triumphant tour of South Africa in the early months of 1903 he astounded the world—and still more his colleagues—by boldly propounding the policy of Imperial Preference or Tariff Reform, and, in so doing, precipitated a Cabinet crisis. Through Knollys, Akers-Douglas warned the King of the likelihood of resignations and made some tentative suggestions about the rearrangement of the Cabinet. The reply shows plainly the King's determination to continue his mother's policy of insistence on having a say in the appointment of Ministers.

Private

Balmoral
13 Sept. 1903

My dear Douglas,

I wrote to the King and told him confidentially what you had said to me as to the possible shuffling of officers in the event of there being any resignations. He was much interested, and, as far as he is concerned, he thinks your ideas are very good ones.

He would however prefer Long at the W[ar] O[ffice] to Forster,[1] as he thinks the former would get on better with a Board, if there is one, than the latter.

He quite agrees that Mr. Chamberlain *must* be Chancellor of the Exchequer, and as regards the vacancy which would then occur at the C[olonial] O[ffice] he thinks that either Ld Balfour of Burleigh, if he remains, or Ld. Selborne would fill it very well.

He says it is *necessary* that Brodrick should be moved from the W[ar] O[ffice], and he thinks that the India Office would be very suitable for him. I thought the King would probably object to Ld. Selborne leaving the Admiralty just now, but he is under the impression that Lord Balfour would be very good there . . .

Yours sincerely,
Knollys.

But actually, impatient at the Prime Minister's noncommittal attitude towards his proposals, Chamberlain had already sent in his resignation on September 9th, although Balfour did not send any answer till the 16th and disclosed nothing even at a Cabinet meeting held on the 14th when he summarily dismissed Ritchie and Balfour of Burleigh from the Government—two ministers who were known to be intransigent Free Traders. On the following day, still in ignorance of the all-important fact, the Duke of Devonshire and Lord George Hamilton—also Free Traders—resigned. Only on the day after that did Balfour reveal Chamberlain's resignation—whereupon Devonshire revoked his resignation and returned to the fold. But the other three Free Trade ministers not unnaturally complained of having been practically tricked into going, not having been told that the man to whose presence in the Government they objected (Chamberlain) had resigned nearly a week before.

Austen Chamberlain then succeeded Ritchie as Chancellor

[1] Rt. Hon. H. Arnold-Forster; Parliamentary Secretary to Admiralty 1900–3; Secretary of State for War 1903–6. M.P. (L.U.) West Belfast.

of the Exchequer and Brodrick succeeded Hamilton at the India Office. As for the War Office, Balfour's first choice was Akers-Douglas, doubtless having in mind his courageous report on Army Education, and this choice was strongly endorsed by the King, who greatly preferred it to his earlier suggestion of Long, but above all wished to prevent Arnold Forster from having it—though in the end he was in fact the man appointed. Akers-Douglas, however, persistently refused in the face of continual pressure from the King and Balfour, and, among others, suggested Wyndham[1] for the post. Knollys wrote:

> I think the King understands what you say about yourself, and he would approve W[yndham] if he felt certain he could be properly spared from Ireland. He is afraid that W's removal would not be popular among the Irish M.Ps, nor among the Irish themselves.

But in any case Wyndham refused to budge.

Owing to the general feeling that recent events had made the War Office a post of the utmost importance, the search for the right man became intense, protracted and rather agonizing. Some idea of the wide implications of the question may be gained from a letter to Akers-Douglas from Balfour's Private Secretary, J. S. Sandars, enclosing a letter from Lord Roberts to Brodrick. Sandars wrote (September 21st, '03):

> . . . Since seeing you, I have had opportunities of listening—and of course only listening—to the observations and talk of outsiders, all of whom concur in the policy of appointing a man to the post unhampered by the allegiance which necessarily will hamper any member of the Government of 1895 now in office. In this connection I send you a copy—very confidentially—of a letter from the C-in-C to St. J. I think that the whole tone of the letter shows something of the difficulty that awaits the new man . . .

The enclosed letter from Lord Roberts ran:

> The conclusion I have come to after a careful perusal of the report of the Royal Commission on the War in S.A. is that the public will not be satisfied until far more drastic reforms have been made than have as yet been attempted, and unless this is done before the next election success will attend that party which will promise seriously to take up the question of Army Reform.

[1] Rt. Hon. George Wyndham, Under Secretary for War 1898–1900; Chief Secretary for Ireland 1900–5.

Lord Esher,[1] and Sir G. Goldie[2] have in my opinion hit upon the two most important points to be dealt with, namely, the necessity for some radical change in the administration of the War Office and the adoption of some scheme for the expansion of the Army in time of war.

With regard to the first point, matters are much the same as when I first took over office; the same delays, the same confusion, the same overlapping of duties, still exist, and will continue to exist until some radical change is made in the present system.

Seeing that Lord Hartington's Commission in 1890, which sat at a time of profound peace, recommended the administration of the War Office being entrusted to a Board, and that a similar recommendation is now made by Lord Esher, Sir George Goldie and Sir John Jackson,[3] three members of Lord Elgin's Commission, which has held a prolonged enquiry at the close of a very serious war, it seems to me very unlikely that the nation would be satisfied unless these views are given effect to.

I can now speak with nearly three years' experience of the War Office, and I am entirely in favour of the proposal to form a Board. It is in fact the inevitable outcome of the change made by Mr. Childers[4], when he removed the Office of the C-in-C from the Horseguards to the War Office, and placed the Duke of Cambridge under the direct control of the Secretary of State. So long as H.R.H. filled the post he was in appearance the head of the Army, but in appearance only, for from the date of his removal to the War Office, the Commander-in-Chiefship practically ceased to exist.

The position of the C-in-C is quite anomalous, a position which no-one else who has been a real C-in-C. or held a high command in the field could possibly fill with advantage to the State or satisfaction to himself. Lord K[itchener] chafes even under the control (necessary and reasonable as I consider it) as exercised by the Military Department in India, and I should be greatly surprised if he remained a year in Office were he ever made C-in-C under existing circumstances.

[1] Reginald, 2nd Viscount Esher, Secretary to Office of Works 1895–1902; served on Royal Commission on War in South Africa under Lord Elgin's chairmanship; Chairman of War Office Reconstruction Committee (the 'Esher Committee') 1903; Permanent member of the Committee of Imperial Defence 1905–18.

[2] Founder of Nigeria; served on Royal Commission on War in South Africa.

[3] Civil engineer; the largest contractor for Public Works of his day.

[4] Rt. Hon. H. C. E. Childers; Security of State for War 1880–2.

It would probably not be the same with the Duke of Connaught. H.R.H. has never filled an important command either in peace or war. The status, the Court functions and the patronage would suffice to keep him happy and contented, and the daily routine might be carried on as it has been for some years past. He could not realise the irksomeness, the nothingness of the position as I do, and as I am sure Kitchener would.

Believe me I am not writing this from a sense of grievance. You have told me more than once, and I am sure it is the case, that I have been treated with greater consideration than former Cs-in-Chief. I am only giving expression to a feeling which I have vainly endeavoured to fight against, a feeling of helplessness, of being throttled as it were by the system in force, and I wish to let you and Mr. Balfour know how prepared I am to fall in with any change which the more drastic reforms I have alluded to would entail. My desire is to do what is best for the Service. I am not only ready but perfectly willing to give up the C-in-Chiefship and retire into private life if it is thought best to abolish the appointment and no suitable position could be found for me in a new form of administration.

With regard to the main theme of the above the following notes may be appended. The Hartington Commission of 1890 had recommended the abolition of the post of Commander-in-Chief, and, as already related in an earlier chapter, in 1895 Campbell-Bannerman, as Secretary for War, had managed to secure the resignation of the old Duke of Cambridge who had held the appointment for close on forty years. This was achieved, however, in the face of very strong opposition, not only from the Duke himself, but from the Queen. The latter had set her heart on the idea of her son Arthur, Duke of Connaught, ultimately succeeding to the Commander-in-Chiefship and therefore insisted on the post being retained. Meanwhile it was filled by Lord Wolseley. When the latter retired in 1900 Salisbury advised the Queen to appoint Lord Roberts, which she eventually did, after a determined attempt to secure the place for the Duke of Connaught.

To return to the original question of the appointment of the Secretary of State for War, Akers-Douglas left copies in his own writing of the numerous telegrams on this subject which passed between himself (at the time in attendance at Balmoral) and

Sandars, the Prime Minister and his brother, Gerald Balfour, between September 21st and 28th. These give a vivid idea of the extent to which the matter preoccupied the Cabinet and the strong feelings aroused by it among the individual members thereof. The selection given here will also show how frequent and almost frantic were the communications hurtling between the protagonists.

J. S[andars] to D[ouglas]. 21 Sep. 1.30 p.m.
Times for what it is worth most anxious for splash. Hood[1] writes in same sense stating that next Session absolutely depends on novel appointment.

D. to J.S. 21 Sept. 2.30 p.m.
Have said all I can in favour of splash—Have told King that all members of Cabinet in 1895 will be greatly handicapped in face of Report [of Royal Commission on War in South Africa] and new man essential at W.O. I think I have convinced him in favour of appointment from outside but find P.M. much more difficult. He prefers me to take it: but have pointed out difficulties and refused. If you can help by letter do so.

S. to D. 21 Sept. 5.24.
Your telegram have written P.M.—am making careful enquiries about Goldie and will report—am very glad to have your message hope that A.J.B. realizes the really great political importance of employing an independent outsider and the weight of the case we have to meet next session.

D. to S. 23 Sep. 12.30 p.m.
P.M. much disappointed about Milner's refusal[2] which means reconstruction much more difficult—He does not smile on Goldie —nor any other heroic appointment. But if really necessary sees much less difficulty and some advantage with Esher. I do not believe he [Esher] would accept even S. of S: but he would certainly decline Under Secretaryship as proposed by King—King very strong about W.O. He again urges me: but would agree to Wyndham or Selborne[3] but not Long or Forster. It seems almost better under these circumstances to leave Brodrick.

[1] Sir A. Acland Hood, Chief Conservative Whip, 1902–11; created Lord St. Audries.

[2] Lord Milner, then High Commissioner in South Africa, was pressed by Balfour to take Chamberlain's place at the Colonial Office.

[3] Under Secretary for Colonies 1895–1900; First Lord of Admiralty 1900–5; as Lord Wolmer was former Liberal-Unionist Whip.

D. to S. Sept. 23. 3.0 p.m.
Chief has wired to Wyndham to ask if he might consider his name for W.O. and if so as to his successor at I[rish] O[ffice]—Also to Chamberlain re Colonial Office—Chief is still pressing me but I am strong against it—If I must yield he wants to bring in Carson[1] —could he and would he go to any other office than H[ome] O[ffice] . . .

S. to D. Sep. 23. 7.0 p.m.
Am not very favourably impressed by suggestion of Carson for H.O. first of all I think his ability is not of the administrative kind. He would no doubt help in debate but . . . again he has no acquaintance I believe by residence or association with traditions of English county or urban life the experience of a successful lawyer was once not a happy one, again how would Sol. Genl. handle Church Bill next session he hated Education Bill on its merits and Church side and he has no Church sympathy—finally if Lord Chancellor died you would have a very new pair of Law Officers . . .

D. to S. 2 p.m. Sep. 24th
Matters do not improve—Selborne declines to move from Admiralty—and Wyndham from Ireland. Esher has been offered and in spite of pressure refuses W.O.—the King still objects to Forster and Long—Long must therefore go to Colonies and Carson H.O.—so Chief says—but I say Walter Long must have H.O. for every reason if I go W.O. Do you think H. of C. would stand both War Office and Admiralty in House of Lords—If not no use approaching Cawdor[2] or Cromer[3] who has been suggested by Chamberlain for W.O.

D. to G. Balfour,[4] Whittinghame. Sep. 24, '03. 7 p.m.
P.M. has asked me to add to his telegram that whole difficulty now centres round W.O. He pressed me strongly when I arrived on Monday to take W.O. Though ready to do anything P.M. desires

[1] Sir Edward [later Lord] Carson; Solicitor General 1900–5; First Lord of Admiralty 1916–17.

[2] Frederick, 3rd Earl of Cawdor; Chairman of G.W.R. 1895–1905; First Lord of Admiralty 1905.

[3] Evelyn Baring, 1st Earl of Cromer; H.M. Agent and Consul General in Egypt 1885–1907.

[4] Rt. Hon. Gerald Balfour, Chief Secretary for Ireland 1895–1900; President Board of Trade 1900–5. The Prime Minister's brother and heir.

I dissented because I felt public would expect some strong outsider. Though many have [been] thought of with one exception—Esher—all have proved impossible. In addition Wyndham and Selborne decline. The King will not agree to A. Forster. The only man is therefore Esher unless I do it. Do you think our colleagues would resent Esher. He wd. bring knowledge and is a useful man. I need not say how much I would prefer to remain at H.O. Send me your views by post.

S. to D. Sep. 25. 7.50 p.m.
Your telegram I am sure House of Commons would stand almost any arrangements which bring new men into War Office—our Daily Telegraph friend was here today and in answer to general question said that appointment to W.O. was more important than that to Colonial because unless new men were brought in the party and the Country would charge us with indifference as we now have an opportunity. I quote this to show that my opinion is shared by a good judge of general outside feeling. If you can secure a Peer would the King allow special appointment of Forster as Under Sec. of State if so this would I think largely meet objection to heads of both departments being in H. of Lords—but if the King is obdurate then Bonar Law[1] or Bromley Davenport[2] would be best for Second in Command. What is the objection if Peer permissible to try Chairman G.W.Rly. [Cawdor]. I would sooner delay than be rushed into unsatisfactory appointment. Chamberlain has just sent for Milner's address so perhaps he is pressing him. I hope Milner may reconsider because Pres.L.G.B. [Long] appointment to Colonial Office does not much smile upon me. He is quite unknown to Colonials. I can hardly think Cromer would accept unless his wife wished to live in England of course he would be excellent.

S. to D. Sep. 26. 1.15 p.m.
I sent off telegram from P.M. last night to Milner this morning early. I have had reply that he remained of same mind but he would come to England . . .

A.J.B. to D. Sep. 26. 8.10
Please tell King that I am going to London Monday night to meet Milner hope to persuade him but am very doubtful.

[1] The future Premier (1922–3) had only entered Parliament in 1900, but was already Parliamentary Secretary to Board of Trade.

[2] Brig. Gen. Sir W. Bromley Davenport, M.P. Macclesfield. Financial Secretary to War Office 1903–5.

A.D. to A.J.B. 28 Sep. 2 p.m.
Esher has written to King today with cut and dried proposal for Com^{ee}. of Reorganization of W.O. with which I could not agree so please do not count upon me as S. of S. for War.

Esher was a very strange—and a very dangerous—phenomenon in the politics of the day—and Akers-Douglas knew it. For in 1895 when the latter was First Commissioner, Esher had become Permanent Secretary to the Office of Works, from which position he was able to obtain, in his own words, 'the tie he was seeking'. This 'tie' was with the Queen and with the future King Edward through pandering to their wishes in matters of Court ceremonials, pageants and monuments. His ambitions appear to have been limited entirely to establishing himself as a sort of *éminence grise* at the Court, and, possessing much flair and address, he quickly achieved his aim. He had failed to make a mark in the House of Commons and studiously avoided all public responsibility; so it is not surprising that his backstairs influence and methods aroused the keenest resentment among some of his contemporaries. The point was reached where, in the words of St. John Brodrick—a minister who was in a real sense a victim of his baneful influence—'by the time any decision had come to the point when the Cabinet could lay it before the Sovereign, the issue had been largely prejudged, on the incomplete premises of an observer who had no official status'.[1]

These remarks will help to explain the tone of the following extract from a letter dated Sept. 25th, 1903, to Akers-Douglas from Gerald Balfour:

> . . . As regards Esher's personal qualifications for the post of S. of S. [for War] you have seen him at work and know that side of him so much better than I do that I hardly like to offer an opinion. Otherwise, I should have thought he had hardly sufficient 'drive' for the position, or that it would have suited his inclination and temperament to accept it.
>
> But in any case I do not think his appointment would produce the exact kind of dramatic effect which is aimed at. It would *surprise* no doubt, but I do not believe it would satisfy, or carry any conviction that a real reform was at hand. Nor do I think it would

[1] Earl of Midleton: *Records and Reactions 1856–1939*, p. 149.

be popular with our own people. I confess that I had imagined Esher to be a Home Rule Liberal so far as he had any pronounced views at all, and certainly he has never borne the heat and burden of the day in any really arduous post. If there is the slightest chance of persuading Milner to reconsider his refusal . . . it seems to me it would be a great mistake to shut the door by appointing Esher to the W.O. . . .

I quite sympathize with your reluctance to leave the H.O. for the W.O., but I should always feel sure that you would not allow personal inclination to stand in the way where there was a chance of helping the Chief out of a difficulty . . .

But Akers-Douglas's final flat refusal settled the matter as far as he and the War Office were concerned and, together with Milner's equally firm refusal of the Colonial Office, broke the vicious circle of proposals and counter-proposals and thereby provided a starting point for the reconstruction of the Ministry. Selborne too showed a marked aversion to leaving the Admiralty for either the War or the Colonial Office and on his strongly backing the Prime Minister in the appointment of Arnold-Forster for the former and Alfred Lyttelton for the latter, the King, who held a high opinion of his judgment, was reluctantly obliged to surrender. How reluctantly is revealed in a letter from Knollys to Akers-Douglas written shortly afterwards.

Confidential

Balmoral Castle
2 Oct. 1903

My dear Douglas,

Many thanks for your letter which I submitted to the King. He is very sorry to think that you are not going to the W.O., but he understands the reasons which you mention for not taking that Post, and he wrote to Balfour yesterday evening to tell him so accompanied by some expressions about you, which I am sure would have given you pleasure to have read.

He also told Balfour that he would not object to Lyttelton but asked whether he thought he would add to the strength of the Govt.

As regards the W.O. he reminded Balfour that over and over again while he was here he had argued with him about A. Forster at that office, and strongly deprecated his going there as Sec. of

State, though he could quite approve of his being Under Sec. for War.

He strongly urged Selborne's app^{t}., as Sec. for War and suggested that Onslow[1] should go to the Admiralty . . . [letter incomplete]

In the previous reign the task of the nightly Parliamentary letter to the Sovereign summarizing the day's proceedings had been the duty of the First Lord of the Treasury. King Edward, however, had excused Balfour owing to the vast and ever-increasing duties of his office and the duty was assigned to Akers-Douglas. The task was an unwelcome extra burden even for the Home Secretary and it would appear that Akers-Douglas put up some resistance. However, Knollys wrote on February 19th, 1903:

> The King thinks it would be a pity to discontinue the practice of a Minister writing to the Sovereign an account of the proceedings in the House of Commons. It is quite true that times are different, but the custom has lasted since the early years of George 3rd's reign, and there might be occasions in which the Press did not give, and would be unable to give, a report of certain circumstances connected with a Debate which the Sovereign ought to know.

At the close of the Session Akers-Douglas received a letter of appreciation from Sir Frederick Ponsonby, Assistant Private Secretary (August 18th, '03):

> The King desires me to thank you for the concise and able summaries which you have written during the whole of this Session which is now at an end. His Majesty is afraid these reports must give you a great deal of trouble but he wishes me to assure you that they are of the greatest interest to him and that as you probably know they have for the last seventy years been kept as a private record for the Sovereign of the proceedings of the House.

Sandars says that Akers-Douglas's 'unadorned and careful version of the debate became a striking contrast to the sprawling, but literary, narrative which had previously been scribbled

[1] William, 4th Earl of; Under Secretary India 1895–1900; Under Secretary Colonies 1900–3, President Board of Agriculture 1903–5.

on his knee by the Leader of the House'.[1] But it is evident that for all that Akers-Douglas did not altogether withhold his personal feelings and opinions, for on one occasion Knollys wrote to him:

H. CAMPBELL-BANNERMAN.

"ORDER IS TIM'S FIRST LAW."

Buckingham Palace
3 March 1905

My dear Douglas,

The King desires me to say with reference to your 'House of Commons letter', that he quite agrees with you in thinking that Sir H. Campbell Bannerman made a gratuitous and ungenerous attack on Mr. Balfour last night. H.M. says he must have known that the Prime Minister was at work in his room, and remarks it is curious that Sir H. C. Bannerman hardly ever opens his mouth without saying something in bad taste.[2]

[1] *Studies of Yesterday, by a Privy Councillor*, 162–3.

[2] It was the night Balfour announced the resignation of George Wyndham from the Irish Secretaryship.

The King likewise thinks that Winston Churchill showed a great want of good taste as well when alluding to Staff Officers, considering that he has been a Hussar Subaltern—what he said too was simple nonsense.

Yours sincerely,
Knollys.

XVIII
THE TARIFF REFORM IMBROGLIO

In regard to that explosive topic which Chamberlain had so unexpectedly lobbed into their midst, Balfour adopted—and maintained for the remaining two and a quarter years of his ministry—an attitude which baffled friends and enemies alike. If he was scarcely a Protectionist, he was equally not a Free Trader. He was in favour of 'investigating' Chamberlain's proposals, but promised that Protection should not be introduced until the Dominions had been consulted at an Imperial Conference. Meanwhile he gave his blessing to Chamberlain's campaign, because he could see that most of the party were following him. Moreover, the appointment of the latter's son, Austen, as Chancellor of the Exchequer was taken as a symbol of alliance between the Government in office and the great Protectionist Crusader.

Balfour's main preoccupation was to avoid splitting his party—as Sir Robert Peel had done on the same issue (only in reverse) in 1846—and to find a formula which would conciliate both Protectionists and Free Traders. In a pamphlet on 'Insular Free Trade' he had accepted tariffs for negotiation and retaliation, whilst not rejecting outright the idea of a full Protectionist policy at some future date. This was really the whole—and only—gist of his speech at Sheffield on October 1st, 1903, which was intended to be a statement of Government policy in the light of Chamberlain's proposals. As he wrote beforehand to the King: 'Mr. Balfour . . . intends to say that though Colonial Preference is eminently desirable in the interests both of British commerce and Imperial unity, it has not yet come within the sphere of practical politics . . .' But he added that he 'ought not to conceal from Your Majesty that in all probability several members of the Government will feel unable to accept it, because it goes too far, or because it does not go far enough'.[1] This forecast, as we have seen, was proved to be only too accurate. Meanwhile he was chiefly concerned to avoid any too definite pronouncements on the whole subject either by his colleagues individually or by the House of Commons as a body.

But, despite Balfour's incomparable dexterity in debate and notorious ability to temporize, even his most devoted followers found it hard to know what the party line really was or how to shape their political conduct and speeches. This is apparent in a letter to Akers-Douglas from his colleague George Wyndham, Chief Secretary for Ireland, on the eve of the Debate on the Address at the outset of the session of 1904.

Confidential

35, Park Lane,
W.
6th Feb. '04.

My dear Bob,

Let me know as soon as it is settled whether Gerald [Balfour] or I follow Morley.

If you are communicating with Arthur on the point we last mentioned viz:—What is to be the Diplomatic and Parliamentary procedure for negotiating treaties and imposing retaliatory duties? —you may care to know that my opinion is *against* pledging the Government to a number of Parliamentary stages involving restriction on action and (2) *against* our whittling down the magnitude of the change advocated by the P.M. as the 'Party Ticket' by using such words as 'the case for imposing such duties may never arise, etc.' We might say that we are the last people to encroach on the real and effective control of the House of Commons over Financial Policy. But I should not like to go much further in that direction.

The bulk of our Party desire a change of greater magnitude. If we 'hedge' too much to keep the 'Free-Fooders' in this debate we are more than likely to split the Party permanently.

The 'Freedom of Negotiation' in respect of Commercial treaties ought to be—I think—as full as the 'Freedom of Negotiation' in respect of territories, e.g. Lord Salisbury's partition of Africa and

[1] Dugdale, I, 354–5.

cases of cession of territory. We had better *not* quote Heligoland but take some cession by the Liberals as an example.

In any case I shall 'sail' strictly to orders and absolutely on the P.M.'s Sheffield and Manchester declarations.

I think we can rally most of the Free-Fooders on that basis if we point out the folly of accepting from the Opposition, and Morley, of all people, a test of uniformity on a number of contingencies e.g. preferential offers from the colonies, which have not arisen.

We do not want a Fiscal Newcastle Programme.[1]

Yrs. ever,
George Wyndham.

John Morley had put down an Amendment to the Address, dealing with the fiscal question, and the debate lasted six days. Unfortunately, the Prime Minister was absent owing to an attack of influenza—and also the Chancellor of the Exchequer through the death of a friend—and the brunt of defending his ambiguous policy falling upon his loyal, but confused, lieutenants, with their varying shades of opinion, the shakiness of the party in power was humiliatingly exposed. Nor, despite their previous consultations, did the sum of their speeches do anything to clarify the Government's attitude to the main question at issue. To crown all Akers-Douglas wound up the debate by an appeal to party unity, which had precisely the opposite effect. This painful and ominous occasion—for the party never really recovered from it—has been described by Balfour's biographer as follows:

> The six-day debate on the Address which opened on February 8th [1904] was conducted from the Ministerial Front Bench much as one of Napoleon's battles might have been if Napoleon himself had been absent from the battlefield. Balfour's brother Gerald, President of the Board of Trade, to whom it fell to make the first exposition of the Sheffield policy given to the House of Commons, transmitted faithfully the Prime Minister's arguments. But he was less convinced than his brother of the immediate impractability of Colonial Preference, and he could not conceal this opinion under the fire of questioning. Otherwise his speech contented the Unionist Free Traders better than the Chamberlainites. These on the other hand were delighted by the tone in which the new Colonial

[1] The ill-advised and top-heavy programme of legislation to which the Liberal Party had committed themselves in October 1891 in anticipation of their return to power in the following year (see ante).

Secretary, Mr. Alfred Lyttelton, pleaded that the door should not be closed upon Preference. The suspicions thus aroused in the Free Traders were increased by the fact that Mr. Austen Chamberlain took no part in the Debate. Finally, the Home Secretary, Mr. Akers-Douglas, failed lamentably in an appeal to Party loyalty. He struck the wrong note with a quavering finger, and the upshot was that some twenty-seven Unionists went into the Opposition Lobby, and seven others abstained from voting.[1]

But Akers-Douglas and his colleagues, though admittedly lacking in the suppleness and adroitness in debate of their absent leader, were the victims of circumstances beyond their control, as well as to some extent, beyond their full apprehension. Each had studiously denied that the issue was merely one of Free Trade versus Protection and stoutly declared that the policy of the Government was not Protectionist. Indeed, it was true to say that Chamberlain's original scheme was directed primarily to Imperial Preference as a means of binding the Empire together rather than to the Protection of home industries. But, under the pressure of big industries at home, the emphasis soon shifted from Imperial Preference to Protection pure and simple —and the latter to the English man-in-the-street, as to his father and grandfather before him, simply meant dearer food and necessities. Thus, although Chamberlain's propaganda was converting the rank and file of the Conservatives, it was not cutting any ice with the masses, despite his efforts to make them see their interest in his new programme. Nor could Imperialism—or the conception of Empire—any longer cast the spell over the country which it had cast in Chamberlain's heyday, when it had smashed the great Gladstone and the mighty Liberal Party. In other words, through an unusually long exercise of power, the Unionist Party and its leaders had become out of touch with the trend of feeling in the country—but were not aware of the fact.

Akers-Douglas was too shrewd not to realize some of these things, but earlier long training as a Whip had inevitably inclined him to rate party loyalty and solidarity above everything else, and to underestimate the necessity for a party and the individuals who composed it from time to time to re-examine their beliefs and tenets in the light of changing circumstances and to ignore the fact that when they did so the crack of the whip or

[1] Dugdale, I, 411.

appeals to their better feelings were more likely to make them rebellious than obedient. But, above all, Whips become accustomed to doing their work behind the scenes and are not used to public controversy, so that they are at a disadvantage when faced with a major issue like Tariff Reform.

Later that year, on October 3rd, 1904, at Edinburgh, Balfour made a further statement of policy which did little to reduce the tension or to enlighten the world—except to convince it that he had no policy at all. He declared that there would be no fiscal change during the currency of the then Parliament; that if he and his friends won the next election the Colonies would be invited to a fiscal conference; and that, if an agreement were come to at the conference, it would be submitted to the country at another general election. This policy of deliberate and organized procrastination naturally pleased no one and when it was accompanied by equally deliberate methods of boycotting the discussion of the whole question in the House of Commons the anger of the Opposition was so much aroused that a powerful stimulus was given to their rapidly reviving spirits and their return at the next election made every day more certain.

The obstinate and repressive mood of the 'old guard' of the Unionist Party is illustrated by the following letter from Akers-Douglas, which is also interesting for its statement of his personal position on the issue.

Private

7th June, '05.

My dear Wollaston,[1]

The habit of the Radical spouter is to extend diminish—or distort for his own purpose any statement made on Fiscal policy so I should be very careful if I were you in dealing with this subject. So far as my views are concerned I have often declared them and they do not vary—I have held them consistently since I was first questioned on the subject in my election of 1885.

Though I am not a protectionist and am opposed to any permanent duties which will in the aggregate raise the price of food of the working classes I was then (1885) and am now in favour of Tariff Reform.

[1] Later Sir Arthur Wollaston, K.C.I.E., Registrar and Superintendent of Records, India Office, 1898–1907.

Tariff Reform is the policy of the Government in the sense laid down [in] Mr. Balfour's declarations at Sheffield and Edinburgh.

The Prime Minister has over and over again explained his position with regard to it and Lord Lansdowne only on Monday night reiterated these views with which I entirely agree.

Yours sincerely,
A. Akers-Douglas.

Despite the outward assurance, the rather vehement tone betrayed the backs-to-the-wall feeling among Balfour's faithful band. It was no good their saying that their party was against Protection, when, to the vulgar eye, unclouded by imperial dreams, this was all that Chamberlain's high-faluting scheme, which they appeared to endorse, seemed to boil down to. Moreover, the awful irony was that Chamberlain, the wayward Radical whom, with sickness in their hearts, they had spent their lives trying to conciliate, had thrust this awkward baby into their arms—and then left them. Worse still, within a couple of years, he was to cease to exist—at least politically—and they were to be landed and branded with a doctrine which had as yet no popular appeal and which was still considered retrograde and scarcely respectable by some of the best intellects of the day on the other side of the political fence. The latter—Asquith, Grey, Haldane, Winston Churchill, Lloyd George—were consequently able to exploit the situation with immense advantage to the long-demoralized Liberal party. In fact it gave the latter a new lease of life.

There was something sublime too about the fact that it should be Chamberlain who brought about the final fall of the venerable régime which he had been principally instrumental in bringing into existence. For, by the autumn of 1905, he was becoming exasperated with the Government's procrastination and ambiguity. On November 3rd in a speech at Birmingham, he declared that he would 'rather be part of a powerful minority than a member of an impotent majority' and demanded a dissolution. Then, encouraged by an almost unanimous vote in favour of his policy at the annual meeting of the National Union of Conservative Associations at Newcastle on November 14th, he issued an ultimatum in another great speech at Bristol (November 21st) insisting that the Unionist Party should fight the election on the fiscal question.

Balfour now saw that the game was up, but, instead of asking for a dissolution, as Chamberlain wished, he resigned office (December 4th, '05). In a memorandum circulated to the Cabinet and dated November 25th[1] he denied that his hand had been forced by Chamberlain's Bristol speech. 'My own leanings towards a December resignation took shape before that speech was delivered'; though he added, 'I do not . . . mean to imply that this speech leaves matters precisely where they were.' Knowing his Cabinet to be divided on the subject of resignation, he wrote: 'We may meet Parliament, and go on until we are beaten, or until our majority is reduced to such obviously exiguous proportions that even the most vehement supporter of the "holding on" policy must feel that resignation is inevitable . . . I still think, however, that in the present state of the party such a course is most undesirable . . . So long as an Administration has such Parliamentary support as will enable it to deal effectually with domestic legislation and foreign policy, let it by all means remain responsible for the government of the country; but if it cannot deal effectually with either it has surely the best of all reasons for asking another Administration to take its place.'

In a speech at the Newcastle meeting, already referred to, Balfour had made an appeal for party unity, but the almost unanimous vote for Chamberlain's policy on that occasion had left him with few illusions. Referring to this in the memorandum he wrote: '. . . The utmost that I now dare expect is that my exhortation may improve our prospects at a General Election. That it will renew the youth of a Parliamentary party seems beyond expectation. But let us by all means wait a little and see. If, however, I be right in my unfavourable forecast, is not the most obviously "straightforward" course to resign place, which has ceased to be power, in time to allow the other side to form their Government, to become acquainted with their various offices, and agree if they can, upon a policy?' This seems effectively to give the lie to those who like Asquith believed that Balfour's resignation was simply one more manoeuvre in the game of 'hanging on' and that he banked upon the Liberals being unprepared to take over and thus exposing their weakness and his own indispensability.[2]

[1] There is a copy of this among the Akers-Douglas papers.

[2] See Asquith: *Studies and Sketches*, 205, and *Fifty Years of Parliament*, II, 32.

King Edward, with characteristic shrewdness and good sense, had meanwhile established excellent relations with Campbell-Bannerman at Marienbad (despite his earlier strictures) and was moreover obviously not sorry to see Balfour go, being out of sympathy with him by nature as well as over his recent handling of affairs. Nor did Campbell-Bannerman hesitate to accept the King's commission to form a government, for he found himself supported in the task by every Liberal of importance—and they were indeed at this time a collection of singularly brilliant men—with the sole, but not surprising exception of Lord Rosebery, whose sun had already set, at least politically.

The retiring Ministers were warned that, in accordance with precedent, they were expected to send the King farewell messages. Akers-Douglas wrote as follows:

> Secretary of State
> Home Department.
>
> Mr. Akers-Douglas with his humble duty to Your Majesty begs leave on the occasion of his relinquishing office to tender to Your Majesty his most grateful thanks for the consideration he has invariably received from Your Majesty. He has deeply felt the responsibility of the important functions it has been his duty to perform, and the honour done him by Your Majesty in entrusting them to his care, and hopes Your Majesty will think he has deserved—as he has always endeavoured to deserve—the confidence Your Majesty has reposed in him.
>
> Mr. Akers-Douglas will always preserve the happiest recollection of the kindness Your Majesty has always shown him, and of the personal relations with Your Majesty into which his office has brought him.
>
> Whitehall.
> 5 Dec. 1905

Knollys replied:

> The King desires me to thank you sincerely for your letter and for the terms in which you express yourself towards him. He desires me to add that he has always been very appreciative of your evident desire to meet his wishes whenever it was possible to do so . . .

In the Unionist debacle at the ensuing General Election, held in January 1906, Akers-Douglas was one of the few Ministers to survive—even increasing his majority—though for the first time since 1885 he found himself opposed. His opponent was a young man named Prescott (later Sir Charles Prescott, Bart.), standing as a Liberal. Something of the old boisterous election spirit manifested itself once again in a jingle improvised for the occasion:

> Vote for Douglas, Vote for Douglas!
> We'll knock young Prescott down
> And we'll roll him round the town!

But such drastic treatment really seemed quite uncalled for, since Prescott was not only of a most amiable disposition, but appeared to be quite won over by his veteran opponent. Acknowledging, after the election, a presentation from a ladies' Liberal club, he declared that 'from the point of view of platform speeches Mr. Akers-Douglas's remarks were his despair. There was not a word of exaggeration, or anything he could take hold of in that way, not a word of personality, and they retained their friendly relations to the end of the contest.' A most refreshing and rather touching episode in the circumstances.

On the other hand Balfour was defeated at Manchester by 2,000 votes and Brodrick, Lyttelton, Gerald Balfour, Walter Long and Bonar Law were other ministerial casualties. The over-all picture was even worse, for out of 369 Unionist members in the former Parliament only 157 retained their seats; on the other hand the Liberals increased their representation from 186 to 377. The Irish Nationalists numbered 83 and—most significant portent—there were 51 Labour members. Even then, however, the Liberals still outnumbered all other parties combined by more than 100.

Until Balfour had found himself another seat the leadership of the House once again temporarily devolved upon Akers-Douglas. But the larger question of the future leadership of the Party now became a subject of debate in wide circles, encouraged by press articles and rumours. For there were many in the Unionist camp who thought that the only chance of the party's survival lay in making Chamberlain the leader. However, apart from the fact that the latter's Radical and ambiguous past made him quite unacceptable to the majority of Conservatives, he himself, immediately after the election, assured Balfour that he would 'refuse the leadership under all circumstances',[1] and cordially joined him in trying to find a formula to reconcile their divergent views before the world. But some of the 'old guard' Tories did not know this and were still racked with suspicions about 'Joe's' motives—as may be seen from the following interesting letter from Akers-Douglas's old friend and fellow-whip, Sidney Herbert, now Earl of Pembroke.

Wilton House,
Salisbury.
February 5th 1906.

My dear Bob,

I am much perturbed at the leadership question. The Unionist M.Ps *may* want Joe, but the mass of the Conservative Party in the country does not quite look upon him as a safe man to whom they can entrust the future of the Party. We polled as many votes at this election as we did in 1900, when we got such a majority, which shows that we had, and have a solid phalanx of Conservative support which is mainly Conservative, and will become more so. The Radicals have got in by the votes of the 'residuum', who can be won back by us, or driven back to us by the mistakes that a Radical Government will make. What I am so afraid of is an attempt by our Party to bid for the so-called 'Labour Vote', which is really the Trade Unions. Let us get the 'Working Man's' vote by all means, quite a different thing. We got it before, and shall get it again, if our policy is guided on strictly economic lines. But I am afraid that Joe Chamberlain will bid for the Trade Union vote, by giving up principles which are the mainstay of our party. Arthur Balfour is absolutely to be trusted. The best leader of the House of Commons whether in, or out of office, that we have ever had, and I devoutly hope that the Party will stick to him. We can only retain the control of our Head Office by this means so far as I can see. Chamberlain has collared the Liberal Unionist Office, and I think that he has got enough. The L.U. so-called Free Traders would permanently split from us, and many Conservatives, like Bob Cecil,[2] would not follow Chamberlain's lead, if the latter is chosen.

[1] Dugdale, II, 25.

[2] Lord Robert Cecil, third son of 3rd Marquess of Salisbury; Under Secretary of State for Foreign Affairs 1915–18; Assistant Secretary of State Foreign Affairs 1918–19; Lord Privy Seal 1923–4; Chancellor of Duchy of Lancaster 1924–27; created Viscount Cecil of Chelwood.

The Fiscal question is not everything after all, and probably, in the present Parliament, it will be less brought up than many equally important subjects.

I do hope therefore that you will use all your influence with our friends to stick to Arthur, in view of the future of the Conservative Party.

Yours,
Pembroke.

In the event Pembroke's hopes were fulfilled, partly for the reasons which he had adduced in this letter, partly because Chamberlain suffered a paralytic stroke little more than a year later and partly also because Balfour himself was not in the least discouraged by the turn of affairs. 'It has made me more violently and pleasurably interested in politics than I remember having been since the Home Rule Bill,' he wrote to Lady Salisbury[1] only a few days after his electoral defeat. It was an indication of his remarkable character, indeed of his greatness, that, far from being alarmed or depressed by the signs of the times, he was genuinely stimulated by them. Thus he could write to Knollys (January 1st, '06) that he was 'so profoundly interested in what is *now* going on' that he would not want to leave politics. 'We have here to do with something much more important than the swing of the pendulum or all the squabbles about Free Trade and Fiscal Reform. We are face to face (no doubt in a milder form) with the Socialist difficulties which loom so large on the Continent. Unless I am greatly mistaken, the Election of 1905 inaugurates a new era.'[2] Again, 'the really interesting development is the organized Labour Party . . .',[3] he wrote to Lord Northcote.

How keen was Balfour's appetite to re-enter the fray and how unimpaired was his energy and ability became abundantly clear from the moment he took his seat in the new Parliament. The Liberal Government introduced an Education Bill designed to reverse the settlement of his own Act of 1902, and he naturally fought tooth and nail to save his own creation. Extensive amendments to the Bill by the House of Lords, who were sedulously coached and advised in the task by Balfour himself, soon

[1] Wife of 4th Marquess, see Dugdale I, 438.
[2] Dugdale, II, 20. [3] Ibid., 21.

involved him in that struggle between the two Houses which was to become the major political issue throughout the next few years. Nor was Balfour in the least inclined to dodge the challenge to the powers of the Upper House which had never been more than dormant since their rejection of the second Home Rule Bill. As in our own day there were those of his party in the Lords as well as in the Commons who advocated reform of the constitution of the Upper House—even at the expense of the hereditary principle—in order to disarm criticism, whilst at the same time strengthening its powers vis-à-vis the Commons. Balfour, however, was in complete opposition to this school of thought—both as a traditionalist and as a 'House of Commons man'.

But, for all the leadership he gave and all the fine fighting qualities he showed with regard to those questions, there was dissatisfaction in various sections of the party, both responsible and otherwise, over his refusal to propound a positive—and preferably progressive—programme for the party and to come off the fence for once and all about the tariff controversy. Already in January 1907 his sprightly and sometimes rather overpowering private secretary, Jack Sandars, was telling him frankly that 'they . . . say that the policy of Fiscal Reform does not fill your heart and mind . . . the rank and file clamour for some broad line of policy above and beyond denouncing a Government no matter how pernicious it may be . . .'[1] But Balfour was dead against 'programmes' in opposition. 'Fiscal Reform', he declared in a speech at this time, 'remains in my view the main constructive plank in the Unionist programme. But do not let us become a party of one idea, for if we become a party of one idea, we shall fail to carry even that idea to a successful issue.'[2]

Later the same year, in October 1907, Austen Chamberlain wrote to him with a further strong plea for a positive programme—including social reform—to cut the ground from under the feet of the Liberals, and suggested lines on which it might be constructed. Three weeks later, at the annual meeting of the National Union of Conservative Associations at Birmingham, resolutions were adopted in favour of fiscal reform and, especially, social reform as a means of combating Socialism and Balfour, speaking at the end, went further than usual in endors-

[1] Dugdale, II, 43. [2] Ibid., 45.

ing these proposals; but he still declined to tie himself to any precise list of priorities or form of tactics. Nevertheless, the general feeling was that the speech had strengthened his position.

These facts provide the background to some interesting letters which Akers-Douglas received from different quarters at this time and which reveal the many shades of opinion even among Balfour's closest associates and the many pressures to which the elusive Premier was consequently subjected. Much care—and cunning—were devoted to the drafting of resolutions for adoption at Unionist meetings up and down the country with a view to claiming the leader of the Party as the foremost apostle of 'whole-hogging'—which he so manifestly was not. Akers-Douglas, Wyndham and Sandars—perhaps his most devoted friends—though as keen as any to make him commit himself more explicitly, sought always to protect and increase his authority; but others were less scrupulous.

Akers-Douglas devised a resolution for adoption at Conservative and Unionist meetings, of which a number took place at the end of the year 1907—notably a great rally of the Kent Division of the National Union of Conservative Associations at Dartford in December at which he presided, supported by Wyndham. In this connection the latter wrote to him:

Private

Saighton Grange
Chester.
2.xi.07.

My dear Bob,

. . . I think your Resolution quite excellent and wish that it might be taken as a model throughout the country. I shall advise its adoption whenever I am consulted.

It is very desirable that A.J.B. should speak on those lines, and, also lead an attack. He ought to speak in Edinburgh on the Scotch Bills and the House of Lords. And I wish he would speak in the Free Trade Hall Manchester, and the Albert Hall, before the session. He is our leader and the only person, besides Rosebery and C.B. who is reported. Anything we say is without authority to our audience and rarely gets beyond that audience except in fragments selected by our opponents' Press.

We suffer from not letting off our 'Big Gun' in the cannonade . . .

Yours sincerely,
George Wyndham.

The struggle over Balfour's body between the intransigent 'whole-hoggers' and the more cautious and doctrinally more tolerant Tory old guard is revealed in all its nakedness in the letters which follow. On November 7th, 1907, Walter Long sent Akers-Douglas—with a request for his opinion—a copy of a letter of remonstrance which he had received from Austen Chamberlain about his (Long's) proposal to speak in favour of a candidate with known anti-Tariff Reform views.

Copy

Highbury,
Birmingham
Oct. 31. '07.

My dear Walter,

We have always spoken very frankly to one another and I think it has been good for us both, and helped to preserve the cordial relations which have always existed between us. May I use the same frankness now? I am rather sorry (though I admit not surprised as I know your views) to see that you are going to speak at Ware for Abel Smith.[1] He is of course a good fellow and in many ways a good party man and I quite understand your desire to help him. But he is not a fiscal reformer and I believe has never voted with us on fiscal reform. We cannot speak in support of all our friends, however active we are, and I rather wish that the support of an ex-Cabinet Minister could be reserved for those who go with Balfour and the Party on this as well as on other questions.

Standing by itself and apart from the character of the speech you may make on the occasion, your visit to Ware must appear rather as an approval or at least a condonation of his attitude and so is somewhat discouraging to those who are bearing the brunt of the fiscal fight there and elsewhere—there (in Hertfordshire I mean) especially, where all the Cecil influence is thrown into the scale against Tariff Reformers. Now I don't for a moment ask or

[1] Abel Henry Smith, M.P. Christchurch 1892–1900, E. Herts. 1900–10. Private Secretary to Walter Long as President of Board of Agriculture 1895–1900.

expect that you should change your plans or give up your visit. But I do venture to urge that you should use the opportunity to appeal both publicly and privately to Abel Smith and others who are hanging back to come into line. You have more than once made an appeal to us who are Tariff Reformers like yourself, not to press our views too hard and to be patient with those who move more slowly. Is not this a good occasion to make a corresponding appeal to the Free Fooders? They must make an advance if we are all to unite and I quite agree with you and Balfour as to the importance of union. I think such an appeal would come well from you. You have earned the right to make it and I believe that you would be listened to. Do try if you cannot help us.

Yours ever,
Austen Chamberlain.

Far from being disarmed by this graceful appeal, Long was irritated, and, moreover, his suspicions of the Chamberlains, which must already have been considerable, were evidently increased by the advice which he received from Akers-Douglas, for he wrote to the latter:

Culworth House,
Culworth,
Banbury.
10.xi.07

My dear Bob,

A thousand thanks for your most helpful letter. Your suggested reply is exactly what, *on second thoughts*, I had intended to write. I will send you my draft tomorrow or next day to the Carlton. I shall not post it to A[usten] C[hamberlain] till after this week as he might show it to some of his confederates and make some mischief. I am delighted and agree with every word you say: I have written Arthur two letters in same vein, as we agreed at Carlton last Wednesday week.

I have also told A. I do not like A.C's methods, that there must be some change and proper understanding before next session, or I, while of course remaining absolutely loyal to A., would prefer to occupy an independent position. I hope you will convince A. and make him take your line. I hear A.C. is to take him to see Joe and I am afraid of all this. A. is so goodnatured and easy-going: he is no match for all these intrigues.

Good luck to you
Yours ever,
W.

Long had also expressed his doubts about Balfour's leadership in terms of real anguish to Sandars, who evidently forwarded the letter to Akers-Douglas, among whose papers it is.

Culworth House,
Culworth,
Banbury.
7.xi.1907

My dear Jack,

. . . I shall be relieved when Birmingham[1] is over—it was a pity some other place was not selected, I told Alick[2] so at the time. However I am not afraid of the extreme Tariff people—they are contemptible!—What I am much more afraid of is that A.J.B. will not assert himself enough and that the trouble will go on steadily increasing and be really more serious in two years time than it is now. There is a general feeling amongst good fellows of *all* classes that he is not strong enough and does not enforce discipline and you and I know there is some ground for this. The Party is certainly in better heart and condition, but wherever I go I have found same feeling about the Chief, in Scotland worse than anywhere! It is too horrible and surely there must be some way of remedying it? To lose him would be the greatest disaster which could happen to our Party. But I am honestly afraid that unless he changes his methods somewhat he will never regain his hold upon the Party and then he will either go, or be a Leader without the real confidence of his followers and either would be disastrous —Still we must remember Dizzy, Gladstone and our late great Chief himself all went through somewhat similar experiences. I earnestly hope the same results may follow but I confess I am very unhappy.

There is much more I could say if we were talking but Heaven knows when I shall get away from here—As you say there are many knaves about and I wish to Heaven the Chief knew how to deal with them. He does *not*. It is magnificent but it is not war.

What do you think about Bonar Law? I am not sure. Tell me but keep this to yourself . . .

Yours
W.

[1] Annual meeting of National Union of Conservative Associations held on November 14th (see above).

[2] Sir Alexander Acland Hood, Chief Unionist Whip.

And Sandars wrote to Akers-Douglas three days later:

Confidential

Darwen Bank,
Torquay.
10. Nov. 1907

My dear Bob,

. . . I am glad to have your view of party expectations, and if you can persuade the Chief to make a rattling attack on the Government I know he can and will do it well—Moreover I expect it will be very much to his taste, and, what is more, it is his idea of what the Opposition ought to do.

But then there are the other counsellors—Austen to wit—who have begged him to go in for an elaborate programme of Social Reform—some replica of the Newcastle scheme which Mr. G. was forced to adopt by *his* advisers.

Now if the Chief makes a good fighting speech—what will happen to the group . . . who clamour for a 'lead'? To bang the Government for their misdeeds, to identify them with their Socialist friends, to expose the shabby manoeuvre of an attack on the House of Lords will be no 'lead'. It will be making a good fighting speech out of the materials which are to everybody's hand. And where will be that constructive programme wherewith to dish the enemy? The Chief may find some way of combining the two plans—but it will be difficult. I think he will incline more to the legitimate method of strong attack and exposure than to the manufacture of a programme.

We shall see *tomorrow*: but I only wish to say that I don't dissent from a single word in your letter.

Au revoir
Ever yours
J. S. Sandars.

Balfour was not oblivious of the hopes and fears, nor even of the criticisms, engendered by his leadership; but he was not the man to let himself be rattled by them. He summed up his attitude defiantly, yet humorously, in a letter to a friend, which is quoted by his biographer.

> . . . I am certainly not going to go about the country explaining that I am 'honest and industrious', like a second coachman out of place! If people cannot find it out for themselves, they must so far as I can see, remain in ignorance.[1]

[1] Dugdale, II, 49.

XIX
LAST BATTLES

It was inevitable that such a debacle as the Unionist defeat of 1906 should have caused not only the leadership, but the whole organization of the party, to come under fire. In fact, almost immediately afterwards (July 1906) a complete re-organization of the National Union of Conservative Associations was carried through. During this process much was said about 'democratizing' the National Union and (shades of Lord Randolph!) 'bringing the Central Office under more effective popular control'. Acland Hood, the Chief Whip, stood firm against these venerable arguments and defended his appointment of an 'Advisory Committee' which included himself and Akers-Douglas, who, in his words, 'had at his fingers' ends the whole history of the committee which once tried to manage the Union and lamentably failed'. The aim of the new scheme was to forestall the old criticisms by a measure of decentralization—by empowering each county (or a group of counties) to form, if it wished, a separate provincial division. The Conservative Central Office itself also underwent certain reforms and changes. But that none of this was enough was proved by the fact that a fresh agitation for reform broke out less than five years later. The great partnership of Akers-Douglas and Middleton[1] in the 'eighties and 'nineties, which had underpinned the long Conservative ascendancy, was no more, and their successors, Acland Hood and Percival Hughes, though diligent and worthy, were lacking in their brilliance and drive.

For a while, however, the course of events tended to

[1] Middleton retired in 1903 and died in 1905.

strengthen Balfour's position as leader of the Unionist Party. The sudden and rather belated awareness shown by the Liberal Government in 1909 of the threat to British naval supremacy from the progressive increase in the German navy provided the Opposition with an absolutely straightforward issue of paramount importance on which to appeal to the nation. Balfour knew how good was his ground when he kept hammering on this subject throughout the year and during the election campaign of January 1910: 'One thing . . . is certain: if we fail in maintaining our sea-power, it does not matter in the least where we succeed, Tariff Reform, Social Reform, all reforms are perfectly useless. As a nation we shall have ceased to count.'[1]

Similarly Lloyd George's 'People's Budget' of May 1909 also put him on firmer ground since, in the succinct phrase of his biographer, it 'changed the antithesis of current politics from Tariff Reform versus Free Trade, to Tariff Reform versus Socialist finance'.[2] True, the Budget led directly to the great collision with the House of Lords, which had thrown it out, but at the resulting General Election (January 1910) the Unionists did regain over a hundred seats[3] and found themselves almost exactly equal with the Liberal victors, who now were at the mercy of their Irish and Labour allies.

When the new Parliament met the rejected Budget was introduced afresh, and—the Irish consenting to overlook the increased whiskey duty in consideration of the Government passing a Home Rule Bill, as well as a Parliament Bill—it passed the House of Commons again and this time was accepted by the Lords. Asquith then produced the Parliament Bill for the purpose of preventing the latter from ever repeating their earlier 'offence' and generally curtailing their powers. However, before much progress had been made with the Bill, King Edward died (May 6th, '10). The shock occasioned by the loss of so sagacious and experienced a monarch imposed a temporary truce upon party warfare. Partly in recognition of the late King's undoubtedly powerful and sincere efforts to avert a major constitutional crisis and partly in deference to the inexperience of his successor, who was faced at the outset of his reign with appalling

[1] Dugdale, II, 53. [2] Ibid., 56.

[3] Akers-Douglas beat his Liberal opponent by 5,386 votes out of a total poll of 13,614.

constitutional problems, an attempt was made to reach agreement by means of a conference between the party leaders. But the conference sat from June to November and then broke up without result. Thereupon Asquith again dissolved Parliament and the second general election of the year was held (December 1910), producing a result almost identical in over-all results (though not in particular details) with that of the one held eleven months earlier. Akers-Douglas was returned this time—which was to be the last time—without a contest.

It was just before this and during the later stages of the Inter-party Conference that Akers-Douglas's position as the *éminence grise* of the Conservative Party was spotlighted for the last time in a somewhat lurid way by Lloyd George. Nevertheless, colossal and terrible as were the implications of the latter's account of the matter, this very fact constituted a great tribute to the remarkable position which Akers-Douglas then held in the party councils.

In October 1910 Lloyd George submitted to the Prime Minister, Asquith, and some of his other Government colleagues—Crewe, Grey, Haldane and Winston Churchill—a memorandum urging that, in view of the impending danger of war, a truce to party conflict should be declared to enable the outstanding domestic questions of the day to be amicably and speedily settled. His colleagues consented to his submitting this proposal to Balfour, who, according to Lloyd George, 'was by no means hostile: in fact, he went a long way towards indicating that personally he regarded the proposal with a considerable measure of approval'.[1] Later Lloyd George understood from him that some of his leading colleagues—i.e. Lords Lansdowne, Cawdor and Curzon and Walter Long and Austen Chamberlain—had given replies which were 'by no means discouraging'. Later still, however, Balfour indicated to him that the bulk of the Tory rank and file in Parliament were hostile and that the principal cause was the personality of Lloyd George himself. The latter thereupon immediately offered to stand out of any coalition ministry which might be formed, whilst giving it wholehearted support. The rest of the story is best given verbatim from Lloyd George's memoirs where it appears under the ominous page-heading 'Akers-Douglas kills it'.

[1] *War Memoirs of David Lloyd George* (Odhams, 1938), I, 22.

> He [Balfour] then told me that there was one other man he felt he would have to consult. He said: 'You will be surprised when I give you his name!' When I heard it I think I was rather surprised that this individual should still hold such an important and influential position in the councils of the Party, for he had retired from active political life for a good many years: it was Mr. Akers-Douglas, who had formerly been Chief Whip of the Conservative Party, and was then Lord Chilston.[1] I remember one of the last things Mr. Balfour said to me on that occasion. Putting his hand on his forehead, looking down and more or less soliloquising, he said: 'I cannot become another Robert Peel in my party!' After a short interval he added: 'Although I cannot see where the Disraeli is to come from, unless it be my cousin Hugh,[2] and I cannot quite see him fulfilling that role!' Mr. Akers-Douglas, however, turned down the project for co-operation in settling these momentous national issues, and there was an end to it. It very nearly came off. It was not rejected by the real leaders of the Party, but by men who, for some obscure reason best known to political organizations, have great influence inside the councils of a party without possessing any of the capabilities that excite general admiration and confidence outside.

Yet Lloyd George's whole assessment of the matter does Akers-Douglas both too much honour and not enough. Balfour's biographer has rightly suggested that greatly as Balfour valued his lieutenant's opinion he had his own opinions and was not the man to allow them to be swamped. He was bound to consult the feelings of his party as a whole and from long experience he knew that Akers-Douglas was the man who could best be trusted to gauge them for him. Moreover, it is more than likely that he found that Akers-Douglas's assessment of the party reaction merely reinforced his own. Lloyd George is naive in laying so much stress on Balfour's apparent air of open-mindedness in the beginning. These were the natural tactics of a highly sophisticated politician—and especially of one by nature so suave and non-committal as Balfour. At the same time Akers-Douglas was not—and had not the slightest ambition to be—the keeper of Balfour's conscience or his 'Svengali'. He was first and foremost a 'party man' and he considered it his duty to give

[1] In fact he was not raised to the peerage until July 1911.

[2] Lord Hugh Cecil, fifth son of 3rd Marquess of Salisbury; created Baron Quickswood.

advice, when asked, on Party matters. He had the great merit of knowing both his own limitations and the limits of his function in the order of things. Among his limitations might indeed be reckoned that partisan outlook by which Lloyd George imagined he bemused his leader and brought to nought the exalted schemes of nobler minds—like that of Lloyd George. It is true, as Sandars wrote of him, that 'he had an *esprit positif* and the philosophy of politics was of no interest to him'[1]—but then was not this exactly the type and the temperament which goes to make a great Whip and party manager?

Though in 1906 Akers-Douglas had allowed it to be understood that his political career was ended, he continued, as we have shown, to render the party great services and at all times to give it the benefit of his advice and unique experience. The maintenance of the party's strength and unity had always been with him the first consideration—as it had also been his job—and it was therefore natural that his advice should be asked whenever this principle was at issue. He therefore gave his opinion to Balfour that the party as a whole was unlikely to be willing to co-operate in Lloyd George's scheme. It was no use his pretending otherwise: neither he nor Balfour could coerce the party. As Mrs. Dugdale rightly says: 'It was, after all, in Balfour's capacity as leader of a great Party that Mr. Lloyd George sought his co-operation. Balfour's own acceptance of office in a Coalition Ministry without his Party's active approval would have been merely an entry into a captivity from whence he could have exerted no influence at all upon the Party strife which it was the object to bring to a close.'[2]

What Balfour had said to Lloyd George about not becoming 'another Robert Peel', he amplified years later to Mrs. Dugdale, thus: 'Peel twice committed what seems to me the unforgivable sin. He gave away a principle on which he had come into power . . . He simply betrayed his Party.'[3] He revealed later that the principle he had in mind in his own case was Irish Home Rule, on which he knew he would be forced to compromise if he joined a Coalition. Indeed, according to a source quoted by Mrs. Dugdale, the condition in respect of Ireland was 'a reasonable federal solution'. But it is difficult not to feel that Balfour was being unduly rigid over this when the extraordinary reason-

[1] *Studies of Yesterday*, 162. [2] Dugdale, II, 73. [3] Ibid., 77.

ableness of the other conditions of the proposed settlement are taken into account. For they included according to this source the proviso that the House of Lords was to 'keep all powers, including money bills', with 'differences to be settled by a joint sitting' of both Houses, which was incidentally an earlier Conservative suggestion; that a Coalition Government was to be formed with Balfour leading the House of Commons and Asquith going to the Lords. Surely, it was the moment for Balfour to heed some words written by his uncle, Lord Salisbury, to Lord Lytton almost a generation earlier, in 1877:

> The commonest error in politics is sticking to the carcases of dead policies. When a mast falls overboard you do not try to save a rope here and a spar there in memory of their former utility; you cut away the hamper altogether, and it should be the same with a policy. But it is not so. We cling to the shred of an old policy after it has been torn to pieces, and to the shadow of the shred after the rag itself has been torn away.[1]

Meanwhile, the dissatisfaction with Balfour's leadership had again spread to criticism of the whole organization of the party. The unfortunate Acland-Hood, who had succeeded Walrond as Chief Whip and who was described as 'the successor to the traditions of Akers-Douglas and the inheritor of his practice and precepts' found himself caught up in a storm of criticism and calumny, which was to prove fatal to his career. Balfour was therefore reluctantly compelled to appoint a Committee to inquire into the organization of the party and very naturally, could think of no better or more appropriate chairman than Akers-Douglas.

Hotel California,
Cannes.
17.1.11

My dear Bob,

I think we must get on with the organization business. For what they are worth my ideas are as follows.

(1) I have no doubt that the Central Office and all connected with it has been unjustly attacked.

(2) *But* I have also no doubt that the system which has been practically unchanged for 25 years requires overhauling. If there

[1] Cecil, II, 145.

were no other reason for this than the relations between the Central Office and the N[ational] Union, that reason would be sufficient.

(3) But there *is* another reason—I mean the widespread feeling in the party that something is amiss. Now I am confident that many of the sins laid to the charge of the C.O. are really due to the N.U.; I am equally confident that many of the remedies proposed are absurd and impracticable. But the only way to make this clear to other people is to have a thorough examination into the real facts of the case.

(4) This can only be carried out satisfactorily by a committee in which the younger and more ardent members of the party have confidence. And they will only have confidence in a committee on which they are strongly represented.

(5) At the same time there must be on the Committee some man of standing, familiar with the traditions of the past, yet not hampered by them, who will have both the knowledge and the authority required to check wild-cat suggestions and impossible projects of reform.

(6) Personally I find it hard to believe that any single person can do the work demanded of a modern head Whip. The Party in the House require more coddling than they did when I was young: and it is the Head Whip who is expected to coddle them. Important local men coming up to London, with or without notice, expect to find an important representative of the Party always at head quarters ready to comfort succour and assist them. This also is the duty of the Head Whip. Constituencies are far more exacting than they used to be—and the Head Whip has to look after his seat as if he had no other duty in life. Correspondence has grown enormously in every department of public affairs. The Head Whip and the Head Office have not escaped the common doom. Depend on it there must be a change of domicile and an increase of staff *as well.*

These are my views as at present advised. Let me know what you think . . .

Yours ever,
A.J.B.

A little later he wrote again:

. . . I entirely agree with you in thinking that the small Committee will not do. I think I shall make a further attempt to get G.C [Lord Curzon] to serve; but probably not as Chairman. I am still disposed to think that you ought to take that place . . .

> I did not press G.C. before I came abroad. He seemed to think that he was full up with work, partly with the Lords' Committee and partly with his Glasgow Address [as Lord Rector of the University]. Now that the latter is over he may be able to reconsider his position.
>
> I should have doubted whether anybody would be jealous of Selborne on account of his being a L.U. He wants, as you know, to join the Carlton . . .
>
> My own rough idea would be yourself, G.C., Willy S. [Lord Selborne], Hayes,[1] Goulding,[2] Maitland,[3] Salvidge,[4] and a Scotchman,—possibly Baird,[5] possibly Reginald McLeod.[6] Will you think over this before we meet . . .

Sandars, in writing later the obituary of Acland-Hood, declared that there had been 'an envenomed intrigue against the Chief Whip', implying that since the latter's enemies were strong on the Committee Balfour was throwing him to the wolves. Of the result he writes:

> There was no mistaking the temper or complexion of the Committee. Steel-Maitland had done his lobbying, and Goulding had perfected his subterranean plot, with the result that the distracted Chairman had to present a Report which sealed the fate of Hood and the Chief Agent.[7]

At any rate Hood immediately afterwards resigned and, in Sandars's phrase, 'submitted himself to the doubtful dignity of a peerage'. Incidentally this expression is accounted for not by the circumstances in which Hood accepted his honour but by the fact that Sandars seems to have had an obsession about peerages being ridiculous rewards coveted by snobbish and worthless politicians—a fact which is best illustrated by his reaction to the acceptance of a peerage by his own beloved master,

[1] William Hayes Fisher, M.P. Fulham 1885–1906; Junior Whip 1895–1902; Financial Secretary Treasury 1902–3; created Lord Downham.

[2] Edward Goulding, M.P. Worcester 1908–22, created Lord Wargrave.

[3] Rt. Hon. Sir A. Ramsay-Steel-Maitland, Bt.; Private Secretary to Chancellor of Exchequer 1902–5.

[4] Archibald Salvidge, Liverpool Alderman, Chairman of Council of National Unionist Association.

[5] J. G. A. Baird, M.P. Central Division, Glasgow, 1886–1900 and 1900–6.

[6] Formerly Chief Conservative Party Agent for Scotland and Permanent Under Secretary of State for Scotland.

[7] *Studies of Yesterday*, 167–8.

Balfour. When this occurred he indited a kind of ironical obituary, declaring that the 'passing of Mr. Balfour, the effacement of the honoured and distinguished designation, and the exchange of the sober broadcloth of the House of Commons for the scarlet robe of a gartered Earl, will long be to the minds of those who have given him their admiration and respect a disappointment and regret'.[1]

Akers-Douglas himself was just about to undergo the same metamorphosis—and no doubt Sandars had the same feelings in his case. Indeed he wrote later in his obituary of Akers-Douglas: 'He wanted nothing for himself; it was with reluctance that he yielded to the persuasion that at the Coronation he should accept a peerage. He would gladly have stood aside for another's claims. His contempt for the appetite for party honours was deep, and he scorned the man who voted in the Government lobby in the hope of being turned into a nobleman.' There is no doubt that this was in essence true, for Akers-Douglas had seen as much as or more than his friends Balfour, Sandars and McDonnell of the ugly and ridiculous scramble for honours among a certain element common to all parties. In fact too great a familiarity with such cases had tended to breed in these men a certain contempt for the prizes themselves. However, no country or system—not even the Soviet Union—has been able to do without some system of honours, and in England, with the creation of peers, there is the added point of replenishing and reinvigorating a body which is an integral part of the Constitution. Moreover, staunch Conservatives like Balfour and Akers-Douglas, if they felt they had themselves been obliged to create so many unworthy peers, owed it all the more to their principles to redress the balance by offering up their own proved talents on this altar. Admittedly, to see the matter really objectively it was necessary to be a great patrician by birth, like the 8th Duke of Devonshire, who is alleged to have once remarked that he could not conceive why anyone wanted an honour, but that, if he did, there seemed no reason why his pretensions should not be gratified! At any rate, whatever Akers-Douglas's views on some of the candidates for peerages who had plagued his earlier career,

[1] Op. cit., 182. Sandars also wrote an article in 1914 on 'The Lords and Party Honours' bearing on this subject which is reproduced in *Studies of Yesterday*, 85.

he was a champion of the rights of the House of Lords as an institution. The fact that the great struggle over the latter happened to coincide with his own imminent membership of it had nothing to do with the views he held on the subject as a whole.

In the interval since the Parliament Bill's first introduction certain peers and certain Conservatives had begun to abandon their original attitude of blank negation and to put forward instead an alternative policy. Sacrificing the principle of hereditary right, Lord Lansdowne, the Conservative leader in the Lords, and Lord Rosebery, the former Liberal leader and Prime Minister, introduced schemes the chief feature of which was that the bulk of the 'Second Chamber' should henceforth be elected by various bodies, or nominated by various authorities. At the same time Lord Balfour of Burleigh sponsored a Bill for the institution of a Referendum for 'organic' or 'constitutional' legislation. Great hopes were founded on these initiatives, which enabled the Conservatives to put before the country at the ensuing election a concrete alternative to the 'Veto' Bill. Nevertheless, when the General Election took place (December 1910), it provided no clear-cut answer to the question, for Liberals and Unionists emerged exactly equal (272 each) and the Irish Nationalists again held the balance.

Despite this situation the Government reintroduced the Parliament Bill in February 1911; it was carried through the Commons, and in May sent up to the Lords. At the very time the Bill was passing through the Commons the Lords were feverishly considering the 'House of Lords Reconstruction Bill', which Lord Lansdowne had framed on the basis of his 'alternative scheme', and the 'Referendum Bill', which Lord Balfour of Burleigh had undertaken to sponsor. But neither Bill got beyond its second reading, for the Government and the Radicals were determined to bring to the test the original issue regarding the powers of the Lords and were not to be distracted by eleventh-hour attempts, however ingenious, to shift the ground.

The second reading of the Parliament Bill had already been debated in the Lords before the Government informed the Conservative leaders of the pledge which they had obtained from the King in the previous December to create as many Peers as might be necessary to pass the Bill. Balfour's indignation at having been kept in the dark was very great, but not so great as that of some of his colleagues, and notably of a section of the Peers led by Lord Halsbury,[1] who resolved to resist the Bill to the last. Balfour counselled caution and moderation in facing the crisis and was followed by the majority of his friends and colleagues in both Houses: but those who would not follow him formed what became known as the 'Diehard Revolt' and included some pretty powerful personalities—e.g. Austen Chamberlain, George Wyndham, Edward Carson and F. E. Smith[2]—and the piquant point is recorded that Akers-Douglas was in spirit with the latter, though he supported Balfour out of personal loyalty.[3]

These facts emerged at a meeting of the Shadow Cabinet held to consider the new development on July 21st, 1911. Akers-Douglas was by then already a Peer—at least in so far as his acceptance of the honour had already been announced (June 20th) and as the official date of the creation was July 6th, 1911. In fact he took his seat five days later, on July 26th, introduced by Viscounts Churchill[4] and St. Aldwyn (the former Sir Michael Hicks Beach).[5] The first division in the Lords in which he voted was on August 8th on the vote of censure concerning the Parliament Bill, moved by Lord Curzon, which read:

> That in the opinion of this House, the advice given to His Majesty by His Majesty's Ministers, whereby they obtained from His Majesty a pledge that a sufficient number of Peers would be created to pass the Parliament Bill in the shape in which it left the House of Commons, is a gross violation of constitutional liberty, whereby among other evil consequences the people will be precluded from again pronouncing upon the policy of Home Rule.

Reviewing the history of the conflict up to date Curzon declared that the Ministers went to the King before the situation

[1] Hardinge Stanley Giffard, 1st Earl of Halsbury; Lord Chancellor 1895–1905.

[2] Later 1st Earl of Birkenhead; Lord Chancellor 1919–22, Secretary of State for India 1924–8.

[3] Recorded in a Diary of Events kept by J. S. Sandars and quoted by Mrs. Dugdale, II, 68.

[4] Victor Spencer, 1st Viscount; Lord Chamberlain, 1902.

[5] Created Earl St. Aldwyn 1914.

had developed and when the Bill had not even been passed by the Commons. The general election and the subsequent proceedings were therefore a farce. 'The Government were about to usurp the prerogative of the Crown in order to extinguish the prerogative of the people.'[1] Lord Crewe, defending the Bill for the Government, maintained that 'nobody was the worse for the conversation [between Asquith and the King] which dealt with purely hypothetical conditions'; but he admitted that 'the whole business was odious to him'. Haldane declared more summarily that the Peers had been 'having a trial of strength with the House of Commons backed by the country, and the latter ought to prevail'. But, in summing up, Lansdowne voiced the basic, and perfectly reasonable, fear of many people far beyond the confines of the House of Lords. He claimed that the 'last resort', as described by the Government, had not yet arisen and argued that the undertaking obtained from the King was so contrived that it would cover anything Ministers might read into the decision of the country at the General Election. They had got a blank cheque to be filled up by the King in accordance with the direction of his advisers. He asked 'whether Ministers would say that the decision of the electors at the last election was that they should not be consulted again on Home Rule'.

Lord Chilston, as Akers-Douglas now was, voted for the motion, which was carried by 281 votes to 68. This was the opportunity for him and others of Balfour's 'old guard' to put on record their protest against a course which they knew they were going to have to accept as soon as the Bill came back for the last time to the Lords. Not only this, but they were going to have to persuade their friends to submit and some of them were even going to vote for the Bill—lest worse befall them.

Meanwhile, the Lords' amendments to the Bill, still proposing a Referendum for Constitutional Changes, had been under consideration in the House of Commons, and, despite powerful and bellicose speeches by Lord Hugh Cecil and Sir Edward Carson, had been rejected. The last round had now been reached when it was necessary for the Lords to decide whether they were to acquiesce in this treatment.

The debate opened on August 9th and Lord Lansdowne, who

[1] This and other quotations from speeches are from the Annual Register, 1911.

had himself been the originator of the amendments, counselled forbearance and submission. Resistance, he said, was useless and detrimental to the public interest—though they took no responsibility for the Bill. To challenge the Government to carry out the threat of creation of Peers would merely bring the British parliamentary system into contempt—and, by association, the Sovereign also. With a down-to-earth touch he added that it would be a misfortune, when he and his party came back into office, to be confronted by a Radical majority of Peers. The Archbishop of York, declaring that he would reluctantly vote for the Government, said that there were times when 'he that ruleth the spirit is better than he that taketh a city'. Other peers spoke reluctantly in favour of submission, including Lord Curzon, and there was 'a somewhat theatrical declaration by Rosebery that he would vote for the Bill but would never enter the House again'.[1]

Nevertheless, a hard core of bitter resisters still manned the barricades, who, despite Lord Morley's solemn announcement that in the event of defeat there would be a 'prompt' creation of 400 Peers, were still obstinately convinced that the Government was 'bluffing'. It was therefore in an atmosphere of intense excitement and uncertainty that the vote was taken. But the motion 'that the House do not insist on the amendment' was finally carried by 131 to 114 votes. The great mass of the Peers had abstained, but 37 Unionist Peers voted with the Government in order to prevent the swamping of their House, and, ironically, it was in fact they who saved the Bill. This, according to Lord Newton, was a pre-arrangement, for he writes: 'As it was difficult to estimate the probable number of Diehards, precautions had to be taken to secure the promise of a certain number of self-sacrificing Unionist peers who would be prepared to save the Bill, if necessary, and these people, who really showed more courage than anyone else, we discovered with some difficulty.'[2]

Akers-Douglas had already smothered his real convictions once out of loyalty to his chief: it was asking too much to expect him to help 'save the Bill'; so he joined the great majority of peers in abstaining. Moreover Balfour's own attitude had undergone certain subtle changes which had been so disconcerting

[1] Lord Newton: *Retrospection*, 186. [2] Ibid., 185.

and bewildering that even his most loyal followers could feel absolved of the necessity of trying to keep up with them. For, though he had published a letter to the party at large (July 25th) supporting the advice that Lord Lansdowne had already given to the Unionist Peers (i.e. to submit under protest and not to challenge the Government's threat to create peers), his biographer reveals that he had also composed another much more freely expressed memorandum intended for circulation among his Shadow Cabinet. But this document, at the strong instance of one or two colleagues (one of whom would surely have been Akers-Douglas), was not circulated even to this limited circle, since it betrayed a curiously ambiguous attitude to the problem which they felt could only confuse his followers and even encourage resistance towards the Bill. For, in it, whilst ridiculing in his worst Balfourian and superior vein the 'Music Hall attitude' of the Diehards and their sympathizers, he blandly asserted that 'the creation of 50 or 100 new Peers is a matter of indifference'.[1] It was another example—as earlier in the Tariff Reform agitation—of his inability to discard the academic and philosophic disquisitions so dear to his nature and, instead, to give his party a clear and practical lead on a topic of burning importance. It had nearly been fatal, as we have seen on the earlier occasion: this time it was quite fatal. He was too shrewd not to sense the gulf which increasingly separated him from his followers and within three months he had resigned for ever the leadership of the party.

The trouble was very much the same as it had been with his uncle, Lord Salisbury—an undoubted intellectual superiority over his fellows and a consequent detachment from and lack of sympathy with their interests and points of view. It was summed up by Acland Hood, the Chief Whip, in the days of the Tariff Reform controversy: 'My complaint is that the Chief thinks his party are as clever as he is. They are not. He doesn't understand their difficulties. I do; and I cannot get him into touch with our men.'[2] But Balfour did realize something of this as is shown by his reply to one who asked him at the end who could succeed him. 'The faculty for readiness in debate is not one which the country demands in a leader. W. H. Smith lacked it. A slower brain would often be welcome to the party as a whole. I see all

[1] Dugdale, II, 69–70. [2] *Studies of Yesterday*, 166.

the factors in the situation. Perhaps this entails want of decision. Some people do not like the qualifications in my speeches. They are not to save myself but to protect my Party in the future, when statements of leaders are recalled to injure the Party . . .'[1] Moreover, although, like Salisbury, he was by nature unsuited to and intellectually uninterested in such pedestrian matters as party management, he had the excuse that, owing to the weakness of his colleagues in debate and his own supremacy therein, he had to assume responsibility for every critical issue in Parliament and had little time to spare for the management side anyway.

As soon as he had made up his mind to resign the leadership Balfour informed Lord Lansdowne, who made strenuous but vain efforts to deter him. After that the first person he informed of his decision was Akers-Douglas, on October 30th. The latter must have found himself in a difficult position at this stage, for his allegiance to Balfour, if a little shaken in the recent crisis, had deep roots. At the same time he was a devoted and life-long friend of Walter Long—a man, incidentally, with whom he had much more in common than with Balfour—and Long was, next to Austen Chamberlain, the most favoured candidate for the vacant leadership. Moreover, Long, who had been restive about Balfour's leadership for several years—as letters already quoted reveal—had just given Balfour a final stab which had moved even that serene personality to bitterness. He had written Balfour a letter severely critical of the party management and of the Leader himself, in which he demanded a radical change of policy and threatened his own retirement from the Front Opposition Bench. Balfour's comment to Lord Balcarres, the Chief Whip, was simple and dignified:

> Now this comes from my oldest colleague, my professed friend and upholder . . . The letter is a bold and brutal invitation to retire. But I do not think the writer can have thought of stepping into my shoes; otherwise he would not have proceeded by such methods . . . Whatever ambitions I have had were satisfied years ago. I know I cannot be evicted from the leadership, and if I resigned I could make trouble, which is of course absurd; but Long asks me to change, and I cannot change.[2]

[1] Dugdale, II, 87. [2] Ibid, 88.

Akers-Douglas, however, left no record of how this rather poignant situation affected him. Publicly, in a speech to former constituents, he paid a final tribute to Balfour and expressed faith in his successor, Bonar Law; but he added that 'he thought they must express thanks to the loyalty, public spirit and generosity of Mr. Austen Chamberlain and Mr. Walter Long, both of whom had undoubted claims to the leadership'. These rather enigmatical words—so characteristically non-committal and solicitous for the integrity of the Party's façade—constitute almost his last comment on public affairs. Even his correspondence, which, over the preceding ten years had been becoming rapidly sparser, now fades out completely. Ever the most reticent of men, divulging the minimum of his real feelings either in speech or on paper, he left no memoirs. Though he had another fifteen years to live, he just quietly left that bustling stage in the centre of which, though his main activities had been in the wings, he had so often been found and illuminated by the roaming spotlight of publicity.

Many references and instances have been cited in these pages representing him as the 'party man' *par excellence*. He was indeed this, but only in so far as through the party he aspired to serve the State; only ambitious in so far as he desired to promote the ideas in which he believed. Born to wealth and high position, he was—like so many other men of his kind and generation—imbued with a deep patriotism and a sense of duty and of the obligations of his class and its traditions. One proof of this is to be found in the constant touch which he maintained with his constituents—even through the twelve hectic years of his whipship—and in his habit of rendering a regular periodical account of his stewardship to them. His genuine interest in the land and genuine sympathy with the problems of those who lived by it and the sincere and unaffected manner in which he expressed himself were among the causes of the enormous popularity which he enjoyed in his county and the consistent support which he received from it for thirty-one years.

At the very end of his career his appearance could evoke scenes of enthusiasm—sometimes highlighted by the same amusing, if crude, little ditties of eulogy which had been such a feature of the hustings of his youth. Thus, during the General Election of January 1910, whilst his Liberal opponent was addressing a meeting in the Theatre Royal, Deal, an impromptu meeting was organized in the streets outside by over a thousand of his own supporters, who were waiting for him to arrive from London. After various impromptu speeches by local Tory leaders 'a ready wit mounted the four-legged platform and to a popular tune sang the following ditty, which is becoming very familiar':

> Who is the man that can put a lot of sense about?
> Douglas! That's him.
> Who is the man that the Radical Party's mad about?
> Douglas! That's him.
> The Tory men are fond of him,
> He beats the Radicals thick and thin,
> Who is the man we Tories want to see get in?
> Douglas! That's him.
>
> *Chorus*
>
> D-O-U-G-L-A-S spells Douglas!
> Proud of all the Tory blood that's in him,
> No Radical man can say a word against him;
> Douglas you see.
> Its a name that is so plain
> That the Radical man will know again,
> Douglas! That's him.
> etc., etc.

Crude—a little ridiculous too, no doubt; but touching in its simple loyalty and warming to a man who had devoted his life to a cause which he firmly believed to be in the best interests of his country.

BIBLIOGRAPHY

A. Biographical Works (Arranged in Order of Subjects)

Asquith, 1st Earl of Oxford and Asquith. *Life of Lord Oxford and Asquith*, by J. A. Spender and Cyril Asquith, 2 vols. (Hutchinson, 1932).

—— *Fifty Years of Parliament*, by the Earl of Oxford and Asquith, 2 vols. (Cassell, 1926).

—— Countess of Oxford and Asquith. *The Autobiography of Margot Asquith*, 2 vols. (Thornton Butterworth, 1920).

Balfour, 1st Earl of. *Arthur James Balfour, 1st Earl of Balfour*, by Blanche E. C. Dugdale, 2 vols. (Hutchinson, 1936).

—— *Chapters of Autobiography*, by Arthur James, First Earl of Balfour (Cassell, 1930).

Beach, Sir Michael Hicks. See St. Aldwyn, Earl.

Beaconsfield, Earl of. *Life of Benjamin Disraeli, Earl of Beaconsfield*, by W. F. Monypenny and G. E. Buckle, 6 vols. (Murray, 1910–24).

—— *The Earl of Beaconsfield, His Life and Times*, by A. C. Ewald, 5 vols. (Mackenzie, 1881).

—— *Letters of Disraeli to Lady Bradford and Lady Chesterfield*, ed. Marquess of Zetland, 2 vols. (Murray, 1929).

—— *Selected Speeches of the late Earl of Beaconsfield*, ed. T. E. Kebbel (Longmans, 1882).

—— *Public Opinion and Lord Beaconsfield*, by G. Carslake Thompson, 2 vols. (Macmillan, 1886).

Brodrick, William St. John. See Midleton, Earl of.

Caine, William Sproston. *W. S. Caine, M.P., A Biography*, by John Newton (1907).

Carnarvon, 4th Earl of. *Life of Fourth Earl of Carnarvon, 1831–1890*, by Sir Arthur Hardinge, Vol. III (Humphrey Milford, Oxford, 1925).

Chamberlain, Sir Austen. *Life and Letters of Sir Austen Chamberlain*, by Sir Charles Petrie, 2 vols. (Cassell, 1939).

Chamberlain, Joseph. *Life of Joseph Chamberlain*, Vols. 1–3, by J. L. Garvin, Vol. 4 by Julian Amery (Macmillan, 1932–51).
—— *A Political Memoir*, by Joseph Chamberlain, ed. C. H. D. Howard (Batchworth, 1953).
Churchill, Lord Randolph. *Lord Randolph Churchill*, by Winston S. Churchill (new edn. Odhams, 1951).
—— *Lord Randolph Churchill*, by Robert Rhodes James (Weidenfeld and Nicolson, 1959).
—— *Lord Randolph Churchill*, by Lord Rosebery (Humphreys, 1906).
—— *Speeches of Lord Randolph Churchill, 1880–1888*, ed. Louis J. Jennings, 2 vols. (Longmans, 1889).
Churchill, Lady Randolph. *The Reminiscences of Lady Randolph Churchill*, by Mrs. Cornwallis West (Edward Arnold, 1908).
Churchill, Sir Winston. *My Early Life*, by Winston S. Churchill (new edn., Odhams, 1947).
—— *Great Contemporaries*, by Winston S. Churchill (Thornton Butterworth, 1937).
Cranbrook, 1st Earl of. *Gathorne Hardy, First Earl of Cranbrook: A Memoir*, by A. E. Gathorne Hardy, 2 vols. (Longmans, 1910).
Devonshire, 8th Duke of. *Life of Spencer Compton, Eighth Duke of Devonshire*, by Bernard Holland, 2 vols. (Longmans, 1910).
Dilke, Sir Charles Wentworth, Bt. *Life of the Rt. Hon. Sir Charles W. Dilke, Bart., M.P.*, by Stephen Gwynne and G. M. Tuckwell, 2 vols. (Murray, 1917).
Disraeli, Benjamin. See Beaconsfield, Earl of.
Edward VII, King. *King Edward VII: A Biography*, by Sir Sidney Lee, 2 vols. (Macmillan, 1925).
Esher, 2nd Viscount. *Journals and Letters of Reginald, Viscount Esher*, ed. M. V. Brett, Vols. II and III (Nicholson and Watson, 1934–8).
Fitzroy, Sir Almeric. *Memoirs*, by Sir Almeric Fitzroy, 2 vols. (Hutchinson, 1925).
Lloyd George, Earl. *War Memoirs of David Lloyd George*, 2 vols. (revised edn., Odhams, 1938).
—— *Tempestuous Journey: Lloyd George, his Life and Times*, by Frank Owen (Hutchinson, 1954).
Gladstone, Viscount. *Herbert Gladstone: A Memoir*, by Sir Charles Mallet (Hutchinson, 1954).
—— *After Thirty Years*, by Viscount Gladstone (Macmillan, 1928).
Gladstone, William Ewart. *Life of William Ewart Gladstone*, by John Morley, Vols. II and III (Macmillan, 1903).
—— *Gladstone: A Biography*, by Sir Philip Magnus (Murray, 1954).

Gladstone, William Ewart. *Gleanings of Past Years*, by W. E. Gladstone, Vol. I (1879).

Goschen, 1st Viscount. *Life of George Joachim Goschen, First Viscount Goschen, 1831–1907*, by A. R. D. Elliot, 2 vols. (Longmans, 1911).

Haldane, Viscount. *Richard Burdon Haldane: An Autobiography* (Hodder and Stoughton, 1929).

Hamilton, Lord George. *Parliamentary Reminiscences and Reflections*, by Lord George Hamilton, 2 vols. (Murray, 1916–22).

Harcourt, Sir William George Grenville Venables Vernon. *Life of Sir William Harcourt*, by A. G. Gardiner, 2 vols. (Constable, 1929).

Hardy, Gathorne. See Cranbrook, Earl of.

Hartington, Marquess of. See Devonshire, Duke of.

Healy, Timothy Michael. *Letters and Leaders of My Day*, by T. M. Healy, 2 vols. (Thornton Butterworth, 1928).

Iddesleigh, 1st Earl of. *Life, Letters and Diaries of Sir Stafford Northcote, First Earl of Iddesleigh*, by Andrew Lang, 2 vols. (Blackwood, 1890).

James of Hereford, Lord. *Lord James of Hereford*, by Lord Askwith (Benn, 1930).

Jeune, Mrs. See St. Helier, Lady.

Labouchere, Henry Du Pré. *Life of Henry Labouchere*, by A. L. Thorold (Constable, 1913).

Lansdowne, 5th Marquess of. *Lord Lansdowne: A Biography*, by Lord Newton (Macmillan, 1929).

Long, 1st Viscount. *Walter Long and his Times*, by Sir Charles Petrie (Cassell, 1936).

Midleton, 1st Earl of. *Records and Reactions 1856–1939*, by the Earl of Midleton (Murray, 1939).

Morley, 1st Viscount. *Recollections*, by John, Viscount Morley, 2 vols. (Macmillan, 1917).

Nevill, Lady Dorothy. *Reminiscences of Lady Dorothy Nevill*, ed. Ralph Nevill (Macmillan, 1906).

—— *Leaves from the Notebooks of Lady Dorothy Nevill*, ed. Ralph Nevill (Macmillan, 1907).

Newton, Lord. *Retrospection*, by Lord Newton (Murray, 1941).

Northcote, Sir Stafford. See Iddlesleigh, Earl of.

O'Connor, Thomas Power. *Memoirs of an Old Parliamentarian*, by T. P. O'Connor, 2 vols. (Benn, 1929).

Parnell, Charles Stewart. *Parnell*, by R. Barry O'Brien, 2 vols. (Smith Elder, 1899).

—— *Parnell and his Party 1880–90*, by Conor Cruise O'Brien (Oxford University Press, 1957).

Pease, Sir Alfred Edward, Bt. *Elections and Recollections*, by Sir A. E. Pease (Murray, 1932).

St. Aldwyn, 1st Earl. *Sir Michael Hicks Beach, Earl St. Aldwyn*, by Lady Victoria Hicks Beach, 2 vols. (Macmillan, 1932).

St. Helier, Lady. *Memories of Fifty Years*, by Lady St. Helier (Edward Arnold, 1909).

Salisbury, 3rd Marquess of. *Life of Robert, Marquis of Salisbury*, by Lady Gwendolen Cecil, Vols. III and IV (Hodder & Stoughton, 1931–2).

—— *Salisbury, 1830–1903: Portrait of a Statesman*, by A. L. Kennedy (Murray, 1953).

Smith, William Henry. *Life and Times of the Rt. Hon. William Henry Smith, M.P.*, by Sir Herbert Maxwell, 2 vols. (Blackwood, 1893).

Victoria, Queen. *Letters of Queen Victoria*. Second Series, Vol. III and Third Series, 3 vols. ed. G. E. Buckle (Murray, 1928–32).

Wolff, Sir Henry Drummond. *Rambling Recollections*, by Sir H. D. Wolff, 2 vols. (Macmillan, 1908).

Wyndham, George. *Life and Letters of George Wyndham*, by J. W. Mackail and Guy Wyndham, 2 vols. (Hutchinson, 1925).

—— *George Wyndham*: *A Study in Toryism*, by John Biggs-Davison (Hodder & Stoughton, 1951).

B. Other Works

Bryant, (Sir) Arthur. *English Saga (1840–1940)* (Collins and Eyre & Spottiswoode, 1940).

Ensor, (Sir) R. C. K. *England, 1870–1914* (Oxford University Press, 1936).

Gorst, Harold E. *The Fourth Party* (Smith, Elder & Co., 1906).

Hanham, H. J. *Elections and Party Management: Politics in the Time of Disraeli and Gladstone* (Longmans, 1959).

Hearnshaw, F. J. C. *Conservatism in England* (Macmillan, 1933).

Jenkins, Roy. *Mr. Balfour's Poodle* (Heinemann, 1954).

Lucy, (Sir) Henry W. *A Diary of the Salisbury Parliament, 1886–1892* (Cassell, 1892).

Marriott, Sir J. A. R. *Modern England, 1885–1945: A History of My Own Times* (4th edn., Methuen, 1948).

Muir, J. Ramsay. *A Brief History of Our Own Times* (George Philip & Son, 1935).

Salter, Sir Arthur. *Personality in Politics* (Faber, 1947).

Sandars, J. S. *Studies of Yesterday, by a Privy Councillor* (Philip Allan, 1928).

Spearman, Diana. *Democracy in England* (Rockliff, 1957).
Taylor, A. J. P. *From Napoleon to Stalin* (Hamish Hamilton, 1950).
Trevelyan, G. M. *British History in the Nineteenth Century and After* (new edn., Longmans, 1944).
Young, G. M. *Victorian England: Portrait of an Age* (Oxford University Press, 1936).

C. Newspapers and Periodicals

1. Newspapers:

Birmingham Gazette
Bradford Observer
Bristol Times and Mirror
Canterbury Journal
Chatham Observer
Cork Examiner
Daily Express
Daily Graphic
Daily Mail
Daily News
Daily Telegraph
Deal Mercury
Dover Chronicle
Dover Telegraph
Dundee Advertiser
East Kent Gazette
Eastern Morning News
Evening Argus (Brighton)
Evening Citizen (Glasgow)
Evening Times (Glasgow)
Folkestone News
Glasgow Herald
Globe
Herne Bay Press
Hull News
Irish Times
Keeble's Gazette
Kent Examiner
Kent and Sussex Times
Kent Herald
Kentish Express & Ashford News
Kentish Gazette
Kentish Mercury
Kentish Observer
Leeds Mercury
Liverpool Daily Post
Liverpool Echo
Liverpool Mercury
Maidstone & Kent County Standard
Maidstone & Kentish Journal
Manchester Courier
Manchester Daily Dispatch
Manchester Guardian
The Morning
Morning Advertiser
Morning Leader
Morning Post
Morning Star
Newcastle Daily Leader
Newcastle Journal
News of the World
New York Herald (London edn.)
Norwich Mercury
Nottinghamshire Guardian
Pall Mall Gazette
Reynold's Weekly Newspaper
St. James's Gazette
Scotsman
Scottish Leader
Sheerness Times
Sheffield Daily Telegraph
Staffordshire Sentinel
Standard
Star
Sun
Sunday Times

1. Newspapers (*contd.*):

The Times
Western Daily News
Western Mail (Cardiff)
Western Mercury (Plymouth)
Western Weekly Advertiser
Western Weekly News
Westminster Gazette
Whitstable Times
Yorkshire Herald
Yorkshire Post

2. Periodicals:

The Bat
The County Gentleman
Court Journal
England
Freeman's Journal
The Hawk
John Bull
Land and Water
London Figaro
The New Age
The Nonconformist
Notes and Queries
The Pelican
Piccadilly
Pictorial World
Political World
Punch
The Record
Review of Reviews
St. Stephen's Review
Saturday Review
Spectator
The Tablet
Truth
Vanity Fair
Westminster Review
The World

INDEX

www.ingramcontent.com/pod-product-compliance
Lightning Source LLC
LaVergne TN
LVHW090801070826
844660LV00022B/1055

* 9 7 8 1 4 4 2 6 3 9 1 1 9 *